SVE
201(
11

GW01237670

Representing private lives of
the Enlightenment

SVEC (formerly known as *Studies on Voltaire and the Eighteenth Century*)
is dedicated to eighteenth-century research. *SVEC* welcomes work across a
broad range of disciplines and critical methodologies.

www.voltaire.ox.ac.uk

Representing private lives of the Enlightenment

Edited by
ANDREW KAHN

VOLTAIRE FOUNDATION
OXFORD
2010

© 2010 Voltaire Foundation, University of Oxford

ISBN 978 0 7294 1003 8
ISSN 0435-2866

The Voltaire Foundation is a department of the University of
Oxford. It furthers the University's objective of excellence in
research, scholarship and education by publishing worldwide.

Voltaire Foundation
99 Banbury Road
Oxford OX2 6JX, UK
www.voltaire.ox.ac.uk

A catalogue record for this book is available from the British Library

Literature / social history / cultural history / art history
Littérature / histoire sociale / histoire culturelle / histoire de l'art

Cover illustration: *Le Bouquet* (detail), engraved by Robert Gaillard,
after a painting by Charles Eisen.

FSC (the Forest Stewardship Council) is an independent organization established to
promote responsible management of the world's forests.

This book is printed on acid-free paper
Printed in the UK by Page Bros (Norwich) Ltd

Contents

Acknowledgements

This book emanates from an interdisciplinary workshop that took place in Oxford in the summer of 2007, organised by myself and Andrei Zorin. For financial support I should like to thank the British Academy; the John Fell Fund, University of Oxford; the Voltaire Foundation, Oxford; the Humanities Division, University of Oxford; and St Edmund Hall, Oxford. The discussions that took place over that long weekend owed their vitality and fresh perspective to the contributors of this volume and to the participation of Wilda Anderson, John Christie, Nicholas Cronk, Nick Davidson, Simon Dixon, Carla Hesse, Ann Jefferson, Colin Jones, Angelica Goodden, Avi Lifschitz, Jonathan Mallinson, John Robertson, Michael Sheringham, Alexis Tadié, Kate Tunstall and Stéphane Van Damme. Nathalie Ferrand, Wes Williams and an anonymous reviewer have also been generous with advice, and Lyn Roberts has provided indispensable editorial support.

List of illustrations

Introduction: The problem of private life

ANDREW KAHN

Representing private lives of the Enlightenment offers a set of case studies. Their common concern is with the discursive strategies and attitudes that men and women adopted from the early eighteenth to the early nineteenth century in order to express an idea of the private. The focus of the chapters is not especially the debate about the public versus the private; or, more generally, about the role of the public paradigm in the scholarly literature that has expanded hugely over the years since the publication, in 1989, of Jürgen Habermas' *Structural transformation of the public sphere* in English translation (the impact of which is surveyed by Sarah Maza in the first chapter). There is a tacit assumption in these chapters, with their focus on literature, art and history rather than on political theory or political economy, that when using the word 'public' the authors have in mind the conceptual framework of civil society as a realm of sociability, described by Habermas and applied in the work of the team headed by Philippe Ariès and Georges Duby in their five-volume *Histoire de la vie privée*, stretching from the Roman Empire to postwar Europe. Although other models like the 'public policy' description or liberal-economist model that juxtaposes the market economy and the state are not taken up directly, some discussions here do presume a market understanding of the 'public'. Mark Ledbury's treatment of the role of objects in painting and in interior design acknowledges the interrelation of the subject as a purchaser and the public as a trading emporium. Similarly, the roles of production, consumption and money-exchange in conferring a private dimension to social spaces and individual identity recurs in chapters on gardens by Andreas Schönle, authorial status by Irina Reyfman, portraits by Shearer West, and juvenile reading by M.O. Grenby. By contrast, the idioms of citizenship, duty and virtue inform Adam Sutcliffe's analysis of the development of friendship as a non-instrumental bond belonging to a different realm of social life from the public. The legal right of the state to investigate the sexual mores of the individual pits a communitarian ethic against libertine philosophy in Larry Wolff's chapter on a Venetian trial. But, in general, the view that the public sphere constitutes the practice of random social exchange by 'heterogeneous individuals and groups [in a] civilized coexistence' or civil society[1] is not contested.

Our common area of interest is in trying to give a more distinctive answer to the question: what is the private? The chapters in *Representing private lives* accept that the pioneering synthesis of Philippe Ariès and Roger Chartier, published originally in *Passions of the Renaissance* (the third volume of the *Histoire de la vie privée*), remains a touchstone.[2] The association in their work of the private with the world of the domestic and the intimate has been an influential roadmap. As a result, the conceptualisation of those very terms and the range of activities that they describe have been subject to much revision: the initial questions and descriptions produced by Ariès and his team have ramified into highly specialised branches of scholarly investigation. Historians, even more extensively in British social history than on the French or Russian side, have put forward a wealth of new evidence and conclusions on various strands that make up the domestic and intimate.[3] This fuller and more complex description of personal life has taught us in greater detail what lives were like in cities and in the countryside, in capitals and in colonies; how parents of all classes and both genders felt about children and how children regarded parents; what labour relations were like; what the impact of class relations on affective relations was; how people married and why or why not; how they grieved and buried and regarded their own mortality; how women breastfed and dressed their children; how servants were treated and treated one another; what the household looked like and how it was managed; how people learnt to read and write, and how those skills shaped the world of children; how often people had sex and what their affective vocabulary meant. The things and empirical reality of the everyday, as well as the descriptive anthropology of different nations and classes, are now more tangible and conceptually rich thanks to the minute recovery and distillation of evidence that has revealed so many private, and therefore hidden, aspects of life in the Enlightenment period.

Such 'thick description' means that a certain amount can be taken for granted now by each author in this volume, writing twenty-five years after the publication of the *Histoire de la vie privée*. The cross-traffic

1. Jeff Weintraub, 'The public/private distinction', in *Public and private thought and practice: perspectives on a grand dichotomy*, ed. Jeff Weintraub and Krishan Kumar (Chicago, 1997), p.1-42 (17).
2. Originally volume 3 in the Ariès-Duby survey, it was published in English as *A History of private life*, vol.3: *Passions of the Renaissance*, ed. Roger Chartier, trans. Arthur Goldhammer (Cambridge, MA, 1989).
3. For a discussion of the topic with extensive bibliographical overview, see Michael McKeon, *The Secret history of domesticity: public, private, and the division of knowledge* (Baltimore, MD, 2005), part 1.

between historians, literature scholars, art historians, linguists, demographers, historians of ideas and economic historians is now an unstoppable dynamic in eighteenth-century studies, and has significantly altered the methods and enriched the conclusions of every field of study. If one were to embark on a new synthesis of private life, in the manner of its first influential theorists, the scale of the project and the size and composition of the team would have to be of a different order. Such a consecutive history is not the goal of this volume, although it does bring together historians, art historians and literature specialists. The heart of the story, however, remains the problem of using this interdisciplinary tool-kit to elucidate a notion of the private. The 'public' lends itself to clearly demarcated models, and the tendency to define the private as the non-public has proven to be tenacious. Equally, the more positive equation of the private with the domestic, by contrast with the impersonal public realm, seems broad-brush. In this collection of chapters, the larger contrast between the intimate domain and the domain of the market and the formal institutions of the public sphere is not challenged. It would be impossible to prise a description of the 'private' away from the 'public'. It should, however, be possible to amplify the meaning of the 'private' by concentrating on the features that look distinctive to social relationships and the individual sense of identity. For Ariès and Chartier, the growth of the public led to the triumph of the family as the quintessential form of 'private life': 'Ainsi la famille devient-elle le lieu par excellence du privé. [...] c'est bien dans le courant du XVIIIᵉ siècle que l'essentiel de l'existence privée se replie sur le for familial, sans discords entre l'individu et les siens.'[4] For the writers in this collection the focus falls much more on individualism.

This collection aims to contribute to the ongoing discussion by preferring a private/public continuum to a starker polarisation, while giving more than usual emphasis to individual constructions of environments. The rethinking and rebalancing are not tendentious and, if anything, may be somewhat cautious. This is because the consensus of the contributors is that there are shades of difference rather than bolder delineations to be drawn. If the chapters implicitly contest the family as the paradigmatic private realm, it is not in order to deny the importance of the companionate family, but rather to suggest a greater range of spaces within that sphere.[5] Secondly, by bringing Russia into the fold, the

4. *Histoire de la vie privée*, vol.3: *De la Renaissance aux Lumières*, ed. Roger Chartier (Paris, 1986), p.400.
5. The tendency to associate solitude and individualism with Romanticism was noted, and given a critique, by R. F. Brissenden, *Virtue in distress: studies in the novel of sentiment from Richardson to Sade* (London, 1974), p.65-72.

case studies offer a comparative framework with more instructive sym-
metries and asymmetries than might have been the case if other Western
European countries had been set alongside the English and French
material that traditionally dominates. Finally, the representation of
private life in the visual arts is an integral component. The art-historical
aims are not to reassert the mimetic values of realism and show how
paintings objectify and catalogue the 'real' element of the private world,
but rather to bring out how representation is a mirror held up to
concepts of private space.

The result is a description of the private largely outside the familial
context, making more room for solitary subjects like the child learning to
read, the woman in her boudoir, portraitists and their subject, the
solitary wanderer in the public garden, the nobleman at the theatre
and in his study, the philosopher recording his dreams, the penitent at
confession and so on. The private is hard to capture because individual
subjects are elusive, and responses hard to collect as the basis of gener-
alisation. The opportunity to take stock of the question in their particular area of the subject has elicited from this volume's authors chapters
that have a focus on how people represented to themselves their
understanding of the private life, much more than on the practical
description of what it was like to lead a private life. At the same time, the
area of enquiry more broadly encompasses Russia, an extension reflected
in this volume that confirms recent efforts to see the Enlightenment as a
pan-European movement, intellectually and socially, while also offering
striking counterpoints.

In scholarship of the 1980s the public–private opposition was a
commonplace, and arguably more rigid, reflex. The fundamental sup-
position shared by the chapters in this volume is that the public nature of
private life, as well as the private nature of public life, needs to be
acknowledged. Throughout the collection we see that establishing what is
private, rather than public, depends very much on point of view,
subjectivity and self-consciousness. Attentiveness to the spheres and
the permeable boundaries of the private/public continuum seems part
and parcel of the classic literary texts of the Enlightenment and their
narrative voices. Eighteenth-century literature in France and in England,
both in fiction and in autobiography, shared the philosophical project
started by Locke and advanced by Hume (*An Enquiry concerning human
understanding*, 1748) of describing a sense of identity that resides in
consciousness or self-awareness of a private self. The status of space as
public or private did not necessarily or exclusively depend on an external designation of function, but on the meanings attributed by viewers of
landscapes and consumers of products. Consider, as a representative
example, how characters in Beaumarchais's *Le Mariage de Figaro* (1784)

create a semiotics of interior spaces by differentiating between public and private. To be sure, like all theatrical settings, Beaumarchais's naturalism is only an illusion. But in making his characters sensitive to the intimate and public dimension of their settings he both embodies the political tensions of the household, and also conveys how actors and viewers perceived subjectively the nature of the intimate and private. When the curtain rises, Figaro and Suzanne, who expect to be married by the end of the day (and end of the play), are shown measuring a room for their bed. Beaumarchais's subversion starts by putting the focus on his servants in a bare setting that can with a few props serve as an intimate space. But the characters assume that the space is liminal, and that its function – as well as their privacy – depends entirely on the intrusiveness of their masters. When the Count and Countess ring for their attention, the space of their conjugal intimacy reverts to being servants' quarters. Yet, when the predatory Count stalks Suzanne, the space is dangerously eroticised. And then again, when the action requires it, virtually the entire cast invades the same space, turning it into a public forum in which characters who have been exchanging insults or jocular remarks revert to a more formal language and observe certain polite conventions. Similarly, at the beginning of act II, the Countess, Suzanne and Cherubin cavort in the Countess' boudoir, a private space marked out by boundaries of propriety. In the famous scene that follows, the Count barges in only to find the Countess alone – Suzanne and Cherubin are hiding in a locked cupboard. When the Countess refuses to surrender the key, the Count vows to expose her. She stands firm and retorts: 'Attirer vos gens, et faire un scandale public d'un soupçon qui nous rendrait la fable du château?' Once intimate affairs are exposed to prying eyes, and once a third party becomes privy to intimate relations, a private space becomes a public one. In fact, any area where an action of general interest can be staged is labelled as public. This is again the case in act III when Beaumarchais's elaborate stage directions transform a corridor into a courtroom. A writer like Beaumarchais ably deconstructs the categories to reveal the degree to which the spheres interpenetrate, bearing out Sara Maza's observation in this volume about 'the complex patterns of mimicry and mirroring between different realms of social existence', and demonstrating ways in which the private can exist within public spaces because individual subjects determine a sphere of intimacy and privacy that ought to be respected.

One common feature of the chapters in *Representing private lives* is the aspiration to indicate positively how individuals from different classes, whether noblemen or servants, wealthy consumers or shopkeepers, illiterate or bookish, urban or gentry, flexibly mapped their social and domestic world. Like Beaumarchais's characters, many of the figures encountered in these chapters construct their sense of identity by beginning with the private. Although the notion of 'separate spheres' has now long been held to be an artificial one, it remains the case that the notion of the private has been harder to pin down and seems amorphous.[6] The public sphere is all about visibility, while the language of accessibility denotes the world of the private. Beyond its spatial–physical dimension, accessibility relates to an awareness of consciousness and the self that becomes most visible in acts of representation such as writing. This is the private realm known to the individual. Writing, which means everything from marginalia on books or ownership inscriptions made to letters and diaries in childhood, is one great technology for describing an essential self. The public spaces of libraries, subscription libraries, gardens, museums and learned societies provided recesses where the individual could withdraw to commune separately. It is in the novel of the period that we begin to see characters in a rounded, three-dimensional portraiture that offers interiority and often subordinates socio-economic descriptions of the individual to an emotional complex. It is no surprise that the figure of the reader is more present, and more evoked, from the middle of the century.[7] When Fielding's narrator in *Tom Jones* stops the plot he addresses the reader as an intimate friend. Whatever the reader's actual location, at home or in a vehicle, that space becomes private by virtue of the new bond between reader and writer which relies on the illusion of uniqueness.[8]

Many types of writing in the first person are shaped around the question of intimacy. Rousseau's great autobiographical project in the *Confessions* and *Rêveries* purports to write the history of the 'je' and make the self transparent both to the writer himself and to all readers.[9] Rousseau can only know himself because he becomes totally accessible to his readers.[10] Sterne's *Tristram Shandy* (1759-1769) experiments with

6. See John Brewer, 'This, that, and the other: public, social, and private in the seventeenth and eighteenth centuries,' in *Shifting the boundaries: transformations of the languages of public and private in the eighteenth century*, ed. Dario Castiglione and Lesley Sharpe (Exeter, 1995), p.1-21.
7. On novel reading in Britain, see Michael McKeon, 'Prose fiction: Great Britain', in *The Cambridge history of literary criticism*, vol.4: *The Eighteenth century*, ed. H. B. Nisbet and Claude Rawson (Cambridge, 1997), p.238-263, esp. p.238-58; for French examples, see Nathalie Ferrand, *Livre et lecture dans les romans français du XVIIIe siècle* (Paris, 2002).
8. See John Bender, *Imagining the penitentiary: fiction and architecture of mind in eighteenth-century England* (Chicago, 1987), p.188-89.
9. For a broad treatment with special attention to Rousseau, see Jean-Marie Goulemot, 'Literary practices: publicising the private', in *Passions of the Renaissance*, ed. R. Chartier, p.363-95.
10. See J. F. Maccannell, 'The postfictional self/authorial consciousness in three texts by Rousseau', *Modern language notes* 89 (1974), p.580-99.

the proposition that the self should be knowable from moment to moment in real time, starting from the moment of conception and inception. It is not embarrassment that creates the hilarity of the description in the opening pages of how the hero was conceived, but the unravelling of the Lockean project to describe consciousness empirically. For Diderot, identity always seems to grow out of responsiveness to another, whether an individual or a social world or oneself as represented in dreams.[11] The self seems inconceivable on its own. Yet there is an intimate world in his correspondence with his mistress Sophie Volland, a correspondence not intended for publication, where the embarrassment of the self that surprises itself when vulnerable to the materialist workings of the body falls away entirely. The absence of embarrassment is the sign that Diderot inhabits a private world made up of shared interests, feelings and experiences that feel unique to the two correspondents. And it is important to Diderot to imagine precisely how Sophie feels when she reads the letters.[12]

At times, the act of writing, as Diderot knew, takes the subject well beyond controllable thoughts into dream language. The frank recording of dreams and desires and their publication occurs at the cost of embarrassment. Similarly, reading makes accessible models to emulate as well as life-writing that serves the reader as a script for his or her own development. It is widely accepted that from the reception of *La Nouvelle Héloïse*, if not earlier, readers emulated the heroes and heroines of fiction in their construction of their own patterns of empathy and sensibility, again subordinating the public domain to private emotions.[13] The age is also one of viewing and scrutinising the self on canvas. Portraiture, perhaps most explicitly of all types of painting, can aim to project the self that painter and sitter wish to project, but often escapes conventional iconography to reveal a more candid view of the subject that defies expectation and seems to share with the viewer the subject's own self-knowledge.[14] Intimate spaces of the house, like the boudoir, are self-consciously demarcated as 'private', even within the already private sphere of the household and the domestic, by the display of portraits and keepsakes of loved ones. Access to places whose purpose was to

11. See Jack Undank, *Diderot inside, outside, & in-between* (Madison, WI, 1979).
12. But Diderot also has a keen eye in *Le Neveu de Rameau* for intermediate spaces like the café and the Palais-Royal gardens, urban spaces of sociability that harbour spaces of intimacy. See 'Introduction', in Denis Diderot, *Rameau's nephew and first satire*, ed. Nicholas Cronk (Oxford, 2006), p.vii-xxx (xviii).
13. Robert Darnton, 'Readers respond to Rousseau: the fabrication of Romantic sensitivity', in *The Great cat massacre and other episodes* (New York, 1985), p.215-51.
14. See Stephen Lloyd, 'Intimate viewing: the private face and public display of portraits in miniature and on paper', in *The Intimate portrait: drawings, miniatures and pastels from Ramsay to Lawrence* (Edinburgh, 2009), p.13-23.

reinforce bonds of feeling was highly regulated and therefore explicitly private. Yet at the same time the same affective props were mobile and could be transferred to more overtly public rooms like a hall or a dining room, thereby extending the privilege of the private to larger circles of friendship and sociability. In civil societies characterised by the institutions of the public sphere identified by Habermas, such divisions between private and public may blur, but they may often need to be defended. In England and France, where the café, the club, the coffee house and the theatre provided an information exchange of an oral kind, the rapid growth from the early eighteenth century of broadsheets and newspapers created and fed interest in the private lives of great men from cradle to grave. The Plutarchan model of exemplary lives had already become subjected to the infusion of less heroic and more anecdotal information and narrative as early as Voltaire. The question of violating privacy or guarding it is a sure sign that contemporaries, depending on class and gender, perceived definite boundaries between the public and private, and this perception operates inside the domestic sphere, outside the house and within public spaces. The generic boundaries between history and biography were porous. Boswell's *Life of Johnson* (1791) marked a step up in the history of life-writing, its documentary thoroughness unprecedented and unmatched for a generation. But other memoirists also aimed to divulge their knowledge of Dr Johnson, even *in extremis*. Francis, barber's *More last words of Dr Johnson* is just one example of a large class of works recording deathbed scenes of celebrities – and not just celebrity authors but celebrity criminals as well. Print culture enabled the commodification of the private lives of celebrities, whether writers, statesmen, royals or crooks, and such accounts (as described by Olivier Ferret), apart from their political purpose, as a form of entertainment enjoyed wide circulation among a readership avid for novels and narrative of all kinds.

The theme of accessing the private and its secrets, the interior space of the mind or the boudoir where sexuality is policed with difficulty, is treated most explicitly in the chapters by Caroline Warman and Olivier Ferret. As Caroline Warman explains, in analysing the typology of the private in the *Encyclopédie*, one meaning of 'privé' is 'secret'. Interestingly, the literary dimension of private life is at its most creative in types of writing that fuse different genres, combining standards of verisimilitude and invention already familiar to the reading public from the novel and the stage. The genre of the *vie privée* referred to a type of life-writing that proliferated widely in France from the reign of Louis XIV to the end of the First Empire. As Ferret shows, the aim of texts bearing the title 'vie privée' was to expose the intimate world of statesmen to the scrutiny of a public, at court and at large, eager to know what made remarkable men and women tick. Like gossip, these texts created a counter-life to official narratives of heroism on display in academic painting and in the postures of statuary and portraiture. However outlandish and outrageous the sexual lives and passions of their protagonists, authors felt little compulsion to corroborate allegations with reference to documentary sources because the style of representation carried its own conviction. The reader was made privy to the inner world of people shown in various states of dress and undress. In the age of sensibility the degree of attention that is paid to the marital and family lives of figures who otherwise look remote is not surprising, and it extends the attention that the novel paid to family relationships. But many of these lives – and the gallery included everyone from national figures like Napoleon to Beaumarchais himself – exploited the private in its meaning of 'secret', and the revelations brought these accounts closer to the pornographic best-sellers in circulation. They narrowed the gap between social classes by exposing, often in salacious detail, the truly scurrilous lives of figures who were otherwise held up as exemplary according to the lights of neoclassical representation.

The *vies privées* of Ferret's account aim to wash dirty laundry in public as a way of authenticating the humanness of remote figures. The marketing techniques of these biographers feed off social tensions that generated a desire to unmask, disgrace and ultimately humanise people in power. Warman turns from definitions discussed in the *Encyclopédie* to their employment in Diderot's quasi-autobiographical fiction. Diderot shows us the degree to which philosophers engaged in thinking about all aspects of human life take themselves as subjects of examination and risk public embarrassment by giving readers access to their innermost and, therefore, most private self. The private in Diderot turns out to be a self, visible in dreams and palpable in the erotic urges of nocturnal emissions, who is beyond the direct control of volition or authorial agency – yet clearly the essential part of one's personality. It is only possible to know this most private self, which is normally hidden from one's explicit awareness, by treating it as a set of reflexes and responses that can be observed from outside, recorded by oneself and sometimes divulged to others. While the very act of fictional representation and autobiographical expression aims at self-knowledge, Diderot shows us how often the subject surprises himself or experiences moments of self-alienation. There is a self about which we lack knowledge (one meaning of 'privé') that is made up of appetites of doubtful civility and is therefore savage (a second meaning). This realisation encourages secrecy (a third meaning). It is through his narratives that Diderot, with a comic touch, reflects on the danger of transparency. Such indiscretion is the stuff of the *vie privée* that satisfied a public appetite for sensation, but Diderot puts his reader on the horns of dilemma between craving to know the private self and fearing the organic volatility of the passions.

Accessibility also evokes the language of surveillance and observation, of social control, exercised by the state. It is difficult now to escape the entrenched and powerful post-Foucauldian view of the Enlightenment as a period which mobilised its institutions of social control to achieve the maximum transparency of motive and behaviour from individuals in their social relations and, where necessary, contain all disorder and unreason. This utopian aspiration to control or eliminate the private self comes up against a very strong counterclaim – that the self possesses a fundamental unknowability, and that, at least philosophically if not legally, remains beyond explanation. The tension between signs that are universally legible and idiosyncratic and individual detail also governs narratives about criminality in the popular literature of *ancien régime* France. As Lise Andries shows in her chapter, while crime in the modern world by definition occurs in the public sphere, and is detected, prosecuted and punished according to judicial systems, writing the lives of criminals is generically complex. Criminal biographies that employed the tropes of roguery tales in which plots and roles were predetermined also assimilated new actual material from documentary sources like broadsheets and judicial documents. Fact and fiction joined forces, and the genre of criminal biographies that developed over the course of the eighteenth century novelised, and in this respect humanised, the lives of criminals whose adventures and deeds acquire a picaresque dimension. Like the heroes of novels, criminals are dynamic agents in the creation of their own fates, but these newer narratives more concretely situate them in a recognisable historical world. Yet, as in the case of painting, the genre of criminal biography often diverged from its documentary sources: the expanded repertory of themes and details about the appearance, sexuality, tastes, strength, haunts and religious confession – in short the private lives of criminals – took on a literary life of their own and projected an image that captured the attention of the public. The tension between the realistic and the symbolic, between the titillation of storytelling as a pleasure to be consumed by readers and listeners and the didactic function of the life as a cautionary tale, remains operative in fictions which intermittently depart from stereotype by penetrating into the interior world of individual criminals. Criminals in turn relished public fascination with their deeds by encouraging their own celebrity. Even the body on which tattoos represented brazen acts or emotional connections, becomes a spectacular record of the biography of criminals.

Larry Wolff's reading of the archival documentation of Gaetano Franceschini's trial on blasphemy charges in 1785 reveals similarities to Ferret's analysis of how sensationalised biographies that circulated in the public sphere owed their power to the private content of the information they revealed. But in this case defamation, unsubstantiated by the evidence, reveals how easily the state could encroach on the private sphere; this is especially true in a city-state the size of Venice, where information on individual activity was accumulated by gossip and filtered through an information network that was uncontrolled by the state and not institutionalised in the public sphere. Although Venetian measures of social control were far less invasive than the type of monitoring described by Viktor Zhivov for the Russian context, popular anxiety about Franceschini's alleged paedophilia suggests, as Wolff explains, a discomfort with the excessive freedoms associated with libertinism.

It is obvious that what communities deemed to be tolerable and acceptable, legally and informally, varied enormously depending on a huge range of factors. Numerous contemporary works treated the anthropology of sexual practice.[15] Among the most famous discussions of the last half of the eighteenth century were Diderot's *Supplément au Voyage de Bougainville* and Rousseau's novel *La Nouvelle Héloïse*. Both explored the negotiation between individual desire, possession and communal interest; the first tests the degree to which travellers can become acculturated to the seemingly natural sexual communism of Tahiti, and adjust their sexual morality to tolerate different attitudes to kinship, cohabitation and promiscuity; while the second tests the limits of a social construct that subordinates private passions, and the possessiveness of individuals, to a form of sexual freedom. Within this radically different context, either exotic or utopian, where family, public and individual interests are meant to be entirely visible to one another and compatible, neither work needs to explore issues of shame and embarrassment, or sees a tension between the private and the public as a key issue. For the sake of experiment, both authors create communities in which perfect transparency between individuals follows from, and supports, a single universe of desires and satisfactions, compatible and uncompetitive interest and self-interest. In the fictional world of Rousseau's Clarens the boundaries of community, family and private passions are relaxed to see whether an erotic utopia can be achieved in which the stability of the community and individual satisfaction coexist.[16] Although 'privation' is spoken of when characters are obliged to

15. On the English context, see G. J. Barker-Benfield, *The Culture of sensibility: sex and society in eighteenth-century Britain* (Chicago, 1992), p.147-61.
16. On sexual desire and the social order in Rousseau, see Thomas Laqueur, *Making sex: body and gender from the Greeks to Freud* (Cambridge, MA, and London, 1990), p.228.

renounce their love interests, the epistolary exchanges of the novel scarcely ever use the word 'privé' because their focus throughout is on creating an equilibrium between individual desire and sharing affection. As Rousseau writes in the *Seconde préface, ou Entretien sur les romans*, 'S'il y a quelque réforme à tenter dans les mœurs publiques, c'est par les mœurs domestiques qu'elle doit commencer.' But the protagonists, as Alison Oliver shows in a close reading of the novel's erotic politics, cannot in the end either deny intuitive taboos, like the dread of incest, or ignore the individual preferences of the passions. The fundamental instability of the private self as an emotional unit that Rousseau describes strained friendship, another form of association as described by Adam Sutcliffe in his chapter.

In Russia, the evidence for a public sphere outside the state would by and large remain sporadic until the reign of Catherine the Great in the last third of the century. Similarly, and reflexively, efforts to trace the emergence of a liberal self-aware individual in Russia have often failed to be frank about the social and intellectual curbs that stymied the emergence of both the public and private spheres in a country where state and church of the early modern period were invasive in prescribing domestic behaviour, religious confession and forms of public decorum. The Russian-centred chapters are particularly innovative, sometimes by way of counter-example, because they capture how in the Enlightenment transitions in status-systems and religious control made it possible for a small educated elite to discover the idea of a private self defined at least partly in terms of subjectivity and self-understanding from within. The Russian example of the relation between the individual and the community lends itself particularly well to Foucault's model of social control as set out originally in *Surveiller et punir* (1975). In their respective discussions of the history of confession and sin, and the ranking of the civil-service hierarchy, Viktor Zhivov and Irina Reyfman examine how these institutions of Church and state in effect shaped and, to some degree, thwarted the capacity of the individual to develop and record a sense of the private detached from, and in critical interaction with, the structures of power. The state aimed to make individuals' motives transparent to the state. Other modes of activity that individuals undertook to make themselves transparent to themselves – through the writing and reading of fiction, theatre, biography – developed only in the second half of the eighteenth century, and with some rapidity. The comparison between penitential practices in Western confessions and Russian Orthodoxy helps to explain the striking divergences between Eastern and European concepts of the private and the public. Zhivov's account begins in the mid-seventeenth century when theological discord, incipient secularisation and the growth of the state at the expense of the Church caused great popular unrest, and also heralded changes that would unfold during the reign of Peter the Great. Penitential discipline in Russia did not share a post-Reformation purpose of inculcating a sense of a private inner self. Access to consciousness through religious ritual like the sacrament of confession could reveal to the communicant and priest a level of thought and intention that seems private. But the degree to which confession felt like a private act rather than an instance of communal piety depended on the degree to which Church and state permitted the creation of a language of feeling, interiority and the private. Against a backdrop of unrest and religious schism that threatened Russia with serious instability in the late seventeenth century, religious discipline aimed to impose order and to promote stability above all: private matters of salvation and a conscientious self-monitoring to avoid sin were secondary concerns in a theology subordinated to the outward demonstration of obedience and meekness in a theocratic state. Instead, the state and Church used their powers of legislation and taxation to persuade and coerce parishioners to attend confession and communion because these rituals made the behaviour of large numbers of people transparent to the authorities whose main concern was to discover any signs of religious dissent and to control and eradicate it. Yet, despite the obvious indifference of ecclesiastical and state authorities to an individual sense of piety, the corpus of confessional texts adduced here attests to the power of personal salvation – inseparable though it is from anxiety about the fate of the Orthodox world – to compel decisions and self-sacrifice that individuals make.

By the reign of Catherine the Great, Peter's secular transformation of the state and court was abetted by the appearance and growth of the Academy of Sciences (founded in 1721) and universities in St Petersburg and Moscow (1755). Travel and education abroad expanded the horizons of the educated gentry. If the numbers remained small until the 1760s, the impact became disproportionately large owing to the huge growth of private presses as well as the state press, the spread of literacy among the gentry, and the relaxation of censorship. There will always be debate about the extent to which a civic sphere existed in eighteenth-century Russia, but the success of the court theatre, the growth of Masonic associations, the development of public urban areas like parks and the tentative success of journals suggest a slow convergence with European examples.[17] In his chapter, Andreas Schönle looks at the public and private dimension of gardens in Russia of the Enlightenment period, charting how the rules of admission to gardens become inflected with

17. Douglas Smith, *Working the rough stone: freemasonry and society in eighteenth-century Russia* (De Kalb, IL, 1999), ch.3.

changing definitions of society. Penitential discipline in Russia did not share a post-Reformation purpose of inculcating a sense of a private inner self. Earlier in the period, the location of gardens and their exclusivity reinforced aristocratic identity and the horizontal bonds of a courtier class bound to the autocrat. Schönle shows how the expanded access to public spaces that was granted by Catherine the Great accompanied a change in function. Gardens were never fully opened to the entire public as the authorities controlled the challenge to order that popular entertainments posed. But some venues like the Summer Garden in St Petersburg and the park at Pavlovsk became a model space of pleasure and entertainment, both a fairground for the population at large and a space of individual freedom that 'blurred the line between the private and public spheres' – a space fit for family idylls and a public space where ostentatious display of public virtues like politeness could be relaxed. The picture of the public/private continuum in this chapter offers one view of the Russian experience. In the following chapter Irina Reyfman discusses the careers of three notable writers and identifies their difficulties and strategies in asserting their 'private' identity as writers in relation to their 'public' identity as defined vertically in the Table of Ranks, the civilian and military hierarchies devised by Peter the Great with a view to encouraging and fixing patterns of social mobility. A commitment to state service, as required by law, operated in tension with notions of authorship which created opportunities for self-fashioning as well as fashioning a relationship with a 'private' body of readers within the small face-to-face world of the cultured elite.

The world of the visual is full of the constant traffic between the public and the private, the things made out in the world and consumed in interior spaces. The world of genre-painting was open to the increased flow of objects that came with the significant growth of liquidity during the Regency in France, and the continual expansion of trade and luxury into global networks over the course of the eighteenth century. Concepts of object ownership and relationship of people to things not only help us compile inventories of consumption, but also reflect the value that worldly goods held for people in the space that was constructed as 'private' and intimate rather than civic and public.[18] Mark Ledbury's survey of historical accounts of consumption and acquisition shows how painting was itself seen as a commodity in circulation. Above all, genre-painting more than any other style has been seen as a literal record of the quiddity of daily life in the domestic sphere, and historians have found in canvases the symbolic representation of the mercantile world in oper-

---

18. For a historical perspective on goods and class identity in Britain of the period, see Maxine Berg, *Luxury and pleasure in eighteenth-century Britain* (Oxford, 2005), ch.6.

ation. But genre-painting is a reflexive mode, self-consciously aware of the part it plays in contributing to an image of the private that becomes standardised in painterly conventions of the genre, while also acting as a semiotic script for viewers and buyers of paintings who use these images to reinforce an idea of intimate space. Within this general observation, genre-painting conveys a spectrum of attitudes regarding the place of possession and accumulation in constructing private space. No painter more than Boucher, the preferred illustrator of objects to his elite patrons, uses the visual representation of luxury to foster a positive view of commerce and glamorise the role of luxury goods as status-markers. Here even Chardin, whose gaze on objects has been prized for the timelessness and patina of age, can be seen to collect objects as a means of freezing the quotidian process. Both painters reinforce for viewers of the paintings and owners of such objects the ethos of bour-geois comfort even in the privacy of the boudoir. In keeping in circu-lation the virtual reality of luxury goods, painting celebrates the aesthetics of private life at least for an elite class and advertises it for those who aspire to the comfort of the home equipped with furnishings that denote taste, worldly goods that remind the owner of his or her own worldliness even when removed from scrutiny. What paintings also disclose obliquely is the relationship servants hold to the objects of their work in daily routine. Like the domestic labourer, the painter is subordinated to objects and their manipulation, and, as Ledbury shows, the focalisation of Chardin's paintings from the servants' viewpoint belies the consensus that Chardin strips objects of their social and historical connotation in order to reveal essential rather than manufactured qualities. By contrast, Greuze's compulsion to create a tableau with a story and moral, and his parodic relationship to genre, lends a theatrical quality to his domestic world. At least on the surface, scenes of social commentary and parable require goods to be de-emphasised against illustrations of universal human behaviour, but closer examination also reveals a tension between Greuze's symbolic language and his command of particular detail.

Alongside fictional and quasi-fictional portrayals of the individual, the eighteenth century was a great age of portraiture. Paintings, however intimate, were almost always intended for more than one viewer, in private as well as in public. The increasing interest in exhibitions of individual and group portraits reflected the impact of sociability in the public sphere where the display of common customs, dress, postures ultimately conveyed a sense of shared values and affective bonds. But, as Shearer West discusses, while portraiture does not necessarily aim to capture the private self in epistemological and Diderotian terms as the profile of elusive consciousness, it does aspire to reveal facets of character hidden from public view and to shed light on identity within the intimate sphere of life and outside the conspicuous display of public acceptability. Like the *vies privées* across the Channel, portraits of fashionable subjects in Britain fed off a taste for celebrity and scandal, and similarly developed new codes of representation in conveying essential truths about character. Behind individual images, from caricature to formal portraits, lay new ideas about the relation between physiognomic detail and character as developed by Lavater whose influence on the theory of portraiture and its practice was pan-European, stretching from England to Russia, and noticeable in prose as well as painting. Reading character from bodily signs enabled assessments about morality, status, class and social fitness. But, if the inner lives of individuals were to be known, it could only be through physical manifestations. Like criminals whose tattoos offered spectacular evidence of their history, eccentrics represented a species of the private whose individuality could be writ large and whose identity was manifest in bodily idiosyncrasies above all. These quirks which the subject carried with him at all times in the traffic between private withdrawal and public appearances became the subject of memoirs and pictures, and are nowhere better encountered than in the memoir literature and portraits surrounding Samuel Johnson. His undeniable oddities posed a challenge to Joshua Reynolds, both as a theorist of painting and as a portrait painter, because the surface anomalies seemed so obviously to emanate from a totally individual psychology, and the challenge in portraying him was to capture both the public self, which was a very real manifestation of Johnson's sense of his own status and dignity, and a private self that could verge on caricature unless rendered with both consummate skill and appreciation for his genius. Whereas Diderot's subject finds himself embarrassed at the exposure of his innermost thoughts to the reader's attention, Johnson's portraits confirm his public stature by eliciting sympathy for an inimitable individuality.

Ideas about the private operate through different sets of oppositions defined by ethical, psychological and moral considerations. Representation of the self is one means of identifying and sometimes reconciling these oppositions. What are Rousseau's *Confessions* about if not the effort to pin down a self whose motivation is subject to misunderstanding by the outside world and by the subject himself unless it can be made transparent through the act of writing? The tensions between sincerity and insincerity, natural behaviour and decorum, individuality and uniformity, deformity and beauty, intrinsic worth and status, virtue and corruption endlessly recur in literature, philosophy and biography of the Enlightenment period, and shape pedagogical theory, encourage the use of intimate forms of discourse like the diary, and promote a reconsideration of the affective bonds like friendship located outside the family but also somewhat apart from the public sphere. In Enlightenment France and England, Montaigne's model of friendship remained an attractive ideal of a reciprocal relationship between equals often pursued for the sake of shared ideals. But at the same time the rise of scepticism and materialism, in particular, subjected friendship, like all forms of sociability, to reconsideration within the materialist account of human ethics. As Adam Sutcliffe discusses, friendship as a private good is continually reformulated as a rallying point for like-minded thinkers rather than a personal affective bond. Montaigne's ideal of friendship as a space of recusal and withdrawal from worldly strife came under pressure from the pessimism of the Jansenists and, in the 1740s, from writers whose materialist bias led them to reappraise the possibility of selflessness in relationships, concluding that it was more realistic to argue that the basis of friendship lay in shared values and mutual necessity. Friendship was seen to have an instrumental value expressed in the formation of group loyalties defined by ideology (for instance, anti-slavery campaigning), ethnicity (Judaism) and political alliance (*fraternité*). It also became increasingly difficult to maintain the admired humanist ideal that separates friendship from love, Platonic affection from sexual intimacy. Sutcliffe effectively contrasts the ideals of conduct literature and friendship manuals with a Spinozist line on friendship pursued by Helvétius, among others, who try to reconcile selfish need with an altruistic ideal of friendship; and with Diderot's materialism and his complex theories of interpersonal relationships in which selfishness driven by biomechanical impulse and reciprocity driven by a need for sociability coexist. The proof that philosophical friendship is unstable, and more public than private, came in the quarrel that openly wrecked Rousseau and Diderot's association. Their contrasting views were played out in a series of squabbles that led to the very public dissolution of a friendship that could not be treated with philosophical disinterest. Their rupture seemed to bear out a more pessimistic view that interpersonal intimacy was always uncertain. Within a larger structure like the family or a club or society, individual friendships could be monitored and placed under the regulating control of concrete obligations. When left as a purely private matter, friendship became subjected to the inherent instability, according to materialist thought, of emotions.

Matthew Grenby reveals how in children's literature in Britain the danger to the subject comes not from within the family or affective bonds, but from an imaginary outside world for which the child must be prepared. Grenby shifts the emphasis away from Enlightenment literature about children to literature written during the long eighteenth century for children, and asks what insight a corpus of English texts can give us into how writers construed the private lives of children – and indeed, based on extant marginalia and inscriptions, how juveniles perceived themselves. A close examination of children's literature written before the late eighteenth century contests the assumption, and often repeated claim, that its function was to reinforce the child's sense of ease and oneness with the cosy domestic sphere. If anything, the plots of fiction published from the 1740s and well into the classics of nineteenth-century writing like *The Swiss family Robinson* unfold outside the home and take child heroes, and with them their readers, into a fantasy world of daring and adventure. And while, by contrast, much children's literature of the period inculcated a rational understanding of the child's place in the family and their familial as well as civic duties, children's literature persisted in removing children from that comfort for the purpose of giving them a taste of what it meant to live in the world, to taste experience and to test boundaries and their individual capacity to survive in the world outside the family unit. For many children the most important experience outside the home would have been school, and Grenby discusses school stories which fall into a dichotomy of tales of home schooling and those of public education that either reinforced a sense of oneness with the nuclear family as the ideal bulwark against the precarious world; or instilled an opposite spirit of exploration and adventure. While ultimately the first type of fiction will become the dominant paradigm, Grenby steps back from one of Ariès's arguments about the balance between family and individualism by looking at children's literature as a commodity written for and consumed by children. His analysis of some important fictions reveals how paratextual devices, like titles, epigraphs and notes, gave the purchaser parent and child consumer instructions on how to read. The act of reading itself was potentially dangerous and needed regulation if it was not to upset the child and disrupt a sense of domestic ease. By contrast, the diaries of the Russian nobleman Andrei Turgenev follow their author out of the home and through the rite of passage of his sexual initiation. Andrei Zorin traces how in the hands of this keen reader of *Sturm und Drang*, Schiller's play becomes a script for his own coming-of-age drama. The self-awareness that Turgenev achieves in writing his diary is refracted through his identification with this theatrical alter ego. It is in the diary that Turgenev balances the contradictory sentiments he feels between respecting and fearing his father, and asserting his own independence through erotic adventure; and subsequently between the rapture of a sentimental education that releases in him feelings of love for a Russian woman he has only fleetingly glanced, and deep anxiety that in losing his virginity to a prostitute he may have contracted a venereal disease and will find himself haplessly emulating Schiller's hero and become a social outcast. Within the Russian context, Turgenev's diary marks a watershed in the discourse of the private, serving as a notable expression of the tension between a private inner world full of remorse and hope and the public projection of a persona.

Historians and eighteenth-century private life: an overview

SARAH MAZA

'Private life' belongs to that species of seemingly obvious but in fact slippery concepts which exist only in relation to their opposite. Shackled to 'public life', its meaning is relational rather than substantive, one term in a fundamental antinomy whose significance varies widely over time and space. What are public and private life? That which happens in the house versus out on the street? The realm of feeling as opposed to that of material concerns? Self-interest versus the public good, civil society as opposed to the state? What is 'privacy', and how far does that notion overlap with the equally elusive concept of 'intimacy'? Little wonder that historians of the eighteenth century, as of other periods, have disagreed creatively about the subject for many years.

The conventional view has it that the Age of Enlightenment brought us not just liberty, equality and fraternity, but the comforts of domesticity as we know them today. The classic historical understanding of 'private life' which prevailed some thirty years ago was loosely derived from Marxist ideas and framed the matter as a contrast between the marketplace and the family, in Christopher Lasch's memorable phrase 'haven in a heartless world'.[1] According to this model, the modern family and the cult of private life developed, starting in the eighteenth century, alongside capitalism as both a form of compensation and an ideological alibi for a world in which impersonal and exploitative economic relations were damaging the fabric of human connections. I will argue in this chapter that this older view has been displaced in the last twenty years by new interpretations whereby the 'family versus marketplace' dichotomy has been replaced by a distinction between the state on the one hand, figured as the public realm, and the market and the family, different but related 'private' entities, on the other. Where earlier generations of historians emphasised the sharp division between private and public realms, those working today are taking pains to bring out the complex patterns of mimicry and mirroring between different realms of social existence.

---

1. Christopher Lasch, *Haven in a heartless world: the family besieged* (New York, 1977).

First, a little history. It has been nearly four decades since the history of
private life, a staple of popular history ('Daily life in past times', 'La vie
quotidienne'), was adopted as a 'serious' topic by academic historians.
Starting in the 1960s, the rise of social history, and later of women's
history, moved the subject of private life into the realm of the respectable, albeit initially only once the topic was taken up by well-established
male scholars like Peter Laslett, Philippe Ariès and Lawrence Stone.[2] At
first the topic derived legitimacy from the social sciences. In the heyday
of quantified, positivistic social history it was widely assumed that anything that could be counted could be proven, and that large numbers of
anything should be relevant to something; the history of private life grew
out of historical sociology and demography, the counting of births,
marriages and deaths, the measuring of fertility and lifespans.[3]

Several different factors pushed historians' enquiries towards the
subjective by the later 1970s. Even in the hands of the most skilled of
stylists – a Peter Laslett, an Emmanuel Le Roy Ladurie – demographic
statistics do not make for the most entertaining fare, and aggregate
numbers cannot usually convey the nature of individual experience. In
response to the influence of cultural anthropologists like Clifford Geertz,
the historical discipline as a whole was moving away from the study or
large 'objective' structures and towards the elucidation of patterns of
meaning. Where the history of private life was concerned, this meant a
shift away from the aggregate data of fertility and death rates and
towards the sort of questions that loomed large, for instance, in
Lawrence Stone's 1977 *The Family, sex, and marriage in England*: how did
people feel about marriage when they did not choose their spouse?
About children when they buried half of them before the age of five?
About death when it could happen any day? About sex when there was
little privacy, and about privacy before they knew such a thing existed?[4]
For a long time now, the history of private life in early modern Europe
has privileged the qualitative over the quantitative, and the result has
been unfortunately but inevitably that the subject now focuses on the
literate elites. Most attempts to document intimate attitudes among the
non-literate – from proverbs, folk tales, police records or simple infer-

---

2. Peter Laslett, *The World we have lost: England before the industrial age* (New York, 1971);
    Philippe Ariès, *Centuries of childhood: a social history of family life*, trans. Robert Baldick (New
    York, 1962); Lawrence Stone's *The Family, sex and marriage in England, 1500-1800* (New York,
    1977) was viewed as a culmination of this first generation of work on family and private
    life.
3. On the general evolution, see Georg G. Iggers, *Historiography in the twentieth century: from
    scientific objectivity to postmodern challenge* (Hanover, NH, and London, 1997), ch.3-7.
4. See n.2, above.

ence from the numbers – have been so controversial as to discourage most historians from venturing into that area of enquiry.

In the 1970s, then, the history of private life was the history of family life exclusively, approached through a combination of quantification and, increasingly, the study of cultural assumptions as pioneered in France by historians of *mentalités*. This moment produced influential histories such as the work of Philippe Ariès, Lawrence Stone and Randolph Trumbach, John Demos' studies of early American families, and pioneering work on sexual attitudes and practices by Jean-Louis Flandrin and Edward Shorter.[5] Histories of cultural attitudes towards death by Ariès and Michel Vovelle belong to this moment and genre as well, although the question of whether death can ever be contained within the private sphere remains an intriguing one. Although written by sophisticated historians who usually knew better, these books never quite escaped a Whiggish narrative whereby children could finally be children (Philippe Ariès), families became cosier (Lawrence Stone) and sex got a whole lot better (Edward Shorter) as one moved into the eighteenth century.

Because of their ground-breaking subject matter and their ambition, these early works almost inevitably came under attack. Critics denounced their 'totalising' aims, their teleological optimism, their arbitrary use of sources, their focus on the upper classes, and most often all of the above. In a famous review in *New society*, E. P. Thompson called Stone's book a 'disaster' for its dismissal of plebeian affect and its trickle-down model of family values, going on to mock it mercilessly: 'The Modern Family is visualized, tanned and beautiful, gazing into each others' companionable eyes and climaxing together.'[6] These kinds of criticisms were probably not, however, what prompted the gradual decline of this model of writing about family life. As the 1970s wore on, the history of private life, now producing a plethora of works about breastfeeding, swaddling, menstruation, ageing and the like, not to mention the ever-infamous psychohistory, came under attack for its alleged triviality and obliviousness to more 'important' questions about class and power.

As early as 1976, Eugene and Elizabeth Genovese were warning of the 'political crisis of social history'. While they specifically exempted Stone from their criticism, they did denounce in colourfully Stalinist language

5. Edward Shorter, *The Making of the modern family* (New York, 1975); Randolph Trumbach, *The Rise of the egalitarian family: aristocratic kinship and domestic relations in eighteenth-century England* (London, 1978); Jean-Louis Flandrin, *Familles: parenté, maison, sexualité dans l'ancienne société* (Paris, 1976); John Demos, *A Little commonwealth: family life in Plymouth colony* (Oxford, 1999).

6. E. P. Thompson, 'Happy families', *New society* 41 (8 September 1977), p.499-501 (499).

the baneful effects of cultural anthropology on the profession: 'By now it ought to be obvious that we view the current fad of "anthropology" as a bourgeois swindle.'[7] Social history as a whole was 'steadily sinking into a neo-antiquarian swamp presided over by liberal ideologues the burden of whose political argument [...] rests on an evasion of class confrontation'. This was especially true of the history of private life: 'The burgeoning interest in the history of marriage and the family owes much to the reigning preference for private satisfaction as against public purpose.'[8] Three years later, Tony Judt chimed in as well in the pages of the *History workshop journal*, writing that a critique of contemporary social history was urgently needed because 'a whole discipline is being degraded and abused'.[9] Judt quoted with indignant relish the editor of the *Journal of social history* who had written that social history would have attained its goals when the history of menarche was recognised as equal in importance to the history of monarchy. 'History is about *politics*', Judt angrily countered, 'the means and purposes by which civil society is organized and governed'. By ignoring this, modern social history had exposed its true nature as 'philistine and conservative'.[10] It is a measure of how much things have changed since the late 1970s that self-professed left-wing feminists like Judt and the Genoveses could not imagine the dynamics of family life as a matter of politics.

It is easy from a distance of more than three decades to poke fun at such myopia, and indeed at all the self-righteous leftism of these critiques, but the truth is that they had a point. If the likes of Stone could keep the big picture in mind, by the early 1980s much social history, including the history of the family and private life, amounted to a scramble for new methods and objects. Where intimate life is concerned, the list of possible topics is not inexhaustible, and once they had run the gamut of experiences ranging from conception to death historians were left with no further new areas of enquiry and the sub-field was threatened with repetitive sterility.

Fortunately, the French academic and publishing nexus can always be counted on to transform yesterday's cutting edge of historical research into a set of expensively produced and lavishly illustrated volumes; and, even more fortunately, when this happened to the history of private life the enterprise fell into some very capable hands. Many, many hands, it must be said, since such publishing ventures boast lists of directors and

---

7. Eugene Genovese and Elizabeth Fox-Genovese, 'The political crisis of social history: a Marxian perspective', *Journal of social history* 10 (winter 1976), p.205-220 (215).
8. 'The political crisis of social history', p.213-14.
9. Tony Judt, 'A clown in regal purple: social history and the historians', *History workshop journal* 7 (1979), p.62-75 (67).
10. 'A clown in regal purple', p.68-71.

contributors that look like the credits for a Hollywood blockbuster. From 1985 to 1987 the Editions du Seuil in Paris brought out a five-volume collective history, directed by Philippe Ariès and the eminent medievalist Georges Duby, of private life in Europe from the Roman Empire to the twentieth century. Volume 3, which will concern us here, *De la Renaissance aux Lumières* (1986) – the title was shamelessly rendered in English as *Passions of the Renaissance* – was edited by the cultural historian Roger Chartier.[11] Ariès, who was supposed to have overseen the volume, died in 1984, but Chartier worked from Ariès's ideas on the subject as laid out in several of his recent writings. The volume broke new ground in avoiding the obvious birth-to-death organisation – it is interesting to compare Stone's *The Family, sex and marriage* to the more expansive definition of private life in the Ariès/Chartier volume, to include civility, taste, literary practices, sociability, customs and honour. Some of it works better in theory than in practice, since some of the chapters were farmed out to mandarins not necessarily very knowledgeable about their topics, and some of the pieces are entirely made up of sentences like: 'On constaterait plutôt une interpénétration constante des espaces, une ambivalence des rôles, avec toutefois une aspiration têtue tout au cours de ces siècles à mieux délimiter les uns des autres.'[12]

This volume of the *Histoire de la vie privée* did represent, however, a major conceptual departure from the Anglo-American model embodied by Stone and others, and I think that departure has had a lasting impact. The Anglo-American model relied implicitly on a central divide between the market and the family. The French, however, do not really have a term for what we mean by 'the market' ('l'économie de marché' is technical and specific), and their thinking accordingly is less prone to the reification of that aspect of social life. Ariès's model follows two evolutions: one is the shift in forms of social life from what he calls 'anonymous sociability' of the street, the marketplace and the neighbourhood, to more closed and structured forms of sociability of which the family is but one instance – others he terms 'groups of choice' like circles, clubs, associations. In the continental model, the emerging modern form of privacy is collective and structured, as in the Habermassian model to which this chapter will shortly turn.

In the *Histoire de la vie privée*, the other, and even more important, evolution in the modern history of private life is the rise of the state. Roger Chartier glosses it thus: 'C'est donc la progressive construction de l'Etat moderne, pas toujours absolutiste mais partout administrative et

---

11. Chartier, *De la Renaissance aux Lumières*.
12. From Nicole Castan's essay 'Le public et le particulier', in *De la Renaissance aux Lumières*, ed. R. Chartier, p. 413-54 (413).

bureaucratique, qui apparaît comme une condition nécessaire pour que puisse être défini, pensé comme tel, ou seulement vécu en acte, un privé désormais distinct d'un public devenu clairement identifiable.' (The Eurocentric nature of the argument does make one wonder how, for instance, it might apply to the American colonies.) There is, Chartier continues, a 'lien essentiel entre l'affirmation de l'Etat et le processus de privatisation'.[13] Neither in Ariès's nor in Chartier's contributions is the link between these two evolutions – the privatisation of social life and the emergence of the state – really spelt out. They seem to occur on different levels, the first as a sort of organic socio-economic evolution – the market may be there, but is not really acknowledged – the other as a purposeful intervention by the ruling elites.

The resulting model is an interestingly complex one, since the effect of state growth on the definition of the private is at least twofold. One is very broadly definitional in that the very nature of the modern state creates in contradistinction not really a private sphere as we usually think of it, but a realm of private interests. Chartier reminds us, and a whole chapter in the volume spells it out, that the opposite of *public* under the Old Regime was less often *privé*, though that term did of course exist, than *particulier*.[14] The *public/particulier* dichotomy imposes a political understanding on the matter of private life, and also productively separates the question of public and private from the spatial metaphors that inevitably dog it, offering the suggestion that the distinction might not refer to what happens inside and outside of the house. The 'private' created by the state would be very different from that delineated by the emergence of the market.

The other way in which the state defined private life was, according to Chartier, through a much more direct process of coercion and model-ling. The early modern state ruled by taking control of certain key aspects of social life. Chartier singles out such areas as the control of violence, and that of expenditure. Drawing on the work of Norbert Elias, Chartier traces the familiar story of the role of court society in establishing widespread norms of civility which undercut aristocratic violence (the outlawing of the duel is the standard example). He also mentions the ways in which sartorial expenditure as a form of power (*le faste*) was repressed to make way for the private and putatively non-political forms of spending (*le luxe*). The state did not just define private life by laying exclusive claim to the public arena; it also told people, at least certain classes of people, how to live.

13. Chartier, *De la Renaissance aux Lumières*, p.22.
14. The following discussion follows Chartier's introductions to the three sections and his conclusion to the volume: *De la Renaissance aux Lumières*, p.22-25, 165-67, 409-11, 618-19.

There were deep differences, then, between the French or continental model of approaches to 'la vie privée' and the Anglo-American one, even as they were taking shape simultaneously in the 1980s. The French rescued private life from the antiquarianism of 'la vie quotidienne' by showing how closely such a concept might be enmeshed in the structures of both state and class power. French scholars Ariès and Chartier drew their conceptual ammunition most explicitly from historical sociologists like Norbert Elias and Pierre Bourdieu, with Michel Foucault hovering mostly unacknowledged on the sidelines. To a large extent theirs is a top-down model, with agency invested heavily in the state. The private is *le particulier*, the broad swath of institutions and practices that flourish outside of the realm of the state. A subset of this private realm of the *particulier* is the individually private known as *l'intime*, which in this volume means sex, the self, and individual religious belief and practice.

What is most conspicuously absent from volume 3 of the *Histoire de la vie privée*? Women. Of course, women are all over the place in the volume, in streets and families, in alcoves and bedrooms and writing cabinets, but they are not present as women. One chapter of volume 3 is devoted to child-rearing, but none to specifically female roles and experiences, and power dynamics within the private realm are never discussed. In the English-speaking world in the 1980s it was feminist scholars like Carole Pateman and Joan Landes who moved private life to the forefront of the historical agenda.[15] In dynastic politics, race – in the sense of bloodlines and sexual access – was what mattered; the modern political model which began to take shape in the eighteenth century, however, was gender-driven. As Jean-Jacques Rousseau famously put it: 'Whether a monarch governs men or women ought to be rather indifferent to him, provided that he is obeyed; but in a republic, men are needed.'[16] In other words, the sex of a subject does not matter, but that of a citizen does. The correlation between gender and political power, the repudiation of kinship for the contract model, is a central reason, largely ignored in the French model, why private life acquired such enormous political resonance in the eighteenth century.

Jürgen Habermas is cited only fleetingly in *Histoire de la vie privée* – in 1986 the rediscovery of his writings on the eighteenth-century public sphere had barely begun. By the 1990s, just about every scholar working on the cultural and literary history of the eighteenth century seemed to be drawing on the ideas laid out forty years earlier in the German

---

15. Joan Landes, *Women and the public sphere in the age of the French Revolution* (Ithaca, NY, 1988); Carole Pateman, *The Sexual contract* (Stanford, CA, 1988).
16. Jean-Jacques Rousseau, *Politics and the arts: letter to M. D'Alembert on the theatre*, trans. Allan Bloom (Ithaca, NY, 1960), p.100-101.

philosopher's *The Structural transformation of the public sphere*.[17] The preceding discussion should suggest how important the Habermassian
model was in bringing separate traditions together: it allowed for the
conjoining of the Anglo-American focus on the market and the intimate
sphere with the continental emphasis on the effect of state power. The
beauty of Habermas' model is that it does not construct a simple
dichotomy of public and private, but a threefold model in which the
separate elements feed into and mirror one another: the public realm of
the state, the essentially private 'public sphere of bourgeois society' and
the really private intimate sphere.

The thesis is so familiar to us by now that we may overlook how
important it was in bringing together, on a first level, the two strands that
remained separate in Ariès and Chartier: private sociability and the state.
As is well known, Habermas identifies such 'institutions of the public
sphere' as salons, Masonic lodges, coffee houses, literary academies and
other non-state semi-public forums. The private 'public' within such
institutions first honed its critical skills on debating the increasingly
commodified products of intellectual and artistic endeavour: literary
and art criticism took off when art and literature stopped being the kind
of sumptuary products generated by patronage to become objects of
private consumption, debated by those who would 'buy' them in either
the literal or the colloquial sense. Eventually, in tandem with the
emergence of a self-conscious civil society, the institutions of the public
sphere turned their criticism against the state. As Michael McKeon has
recently emphasised, the relationship between the public sphere and the
state is not a matter of strict separation but of 'interpenetrative conflation': 'Habermas's category of the public sphere names the historically
unprecedented space opened up between political authority and political subjects, whereby the latter may participate in the former without
being of it.'[18] McKeon also calls this a relationship of mimicry or parody,
of 'repetition with difference'. The public sphere does not just critique
the state, it also cannibalises it by taking on its form.

Habermas shows, much better than do Ariès and his collaborators,
how the elite institutions of private sociability grow out of the state: the
Freemasons in imitation of state-sanctioned guilds, for instance, or the
salons as breakaway elements of court culture – these one-time creations
of the state then turn against it Frankenstein-like by declaring their
difference. But Habermas also demonstrates how *l'intime* articulates with
le particulier, laying enormous stress on the role of private experience and

---

17. Jürgen Habermas, *The Structural transformation of the public sphere: an inquiry into a category of
    bourgeois society*, trans. Thomas Burger and Frederick Lawrence (Cambridge, MA, 1989).
18. McKeon, *The Secret history of domesticity*, p.48.

the literary imagination in the emergence of the 'public sphere'. Within the private realm, the intimate sphere of the family takes on a particular character and intensity because of its increasing separation from civil society as defined by market exchange. Habermas locates the birthplace of modern public opinion in this 'intimate sphere' because, for private persons with no direct access to the public realm, the most natural topic of discussion was their common experience as lovers and spouses, parents and children: 'Before the public sphere explicitly took on its political role [...] there appeared under cover of this public sphere an apolitical public opinion – a blueprint, literary in the widest sense of the term – of what the political public sphere would become.'[19] I have endeavoured to illustrate this proposition in one of my own works by demonstrating the impact of highly publicised private court cases in France in the two decades before the Revolution: stories of seduction, adultery and class-based injustice involving ordinary French people became, in the 1770s and 1780s, fodder for political debate because a literate 'public' with no access to state power learnt to debate questions about the nature of authority through the prism of 'private affairs'.[20]

The model proposed by Jürgen Habermas therefore provides for a brilliant synthesis between the Anglo-American preoccupation with affect, subjectivity and intimate power dynamics on the one hand, and the French or continental definition of the private as simply non-state. Literary critics have been more interested than historians in the role of intimate experience in the rise of the modern public sphere, perhaps understandably since therein lies a major theory of the eighteenth-century rise of the novel. Historians, at least those of eighteenth-century France, tend to divide between those who study political culture (political and literary institutions) and social historians who explore family dynamics. This separation may explain how few historical works make a link between intimate experience and politics in the eighteenth century.

Yet as we know the line between intimate life and the state, as processed in between by the 'public sphere', became highly politicised in the eighteenth century, in a process that worked in two directions: the lives of the famous were privatised, and those of the obscure made into models for civil society and the state. In France, the sort of books labelled 'vies privées' of the great proliferated in the decades before the Revolution. Several dozens appeared in print, and Robert Darnton counts six of them among the seventy best-selling books of the decades from 1769 to 1789, with one of them, Mouffle d'Angerville's *Vie privée de Louis XV*,

19. Habermas, *The Structural transformation*, p.40.
20. Sarah Maza, *Private lives and public affairs: the causes célèbres of prerevolutionary France* (Berkeley, CA 1993).

appearing regularly among the top best-sellers.[21] Darnton has suggested that these texts need to be understood within a system of urban communication in which written and printed matter and oral rumour and gossip were connected in an endless loop.[22]

A great deal has been written about the 'desacralisation' of the monarchy in connection with these texts, perhaps never so eloquently as in the introduction to the text of the *Vie privée de Louis XV* itself:

[S]i l'intérêt d'un récit depend du retour secret que l'on fait sur soi-même en l'écoutant...quel peut exciter celui des infortunes & des prosperités d'un prince éprouvant des malheurs que le lecteur néprouvera jamais, ou rayonnant d'une gloire à laquelle il n'a pas le droit d'atteindre? Au contraire, dépouillez-le des ses dignités & de ses grandeurs, ne montrez que l'homme; nécessairement tous les ordres des citoyens, tous les individus s'entretiendront avec avidité de ses peines & de ses félicités domestiques, gémiront des unes, se réjouiront des autres: toutes leur devriendront en quelque sorte communes par la possibilité des les éprouver.[23]

The question as to exactly why stories about the intimate lives of the great packed such a political wallop at this time admits to more complicated explanations than one might imagine. Many good theories have been advanced, such as the scandalous privatisation of traditional patterns of ruling-class fornication – nobody ever wrote a *vie privée* of Louis XIV, even though that monarch enjoyed an abundance of it; the imperviousness of Louis 'the Great' to sexual slander has to do with a lot more than just matters of print culture and censorship.[24] I would also suggest that we take into account the other French sense of 'privé': deprived. In these texts the great become creatures of compulsion, robbed of control over their actions. Sexual activity as a form of control over the aristocracy and its women, as in the case of rulers like Henri IV or Louis XIV, served to accrue the ruler's authority. Conversely, the erotic addiction attributed to the likes of Louis XV makes one *privé*, or deprived, of the rational capacities indispensable to successful monarchical rule. (Naturally, the actual inclinations and behaviour of different monarchs mattered less in the end than the form and context in which these were described by apologists and detractors.)

In the eighteenth century, writings which breached the divide between matters of state and private affairs were often politically fraught. The trajectory from the state to the intimate sphere, as shaped by Habermas'

---

21. Robert Darnton, 'Mlle Bonafon et "La Vie privée de Louis XV"', *Dix-huitième siècle* 35 (2003), p.369-91 (369).
22. 'Mlle Bonafon', p.390.
23. Barthélémy-François Mouffle d'Angerville, *Vie privée de Louis XV, ou Principaux événements, particularités et anecdotes de son règne*, 4 vols (London, J. P. Lyton, 1781), vol.1, p.6.
24. See Maza, *Private lives*, p.177-82.

'literary/political public sphere' (pamphleteers and their eager reading public) cut the great down to size by exposing their scandalous 'private lives'. Conversely, conjugal and family matters came to be seen as politically foundational, most typically the analogy between marriage contract and social contract: forward-thinking writers in the Age of Enlightenment argued that individuals ought to be able freely to enter and exit a marriage just as they were at liberty, faced with arbitrary government, to dissolve the social contract.[25] Scholars have also in recent years highlighted the function of sentimentalism and the cult of sensibility as critiques of established social and political norms.[26] Writers ranging from the novelist Samuel Richardson to the playwright Louis-Sébastien Mercier argued that sensibility could erode class distinctions, and offered the sentimental family as a model for the emerging idea of a civil society independent of monarchy: the eighteenth century invented 'the social' as an autonomous sphere whose imagined cement was love in all of its forms. In France, Mercier imagined love and marriage as the solvent of social inequality but also a way of knitting together society, as he explained in the preface to his play about social miscegenation, *La Brouette du vinaigrier*: 'Qu'il est beau, meme en speculation, de voir certaines familles descendre d'une hauteur démesurée, tandis que d'autres monteraient...& se régénéreraient. Cette espèce d'échange de biens seroit fort avantageux à la Nation.'[27]

Love matches, in Mercier's view, were an exchange of goods which would benefit the nation in the same way as the circulation of commodities. Wherever there is talk of sentimentalism in the eighteenth century, commerce is never far away. As McKeon points out, market activity is an ambiguous category, private in relation to the state, but public in relation to the family.[28] Indeed, I would suggest that this Janus-like quality of the category 'market' was precisely why the question of 'luxury' caused such hysteria in the eighteenth century: how could one classify, judge and contain a force that liberated private life – 'luxe' was etymologically close to 'luxure', debauchery – while threatening to destroy public values?[29]

25. Maza, *Private lives*; see also Francis Ronsin, *Le Contrat sentimental: débats sur le mariage, l'amour, le divorce de l'ancien régime à la Restauration* (Paris, 1991). For a different instance of the politicisation of private lives see Mita Choudhury, *Convents and nuns in eighteenth-century French politics and culture* (Ithaca, NY, 2004).

26. For examples of arguments in this vein see for instance Scott Bryson, *The Chastised stage: bourgeois drama and the exercise of power* (Stanford, CA, 1991) and David Denby, *Sentimental narrative and the social order in France* (Cambridge, 1994).

27. Louis-Sébastien Mercier, *Théâtre complet*, 4 vols (Amsterdam, 1778-1784), vol.3, p.114.

28. McKeon, *The Secret history of domesticity*, p.10.

29. Sarah Maza, *The Myth of the French bourgeoisie: an essay on the social imaginary, 1750-1850* (Cambridge, MA, 2003), p.53-61.

For Habermas, the market falls squarely within the private sphere, forming the crucible of civil society. The historians who rediscovered Habermas' writings on the public sphere in the 1990s mostly ignored the role of capitalism in his argument as well as his resolute, embarrassingly old-fashioned, use of the term 'bourgeois'. This was especially true in eighteenth-century French history where, in the 1990s, anti-Marxist 'revisionism' was still in full swing, and most of us were eager to latch onto Habermas' argument about communication networks, to write the history of salons, pamphleteers and courtroom literature, while skipping over those parts of Habermas' thesis that looked ponderously *marxisant*. As Colin Jones rightly pointed out in 1991, the embrace of Habermas by anti-Marxist historians was 'richly and wondrously ironic [...]. Like a bad relation, the bourgeoisie has been banished from the front door of eighteenth-century studies, only to jump back unnoticed through a side window.'[30]

If the 'bourgeoisie' has perhaps not made a triumphal return to the centre stage of eighteenth-century studies, the market certainly has. If historians are still wary of reintroducing 'capitalism' as a category in the eighteenth century, they are eager to point to commerce and consumerism as pivotal forces in both material and cultural terms. Habermas, once again, had anticipated the point: the public sphere, in its literary and political forms, he suggested, was a sort of genie brought forth by the friction between civil society and the absolutist state. And civil society, Habermas explained, relying heavily on the arguments of Hannah Arendt, is begat by market relations: 'Society is the form in which the fact of mutual dependence for the sake of life and nothing else assumes public significance, and where activities connected to sheer survival are permitted to appear in public.'[31] Those material activities confined to the *oikos*, Arendt had argued, were originally deemed because of their purely material nature to be *privé* – deprived – of freedom. Once separated from the domestic sphere, activities involved in the repro-duction of human life partook of the freedom of the public sphere, yet they were closely implicated with the private realm.

With the flowering of a large body of literature on eighteenth-century consumer culture, historians have in recent years increasingly pointed to the mutual implication of private life and the market. Indeed, since so many of the items most prized in the Age of Enlightenment came from Europe's colonial possessions, traces of European rule and slavery can be found in the most personal of objects and practices: silk stockings,

30. Colin Jones, 'The return of the banished bourgeoisie', *Times literary supplement* (29 March 1991), p.8.
31. Habermas, *The Structural transformation*, p.19.

intimate breakfasts, rococo Buddhas (on such interiors, see the chapter by Mark Ledbury). The links between the market and private life in the eighteenth century were anything but abstract and symbolic. As Sarah Pearsall shows in her book on family correspondence across the eighteenth-century Atlantic, we need to think about the connection between separation in pursuit of imperial and commercial profits and the importance of sentimental styles in managing the chaos of long-distance relationships. The performance of sentiment among eighteenth-century loved ones has many meanings, but some of it surely has to do with the ways in which markets scattered kinsfolk and threatened to weaken family ties.[32] Goods shaped private roles and behaviour, both face to face and at a distance, and their binding social effects could be politically charged. T. H. Breen's *The Marketplace of revolution*, for instance, tells the story of the ways in which the American colonists were at first shaped by British goods, learning with them how to dress, eat and behave, before using those very goods to throw off British rule in a series of consumer boycotts.[33]

It may not be a surprising conclusion to offer that Habermas, even more than the *Histoire de la vie privée* team, has reshaped historians' approach to the history of private life; but I do think that is the case. Where a generation ago we still approached the question in classic dichotomous terms of public and private, the revival of the German philosopher's 1962 classic, along with the more general emphasis of continental scholars on the importance of the state, has considerably enriched the analytical models upon which historians now draw. Habermas especially, with his multi-part model and his insistence on distinguishing civil society, intimate life, the public sphere and the state, has forced us to draw distinctions as well as to see unexpected connections. The study of private life has opened up from its classic location in social history to the domains of political culture and commodity exchange. Thanks to recent work we are now aware that 'private' in the eighteenth century meant many things – intimate, deprived, self-serving, protected, particular. The wealth of meaning contained in this simple term leads naturally to the profusion of subjects and perspectives to be found in this volume's chapters.

---

32. Sarah M. S. Pearsall, *Atlantic families: lives and letters in the later eighteenth century* (Oxford, 2008).
33. T. H. Breen, *The Marketplace of revolution: how consumer politics shaped American independence* (Oxford, 2005).

Intimate, deprived, uncivilised: Diderot and the publication of the private moment

CAROLINE WARMAN

This chapter explores the three distinct meanings of the term 'privé' in eighteenth-century French and delves into the overlaps so startlingly explored by Diderot, using as a starting point the entries on 'privé' in Diderot and D'Alembert's *Encyclopédie, ou Dictionnaire raisonné des sciences, des arts et des métiers*, that frequently cited monument to the progressive aims of the Enlightenment, published through thick and thin between 1751 and 1772. The fact that the term 'privé' has three quite distinct meanings makes it no obvious matter to determine what a private life in French – *une vie privée* – might be. This is the reason for the present discussion on the French context despite the wider European optic of the volume as a whole, the ambivalences existing in the French language not being replicated in the same way elsewhere. Having looked at the way in which these *Encyclopédie* definitions clearly pull the idea of a what a private life might be in very different directions, I will then investigate how Diderot in his other work illuminates and plays with the idea of the private life, arguing that he shows that the various meanings converge as much as they diverge. His purpose is to elucidate and complicate our idea of what a private life might be. I will then try to understand the extent to which the making public of private moments, a topos which repeatedly shapes the narrative, is also their publication.

The *Encyclopédie* definitions run as follows:

PRIVÉ, APPRIVOISÉ, (*Synonymes*) les animaux *privés* le sont naturellement, & les *apprivoisés* le sont par l'art & par l'industrie de l'homme. Le chien, le bœuf & le cheval sont des animaux *privés*; l'ours & le lion sont quelquefois *apprivoisés*. Les bêtes sauvages ne sont pas *privées*; les farouches ne sont pas *apprivoisées*.[1]

---

1. This first paragraph is lifted from l'abbé Girard's influential (and much cited) *Synonymes françois et leurs différentes significations*, 3rd edn (Paris, Vve d'Houry, 1741), word for word. The rest of the entry is Jaucourt's own, so far as can be established from a comparison with the *Dictionnaire universel des synonymes de la langue française contenant les synonymes de Girard [...] et ceux de Beauzée, Roubeaud, D'Alembert, Diderot, et autres écrivains célèbres*, 2 vols (Paris, Félix Locquin, 1837), which credits it to Jaucourt: this work reuses most synonyms from the *Encyclopédie* and is therefore a helpful although not definitive resource for tracking them. It summarises the entry 'Privé, apprivoisé', citing this first paragraph and

Le verbe *apprivoiser* s'employe fort bien au figuré pour signifier *manier les esprits, les adoucir*. Solon sçut insensiblement *apprivoiser* avec les idées de justice, d'ordre & de loi, un peuple nourri dans la licence; ce mot se dit aussi avec le pronom personnel pour *s'accoutumer*. L'habitude nous *apprivoise* à tout; j'admire ceux qui savent *s'apprivoiser* avec tout le monde, rien n'est plus commun dans notre nation; mais il s'y trouve aussi des gens si farouches, qu'on ne peut les *apprivoiser*. (*D. J.*)

PRIVÉ, PARTICULIER, SECRET, adj. (*Gramm.*) en ce sens il s'oppose à *public*; & l'on dit après s'être livré aux affaires de l'état, il s'est retiré, & il jouit des douceurs d'une vie *privée*.

Il est synonyme à *propre*; il a fait cet acte de son autorité propre ou *privée*.

Il se prend aussi dans le sens du substantif *privation*. Le dogme chrétien *prive* du salut éternel tous ceux qui n'ont pas eu la foi en Jesus-Christ, & même les enfans morts sans avoir reçu le baptême.

PRIVÉ Conseil, (*Jurisprudence*) se disoit autrefois pour *conseil privé*, voyez au *mot* CONSEIL, *l'article* CONSEILS DU ROI. (*A*)

PRIVÉ, (*Archit.*) *voyez* AISANCE. [i.e. privies, latrines]

PRIVER, v. act. (*Gramm.*) ôter quelque chose à quelqu'un. Il se dit des choses & des personnes. Dieu nous *prive* de ses graces; notre imprudence nous *prive* de plusieurs avantages. Je me suis *privé* quelquefois des choses essentielles à la vie pour le soutenir.[2]

The authors, in so far as they are given, are the chevalier de Jaucourt ('D. J.') for 'Privé, Apprivoisé', and Boucher d'Argis for 'Privé, Conseil'. 'Privé, particulier, secret', 'privé' and 'priver' are not signed. This is of course not an uncommon feature of the 1765 volumes (vol.8-17), in which authors were not quick to identify themselves for fear of retribution. More significant perhaps is the fact that the two definitions containing the adjective in question, 'Privé', are both synonym strings. When a string of synonyms introduces an *Encyclopédie* article in this way, giving it a multiple heading, we can be relatively confident that there is a reason, which is not necessarily a commonsensical one simply indicating multiple words for a single meaning, that is, a true synonym. In their influential treatises on synonyms and tropes, the grammarians Girard and Du Marsais had argued in 1718 and 1730 respectively that true synonyms do not exist.[3] The *Encyclopédistes* had adopted this line with zeal, seeing it as their duty in a 'dictionnaire raisonné' or 'rational dictionary'

---

then explaining that an animal to be 'privé' must first be 'apprivoisé' and that, once 'apprivoisé', it will be 'privé'. *Dictionnaire universel des synonymes*, vol.2, p.209.

2. *Encyclopédie, ou Dictionnaire raisonné des sciences, des arts et des métiers, par une société de gens de lettres*, ed. D. Diderot and J. D'Alembert, 17 vols (Paris and Neufchâtel, Briasson, 1751-1765), vol.13 (1765), p.388.

3. Gabriel Girard, *La Justesse de la langue françoise, ou les Différentes significations des mots qui passent pour synonimes*, 1st edn (Paris, L. d'Houry, 1718); César Chesneau Du Marsais, *Traité des tropes, ou des différents sens dans lesquels on peut prendre un même mot dans une même langue*, 1st edn (Paris, Vve J.-B. Brocas, 1730).

to pin down the meaning of each and every separate term and restore the range of terms available to their distinctness and precision.[4] Moreover, the synonym strings seem to draw the eye to their article and therefore give it a prominence on the page which single-word articles lack. I would argue therefore that they constitute a subtle but clear indication of *Encyclopédie* rhetoric, that is, of its own particular art of persuasion and emphasis. The fact that the headwords of these articles are not single but multiple means that they draw the eye more than single headwords, and thus that the page layout itself directs attention. In support of this thesis, we note that there are not one but two multiple headwords on the same page. The reader cannot avoid their presence on the page, clustering in capitals around the term 'PRIVÉ'.

The definitions themselves can be rapidly summarised. The first one, translated as 'domesticated', 'tamed', explains that 'privé' refers to domesticated animals such as the dog, the cat, the horse, and that 'apprivoisé' refers to tamed animals such as bears or lions; because they are fundamentally wild, the term indicating that they are now under the control of man is different from that used for farmyard animals. This article carefully differentiates techniques of human control over animals according to their initial degree of wildness. The second paragraph extends this notion of control – via the term 'apprivoiser', meaning 'to tame' – from wild beasts to the manipulation – 'manier' – or sweetening – 'adoucir' – of minds. The examples the chevalier de Jaucourt gives us do not all tend in the same direction, either to approve or condemn. Manipulation and sweetening are negative and positive respectively; the picture of Solon calming his people and bringing the licentious into the realm of justice, order and law (note the entirely secular recasting of this ancient story) is entirely praiseworthy, while habit does not just make us used to things, it tames us; thus the original synonym string multiplies, and is now 'privé, apprivoisé, accoutumé' or 'domesticated, tamed, accustomed'. The authorially personalised remark 'I admire those who are able to tame themselves so well that they get along with everyone' is double-edged, ironically pointing to insincerity, and thus the final

---

4. Indeed Du Marsais contributed much-admired articles on the subject of grammar until his death in 1756, when they were given to the grammarians Beauzée and Roubaud. Beauzée, the author of the article 'Synonyme', quotes Du Marsais's famous sentence: 'S'il y avoit des synonymes parfaits, il y auroit deux langues dans une même langue. Quand on a trouvé le signe exact d'une idée, on n'en cherche pas un autre.' See Beauzée, 'Synonyme', in *Encyclopédie*, vol.15 (1765), p.757, Du Marsais, *Traité des tropes*, p.309, and also Girard, 'Préface', in *La Justesse de la langue françoise*, 2nd edition and onwards. Using the exact word 'facilite l'intelligence et la communication de la vérité'. More than this, Beauzée declares that the task of differentiating and defining terms is the definition of the *philosophe*'s main job, 'parce que l'esprit de justesse est le véritable esprit philosophique', 'Synonyme', p.757.

statement, that some people are so wild they cannot be tamed, looks in
contrast like approval of wild nature as opposed to smooth civilised
artificiality. The article skates between different evaluations of the notion of taming, and serves to underline by inference that whatever tamed
or domesticated is, it is not necessarily originary or natural, while in the
process some particularity is lost.

The second sub-heading is 'PRIVÉ, PARTICULIER, SECRET'. It is
unsigned.[5] This article, in sharp contradistinction to Jaucourt's, does
not give separate explanations for the different terms, nor does it elucidate them, other than by defining private as the opposite of public, and by
presenting the morally worthy scenario of a public man serving his
country and retiring to the sweet enjoyment of a private life. The only
overlap with our previous definition is in the reference to sweetness –
before we had Solon sweetening the minds of his licentious people; here
we see this hard-working public man now enjoying the sweets of private
life. Its second paragraph, consisting in a single short line, adds a further
synonym to those already in view, 'propre', to be understood as 'personal':
the notion of 'personal authority' is given to exemplify it, standing in tacit
contrast to the notion of divine authority which follows. The third part of
this definition is therefore devoted to Christian doctrine, and the dogma
by which it is ordained that those 'deprived' of baptism can never be
admitted to heaven; the element most focused on refers to the emotive
issue of unbaptised children being 'deprived' of eternal salvation. The
earlier article 'Privation' goes into this in more detail.

The terms 'particulier' and 'secret' are not investigated in the slightest,
and simply serve to indicate an absence. The moral private life alluded to
is as near as we get – it may or may not contain or contrast with whatever
a secret life may be. The meanings of 'particulier' and 'secret' remain
uninvestigated, closed, possibly in tacit ironic acknowledgement of their
unknowability. We will return to this point in our discussion of the *Lettre
sur les aveugles*, a text which probes the important shifts between these
supposedly synonymous terms.

The remaining definitions draw an extraordinary trajectory between

---

5. Neither Schwab nor Lough give it as one of the articles they think Diderot did write or
    might have written. See Richard N. Schwab, W. E. Rex and J. Lough, *Inventory of Diderot's
    Encyclopédie*, SVEC 80 (1971), 83 (1971), 85 (1972), 91 (1972), 92 (1972), 93 (1972), 223 (1984):
    Schwab and Rex identify 'Privé, particulier, secret' as vol.13, no.1503 (see *SVEC* 91, p.838);
    it is not recorded as being either definitely by Diderot (*SVEC* 93, p.93) or possibly
    attributable to him (*SVEC* 93, p. 94). See also John Lough, *The Encyclopédie* (London, 1971),
    see especially under 'Diderot, Denis' in his Index which lists all the articles he attributes to
    Diderot, p.416-18; nor does the 1837 *Dictionnaire universel des synonymes* cite it under any
    one of the key words. Nonetheless, for reasons that will become clear, it seems quite
    plausible that Diderot penned it.

different sorts of human and divine self-organisation, from law courts, to latrines, to grace. Thus from the 'privy council', we turn to 'privies' – here the English echoes the French very clearly – and 'being deprived of something': in this way we return to the idea of being deprived of grace. From divine agency we descend to human agency, the accent being clearly on human fallibility, and we end with a slightly cryptic return to the first person: 'je me suis *privé* quelquefois des choses essentielles à la vie pour le soutenir.'

Summarising the picture we see that we have three principal ideas under the word 'privé' and cognates: 'control' as in taming, domesticating, manipulating, habituating; 'private' as in 'private life', which is given as the opposite of 'public life' and associated in unexplicit ways with the 'particular' (meaning either 'individual' or 'personal') and the 'secret', and lastly the notion of 'deprivation'. Finally, we have some sense – via the eye-drawing power of the synonym strings – that these definitions are of some importance.

It is under the three headings of control, private and deprivation that we will now inspect Diderot's various writings to see whether the light that they shed in turn illuminates the central question of what a private life might be understood to be. In fact we find that all of these aspects feature powerfully in Diderot, united in each case to an overarching notion of the private self, understood as intimate experience. We see the question of control and taming quite explicitly linked to private lives in Diderot's erotic novella the *Bijoux indiscrets* wherein we find Mangogul, the sultan of Congo, slightly bored and rather curious, turning a magic ring on the women of his court which makes their 'jewel' – that is to say, their private parts, their sex – speak its adventures and desires. The jewel's devastating frankness threatens not only embarrassment but in fact destroys marriages and reputations. Mangogul finds it simply amusing: the privacy that he invades is at his service as he sees it; the separate and private lives that are uncovered are not theirs to call their own. Thus he declares that: 'Et que m'importent à moi ces maris détrompés, ces amants désespérés, ces femmes perdues, ces filles déshonorées, pourvu que je m'amuse? Suis-je donc sultan pour rien? [...] Prenez sur vous de vous familiariser avec ces nouveaux discoureurs.'[6] This is the Solon of the *Encyclopédie* definition

---

6. Les Bijoux indiscrets, ed. Jean Macary and Aram Vartanian, in Œuvres complètes (henceforward DPV), ed. Herbert Dieckmann, Jacques Proust, Jean Varloot et al. (Paris, 1975-), vol.3 (1978), p.51 (end of ch.6). The reader may find it useful also to have the reference to the Pléiade edition: Contes et romans, ed. Michel Delon et al. (Paris, 2004), p.18. In order to minimise readerly inconvenience with respect to Diderot editions, we have chosen to reference the definitive but as yet incomplete DPV edition, except in the case of the Lettre sur les aveugles where more recent work has superseded it. Where Delon's edition is available, we give that too.

gone mad: Mangogul's pursuit of knowledge does not lead him to calm the licentious behaviour of his subjects, as Solomon does, but turns it into the object of the enquiry itself. His subjects' behaviour to a certain extent becomes irrelevant because their subjectivity is overridden by their subjection – these women and by extension their lovers are Mangogul's performing animals; they are reduced to and treated as beasts. The conclusion of the book righteously puts everything back in order (but only after a titillating thirty twists of the ring!) by restoring trust and privacy to the courtiers, and it is on this basis that a healthy reign over unviolated private individuals is established. The hypochondriac genie who gave it to Mangogul disappears in a puff of smoke. *Les Bijoux indiscrets* viewed in this way becomes a fable of the relationship between the controlled and the controller, of the duties and responsibilities involved in taming one's subjects, and the extent to which one can be allowed to control them: the privacy and inviolability of the private life becomes in turn the focus of attention and the indicator of health. Mangogul is a ruler who knows about his subjects' private lives but does not accord them privacy until the close of the tale when he returns the ring. The tale thus constitutes an important marker of the moment when detailed state control of the population comes to be seen as unacceptable, as pornographic and voyeuristic. Allusion is clearly being made to Louis XV's voyeuristic habit of reading police reports detailing sexual deviancy in the capital, yet Diderot is also looking forward to nineteenth-century institutions of control and observation, particularly with respect to sexual mores, and to the tight relationship between law, police and medicine that is so often the subject of Michel Foucault's influential analyses. Finally, we see Diderot indicate that the freedom of individuals in society is based on their right to a private life, the series of individuals here being very specifically female. It is interesting to note, moreover, that the freedom of women is shown to be particularly threatened: the position of woman, as very often in Enlightenment writing, is used to explore abuses of power.

We now turn to our second meaning, that is, the private life which is defined in opposition to public service. In one of his letters to his long-term 'amie' Sophie Volland, Diderot depicts this pressurised polarity with great lucidity:

> Je suis accablé de visites; je suis interrompu à chaque ligne, et je ne souffre pas patiemment qu'on vienne me distraire quand je suis avec vous. Adieu, adieu; il faut que je vous quitte pour des prêtres, des moines, des avocats, des juges, des animaux de toute espèce et de toute couleur, mais je ne vous quitterai pas sans vous protester que je ne vis que par la tendresse que j'ai pour vous.[7]

7. *Lettres à Sophie Volland*, ed. Jean Varloot (Paris, 1984), p.53 (27 July 1759). We have followed

His public affairs could not be better contrasted with his private desires in this passage, which makes explicit that his private life – understood as his emotion for Sophie and his letters to her – stands in sharp contrast to his public duties. As a tableau of the conflict between private and public, sharply critical of public demands on him, it is closest to the untranslatable English term 'privacy', which implies the right to protected, uninvaded private life and space. And Diderot locates his real life – the fact that he lives at all – in this tender relationship. What he is therefore is not his public work: his self is private and is moreover not only inaccessible to the stream of visitors he receives, but presumably also invisible to them. His real self disappears from public view while remaining strongly perceptible to him alone: its voice can only be heard in the language of thoughts and emotion which the letters convey, unless of course it is caught out and witnessed by magic – as in the *Bijoux* – or by curiosity and trickery, as in *Le Rêve de D'Alembert*. The self is internalised. It is at this level that language spoken and transcribed becomes the only lasting evidence of private experience and real, as opposed to public, life. Yet the feelings which are manifested by the sensitive body – the *corps sensible* – need to be witnessed by words or observers or both for the private life to be properly comprehended. A last point in this section: the interiorised self and its alignment or association with love is consistent with *Les Bijoux indiscrets*: in that earlier text, we saw the private life tightly bound to sexual desire, as is the convention in numerous salacious texts, whether clearly advertising themselves as pornographic fiction, or whether maintaining some tenuous relation to the supposed truth of the lives of the great (and not very good). In relating the violation of sexual privacy to the violation of intimate desires and thus to the violation of selfhood, however, *Les Bijoux indiscrets* associates the private life with the self, and the self with emotional desire. This is what we also witness in Diderot's letters to Sophie.

We now come to the final meaning that the *Encyclopédie* lays out for us: 'privé' as 'deprived'. It is manifested perhaps most clearly in *La Religieuse* and in the *Lettre sur les aveugles*. The protagonist Suzanne is deprived of amorous or simply internal private life and also of her freedom by being sent to the convent where she is watched and coerced unremittingly.

Varloot's later edition rather than the complete *Correspondance*, ed. Georges Roth and Jean Varloot, 16 vols (Paris, 1955-1970), because Varloot does not impose modern paragraphing on the text as Roth had done, instead retaining Diderot's own system which varies widely from exclamatory new paragraphs with every sentence to much longer chunks of text. Varloot explains this in his textual notes: see *Lettres à Sophie Volland*, p.363. With respect to the passage cited, Roth introduces a new paragraph at 'Adieu, adieu' which quite interrupts the flow: see Diderot, *Correspondance*, vol.2 (1956), p.185.

Moreover, her status of gracelessness is ironically underlined by her steadfast denial of vocation. Her characterisation as an extreme example of victimhood, exploitation and consistently thwarted self-determination is only reinforced by the notorious *préface-annexe*: Suzanne's first-person narrative ends on a piteous and desperate note which is brutally debunked in the *postface*, explaining that Diderot and his circle made the whole story up as a joke. Suzanne's position as other people's plaything rather than being belied is in fact confirmed by this afterword. The *préface-annexe* deprives her even of her voice.

In Diderot's early philosophical text, *La Lettre sur les aveugles* (1749), the notion of deprivation is even more centrally organising: here Diderot considers what humans who are deprived of the notion of sight actually are; whether they are the same as other humans or more or less and in what ways. The publication of the *Lettre* marked a turning point in his career: it was the first and the last time that he wrote anything extended and explicit about his own philosophy, and it sent him to prison for three months on a charge of suspected atheism and thereby imperilled the work on the *Encyclopédie*. But explicit does not mean straightforward: his explicit subject is the Molyneux problem, a question first raised by a correspondent of Locke, Mr Molyneux, which asked something crucial about the theory that all knowledge comes through the senses, as Locke had argued in his *Essay concerning human understanding* (1690). Molyneux asked whether someone who was blind from birth and was suddenly able to see would be able to tell the difference between a cube and a sphere without touching them. The premise of the *Lettre* is that Diderot and his correspondent, 'Madame', were hoping to have had the opportunity of witnessing a cataract operation on a young girl, blind from birth, and would thus be able to find out the answer to the question by seeing it for themselves in a perfect example of Enlightenment observation, experiment and experience. However, in the event, they are not allowed to watch the operation, and the *Lettre* constitutes Diderot's philosophical, rhetorical and partly fictional answer to the question. He concludes that the girl would be unable to tell the difference between the cube and sphere merely on seeing them, because she would not yet have learnt how sight works or what information it gives. But, arguably, Diderot shifts the ground of the investigation entirely. Crucially, he pushes the idea of the Lockean subject to its farthest extent to see whether not just knowledge but also morality derives from the senses; and whether this implies that a person with fewer senses will be less moral. He concludes that this would be the case, asserting that the feelings of sympathy and pity which are supposed to be most particularly human are much diminished in the blind person because s/he cannot witness suffering in the same immediate way that sighted people can. The argument is that when we cannot see someone suffering, we do not care in the same way, and that what Diderot explicitly calls the 'privation de la vue' has this effect on the blind. The passage is worth quoting: 'Nous-mêmes, ne cessons-nous pas de compatir, lorsque la distance ou la petitesse des objets produit le même effet sur nous, que la privation de la vue sur les aveugles? Tant nos vertus dépendent de notre manière de sentir, et du degré auquel les choses extérieures nous affectent!'[8]

The important implication is that if things are to have an effect on us we need to see them up close. In order for us to understand things fully we need to feel them, they need to affect us personally. This locks the idea of the *privation de la vue*, being deprived of sight, back into our primary idea of *la vie privée*, the private life: in order to understand things we need to experience them intimately. The ruthless logic which Diderot deploys to conclude that blind people are less moral than those in enjoyment of all their senses is deliberately compromised here, as much of the *Lettre* is given over to the discussion of the personalities, private lives and experience of various blind people. If the stated moral problem is whether blind people are capable of feeling compassion, given that they cannot witness it, then surely this is in direct contradiction with the *Lettre*'s opening scene, which starts with Diderot's frustrated apology to 'Madame' that they will be unable to witness the operation to remove the cataracts of a young girl. Nowhere there is the issue of witnessing pain mentioned, although it forms the explicit concern of the following extraordinary question, and the grounds for the ensuing moral condemnation of the blind quoted above: 'Quelle différence y a-t-il pour un aveugle entre un homme qui urine et un homme qui sans se plaindre verse son sang?'[9] From this point of view, the experience of witnessing a cataract operation could not be primarily about the acquisition of knowledge, in this case defined as the resolution of a philosophical problem of perception: it would also necessarily involve seeing pain and feeling compassion, unless of course, one was 'blind' and the patient mute.

We are obliged to conclude that compassion and its relation to knowledge is a new problem which displaces the Molyneux problem, and which we might formulate thus: what is one's ethical responsibility to or relationship with the knowledge one wishes to acquire but cannot

8. Diderot, *Lettre sur les aveugles: à l'usage de ceux qui voient; Lettre sur les sourds et muets, à l'usage de ceux qui entendent et qui parlent*, ed. Marian Hobson and Simon Harvey (Paris, 2000), p.38, l.343-348: as this edition helpfully indicates line numbers, we give them too. All our references to the *Lettre sur les aveugles* are to this edition which supersedes and replaces all previous editions. We do not therefore reference DPV in this case.

9. Diderot, *Lettre sur les aveugles*, p.38, l.341-343.

experience? Diderot draws our attention to this problem by means of the double lacuna so clearly advertised at the beginning of the *Lettre*, almost in the form of a paradox: Diderot and 'Madame' will not be allowed to see the operation for the removal of cataracts, supposedly to allow the patient to see and hence to resolve the Molyneux problem. The problem itself is one of perception and experience: they will neither see nor experience the experiment (the reader will remember that 'experience' and 'experiment' are both rendered by the same term, 'expérience', in French), and will be unable to experience witnessing the young patient's experience. This seems to suggest that the 'answer' to the Molyneux problem may not be divorceable from the circumstances of its experience: one is then forced to ask whether that experience, necessarily singular, can be generalisable. This seems to be the question that the section devoted to Saunderson repeatedly asks: what is his experience/perception? What does that tell us? Can we get access to it? Does it influence his mathematics? Thus Diderot repeatedly tries to winkle out details of Saunderson's – or the blind man of Puiseaux's, or Mélanie de Salignac's – private or personal life, the 'vie particulière' of someone who is 'privé de la vue'.[10] 'Privé' as 'deprived' and 'privé' as 'personal' are clearly brought together here.[11] In the following passage, Diderot tells how he scoured Saunderson's mathematical works for details of his personal experience:

> J'ai parcouru les éléments d'algèbre de Saunderson, dans l'espérance d'y rencontrer ce que je désirais d'apprendre de ceux qui l'ont vu *familièrement*, et qui nous ont instruits de quelques *particularités* de sa vie; mais ma curiosité a été trompée, et j'ai conçu que des éléments de géométrie de sa façon

10. Interestingly, mentions of the specific term 'privé' refer exclusively to the meanings around 'deprived'. There are thirteen instances, as follows (emphasis added): 'celui qui est *privé de la vue*', p.34, l.169-175; '[n]otre aveugle nous dit à ce sujet, qu'il se trouverait fort à plaindre *d'être privé des mêmes avantages que nous*', p.34, l.190-194; '*la privation de la vue*', p.38, l.343-348; '[e]n effet, Saunderson parlait à ses élèves comme s'ils eussent été *privés de la vue*', p.53, l.738-742; 'Saunderson était *privé non seulement de la vue, mais de l'organe*', p.58, l.950-955; '*les dieux jaloux les en privèrent*, de peur d'avoir des égaux parmi les mortels', p.59, l.983-988; 'Qu'avions-nous fait à Dieu, vous et moi, l'un pour avoir cet organe, l'autre *pour en être privé?*', p.62, l.1096-1104; '*Ils ont des yeux dont Saunderson était privé*', p.63, l.1157-1164; '*la privation de la vue et du spectacle de la nature*', p.63, l.1168-1171; 'Je renonce sans peine à une vie qui n'a été pour moi qu'un long désir, et *qu'une privation continuelle*', p.64, l.1196-1199; '[c]'est peut-être par cette raison que les enfants se consolent si promptement *des jouets dont on les prive*', p.70, l.1424-1438; 'Il n'en est pas du bonheur et du malheur ainsi que des ténèbres et de la lumière; l'un ne consiste pas *dans une privation pure et simple de l'autre*', p.76, l.1679-1681; 'Il n'en serait cependant pas moins essentiel, lorsqu'on se proposerait la démonstration de quelque proposition d'éternelle vérité, comme on les appelle, *d'éprouver sa démonstration en la privant du témoignage des sens*', p.81, l.1869-1878.

11. Some examples might be: 'un détail qui vous amuserait sans doute', p.39, l.362; 'ceux qui l'ont vu familièrement', p.56, l.860; 'd'autres particularités intéressantes', p.63, l.1174.

auraient été un ouvrage plus singulier en lui-même, et beaucoup plus utile pour nous.[12]

Having been unable to find details relating the profile and character of the work to a personal perspective, Diderot muses about what such a text would have looked like, and later comes back to the subject, again regretting that he cannot provide 'Madame' with 'd'autres particularités intéressantes'.[13] The eager praise he expresses for the book entitled *The Life and character of Dr Nicholas Saunderson late Lucasian Professor of the mathematics in the University of Cambridge, by his disciple and friend William Inchlif, esq* is all directed at the fact that it gives us the personal details elsewhere lacking: in fact, as we know, no such book exists, and Diderot made up the reference entirely.[14] Speaking of the book, he writes that:

> L'Angleterre est le pays des philosophes, des curieux, des systématiques; cependant sans M. Inchlif, nous ne saurions de Saunderson que ce que les hommes les plus ordinaires nous en auraient appris; par exemple, qu'il reconnaissait les lieux où il avait été introduit une fois, au bruit des murs et du pavé, lorsqu'ils en faisaient, et cent autres choses de la même nature qui lui étaient communes avec presque tous les aveugles.[15]

This is the paragraph which seems to promise the personal details which otherwise are lacking ('sans M. Inchlif, nous ne saurions de Saunderson que') and which in fact proceeds to tell us the opposite, that is, only those experiences and tricks which he shares with all blind people, and which are well known. Is this a Diderotian trick? Why does he invent books which do not exist, only to tease us with references to unique revelatory information which he then does not reveal? Is it a repeated structure of information both advertised and withheld, such as Réaumur is charged with in the opening pages? Is he saying that such information does not exist or that it is secret, or that secrets are just a trick, a fiction of withheld information, and behind them is nothing? Is he saying, when he refers to Saunderson's personal experience and then supplies information about a whole group of people, that singular, unique unrepeatable personal experience does not exist, that Saunderson is simply at one (educated) end of a spectrum of similar experience, and that what we might want to call his individual identity is merely that of an *aveugle-né*, a man born blind? Thus uniqueness, singularity, do not exist, firstly because all 'individuals' are part of a collectivity, their identity contingent on their organisation; and secondly because *la vie particulière* –

12. *Lettre sur les aveugles*, p.56, l.858-864 (emphasis added).
13. *Lettre sur les aveugles*, p.63, l.1174.
14. *Lettre sur les aveugles*, p.64, l.1183-1186.
15. *Lettre sur les aveugles*, p.64, l.1207-1214.

private life, or individual experience – is played out in public, as witnessed by others, and systematically conforms to the demands of social convention.[16] The wearing of clothes, which sighted people feel they need to do, but blind people and, in this case, l'aveugle du Puiseaux, are mystified by, other than for purposes of warmth, would be one such example.

Another might be the case of Saunderson's deathbed speech, a perfect example of a conventional genre, at once seemingly intimate and necessarily public.[17] One has no sense of penetrating the realm of personal feeling, of interiority. Thus one comes back again to the synonymous trio, *privé, particulier, secret*, which with reference to Saunderson might be translated as 'deprived, personal, secret'. His individual experience relies on his status as a member of that group of people deprived of sight, while his interiority remains inaccessible, secret. Secret in this light is redefined as the inaccessible, the invisible. A secret can be stolen or violated; we note, moreover, that the prospective patient in the *Lettre sur les aveugles*, whose Molyneux secret is about to be violated, is in fact a 'jeune fille'. Her virginal girlhood makes her all the more vulnerable, or violable, as the topos of the young girl in pornographic fiction makes abundantly clear. So she and her secret – stealable, violable – are in a fragile position. But secrets can also be confided. This Saunderson does on a single occasion when, as part of his deathbed speech, he diverges from convention for one sentence, saying: 'Je renonce sans peine à une vie qui n'a été pour moi qu'un long désir, et qu'une privation continuelle.'[18] Stoically conventional as such sentiments may be, it is a declaration of suffering which stands in stark contrast to the rest of his behaviour and sayings as recounted by the *Lettre*, which systematically paint him as a virtuous, enlightened, practical mathematical philosopher whose life is devoted to public service and

16. See for example the following extract from the *Rêve*: 'Je suis donc tel, parce qu'il a fallu que je fusse tel. Changez le tout, vous me changez nécessairement; mais le tout change sans cesse. [...] L'homme n'est qu'un effet commun; le monstre qu'un effet rare; [...] Tous les êtres circulent les uns dans les autres, par conséquent toutes les espèces [...] tout est en un flux perpétuel... [...] Et vous parlez d'individus, pauvres philosophes! laissez là vos individus', *Le Rêve de D'Alembert*, ed. Jean Varloot and Georges Dulac, in DPV, vol.17 (1987), p.137-38.
17. Kate Tunstall's articles on the figure of the *aveugle-né* in philosophy from classical times onwards provide a particularly suggestive counterpart to this point: these 'real-life' *aveugles-nés* whose 'real-life' experience is the object of discussion, are in fact part of a long self-referential philosophical tradition. See Kate Tunstall, 'Pré-histoire d'un emblème des Lumières: l'aveugle-né de Montaigne à Diderot', in *Les Lumières en mouvement: la circulation des idées au XVIIIᵉ siècle*, ed. Isabelle Moreau (Lyon, 2009), p.173-98; 'L'aveugle qui suit l'aveugle qui suit l'aveugle: la philosophie intertextuelle de la *Lettre sur les aveugles*', in *L'Aveugle et le philosophe*, ed. Marion Chottin (Paris, 2009), p.20-28.
18. *Lettre sur les aveugles*, p.64, l.1197-1199.

who shows himself to be ready to do anything to advance human knowledge, even by so little as an iota. This virtuous public servant, great mathematician and family man, the very portrait of worthy success, reveals here in one sentence a world of internal feeling which profoundly alters his profile. Needless to say, Diderot made this sentence up: it is a completely fictional insight into the world of interiority, and it alerts us to the possible role of fiction within philosophy, a subject which Kate Tunstall illuminates in her study of the forms Diderot's philosophical dodges and weaves take on in this same *Lettre sur les aveugles*.[19]

The investigation into whether Saunderson's extraordinary mathematical achievements derive from genius or from organisation seems to resolve that he is a member of a group, although a particularly talented and educated one, rather than unique. His perception is repeatedly explained by reference to collective rather than singular experience. Yet this does not preclude his having interiority, a private life, which is strictly imperceptible to others unless given a voice (as in the case of Diderot's letter to Sophie Volland), or if recreated by means of imaginative empathy or, as Diderot might call it, *compassion*.

So we are left with two problems here: a philosophical one, framed by Diderot, which asks how we perceive something imperceptible (the internal life of others), and a critical one, which asks how important these questions clustering around the different meanings of the *vie privée* are for Diderot. We are forced, in the face of abundant evidence, to accept that the answer to this second question is that they are important and, moreover, that his writings combine to suggest that personal internal experience determines one's selfhood, and constitutes one's life, while the notion of the unique self, deriving from the theology of the soul, is revealed to be completely illusory. Thus privacy overtakes grace.

With respect to the former question, how to reach into and even experience the private lives of others, one answer Diderot supplies is that in each case where we witness privacy, it is inevitably, or always already, a violation of it. Beginning to justify or explain this view, perhaps I might turn again to the texts. The *Bijoux indiscrets* as already discussed provides a clear dramatisation of these issues, and the narrative is constructed very explicitly from repeated scenes of this nature where a woman's private life is shockingly exposed in front of multiple witnesses. The *Rêve de D'Alembert* provides us with a similar case, violating personal experience. It opens with a conversation about generation between Diderot and D'Alembert wherein Diderot introduces his friend to the farther reaches

19. Kate E. Tunstall, 'Ethics and the work of fiction: Diderot's answer to Molyneux's problem', in *Fiction at the frontiers of knowledge: law, literature, and philosophy in early modern Europe*, ed. Alexis Tadié and Richard Scholar (Burlington, VT, 2010), p.186-203.

of materialism, and which is supposed to have such an effect on D'Alembert that he raves all night long, to the extent that his companion Mlle de Lespinasse calls for the doctor Bordeu, reads out to him her on-the-spot record of the streams of words and uninhibited gestures that had emanated unconsciously from her companion during the course of the night and which she – as a proper witness – had noted down, asking for explanation, which Bordeu provides. In the final section Lespinasse thinks through the consequences of this theory of material generation with Bordeu. At one level, *Le Rêve* constitutes a skilful but also obvious exercise in persuasion, following the pedagogical tenet that everything should be repeated three times in order to be understood. At another level, it is also the dramatisation of the effect of apparently abstract ideas on the mind and body of a named individual. A corollary of this point is that *Le Rêve* works neatly in parallel to the discussion in the *Lettre sur les aveugles* of the idea that in order to understand something you have to look at it up close and personal. So D'Alembert's experience of the ideas is deeply personal and intimate – not as upright philosopher but as recumbent dreamer – and Mlle de Lespinasse is the necessary witness who gives his private life public reality. Her notation of what he said and her reactions to his words, both as she recalls them, and as she comes back to them with Bordeu, make explicit that she is witnessing thoughts and experiences which are interiorised and private. This is perhaps most embarrassingly the case when she recounts ever so innocently and in defamiliarised terms what is very clearly D'Alembert's desire for her. And so he masturbates:

> 'Qui sait les races d'animaux qui nous ont précédés? Qui sait les races d'animaux qui succéderont aux nôtres? Tout change, tout passe, il n'y a que le tout qui reste. Le monde commence et finit sans cesse; il est à chaque instant à son commencement et à sa fin; il n'en a jamais eu d'autre, et n'en aura jamais d'autre. Dans cet immense océan de matière, pas une molécule qui ressemble à une molécule, pas une molécule qui ressemble à elle-même un instant: *Rerum novus nascitur ordo*, voilà son inscription éternelle...' Puis il ajoutait en soupirant: 'o vanité de nos pensées! o pauvreté de la gloire et de nos travaux! o misère, o petitesse de nos vues! il n'y a rien de solide que de boire, manger, vivre, aimer et dormir... Mademoiselle de Lespinasse, ou êtes-vous? – Me voilà.' Alors son visage s'est coloré. J'ai voulu lui tâter le pouls, mais je ne sais où il avait caché sa main. Il paraissait éprouver une convulsion; sa bouche s'était entrouverte, son haleine était pressée; il a poussé un profond soupir, et puis un soupir plus faible et plus profond encore; il a retourné sa tête sur son oreiller et s'est endormi. Je le regardais avec attention et j'étais tout émue sans savoir pourquoi, le cœur me battait, et ce n'était pas de peur.[20]

---

20. *Le Rêve de D'Alembert*, p.128-29.

Of course the innocent voice recounting an erotic scene in defamiliarised terms is an old technique in pornography, and one which Diderot also deploys in *La Religieuse*. It is a scene which takes the idea of the private life of a person, and violates it by making it public, firstly to the witnesses in the dialogue – Lespinasse and Bordeu – and thence as text to us, the readers. It brings together abstract philosophy and the bodily actuality of our responses to philosophy in a way which is as cheeky as it is Lockean. It makes ideas manifest by making them personal and private. It is also a passage – and a dialogue – which brings us back to one of our initial definitions, that of being tamed and domesticated. As D'Alembert follows the ideas through, he is confronted ceaselessly with the depiction of atomistic nature at work, reproducing, splitting, forming, feeling affinity, joining together and so on. His own nature is part of that nature, and thus the masturbation scene is essential in connecting him – his ideas, his socialised self – with his embedded instincts and behaviour, and thus we find the notion of *privé* dramatised as at once natural, untamed and by association bestial, and also as private. Sex is obviously a key way of associating these ideas, and furthermore is a powerful way of reinforcing the sense of uncrossable boundaries between what we need to see in order to understand that something is real because we want to see and enjoy it, and something we feel we ought not to see because it is private. As in the *Lettre sur les aveugles*, this method of acquiring knowledge seems to be ethically compromised, while also being the only authentic means of learning anything at all. We need to eavesdrop on private lives, as Mangogul did illicitly. Access to knowledge and questions of political control, or exploitation, are absolutely imbricated.

An even starker example of eavesdropping is related in *Jacques le fataliste*. Jacques has been wounded in the knee and taken in by a peasant woman whose husband grumbles at the expense. Jacques on a pallet bed on the other side of a thin partition overhears a very private scene in which the wife asks her husband not to make love to her since they have not got enough money to raise another child. He berates her in turn for taking someone in because there is not enough money to pay for the doctors. Needless to say, they do have sex and the woman is in despair at falling pregnant. It is a hilarious scene and a really inimitable piece of Diderotian *vraisemblance*. The idea of poverty – another form of deprivation – is made real and understandable via a witnessed and recounted scene of sexual intimacy. Jacques is narrating the episode:

> Me voilà pansé, un peu soulagé, le chirurgien parti, et mes hôtes retirés et couchés. Leur chambre n'était séparée de la mienne que par des planches à claire-voie sur lesquelles on avait collé du papier gris et sur ce papier quelques images enluminées. Je ne dormais pas, et j'entendis la femme qui

disait à son mari: 'Laissez-moi, je n'ai pas envie de rire. Un pauvre
malheureux qui se meurt à notre porte! – Femme, tu me diras tout cela
après. [...]'
Après une assez courte pause, le mari prit la parole et dit: 'Là, femme,
conviens donc à présent que par une compassion déplacée tu nous as mis
dans un embarras dont il est presque impossible de se tirer. L'année est
mauvaise, à peine pouvons-nous suffir à nos besoins et aux besoins de nos
enfants. Le grain est d'une cherté! [...]'
– Oui, voilà qui est fort bien dit; et parce qu'on est dans la misère vous me
faites un enfant, comme si nous n'en avions pas déjà assez. – oh! que non. –
Oh! que si; je suis sûre que je vais être grosse! – voilà comme tu dis toutes les
fois.– et cela n'a jamais manqué quand l'oreille me démange après, et j'y sens
une démangeaison comme jamais... – Ton oreille ne sait ce qu'elle dit. – Ne
me touche pas! Laisse là mon oreille! Laisse donc, l'homme, est-ce que tu es
fou? Tu t'en trouveras mal.– Non, non; cela ne m'est pas arrivé depuis le soir
de la Saint-Jean. – Tu feras si bien que... et puis dans un mois d'ici tu me
bouderas comme si c'était de ma faute. – Non, non. – C'est toi qui l'auras
voulu. – Oui, oui. – Tu t'en souviendras, tu ne diras pas comme tu as dit
toutes les autres fois? Oui, oui...' Et puis voilà que de non non en oui oui cet
homme enragé contre sa femme d'avoir cédé à un sentiment d'humanité...[21]

Here, as before, we see that natural, untamed instinct is at play, as well as
at loggerheads: which is more natural – compassion, such as the woman
felt for Jacques, or egotistical desire, such as the man felt for his wife? It is
typical of Diderot that his writing both captures contemporaneous
polemic and refracts it into new contexts where it takes on new (and
generally surprising) forms. Either way, the socio-economic context
requires the man and woman to choose and control their instincts,
and this choice is not an uncontested one, given that material consequences will ensue. And the couple's perception and experience of their
lives is only acquired by virtue of Jacques's unintended eavesdropping.

   A preliminary conclusion to this section would accept that the three
meanings of 'control', be it self-control as in the scene from *Jacques*, or
governmental control and manipulation as in *Les Bijoux*, *private life* and
deprivation are all explicitly, even centrally, dealt with by Diderot, and that
in each case they are linked back to what begins to look like a sustained
meditation on the notion of self and what is necessary or fundamental to
it with relation to issues of intimacy, privacy, internalised inhibition and
external control, self-expression and conversely invisibility.

   To summarise: Diderot in his writings reflects the diversity of associations and meanings which cluster around the term 'privé' and does it in
ways which complicate our idea of what a private life could be. We think
we can assume quite unproblematically that a private life probably refers

21. *Jacques le fataliste*, ed. Jacques Proust, in DPV, vol.23 (1981), p.39-40; *Jacques le fataliste*, ed. M.
   Delon (Paris, 2004), p.682-83.

to the domestic relations described in the third volume of the *Histoire de la vie privée*. What Diderot forces us to consider is whether in fact a private life implies a reversion to nature or is an indicator of having been tamed, socialised. Is it something the unviolated existence of which guarantees a healthy society of self-determining individuals? Is it something that denotes lack, or is it the location of the real self? Is it interiorised and invisible while being at one and the same time the site of the perception, actualisation and personalisation of otherwise elusive ideas? In order to be properly private, does it need to be witnessed in public? And can the text perform that witnessing, be that audience? And, finally, what sort of provocative role do Diderot and his texts play in this dramatisation and making public of the private moment? Surely, a crucial part of their polemical and often censored character derives from the transgressive way in which they put the private life centre stage. In conclusion, I would suggest that the private life is a core notion for Diderot, and that the way in which he looks at its tensions and contradictions fundamentally illuminates our own understanding of what is at stake.

Inventing private lives: the representation of private lives in French *Vies privées*

OLIVIER FERRET

While the French expression 'vie privée' refers to the cultural notion treated more broadly in this volume, it is the literary genre that will concern us. From the late 1720s to the 1830s, approximately 140 texts were published with titles including this exact phrase. These *Vies privées*, which exhibit notable similarities, are biographies that narrate the life of the person named in the title, from birth to death, or in cases where the subject was still living, then at least to the date of publication. The work of anonymous authors, the typical *Vie privée* text can be read as a pamphlet. Its subject is a politically influential man or woman, a soldier, a clergyman, who becomes the target of satirical attacks dealing with his (or her) public actions and, of course, his (or her) private life.[1] If we leave to one side the earliest texts, most of which narrate the lives of criminals,[2] we can distinguish three different periods in the history of this prolific genre: the *ancien régime Vies privées*, the model for which is probably the well-known and successful *Vie privée de Louis XV*, published in 1781 and attributed to Mouffle d'Angerville;[3] the mass of texts written during the Revolution period; and last but not least the *Vies privées* devoted to Napoléon Bonaparte. The degree of censorship that was imposed varied during these periods, notably affecting the distribution of texts. But they nonetheless display a common rhetorical shape, a fact that justifies a study grounded on narratology, discourse analysis and history of ideas.

In treating the representation of private lives in the French *Vies privées*, this chapter will consider the relationships between the two meanings of

---

1. On this genre, see the *Dictionnaire des Vies privées*, set up by the LIRE research team in Lyon: *Vie privée et politique (1770-1830)*, suivi de *Dictionnaire des Vies privées*, ed. O. Ferret, A.-M. Mercier-Faivre and C. Thomas, publishing in February 2011 (*SVEC* 2011:02). Numerous ideas developed in this chapter derive from collective discussions among the members of this team during the preparation of the book. I must especially thank Claude Labrosse, whose reflections on the notion of private in the *Vie privée du maréchal de Richelieu* were very helpful. See also Robert Darnton, *The Devil in the holy water, or the Art of slander from Louis XIV to Napoleon* (University of Pennsylvania Press, 2009).
2. See the chapter by Lise Andries in this volume.
3. [Barthélemy-François-Joseph Mouffle d'Angerville], *Vie privée de Louis XV*. On this text, see Darnton, 'Mlle Bonafon'.

the expression, that is between the notion and the genre. Which facts in the character's life can be defined as 'private'? Are there private 'biographèmes', in Roland Barthes's sense of the word? Is there an evolution in the representation of private life between the 1780s and the mid-1800s, and can we make a connection between this evolution and the cultural changes described by historians? In so far as these texts contain a substantial fictional element, they must not be considered as documents. But, even when the representation of the private is distorted, it may throw light on fantasy and perhaps on collective mentality. It may equally disappoint certain expectations. Are the authors really interested in evoking private life in itself, or does the private image built up by these satirical texts aim only at destroying the public image of their targets? Let us first consider problems faced by authors in presenting private matters, move onto a discussion of the position of the reader and narrative approaches, and finally touch on ideological content. These texts openly aspire to influence the public, but underlying the interaction between public and private spheres is a conception of politics and a sense of history.

Definitions given by French dictionaries help pinpoint the difficulty in describing the 'private' in the *Vies privées*. The 1762 edition of the *Dictionnaire de l'Académie* is interesting: 'privé', as an adjective, means 'qui est simple particulier, qui n'a aucune charge publique' and the expression 'vie privée' is said to be used to evoke 'la vie d'un homme qui est éloigné de toutes sortes d'emplois'. Therefore, this expression seems to be irrelevant to most of the lives narrated in the texts named 'Vies privées', since they concern persons who are known because of their (public) activities. Associating private and public fields, some texts are entitled 'Vie privée et publique' ('de Louis XVI' or 'du ci-derrière marquis de Villette')[4] or 'Vie publique et privée' ('de M. le marquis de La Fayette', 'du comte de Mirabeau', 'de Joachim Murat', 'de [...] Vergennes').[5] We also find adjectives that are more specifically connected with the (public) activities of the person: a 'Vie privée, politique et militaire' is devoted to the 'prince Henri de Prusse' and a 'Vie militaire, politique et privée' to the 'demoiselle Charles-Geneviève-Louise-

---

4. [Jean-François André? Auguste Danican?], *Vie privée et publique de Louis XVI, roi de France*, (Paris, chez tous les magasins de nouveautés, 1800); *Vie privée et publique du ci-derrière marquis de Villette* (n.p., n.d.).

5. *Vie publique et privée de M. le marquis de La Fayette, avec des détails sur l'affaire du 6 octobre, etc.* (n.p., 1791); *Vie publique et privée de Honoré-Gabriel Riquetti, comte de Mirabeau, député du tiers état de la sénéchaussée d'Aix* (Paris, Hôtel d'Aiguillon, 1791); [Antoine Sérieys], *Vie publique et privée de Joachim Murat, composée d'après des matériaux authentiques, la plupart inconnus, et contenant des particularités inédites sur ses premières années, par M. **** (Paris, J. G. Dentu, 1816); Charles-Joseph de Mayer, *Vie publique et privée de Charles Gravier de Vergennes, ministre d'Etat* (Paris, Maradan, 1789).

Auguste-Andrée-Thimotée Eon, ou Eon de Beaumont' (who, by the way, is presented as a woman);[6] a 'Vie privée et politique' is devoted to the 'général Dumouriez', to the 'roi Isaac [Le] Chapelier', to Condé, to Conti, to Hébert and to the 'citoyen Lenoir' and, in a more specific way, the life of Calonne and the life of Necker, whose public office ('directeur général des finances') is mentioned, are related in a 'Vie privée et ministérielle'.[7] It is not surprising that the Genevan scientist Charles Bonnet is the subject of a 'Vie privée et littéraire', and Beaumarchais of a 'Vie privée, politique et littéraire'.[8]

The association of these terms ('politique', 'militaire', 'ministérielle', 'littéraire' or simply 'publique'), which are related to the public life of the character, with the word 'privé' raises the question of the distinction between the public and the private. We will see later that one of the ideological meanings of these texts concerns a peculiar relationship between the two fields. For the moment, the existence of this association encourages us to define more closely our definition of private life. Information provided in the titles and in the paratexts may be useful. For instance, according to the title, the aim of the *Vie privée, politique et littéraire de Beaumarchais* is to 'bring to light' his 'character' and his 'wit'.

6. [Louis-Joseph Bouillé du Charol? Jean-François Roger?], *Vie privée, politique et militaire du prince Henri de Prusse, frère de Frédéric II* (Paris, Delaunay, 1809); [La Fortelle? Peyraud de Beaussol?], *Histoire du chevalier d'Eon: la vie militaire, politique et privée de demoiselle Charles-Geneviève-Louise-Auguste-Andrée-Thimotée Eon, ou d'Eon de Beaumont, écuyer, chevalier de l'ordre royal et militaire de Saint Louis, ancien capitaine de dragons et des volontaires de l'armée, aide de camp du maréchal et comte de Broglie; ci-devant docteur en droit civil et en droit canon, avocat au parlement de Paris, censeur royal pour l'histoire et les belles-lettres, envoyé en Russie d'abord secrètement, puis publiquement avec le chevalier Douglas [...] secrétaire d'ambassade, [...] ambassadeur extraordinaire [...] et connue jusqu'en 1777 sous le nom de chevalier d'Eon* (Paris, Lambert, Onfroi, Valade, Esprit et chez l'auteur, 1779). On this last text, see Anne-Marie Mercier-Faivre, 'Les vies privées du chevalier d'Eon', in *The Chevalier d'Eon and his worlds: gender, politics and espionage in the eighteenth century*, ed. S. Burrows (London, 2010).
7. *La Vie privée et politique du général Dumouriez pour servir de suite à ses mémoires* (Hamburg, B. G. Hoffmann, 1794); *Vie privée et politique du roi Isaac Chapelier, premier du nom, et chez des rois de France de la quatrième race en 1789, Louis XVI étant roi des Français; précédée d'une introduction, et ornée du portrait de Sa Majesté* (Rennes, n.p., 1790); *Vie politique et privée de Louis-Joseph de Condé, prince du sang* (Paris, chez les marchands de nouveautés, 1790); *Vie privée de Louis-François-Joseph de Conti, prince du sang, et sa correspondance avec ses complices fugitifs* (Turin [Paris], Garin, 1790); [Pierre Turbat], *Vie privée et politique de J.-R. Hébert, auteur du Père Duchêne, pour faire suite aux Vies de Manuel, Pétion, Brissot et d'Orléans* (Paris, Franklin, An II [1794]); *Vie privée et politique du citoyen Lenoir, à ses concitoyens* ([Paris], Clément, n.d. [1793?]); Jean-Louis Carra, *Vie privée et ministérielle de Calonne* (Paris, Guillemard, 1791); [James Rutledge], *Vie privée et ministérielle [Supplément à la] de M. Necker, directeur général des finances, par un citoyen* (Geneva, Pellet, 1790).
8. [Jean Trembley], *Vie privée et littéraire de Charles Bonnet en réponse à quelques pamphlets* (Bern, Société typographique, n.d. [post 1793]); [Charles-Yves Cousin d'Avallon], *Vie privée, politique et littéraire de Beaumarchais, suivie d'anecdotes, de bons mots [...] propre à faire connaître le caractère et l'esprit de cet homme célèbre et singulier* (Paris, Michel, An X [1802]).

The interest for the 'character' of the person, especially when the text deals with a 'well-known' and 'singular' man, is also mentioned in the *Vie privée et criminelle de Henri-Augustin Trumeau*: in the histories of famous criminals, the public can read 'leur véritable physionomie, leur caractère, leurs mœurs, leurs penchants. Les lecteurs les suivent avec intérêt dans le labyrinthe de leurs passions.'[9] Yet the task is to decide whether the main interest is to define the singularity of the person or decide that the character of this person is interesting because of his inclusion in a broader category such as criminals. Although it is in a different way, the same problem arises in the *Vie privée du comte de Buffon* when the author explains his project: 'C'est de l'homme et de sa vie privée seulement que j'ose ici vous occuper', he writes: 'ses mœurs, ses habitudes, sa conduite et ses principes domestiques; voilà le but de cet écrit.' There seems to be a clear distinction between the supposedly public activities of the man of letters and the scientist, and his private life as a person:

> Dès qu'il prendra la plume, je me retirerai modestement; mais j'attendrai en silence sa sortie du cabinet, pour observer ce que va dire et faire avec ses amis, ses parents, son procureur, son curé, l'homme qui vient d'embrasser la généralité des êtres et de calculer l'infini. Je dirai tout, l'heure de son réveil, la manière dont il s'habillait, ses repas, ses bons mots, ses amours, ou, si vous aimez mieux, ses jouissances; car il ne croyait qu'à cela.
> Qui n'apprendrait avec le plus vif intérêt les entretiens de La Fontaine avec sa femme Honnesta? Ce que disait Fénelon à son valet de confiance, et Crébillon à ses chats? Qui lirait donc sans intérêt les entretiens du comte de Buffon avec le P. Ignace et Mlle ***? Le premier desservait la chapelle de M. le Comte; et M. le Comte, la chapelle de l'autre.[10]

The examples given in the text show that the main interest is to be found in the person's intimacy and specifically in his sexuality:

> L'homme qui a porté la plus forte atteinte à l'empire des femmes, puisqu'il a voulu réduire le bonheur de l'amour au physique, et qu'il a prétendu prouver que le moral n'en valait rien, a été dans son jeune âge comme dans sa vieillesse, l'un de leurs plus vigoureux courtisans: il cherchait ses jouissances journalières dans une classe de femmes peu faites pour l'enlever à la gloire, sa grande maîtresse, et qui ne lui prenaient de temps que les deux minutes où les anges, dit-on, se couvrent de leurs ailes pour ne pas être jaloux de nos plaisirs.[11]

If the author of the *Vie privée du comte de Buffon* uses periphrasis and does not give details about such sexual episodes – perhaps because they are

---

9. *Vie privée et criminelle de Henri-Augustin Trumeau* ([Paris], Renaudière, n.d. [1804?]), p.6.
10. Joseph Aude, *Vie privée du comte de Buffon, suivie d'un recueil de poésies, dont quelques pièces sont relatives à ce grand homme* (Lausanne, n.p., 1788), p.5-6.
11. *Vie privée du comte de Buffon*, p.37-38. The author adds later on: 'Les jeunes filles, les femmes niaises étaient fort de son goût' (p.41).

obviously quick, Buffon being rather a busy genius – other authors of *Vies privées* are more explicit. Sexuality is indeed a very important aspect of private life, to such an extent that some texts deal mainly or entirely with the character's love affairs: *Amours secrètes de Napoléon Bonaparte*; *Vie privée, amoureuse, secrète et authentique de Napoléon Bonaparte et des princes et princesses de sa famille*, for example, promises to reveal, according to its title, 'leurs liaisons particulières et leurs intrigues galantes avec divers personnages de tous rangs et de toute renommée'.

The *Vie privée du comte de Buffon* also shows that the representation of private life includes domestic considerations, an aspect which is also part of the *Vie privée, impartiale, politique, militaire et domestique du marquis de La Fayette.*[12] Details about everyday life need to be given about the way the person is dressed, the way the person eats and so on. These activities are the main topic of the *Histoire de la vie privée des Français*, a work commissioned by the marquis de Paulmy. Although unfinished, its plan contains rubrics for food, housing, dress, games and entertainment, which are said to contain 'tout ce qu'on peut dire sur la vie privée'.[13] It is clear that, because the interest in the private encompasses domestic and even everyday life, it raises the same kind of problem we have already met concerning private lives of criminals. Although the person may have original ways of behaving, the characterisation of private life is most often generic. Furthermore, one of the issues the author confronts is how to provide details of sufficient interest to hold the reader's attention: the more common the evocation, the more boring the text risks being. The authors do not always succeed in rising to the challenge. Even if we should be convinced that 'tout intéresse dans la vie d'une femme extraordinaire',[14] as the author puts it in the *Vie militaire, politique et privée [du] chevalier d'Eon*, the reader must be disappointed by the platitude of the narration: the private life of the chevalier d'Eon in London consists of commonplace activities, a studious and stay-at-home life during the winter and a timetable shared between studying, hunting and horsing during the summer – in short, everything but the virtually fictional life of a spy who is a sexually ambiguous character as well!

---

12. *Vie privée, impartiale, politique, militaire et domestique du marquis de La Fayette* [...] *pour servir de supplément à la nécrologie des hommes célèbres du dix-huitième siècle et de clef aux révolutions françaises et américaines* (Paris, Bastide, 1790). See also [Charles Doris], *Chagrins domestiques de Napoléon Bonaparte à l'île de Sainte-Hélène; précédé de faits historiques de la plus haute importance; le tout de la main de Napoléon, ou écrit sous sa dictée* [...], *suivi de notes précieuses sur les six derniers mois de la vie de Napoléon* (Paris, G. Mathiot, 1821).

13. Pierre-Jean-Baptiste Legrand d'Aussy, *Histoire de la vie privée des Français, depuis l'origine de la nation jusqu'à nos jours*, 3 vols (Paris, Ph.-D. Pierres, 1782). The only section published deals with food and contains additions on fishing, hunting and gardening.

14. [La Fortelle? Peyraud de Beaussol?], *Vie militaire, politique et privée [du] chevalier d'Eon*, p.35.

In any case, the tension between the general and the specific is central to the definition of private life. Like the *Dictionnaire de l'Académie* already quoted, Diderot and D'Alembert's *Encyclopédie* repeats that the word 'privé' 's'oppose à *public*': 'on dit après s'être livré aux affaires de l'Etat, il s'est retiré, et il jouit des douceurs d'une vie *privée*'. But the article stresses that the word is synonymous for 'propre' and 'particulier', and the entry for this last term contains the expression 'la vie *particulière*', in which '*particulier* s'oppose à *public*'.[15] Littré's dictionary gives this interesting example as well: 'La vie privée doit être murée, il n'est pas permis de chercher et de faire connaître ce qui se passe dans la maison d'un particulier.' Such an example seems contradictory with the evocation, immediately afterwards, of the genre: 'Vie privée', 'titre de certains ouvrages où l'on raconte les actions privées d'un personnage public'. Indeed, as Caroline Warman has shown, the word 'privé' in the *Encyclopédie* is already connected to 'secret', a word we also find in the title of several *Vies privées*: *Vie privée, amoureuse, secrète et authentique de Napoléon Bonaparte* (1836), mentioned above; some texts are even entitled 'Vie secrète et politique' ('de Brissot', 'de [...] Monsieur, frère de Louis XVI'), 'Vie secrète, politique et curieuse' ('de [...] Robespierre') or simply 'Vie secrète' ('de [la] duchesse d'Orléans', 'de Pierre Manuel').[16] The *Vies privées* therefore pretend to reveal things that are hidden and, by publishing them, paradoxically make public what should remain secret, which is another interesting tension in the definition of the genre. If the 'escalier secret, escalier dérobé' leads to 'des parties d'une habitation qui est fermée au public', as mentioned by Littré, the reader is asked to enter the person's privacy and intimacy, even to break into remote places like a burglar, or a voyeur. This is, of course, one of the main points on which authors insist in a conscious bid to advertise their works: the reader must know that he will find in the work something really new and learn facts that have not yet become public.

Although the notion of the private is clearly opposed to the public in the definitions given by the dictionaries, the representation built up in the texts of the *Vies privées* is certainly more complex and is probably evolving through the period. The most striking phenomenon may be the

15. *Encyclopédie*, articles 'Privé', vol.13 (1765), p.388, and 'Particulier', vol.12 (1765), p.103.
16. [P. Turbat], *Vie secrète et politique de Brissot* (Paris, Franklin, An II [1793]); *Vie secrète et politique de Louis-Stanislas-Xavier, Monsieur, frère de Louis XVI* (Paris, Au manège des Tuileries, 1790); [L. Duperron], *Vie secrète, politique et curieuse de M. J. Maximilien Robespierre [...] jusqu'au 9 Thermidor l'an deuxième de la République [...], suivie de plusieurs anecdotes sur cette conspiration sans pareille* (Paris, Prévost, An II [1794]); *Vie secrète de Louise-Marie-Adélaïde Bourbon-Penthièvre, duchesse d'Orléans, avec ses correspondances politiques* (London, Werland, 1790); [P. Turbat], *Vie secrète de Pierre Manuel, ci-devant procureur-syndic de la commune de Paris, et député à la Convention nationale* (Paris, Franklin, n.d. [1793]).

growing importance of family among the evocation of domestic life. Following an evolution described by historians of private lives,[17] the authors of *Vies privées* seem to lay stress on the relationships within the family at the beginning of the nineteenth century: this can be seen, for example, in the texts devoted to Napoléon Bonaparte. It is of course difficult to say whether the importance of family life is the consequence of a broader evolution of mentalities, and whether it is connected with the particular situation of the character or is better explained by the matters of interest to Charles Doris, the author of most of these *Vies privées*, whose literary production tends to specialise itself in works connected with the private life of Napoléon and the different members of his family as published under various pen names from 1814 to the early 1840s. It is certain, however, that among the prolific production of texts narrating Napoléon's private life, a significant number deal with the character's family. This looks like an innovation when compared with the *Vies privées* published during the previous periods. The *Mémoires pour servir à la vie d'un homme célèbre*[18] give a lot of precise details about Napoléon's everyday life (his character, his terrible fits of anger and his bubbling over with high spirits, his charity, his familiar habits), including considerations of his behaviour towards his close family (his fatherly tenderness, for instance). Other texts are partly or entirely devoted to the members of Napoléon's family: *Amours de Napoléon et des princes et princesses de sa famille*; *Amours secrètes de Napoléon et des princes et princesses de sa famille*, exclusively dealing with a succession of love affairs involving Napoléon, his brothers and sisters; the *Histoire secrète des amours de la famille Bonaparte* consists in the narration of a series of evenings during which each member of the 'sainte famille' Bonaparte, from Laetizia to Napoléon, tells about his life and love affairs;[19] the *Vie privée, amoureuse, secrète et authentique de Napoléon Bonaparte et des princes et princesses de sa famille*, already mentioned, contains numerous episodes on family life, love affairs and married life and on the conflictual relationships between Napoléon and his brothers and sisters. Some texts are entirely

17. See R. Chartier's introduction in *De la Renaissance aux Lumières*: 'Ainsi la famille devient-elle le lieu par excellence du privé. [...] c'est bien dans le courant du XVIIIᵉ siècle que l'essentiel de l'existence privée se replie sur le for familial, sans discords entre l'individu et les siens' (p.411).

18. [Regnault-Warin], *Mémoires pour servir à la vie d'un homme célèbre* [Napoléon Bonaparte], *par M. M****, 2 vols (Paris, Plancher, 1819).

19. [C. Doris], *Amours de Napoléon et des princes et princesses de sa famille: ouvrage rédigé d'après les mémoires modernes et les matériaux authentiques communiqués à l'auteur*, 2 vols (Paris, B. Renaud,1835); [C. Doris], *Amours secrètes de Napoléon et des princes et princesses de sa famille, d'après des documents historiques de M. de B***, ornées de gravures historiques*, 2 vols (Paris, B. Renault,1842); *Histoire secrète des amours de la famille Bonaparte* (Paris, Davi et Locard; Delaunay, 1815).

focused on one or several members of the family except Napoléon himself.

If the notion of private life seems to grow richer with developments in family life at the beginning of the nineteenth century, its constitutive elements were already evident earlier. Authors take visible interest in evoking characters and give numerous details about domesticity and everyday life; their favourite subject, however, is the evocation of intimacy and especially sexuality, to which the representation of private life is sometimes reduced. When they expand the notion of private life to the most commonplace elements of everyday life, the authors face the risk of platitude since it cannot be taken for granted that everything is interesting in the life of a famous person. Is curiosity for private life strong enough to hold the reader's attention when the facts and situations evoked seem uninteresting? The solution may be found in the secret dimension of private life, and the illusion that the reader can fathom a secret by seeing through the public person and learning things that nobody should know. Typically, the text shows the reader 'le héros en déshabillé' and at odds with his public image; and in so doing the author reveals aspects that have always been hidden behind closed doors or behind a mask.[20] But, on the other hand, while playing on the reader's voyeurism, the authors must contend with gaps in available knowledge of the non-public life. In this matter, imagination is obviously needed, and a reading of the *Vies privées* persuades us that the main task of the author consists in inventing the private life of the public person whose literary treatment transforms him (or in rare cases her) into a fictional character.

The authors are indeed well aware of the importance of the readership: they develop narrative strategies to catch the reader's attention – that is one of the functions of the expected episodes dealing with sexuality – and to make them credible through both justifying procedures used in historical works and literary techniques used in the novel. These strategies have decisive consequences for the definition of the genre. By borrowing from the previous codified genres of history and novel, the *Vies privées* emerge as a complex genre. But the point here is to see that the proximity with other genres is the result of the narrative treatment of private matters aimed at the reader: how to make the reader believe in the facts and situations that are the author's inventions? That is, how to create the illusion that these fictitious private episodes are credible?

20. Note the title, for instance, of [de Beaunoir], *Les Masques arrachés, ou Vie privée de L. E. Vander-Noot et Van Eupen, de S. E. le cardinal de Malines et de leurs adhérents par Jacques Le Sueur, espion honoraire de la police de Paris, et ci-devant employé du ministère de France en qualité de clairvoyant dans les Pays-Bas* (London, n.p., 1790).

Titles and paratexts explicitly seek to convince the reader that what is stated in the *Vie privée* is both original and reliable, at least in so far as history is concerned. Indeed some authors define themselves as historians: they insist on their impartiality and the exactness of the facts they are relating. The author of the *Vie privée de J.-P. Marat* pretends to steer a course between a (rejected) conception of the historical genre, 'avili par la bassesse et l'adulation', and the pamphlets written by 'de vils calomniateurs': the truth of facts should be his sole guide.[21] The author of the *Vie politique et militaire de M. le maréchal duc de Belle-Isle* also strongly condemns the partial views of pamphleteers, but he objects that his work is different from that of the 'gazetiers' as well. 'Ce n'est point ici une fade compilation de gazettes, ni un recueil de faits dépourvu d'intérêt et de vérité', he says and adds: 'j'ai travaillé sur de bons mémoires.'[22] In the *Vie privée de [...] Conti*, a 'discours préliminaire' builds up the ethos of the author as a historian: 'le premier devoir d'un homme de lettres qui écrit l'histoire est d'être véridique.'[23] We should not automatically trust such statements, especially in a text which sometimes retains the tone of a pamphlet. We should instead notice that the author intends to multiply the signs which make his text look like an authentic historical work: footnotes[24] – some up to three pages long – and a series of documents ('pièces justificatives'), at the end of the volume. Some *Vies privées* bolster their authority by showing the sources used by the author, sources which are given as an authority. For instance, in the *Vie privée, amoureuse, secrète et authentique de Napoléon Bonaparte et des princes et princesses de sa famille*, the author sets up an intertextual device in order to justify the veracity of the related facts and refers to well-known and authorised works on Napoléon (Constant's *Mémoires*, Las Cases' *Mémorial de Sainte-Hélène*) as well as quoting and citing other memoirs. According to the title, this text is reputed to be the 'seul ouvrage impartial et complet publié d'après des renseignements exacts et les divers mémoires du temps et notamment ceux publiés par Constant, ex-valet de chambre de l'empereur'. The title of the *Amours de Napoléon et des princes et princesses de sa famille* (1835) also underlines that the work has been written 'd'après les mémoires modernes et les matériaux authentiques communiqués à l'auteur', that is, partly some of the more or less known memoirs mentioned above, and partly some of the previous productions of the author, Charles Doris,

21. *Vie privée de J.-P. Marat, député à la Convention nationale* ([Paris], Lerouce and Berthelot, n.d. [1793?]), p.1.
22. François-Antoine Chevrier, *La Vie politique et militaire de M. le maréchal duc de Belle-Isle, prince de l'empire, ministre d'Etat de S. M. T. C., etc., etc., publiée par M. D. C**, éditeur du testament et du codicille* (The Hague, Veuve Van Duren, 1762), p.v-vi.
23. *Vie privée de [...] Conti*, p.10.
24. See Antony Grafton, *The Footnote: a curious history* (Cambridge, MA, 1997).

alias 'baron de B***': the *Amours secrètes de Napoléon Bonaparte* (1815) and
the *Amours secrètes des quatre frères de Napoléon* (1816) in particular.

We must say a word about the category of the 'pièces justificatives'
which are often added to the text, mostly at the end of the volume, and
only sometimes mentioned in titles. This is one of the characteristics of
the *Vie privée de Louis XV*, whose influence on the *Vies privées* of the *ancien
régime* was noticeable. In this case, these 'pièces justificatives' contain
heterogeneous texts: memoirs, relations, official or non-official letters,
lists, pamphlets. The *Vie privée du maréchal de Richelieu*[25] shows a collection
that may seem less diversified since each of the three volumes ends with
letters from various correspondents. These include women such as Mme
d'Averne, Mme de Tencin and Mme Du Châtelet because of the fascination the maréchal exerts on them, and also feature letters from
Richelieu himself, Voltaire or Louis XV. Actually it is not surprising
that letters should be quoted as 'pièces justificatives': since the correspondence is a private genre, it is supposed to give the reader the
impression that he has intimate access to the person, and whether these
letters are authentic or forged does not really matter here.[26] The point is
to invent more or less credible reasons to explain how the letters came
into the author's hands.[27] The process of corroboration impinges on the
narration itself: if adopting the attitude of the historian can be a way of
convincing the reader that the facts advanced are authentic, the authors
often play on the characterisation of the narrator. Thus the story is
frequently related by a witness, close enough to the person to be well
informed of his private life. The technique is rarely effective. The *Vie
privée du comte de Buffon* is indeed written by 'M. le chevalier Aude, de
l'Académie des arts et sciences de Sicile' who was really Buffon's sec-
retary, but only during his two last years (1786-1787). His main purpose is
to tell the story of an old and famous Buffon, but he feels compelled to
invent material concerning Buffon's childhood and youth in order to
create the impression of a biography. Most of the time, the witness is a
creation of the author.

A series of *Vies privées* use the first-person subject to tell the story. This
literary technique is particularly effective because it suggests a generic

---

25. [Louis-François Faur], *Vie privée du maréchal de Richelieu contenant ses amours et intrigues, et tout
    ce qui a rapport aux divers rôles qu'a joués cet homme célèbre pendant plus de quatre-vingts ans*, 3 t. in
    1 vol. (Hamburg, P.-F. Fauche, 1791).
26. Since they are selected on purpose, even authentic letters can be used to give a realistic
    touch to a fictitious story.
27. See, for instance, the *Vie privée de* [...] *Conti*, p.95: 'nous avons lu sa lettre, dont on nous a
    montré une copie, mais nous nous en rappelons l'esprit. Nous nous empressons d'en
    donner à nos lecteurs une idée, pour qu'ils sachent à quoi s'en tenir.'

affinity with autobiography and first-person memoirs.[28] In some cases the illusion is not total since the reader cannot ignore that the text, written in the first person, is a creation. According to its title, the *Histoire amoureuse de Napoléon Bonaparte* is said to have been 'extraite des mémoires particuliers composés par lui-même, pendant son séjour à l'île d'Elbe', which is supposed to guarantee the authenticity of the events but which also supposes the existence of someone who has done the work, someone presented as 'un ancien officier de sa maison qui ne l'a quitté qu'au moment de monter sur le Northumberland'. We find again the character of the eye-witness: the text will first 'laisser parler Napoléon', then the 'éditeur' will speak in the name of the emperor and recall the last three months of his reign, hence covering the whole life of Napoléon, from his childhood to his exile.[29] The same period and the same fiction based on a topic – during his exile, the emperor has enough time to think about his past and write his memoirs – is used in the *Amours secrètes de Napoléon Buonaparte*, except there is no intermediate character involved: the reader must have the illusion that he is reading a text written on the island of Elba. In all these works, therefore, the hero narrates his own life and divulges intimate sexual detail. This was already the case in the multi-volume *Vie privée du maréchal de Richelieu*, which is unusual in combining two sorts of texts. In the first two volumes an anonymous narrator relates the political, military and sentimental life of the maréchal, whereas in the third it is the maréchal himself who narrates, in the first person, his numerous love affairs, from his first presentation at court to the end of the Regency.

We can see that the aim of the narrative strategies developed by the authors is to give the reader the impression that he is penetrating the intimate world of the character. This process, which is a matter of

---

28. On the 'mémoires d'histoire', see Madeleine Foisil, 'L'écriture du for privé', in *De la Renaissance aux Lumières*, ed. R. Chartier, p.332-33. J.-M. Goulemot also speaks about what he calls 'un genre aristocratique', but he opposes the autobiography, connected to 'l'intime et le privé', and these memoirs, connected to 'l'espace public'; indeed he stresses the fact that 'les Mémoires s'arrêtent là où commencent le privé et l'intime. [...] ils nous laissent entendre que le privé et l'intime n'existent pas ou qu'ils sont dénués d'intérêt et interdits de discours' ('Les pratiques littéraires ou la publicité du privé', in *De la Renaissance aux Lumières*, ed. R. Chartier, p.390). This is obviously not the case in the *Vies privées*.

29. *Histoire amoureuse de Napoléon Bonaparte, extraite des mémoires particuliers composés par lui-même pendant son séjour à l'île d'Elbe, et continuée jusqu'au 14 juillet 1815, par un ancien officier de sa maison qui ne l'a quitté qu'au moment de monter sur le Northumberland*, 2 t. in 1 vol. (Paris, Le Dentu, 1815). In the *Chagrins domestiques de Napoléon Bonaparte*, the text is supposedly written 'à l'île de Sainte-Hélène', 'de la main de Napoléon, ou [...] sous sa dictée', but from time to time the editor, who pretends to maintain Napoléon's style inaccuracies, is openly in charge of the narration and explains in footnotes that the details he gives are 'calqu[és] sur les communications qui nous ont été faites par un témoin oculaire' (p.204, n.1).

narration, is inherited from eighteenth-century fiction and especially from the fictional techniques used. Although the general orientation followed by the *Vies privées* is that of a biographical story, punctuated in a chronological order by the main stages of the character's life, the structure of the texts can be described as a series of episodes linked together. These episodes often correspond to the anecdotes praised here and there in the titles, but which seem to be characteristic of the genre:[30] the *Vie privée de Louis XV* contains the 'principaux événements, particularités et anecdotes de son règne'; the *Vie privée, amoureuse, secrète et authentique de Napoléon Bonaparte et des princes et princesses de sa famille* contains 'un grand nombre d'anecdotes curieuses sur des familles et des personnes qui jouent encore un grand rôle dans le monde'. These anecdotes can be considered as ornaments. According to the author of the *Vie privée et ministérielle de M. Necker*, these anecdotes, 'dont les témoins ont pu seuls nous fournir les détails', are meant to 'rendre cet ouvrage plus piquant'.[31] They are sometimes placed in footnotes[32] or rejected at the end of the volume,[33] but most of the time they are part of a concatenated narrative. This kind of storytelling, which is supposed to particularise the subject, is indeed closely connected with the evocation of private events: it is even, we may assume, the form which fits private things best since something particular is detailed and specific circumstances are given.

In Genette's terminology, the anecdotes are sometimes presented as summaries ('sommaires'), and these episodes frequently use literary topics. For instance, clergymen's lives often exploit the image of the ribald priest popularised by the literary tradition familiar since Rabelais (and even earlier) and reinvented in the eighteenth-century pornographic novel. One of the recurrent episodes thus is the seduction of the penitent or the pupil, as illustrated by the *Vie privée de l'ex-capucin Chabot*, which provides the reader with details about 'l'histoire crapuleuse de sa vie libertine'.[34] Among the predictable topoi are the pregnant young woman and the libertine afflicted by sexual disease in flight from

---

30. See Darnton, *The Devil in the holy water*, ch.22.
31. [J. Rutledge], *Vie privée et ministérielle de M. Necker*, p.6.
32. See *Mémoires secrets sur la vie privée, politique et littéraire de Lucien Buonaparte, prince de Canino, rédigés sur sa correspondance et sur des pièces authentiques et inédites* (Paris, n.p., 1815; Brussels, n.p., 1818): for instance, Napoléon pinching the money his mother had hidden behind a painting.
33. In the *Amours secrètes de Napoléon et des princes et princesses de sa famille*, we find a collection of 'Anecdotes détachées' on Napoléon and Joséphine, Lucien, Jérôme and the 18 Brumaire, from p.90 of vol.2 onwards.
34. [P. Turbat], *Vie privée de l'ex-capucin Chabot et de Gaspard Chaumette, pour servir de suite aux Vies des fameux scélérats de ce siècle* (Paris, Franklin, An II [1794]), p.32.

the 'temple de Cythère aux ateliers d'Esculape' (p.23). The episodes often stage the endlessly inventive trio made up of the seducer, the woman and her wooer or her husband, to whom the author sometimes gives an identity: Chabot seducing the 'aimable Rozette', the elder daughter of the doctor who cured him, and planning her kidnapping whereas her parents are trying to marry her to a young soldier named Belleval (p.24-30); Chabot abandoning an 'ex-marquise un peu avancée en âge' but very rich for her maid ('la borgne Julie'), facing 'la jalousie du valet d'écurie Lafleur' and being chastised (p.35-37); Chabot living in concubinage with a young woman engaged to a young man who, being desperate, killed himself on the 2 August 1793 (p.38). More generally, the *Vies privées* which focus on sexual life always contain key episodes relating to the initiation of the hero. For instance, the *Histoire amoureuse de Napoléon Bonaparte* is structured as a succession of detailed episodes illustrating the most different aspects of erotic relationships: the traditional initiation of the child who is spectator to a coitus scene in a grotto between his godmother and, improbably, Pascal Paoli; the equally traditional seduction of the hero by a mature woman as well as the spectacle of lesbian relationships; the burlesque attempt at seduction of a financier's woman who is the daughter of a greengrocer; the simple love affair in a modest family living in Besançon; but also complex stories including a duel, in which only Napoléon succeeds in hoodwinking lovers and husbands. For the sake of completeness, I shall also mention an exotic affair with the daughter of the governor in Cairo who pretends to marry Napoléon, the revenge of a German woman using the 'poison américain' against the man who wiped out her family as well as actresses giving Napoléon 'le germe de la corruption', a few rapes and, from time to time, some gun shots aimed at those who resist Napoléon's desires.

Unsurprisingly, some of these anecdotes take the form of a 'scène', in Genette's terminology, which implies a specific literary treatment of the episode. This is the case, for instance, in the *Vie privée du maréchal de Richelieu*. As a matter of fact, Richelieu is said to impose on himself a regime befitting his entire sex life: 'Il observa un régime particulier tous les printemps; comme il voyait une grande quantité de femmes de toute espèce, et même des filles, il croyait prudent de se régénérer toujours au renouvellement de la belle saison, et de ne conserver aucune des souillures de la précédente année.'[35] It is worth noticing that the references to the character's body are not only a means of making credible the amazing collection of his love affairs: they reinforce the physical presence of Richelieu in the text.[36] Nevertheless the scenes recur in an

---

35. [L.-F. Faur], *Vie privée du maréchal de Richelieu*, vol.2, p.107.
36. Another striking detail is given: Richelieu suffers from a 'dartre vive', that is a sort of

emblematic range of places: 'petite maison', 'appartement', 'cabinet', 'chambre', 'boudoir', 'réduit', 'garde-robe', 'lit', 'canapé', etc. where the same basic characters have access by 'escaliers', even by 'cheminées tournantes'. Different tonalities can be heard within this schema. When Richelieu, made up as a door-to-door vendor, joins his former mistress who is now the duchess of Modena, the narrator describes the meeting place as decorated by the woman (vol.1, p.120):

> La duchesse avait fait préparer la veille un cabinet délicieux [...]. Des emblèmes allégoriques, que Richelieu et elle seule pouvaient expliquer, leur rappelaient ces premiers plaisirs, dont le souvenir est toujours enchanteur, qu'ils avaient goûtés à Paris. Une tresse de cheveux, qu'elle avait alors dérobée à son amant, était sur un petit autel surmonté d'une couronne où l'on voyait deux cœurs enlacés. Elle lui montra ce trésor, lui dit qu'il avait été depuis son mariage son unique consolation.

Although the evocation of this little private monument contains details familiar from the sentimental novel,[37] other passages describe seduction scenes reminiscent of Baculard d'Arnaud's works. Hence the following episode, narrated in the historic present, where Richelieu and a young widow from Bordeaux find themselves locked in a room (vol.2, p.148):

> Elle veut ouvrir la fatale serrure [...] ses efforts sont inutiles. Le Maréchal est à ses pieds [...]. En parlant, il veut agir [...]: elle est à ses genoux en lui tendant les bras.
> Le Maréchal la relève, la fait asseoir, la supplie de calmer son agitation [...] ses beaux yeux la trahissent, en décelant l'ardeur qu'elle éprouve; Richelieu s'en aperçoit aussitôt [...]. L'attaque fut rapide, et la victoire complète.

In such scenes the construction of private life draws its inspiration from literary tradition, borrowing from sentimental, libertine and even por-nographic-literature[38] situations (and even some characters), which function as 'scripts', in Eco's sense of the word. In Richelieu's *Vie privée* he is dubbed (through the trope of antonomasia) the 'Nestor de la

---

leprosy that develops on the face and spreads on the whole body: 's'il eût été jeté sur un fumier, [il] aurait parfaitement représenté Job', the author writes. And he goes on with details: 'On lui appliquait continuellement du veau sur les endroits dartreux, et le pansement exhalait une odeur infecte.' The medicine seems powerful, however: 'Ce qu'il y a de certain, c'est que tous ses valets de chambre attesteront que, jusqu'à sa mort, il a eu le corps très blanc, sans aucun bouton [...] et qu'à la surdité près, il était comme un jeune homme' (vol.2, p.105-107). Luckily then the succession of Richelieu's love feats can continue until the age of eighty.

37. A vein that is also exploited, for instance, in the *Amours secrètes de Napoléon et des princes et princesses de sa famille*, when the history of the doleful love between Louis and Hortense de Beauharnais is related.

38. On the way the pornographic novel is connected with 'la publicité de l'intime'; see Goulemot, 'Les pratiques littéraires', p.402-404.

galanterie' (preface, p.iii).[39] Olga Wormser suggests that the protagonist of Laclos's *Liaisons dangereuses* may have served as a model for Richelieu who appears as a 'fantôme déguisé' in the text.[40] Although such precise identifications may be a matter of argument, we must agree that literary genres of fiction profoundly shape the private episodes represented in the *Vies privées*. In the *Vie privée* [...] [*du*] *duc de Chartres* (the later duke of Orléans, then Philippe Egalité), while public and private spheres are closely overlapping, we can surmise that the reader's attention will focus on 'les lieux les plus secrets et les plus retirés'.[41] The indication of the action scenes seems programmatic: the text mainly deals with episodes which take place in the intimacies of the alcove and the boudoir, where typical characters like the lover and his mistresses take the stage. A large number of such scenes can be found in the *Vies privées* in which the dramatisation is intensified by the introduction of dialogues.

The connection between the (invented) representation of private life and fiction can be observed finally through the literary treatment of characters. Indeed, to a greater or lesser extent, the person whose life is related in the *Vies privées* becomes a character, whose (invented) feelings and thoughts are interpreted from the inside. As in the novel, the narrative voice analyses the secret logic of the character's psychology. The *Vie privée du maréchal de Richelieu* throws light on the inner lives of the hero and his associates. During an episode in Vienna, the reader catches Richelieu's reaction towards the duke of Riperda: 'Richelieu [...], dans son for intérieur, le traitait de faquin.'[42] He is led into the confidence of the princess of Conti when she tells Richelieu about her lover La Fare: 'Elle lui dit qu'une première impression s'effaçait difficilement, et que la vue et le repentir de son amant avaient ranimé en elle des sentiments qu'elle croyait éteints' (vol.1, p.135). A moment before, the narrative voice explained the secret movements affecting the character's interiority (vol.1, p.134):

> La princesse étonnée suivit une impulsion qu'elle prit pour de l'amour. Elle avait besoin que l'ivresse de ses sens lui ôtât tout autre souvenir [...]. Elle avait des remords qu'elle ne pouvait éloigner, et malgré elle, ils l'assiégeaient sans cesse. [...] Il [La Fare] n'avait jamais cessé de l'être [aimable] à ses yeux; la

---

39. In the same way, the *Histoire secrète des amours de la famille Bonaparte* narrates the venture of 'Lovelace Napoléon'.
40. See Olga Wormser's edition of this text under the title: *Amours et intrigues du maréchal de Richelieu* (Paris, 1955).
41. [Charles Théveneau de Morande], *Vie privée, ou Apologie de très sérénissime prince monseigneur le duc de Chartres contre un libelle diffamatoire écrit en mil sept cent quatre-vingt un, mais qui n'a point paru à cause des menaces que nous avons faites à l'auteur le déceler, par une société d'amis du prince* ([London, J. Hodges and W. Reeves], 1784), p.134.
42. [L.-F. Faur], *Vie privée du maréchal de Richelieu*, vol.1, p.164.

jalousie lui avait seulement ôté ses attraits pour quelques moments. Le cœur
était à lui; ce cœur avait été égaré par des désirs qu'un homme adroit
[Richelieu] avait fait naître.

The authors of the *Vies privées* often resort to inventing details of private
life. Yet they promise the reader the revelation of truthful secrets.
Reconciling these contradictory requirements may consist in the exploitation of what critics called the suspension of disbelief. There is indeed a
close connection between the private episodes related in the *Vies privées*
and techniques, situations and even characters which can be found in the
novel. One may assume that the process exploits the benefits of the 'effet
de réel' and, more generally, of what Goulemot calls the 'nouveaux
systèmes de crédibilité de l'écriture romanesque'[43] built up in order to
create referential illusion. Invented 'facts' must be true because they
resemble what can be read in the novel.

It is difficult to know what this invented representation of private life
does reveal. An easier question to ask of these texts would be to enquire
what it is meant to reveal. The characterisation of the person and the
evocation of his or her private life is not totally without any purpose,
since the narration always seems to be underlined by an authorial
discourse: the *Vies privées* are strongly biased texts. Although the author
of *Napoléon Buonaparte, sa vie civile et militaire* pretends to reduce the
narration to the 'seuls faits' and adorn it with 'anecdotes pour et contre
ce personnage célèbre',[44] such a neutral position is in fact rare. The given
facts never speak for themselves as they always result from a biased
process of selection. Even when texts stage debates for and against,
neutrality and discretion are only an illusion. By and large most of the
Vies privées are clearly for or – most often – against the person. In any
case, the sole existence of a debate indicates that the person (and
Napoléon maybe more than anyone else) is at the heart of an argument
in which a position must be taken. The *Vies privées* are decidedly
polemical works, even those which can be considered as apologies.
This point is illustrated by the *Vie privée, amoureuse, secrète et authentique
de Napoléon Bonaparte et des princes et princesses de sa famille*, whose moder-
ation must be interpreted by taking into account the way its author
denounces the 'vils pamphlets', 'réceptacles impurs de basses calomnies
et de dégoûtants mensonges',[45] that were published in 1814 at the

43. Goulemot, 'Les pratiques littéraires', p.392.
44. [C. Doris], *Napoléon Buonaparte, sa vie civile et militaire réduite aux seuls faits, depuis l'instant de sa
     naissance, jusqu'à celui de sa retraite dans l'île d'Elbe; avec une foule de détails intéressants et officiels
     sur les expéditions d'Egypte, d'Espagne et de Russie, suivie d'anecdotes pour et contre ce personnage
     célèbre, puisées dans les meilleures sources, par Charles D***, auteur des Vies de Henri IV et de Sully*
     (Paris, L'Ecrivain, Le Dentu, Delaroque,1814).
45. *Vie privée, amoureuse, secrète et authentique de Napoléon Bonaparte et des princes et princesses de sa*

moment of Napoléon's fall: in particular the author's accusations are directed against the *Histoire secrète des amours de la famille Bonaparte* and the *Histoire amoureuse de Napoléon Bonaparte*. Therefore the aim of this *Vie privée* is more to counterbalance a satirical representation of its main character than to praise him with an apology. This does not seem to be the case of the *Vie secrète de Louise-Marie-Adélaïde Bourbon-Penthièvre*, whose tone is extremely laudatory: 'Soumission, douceur, sensibilité, reconnaissance, générosité, candeur, affabilité, tels sont les précieux attributs qui caractérisent cette princesse aimable', the author writes, adding that 'tant de qualités, tant de perfections s'accrurent encore avec les années.'[46] The hyperbolical praise given to one character may be regarded then as the counterpoints of the well-founded distrust the reader is invited to share in the case of another character obviously related to the main one. The duke of Orléans, formerly duke of Chartres, is precisely, we should recall, the subject of a *Vie privée* that is described as an 'apologie' officially written 'contre un libelle diffamatoire'. Although this subtitle may give the reader the impression that the aim of this *Vie privée* is to condemn a pamphlet previously published, it is partly misleading: the end of the subtitle irrelevantly explains that the 'libelle' in question 'n'a pas paru à cause des menaces que nous avons faites à l'auteur de le déceler'. What would be the point of replying to a pamphlet that was never published? The reader must understand that the real pamphlet is the text he is about to read, and that the term 'apology' is only ironical and antiphrastic.

By and large the *Vies privées* have a satirical aim. We have seen that the *Vies privées* insist on the taste of the character for lust and dissolute living: according to the text, Richelieu is mainly interested in gambling, drinking and having sex with women, for instance. We should add that the *Vies privées* also denounce various other vices. Cupidity is one of the recurrent characteristics: the 'ci-devant duc d'Orléans' is known for his speculations in building on land near the Palais-Royal; the text also mentions the way he used to deceive his gambling partners and his passion for horse-racing.[47] All the members of Bonaparte's family are stigmatised for their irrepressible taste for debauchery and money:

famille, faisant connaître leurs liaisons particulières et leurs intrigues galantes avec divers personnages de tous rangs et de toute renommée [...], contenant un grand nombre d'anecdotes curieuses sur des familles et des personnes qui jouent encore un grand rôle dans le monde; ainsi que des lettres de Napoléon et de Joséphine; seul ouvrage impartial et complet publié d'après des renseignements exacts et les divers mémoires du temps et notamment ceux publiés par Constant, ex-valet de chambre de l'empereur, 2 t. en 1 vol. (Paris, Terry, 1836), p.vi.

46. *Vie secrète de Louise-Marie-Adélaïde Bourbon-Penthièvre*, p.10-11.

47. [P. Turbat], *Vie de L.-P.-J. Capet, ci-devant duc d'Orléans, ou Mémoires pour servir à l'histoire de la Révolution française* (Paris, Franklin, An II [1794]).

Laetizia and her daughters own a gambling and prostitution den; others
are accused of stealing money in the exercise of their governmental
duties.[48] Money issues recur in the *Vies privées* devoted to Bailly and
Barras, which insist on the illegal ways they have come to their wealth, or
in the *Vie et aventures de Joachim Murat* (1816), which denounces the
misappropriation of public money for his personal use.[49] The *Vie secrète
de Pierre Manuel* explains in detail his swindling which depicts 'une âme
vénale et sordide' incapable of refraining from the 'attraits de la fortune
et de la paresse'.[50]

Luxury, cupidity and laziness are vices to be denounced. In some cases,
the character is presented as an expert deceiver: this is the main
characteristic of Manuel, for instance, and Pétion is presented as 'un
fourbe qui trompe tout le monde, pour voler tout le monde, et conserver
sa réputation'.[51] Reputation is at stake, and the *Vies privées* aim at
influencing it. The more the character wears a mask, the more the text
is supposed to tear it away: 'il est des hommes qu'on ne doit pas
démasquer à demi; ce sont des hydres, dont il faut écraser, s'il est
possible, toutes les têtes', the author of Fouché de Nantes's *Vie privée*
writes in the preface.[52] Denouncing the scandals hidden behind the
closed doors of private life or the political hypocrisy of the characters,
the polemical *Vies privées* will tell everything compromising the public
image of the person. That is why the aim of the underlying discourse is
close to that of a trial: even the 'pièces justificatives' given can be read as
documents for some kind of prosecution.[53]

Although they are mainly narrative texts, we must read the *Vies privées*
as rhetorical works which aim to influence public opinion. The author of
the *Vie secrète de Pierre Manuel* wants to open the eyes of his fellow
countrymen so that they will no longer be seduced by 'des dehors
trompeurs, et les cris des enthousiastes et des prôneurs qui sont si

---

48. *Histoire secrète des amours de la famille Bonaparte.*
49. Detrou, *Vie de M. Jean-Sylvain Bailly, premier maire de Paris, dédiée et présentée à l'Assemblée
    nationale* (Paris, Imprimerie de la Liberté, de la Vérité, et surtout de l'Impartialité, 1790);
    [C. Doris], *Amours et aventures du vicomte de Barras, ex-membre du Directoire exécutif, avec
    Mesdames Joséphine de B***, Tallien, la douairière Du Baillet, Mlle Sophie Arnoult, etc., etc., par M. le
    baron de B****, 3 vols (Paris, G. Mathiot, n.d. [1815-1817?]); [A. Sérieys], *Vie et aventures de
    Joachim Murat depuis sa naissance jusqu'à sa mort par M. L.* (Paris, J.-G. Dentu,1816).
50. [P. Turbat], *Vie secrète de Pierre Manuel*, p.55 and 44.
51. [P. Turbat], *Vie politique de Jérôme Pétion, ci-devant maire de Paris, ex-député de la Convention
    nationale, et traître à la République française* ([Paris, Franklin], n.d. [1793]), p.16.
52. [A. Sérieys], *Fouché (de Nantes), sa vie privée, politique et morale, depuis son entrée à la Convention
    jusqu'à ce jour, avec son portrait* (Paris, G. Mathiot, 1816), p.vi-vii.
53. Some texts explicitly or implicitly show the marks of judiciary eloquence. The most
    striking example may be the *Vie privée et ministérielle de M. Necker*, whose author refers to
    another of his works (*Dénonciation sommaire faite au Comité des recherches de l'Assemblée nationale
    contre M. Necker*) written in order to prove his innocence and the minister's guilt.

richement intéressés à [les] abuser'.[54] According to the 'Discours préliminaire', the aim of the *Vie politique de Jérôme Pétion* is to enlighten the 'fidèle patriote' so that he will not be deceived anymore by 'les odieuses et infernales manœuvres des traîtres qui ont joui de sa confiance'.[55] In the 'Avant-propos', the *Vie privée des cinq membres du Directoire* makes a close connection between the interest in private life – which is the main purpose of such a text – and, from the public's point of view, a significant change in the political mentalities:

> Le temps n'est plus où, dans un fol enthousiasme, le peuple, séduit par des apparences, idolâtrait ceux qui tenaient le pouvoir entre leurs mains. Les Français, éclairés par leurs malheurs, n'estiment plus que par des motifs d'estime, n'aiment plus sur parole et ne haïssent plus par prévention. C'est là sans doute ce qui explique l'avidité avec laquelle ils recherchent tout ce qu'ils peuvent recueillir de renseignements sur les hommes qu'ils ont revêtus de l'autorité suprême, et saisissent tous les moyens qui se présentent de sonder le cœur de leurs premiers magistrats: de démêler leur caractère de leurs habitudes, leurs systèmes de leurs liaisons et de calculer ce qu'on doit attendre de chacun d'eux par ce qu'on connaît de leur vie privée.[56]

The author suggests that details of the private life can be helpful in appreciating the action of the person in the public sphere, which confirms that in these texts the distinctions between the private and the public are blurred.

From an ideological point of view, it is interesting to note that the representation of private life in the *Vies privées* operates a specific conception of public life. We have just seen that the authors take for granted that the character of the person has a great influence on his public activities. In the *Vie politique, militaire et privée du général Moreau* (1814), which happens to be a real apology, the first-person narrator, whose voice overlaps with the third person from time to time, declares: 'Tel a été mon caractère, telle a été ma vie entière. Je proteste à la face du ciel et des hommes l'innocence et l'intégrité de ma conduite: vous savez vos devoirs, la France vous écoute, l'Europe vous contemple, et la postérité vous attend.'[57] This is confirmation that a close connection has been established in the text between the public role played by the person and his life and character. The satirical texts also insist on the

---

54. [P. Turbat], *Vie secrète de Pierre Manuel*, p.5.
55. [P. Turbat], *Vie politique de Jérôme Pétion*, p.[3].
56. [Joseph Despaze], *Vie privée des cinq membres du Directoire, ou les Puissants tels qu'ils sont* ([Paris], de l'imprimerie du bureau central des abonnements, n.d. [1795]), p.1.
57. Alphonse de Beauchamp, *Vie politique, militaire et privée du général Moreau, depuis sa naissance jusqu'à sa mort; avec des pièces justificatives et ses discours au tribunal; suivie de son éloge funèbre prononcé à Saint-Pétersbourg et d'une notice historique sur Pichegru, ornée du portrait du général Moreau* (Paris, F. Le Prieur, 1814), p.280.

consequences of the passions of the person on his public actions: just as criminals' behaviour is explained by the 'labyrinthe de leurs passions',[58] so personal ambition, for instance, seems to be the key to understanding the political choices of politically influential men such as the 'ci-devant duc d'Orléans'.[59] Since private life is often reduced to sentimental and sexual life, the *Vies privées* insist on the influence of mistresses on political life and decision-making at the highest level. The *Vie privée de Louis XV* underlines the political power of the royal favourites. Mme de Pompadour 'expira, pour ainsi parler, les rênes de l'Etat encore dans les mains': 'Elle nommait les ministres, les généraux, recevait les ambassadeurs, était en correspondance avec les puissances étrangères.'[60] The same idea is repeated in the *Vie privée du maréchal de Richelieu*: the text denounces the skilful manoeuvres of the kings' mistresses who emasculate royal power which is proved incapable of guaranteeing the welfare of the state. Mme de Pompadour not only reigns over Louis XV's pleasure but intends to maintain by any means 'l'ascendant qu'elle avait pris sur son esprit'.[61] As far as Louis XIV is concerned, the blame is laid mostly on the devout Mme de Maintenon, responsible for the revocation of the Edict of Nantes: '[elle] commandait dans l'intérieur, sans vouloir paraître jouir d'aucune autorité', the author writes (vol.1, p.46), which is symbolised by the fact that the *Conseils du roi* take place in her own apartments. The general orientation of the text reinforces the link between private affairs (that is love affairs) and political events: as far as the Cellamare conspiracy (vol.1, ch.6), the intrigues concerning Louis XV's wedding (vol.1, ch.12), the underground plans about military nominations during the Rhine campaign of 1757 are concerned, the narration evokes private reasons, described as 'particulières', to explain successes and disgraces. In a word, according to the author, the private allows the reader to 'comprendre les événements'. A similar explanation is given for Napoléon's action. While the purpose of the *Vie privée, amoureuse, secrète et authentique de Napoléon Bonaparte et des princes et princesses de sa famille* is to show 'Napoléon dans un boudoir, en robe de chambre et en pantoufles', since 'si l'on veut connaître à fond l'empereur, il faut le voir là aussi',[62] it is to insist on the influence of the man on actions which follow only 'l'intérêt de son ambition', according to the *Précis historique sur Napoléon*

---

58. *Vie criminelle de H.-A. Trumeau, [...] ancien apprenti de l'empoisonneur Desrues* (Paris, Rochette, An XI [1803]), p.6.
59. [P. Turbat], *Vie de L.-P.-J. Capet, ci-devant duc d'Orléans*.
60. [B.-F.-J. Mouffle d'Angerville], *Vie privée de Louis XV*, vol.4, p.25-26.
61. [L.-F. Faur], *Vie privée du maréchal de Richelieu*, vol.2, p.157.
62. *Vie privée, amoureuse, secrète et authentique de Napoléon Bonaparte et des princes et princesses de sa famille*, p.v.

Buonaparte.[63] The author of the *Amours secrètes de Napoléon Bonaparte* can also draw an interesting parallel between the emperor's tactics in seducing women and the way he used to run the Empire: his erotic strategy is based on the same qualities (determination, quickness, authority) that made him successful 'en politique et dans les champs d'honneur'.[64] Furthermore, in the *Mémoires secrets sur Napoléon Buonaparte*, the private characteristics of the man are said to make the reader understand the political regime. Indeed, the analysis of Napoléon's character and behaviour derives from 'une étude constante, suivie et raisonnée de toute la personne de Bonaparte', the author says, and the aim of his work is to study the 'mécanismes' of Napoléon's 'aberrations' and 'disparates continuelles' in order to understand 'la machine despotique': his own researches allowed the author to reach 'la science du cœur humain' because 'de l'âme du maître, il était facile de descendre dans le cœur des courtisans et des valets'.[65]

According to the underlying discourse of the *Vies privées*, knowledge about the private life and the passions of public men or women is presented as a means of revealing secrets about political life. Therefore, given the treatment of private life, these texts tend to deliver a message shaped by ideological conceptions of politics: since politics is made by men or women, revealing 'les actions les plus cachées des personnages historiques',[66] showing the readers the naked truth means revealing the mystery of politics. Although the construction, by the author, of an ethos of the historian is certainly a rhetorical means of making credible invented facts or situations, as we have seen, such a connection between the *Vies privées* and historical genres may be seriously considered in so far as narrating the private life of a historical character is a way of writing history. It is interesting to note that the author of the *Mémoires secrets sur la vie privée, politique et littéraire de Lucien Buonaparte* links his work with the genre of the 'mémoires historiques', which leads us to wonder if we could not discern, through the relationships between private and public spheres built up in the texts, the underlying presence of a sense of history. The author of the *Vie privée de Louis XV* underlines that it is difficult to write the history of his reign: one should have access to the 'archives du ministère' and enjoy the same liberty 'dans les autres cabinets de l'Europe' to deal with current events; 'nous courrions risque

63. [C. Doris], *Précis historique sur Napoléon Buonaparte: jugement porté sur ce fameux personnage, d'après ce qu'il a dit, ce qu'il a fait, le tout extrait des mémoires d'un homme qui ne l'a pas quitté depuis quinze ans* (1814; Paris, G. Mathiot, 1816), p.84.
64. [C. Doris], *Amours secrètes de Napoléon Bonaparte par M. le baron de B****, 2 vols (Paris, G. Mathiot,1815), vol.1, p.106.
65. [C. Doris], *Mémoires secrets sur Napoléon Buonaparte*, p.48-49 and 51.
66. *Mémoires secrets sur la vie privée, politique et littéraire de Lucien Buonaparte*, p.viii.

de composer un ouvrage imparfait, partial du moins', he writes. Since Louis XV is dead, it is possible, however, to write 'la *vie privée* d'un monarque', which would have been too dangerous if it had been done 'sous ses yeux': 'on ne saurait trop tôt recueillir une multitude de faits qui la composent, et ne se conservent souvent que par une tradition orale, dont les traces fugitives s'affaiblissent, et se perdent quelquefois tout à fait avec leurs témoins.' Although the historical ambition is beneath that of what the author calls the 'grandes masses de l'histoire', the aim remains to write some kind of history, grounded on important 'recueils d'anedotes' provided they are constituted 'avec défiance et discernement'.[67] The author of the *Vie de L.-P.-J. Capet, ci-devant duc d'Orléans* also fixes a limited purpose to his work: the 'mémoires' he wrote could 'servir de matériaux à l'homme de génie qui composera notre histoire en grand'.[68] This notion of 'matériaux' seems to be consistent with the structure of the texts which mainly consist in a collection of anecdotes.

Indeed, the specific way of writing history in the *Vies privées* emerges through the interaction between the private and the public within the reduced form of the anecdote. Since, as we have seen, the focus is on the public actions of historical characters, the tendency is to explain important political events and characteristics of the political regime through the subjects' character or through private episodes. The *Vies privées* are connected with a conception of history based on the influence of passion and on the existence of secret keys which have to be found to understand the course of events. Such a conception according to which small causes can have big effects, is certainly beyond all doubt old-fashioned. At least it is the opposite of the philosophical conception of history developed in the middle of the eighteenth century by historians like Voltaire: a conception which, in theory but also in practice, deems that the movement of history depends not only on the actions of individual characters but also on what the author of the *Essai sur les mœurs* calls the 'esprit des nations'.

In conclusion, what is striking when we consider the connections between the French genre of *Vies privées* and the notion of private life is that in these texts the attention given to the private life of the characters never implies that private life has an interest in itself. Studies like the *Histoire de la vie privée* certainly show the growing interest in the private sphere during the eighteenth century. Yet, beneath a narration which often gives priority to private episodes, the *Vies privées* remain polemical texts in which rhetorical strategies aim at having a practical impact on

---

67. [B.-F.-J. Mouffle d'Angerville], *Vie privée de Louis XV*, vol.1, p.1-2.
68. [P. Turbat], *Vie de L.-P.-J. Capet, ci-devant duc d'Orléans*, p.vi.

the reader. These texts reveal a series of tensions which make the *Vies privées* a fundamentally ambiguous genre. Behind the guise of the trustworthy historian, writers deployed literary techniques to create credible narratives from invented material. The result is that the historical person becomes a fictitious character, and the genre falls halfway between history and novel. In the words of one such author, these *Vies privées* are 'productions informes et amphibies qui n'appartiennent ni au roman ni à l'histoire'.[69] The ambiguities can also be observed in the way the *Vies privées* blur the distinctions between the private and the public. Not only do the texts make private facts and situations become public through their publication, not only does the evocation of private life aim to have repercussions on the public and maybe on public opinion: the evocation of the private hopes to give to the reader keys to understanding the public actions of the characters. Consequently, from an ideological point of view, these texts are informed by a specific conception of politics and seem to be underlined by a sense of history which is fundamentally reactionary, even in texts written after 1789 in which History, at last set in motion by the Revolution, is celebrated. Finally the *Vies privées* seem to set up an ambiguous relationship with the reader. On the one hand, the texts – at least, the satirical ones – create a repellent image of the character. On the other hand, the authors assume a readership for the stories of these public characters, and deliberately play on the curiosity for supposedly secret details about the private lives of famous persons and even on the reader's voyeurism. A trivial explanation would be that the intentionally crude episodes are a means of catching and holding the reader's attention: sex makes the works sell even though they are recycling topical scripts. But it also means that the reaction of the reader towards the character is a mixture of repulsion and fascination: whereas the texts' explicit purpose is to hold famous persons up to public obloquy, they also exploit and pander to the reader's fascination. From this point of view, the French eighteenth-century *Vies privées* can be considered as an early form of later scandal sheets and tabloid newspapers.

---

69. *Mémoires secrets sur la vie privée, politique et littéraire de Lucien Buonaparte*, p.10.

The private life of criminals

LISE ANDRIES

The study of the private life of criminals is a paradoxical endeavour because it is in the very nature of their lives and actions to be public. The main aim of all the documents about them, whether judicial archives, pamphlets, newspapers or engravings, is to publicise their deeds. From the reading of these documents we may, nonetheless, deduce certain aspects of their life in its everyday course, and learn a little more about their 'private life', particularly when considered from an anthropological point of view. That means asking questions about how and where criminals in France of the eighteenth century used to eat, drink, sleep, how they dressed, what kind of domestic, social and sexual relationships they had, and so on.

This chapter is based on three kinds of documents: broadsheets distributed by pedlars in the streets; criminal biographies, the majority of which were anonymous; and judicial archives which are held in the Archives nationales (and especially the Acts of the Parlement de Paris, AD III 2 to 7 series for the years 1720 to 1740). I shall therefore concentrate on the criminals who meandered the streets of Paris and its surroundings in the first half of the eighteenth century, and I shall compare them when necessary to English criminals of the same period.

The term 'criminals' is taken here in a broad sense, indicating both highwaymen and burglars, simple thieves and pickpockets, implying theft with or without violence. It would be simplifying the criminal world to divide it into two different groups, highwaymen roaming in the countryside, on the one hand, and city robbers, on the other. In fact, gangs usually operated both in towns and in the rural surroundings of towns. The range of criminal activities was wide, encompassing petty theft and burglary, brutal murder and upper-class larceny. The last point to make in this brief introduction is that studying criminals is a complex topic interweaving imaginary representations with social, economic and judicial elements. It treats the way in which society of this period tackled crime, dreamt about it and fought it. That is why criminals are often both real and mythified in the texts. In criminal biographies especially, fact and fiction are so closely linked that it is difficult to distinguish between judicial documents and literature.

Physical constraints

Studying criminals means dealing with bodies. The body is central to their lives and it is always a spectacular object. On the one hand, there is their own performing body – running, fighting, riding a horse or being tortured on the scaffold – on the other, the passive body of their victims – knocked down, wounded or killed. The archives speak of men (and sometimes women) who are strong, young, full of life and energy. As the judicial archives show, the majority of those executed were under thirty. Cartouche, a famous Parisian criminal, died in 1721 on the wheel at the age of twenty-eight; Raffiat, the chief of a gang of burglars, at the age of twenty-one; and Mandrin, a murderer and a smuggler, at thirty. In his contemporary chronicle, Michel Forest, a merchant of Valence, describes Mandrin thus: 'Il avait beaucoup d'esprit [...], la physionomie des plus guerrières et des plus hardies, l'œil vif; enfin sa figure montrait qu'il était capable d'entreprendre ce qu'il avait fait; de la taille de cinq pieds et quatre à cinq pouces, cheveux blonds, les épaules larges, bien tourné et une jambe des mieux.'[1]

Texts also speak of the capacity of criminals to move so swiftly as to give the illusion of being in different places at the same time. Mandrin's criminal biography, *Histoire de Louis Mandrin depuis sa naissance jusqu'à sa mort*, says that 'On le vit en peu de tems fondre de la Savoie dans le Bugey, se porter aux Bureaux de Nantua, de Bourg en Bresse, de Châtillon-les-Dombes, de Charlieu, de Roanne, de Thiers, d'Amberg, de Marsal, d'Arlan, de la Chaise-Dieu',[2] which means that he covered a vast territory extending to 300 square kilometres. Other biographies describe the extraordinary strength of some criminals. Cartouche, for example, succeeded in escaping from the prison of the Châtelet by breaking his irons with his hands, in the same way that Jack Sheppard escaped from Newgate in 1724: 'He first took off his handcuffs, and then opened the padlock that fastened the chain to the staple. He next, by mere strength, twisted asunder a small link of the chain between his legs, and then drawing his fetters high as he possibly could, he made them fast with his garters.'[3] In criminal biographies, ubiquity and strength seem to be typical of famous bandits and they appear as kinds of supermen. Some texts even wonder whether they are protected by a 'familiar genius' which gives them their supernatural powers. In the *Histoire de la vie,*

---

1. Michel Forest, *Chroniques d'un bourgeois de Valence au temps de Mandrin*, ed. Roger Canac (Grenoble, 1980), p.43.
2. *Histoire de Louis Mandrin, depuis sa naissance jusqu'à sa mort* (Troyes, Vve Garnier, 1755), reprinted in *Histoires curieuses et véritables de Cartouche et de Mandrin*, ed. H. J. Lüsebrink (Paris, 1984), p.157-221 (211).
3. G. Thompson, *Newgate calendar containing the lives of the most notorious characters* (London, 1842), p.77.

grandes voleries & subtilitez de Guilleri et de ses compagnons, et de leur fin lamentable et malheureuse, one of the first criminal biographies published in the *Bibliothèque bleue* which tells the story of a highwayman at the time of Henri IV, the text says: 'Plusieurs tiennent qu'il avoit un esprit familier, qui le conduisoit en ses entreprises.'[4]

Criminals are, of course, not only strong but skilful and nimble. They can run fast, they know how to fight and to use weapons. In a word, they are accomplished sportsmen. This is especially true of highwaymen, not the poor devil whom Tom Jones meets on a highway towards London and who tries to threaten him with a rifle which is not even loaded, but famous highwaymen in England like Claude Du Vall in the 1660s or Mac Lean, in the 1750s, who was the son of a parson. Novels and criminal biographies tend to describe highwaymen as ruined noblemen who chose that career because of need. This stereotype is not surprising: highwaymen know how to ride a horse and to use a sword, two skills which supposedly prove a gentleman's education. Highwaymen are usually described as generous and polite, as noble-hearted bandits and not murderers, who steal money from the rich and give it to the poor in the manner of Robin Hood. But this is a stereotype which is more frequently found in English criminal biographies than in French ones, less influenced by the legend of Robin Hood. In *The Memoires of Monsieur Du Val*, a famous highwayman who was French and was hanged in London in January 1670, the English text describes one of his elegant robberies. Having followed on a moor near London a coach carrying a knight and a lady, and knowing that they had in their possession 400 pounds, Du Vall obliged the coach to stop and invited the lady to come out and dance with him. Of course, after the dance, he asked the knight to pay for the dance. The text says: 'Du Vall leaps lightly off his horse, and hands the lady out of the coach. They danc'd, and here it was that Du Vall performed marvels; the best master in London, except those that are French, not being able to shew such footing as he did in his great riding French boots.'[5]

Being a gallant gentleman-robber and a good dancer, Claude Du Vall naturally deserves the epitaph which the pamphlet quotes as a conclusion:

> Reader, if Male thou art,
> Look to thy purse; if Female, to thy heart.

---

4. *Histoire de la vie, grandes voleries & subtilitez de Guilleri et de ses compagnons, et de leur fin lamentable et malheureuse* (Troyes, Vve Pierre Garnier, [1728]).
5. *The Memoires of Monsieur Du Val: containing the history of his life and death, whereunto are annexed his last speech and epitaph* (London, printed for Henry Brome, at the Gun near the west end of St Paul's, 1670), p.12.

Because of their strength, their agility and sometimes their good looks, criminals are attractive characters too. Just as they do today, they exerted a real fascination on people, and especially on women. Eyewitness statements from the eighteenth century speak of the crowd of visitors, among whom there numbered a great many noble men and women, who went and visited Cartouche or Mandrin in their prison. Both had their portraits drawn by engravers. Biographies as well as poems, songs and plays were written about them. Legrand for instance, a French play-wright, met Cartouche in the Conciergerie, interviewed him and wrote a play entitled *Cartouche, ou les Voleurs* which was played a month before his public execution.[6] It shocked the magistrates and the play was soon suspended. According to Cartouche's biography, the *Histoire de la vie et du procès du fameux Louis-Dominique Cartouche, et plusieurs de ses complices* published in 1722, at the time of his arrest he had three mistresses, his favourite one being a fishmonger from Les Halles.[7]

One of the reasons why criminals are fascinating, especially in *ancien régime* France, is that they seem to have chosen their life, a life of freedom and recklessness, at a time when most people's fate was to live the same sedentary life as their parents and grandparents. The dynamism of criminals, their mobility and agility were perhaps, in the collective consciousness, the enviable opposite of the quiet life of ordinary people, emblematised clearly in the way that Claude Du Vall's 'great riding French boots' contrasted with the wooden clogs of most French ploughmen.[8]

Physical achievement and strength are also linked with violence. In the unforgiving society to which criminals belonged, physical superiority was one of the necessary conditions to be respected and to become a member of a gang. Such displays were often characterised by outrageousness and excessive behaviour, including uncontrolled sexual appetites as well as enormous feats of gluttony and drinking. These aspects of criminals' 'private life', however, are more often described in novels and in criminal biographies than in judicial archives, and it is difficult to know whether they are the products of fantasies or of reality. In the first volume of Lesage's picaresque novel, the *Vie de Gil Blas de Santillane*, published in 1715, the hero is captured by a gang of highwaymen who meet in a wood.

6. See Marc-Antoine Legrand, *Cartouche, ou les Voleurs: comédie* (1721) and John Gay, *L'Opéra du gueux* (1728), trans. A. Hallam (1750), ed. Christian Biet with Martial Poirson and Romain Jobez (Vijon, 2004).
7. *Histoire de la vie et du procès du fameux Louis-Dominique Cartouche, et plusieurs de ses complices* (Rouen, Pierre Machuel, 1722).
8. On this point, see Nicole Pellegrin, 'Corps du commun, usages communs du corps', in *Histoire du corps*, ed. A. Corbin, J. J.Courtine and G. Vigarello, 3 vols (Paris, 2005), vol.1, p.131-32.

They keep him prisoner in the cave where they hide their booty, and he is obliged to serve their wine during the countless feasts they organise following their exploits.

The archives tell a different story. They talk of misery and deprivation rather than of a world of plenty. In Paris, criminals sleep in furnished rooms like the majority of workmen and craftsmen: in 1722 Jean-Baptiste Barré, one of the men arrested as an accomplice of Cartouche, is the owner of furnished rooms costing 2 sols per night (2 pence). He is accused of having 'retiré et logé chez lui Louis-Dominique Cartouche et les autres voleurs ses complices'.[9] In the *Histoire de la vie privée*, Arlette Farge describes such lodgings: 'Les soupentes ou garnis sont loués par des logeurs à deux ou trois sols la nuit. On y vit à plusieurs, sur matelas ou paillasses, rangeant son pécule sous draps et linges ramassés souvent à même le sol.'[10] As for the places where criminals usually congregated and caroused, they seem akin to the seedy taverns described by Louis-Sébastien Mercier in 'Cabarets borgnes' in *Le Tableau de Paris*:

> Sur les dix heures du soir, je vis tout à coup entrer tumultueusement dix-neuf pendards, seize créatures et dix enfants, qui s'emparèrent de la table, la chargèrent de débris de viande, poissons, légumes, morceaux de pain; puis l'on fit venir du vin, qui [...] fut servi dans des vases de grès. [...] De ces femmes, plusieurs avaient des enfants qu'elles allaitaient et torchaient. Les chiens étaient de la partie.[11]

The archives also speak of violence. After an attack on the post from Lyon to Paris on 5 August 1726, the Act of the Parlement speaks of 'plusieurs particuliers à cheval qui, après avoir lié les mains [du courrier et du postillon] derrière le dos, leur ont coupé la gorge; & ayant ouvert la Malle, ont pris l'or & l'argent & les autres effets qui y étoient renfermez.'[12] In 1743, another judgement condemns Nicolas Branche, 'convaincu d'avoir été chez la Veuve Gallet, hôtellière au village de Lognes, près Lagny, ayant deux pistolets, d'avoir fermé la porte sur lui et tenant les deux pistolets dans ses mains, d'avoir forcé ladite Veuve Gallet de lui donner de l'argent'.[13] Indeed, unlike novels and biographies, judicial archives insist on the violence committed by criminals rather than on their sex appeal or good looks. It is important to emphasise that

---

9. *Arrêt de la Cour de Parlement*, BnF, Inventaire F 23672.
10. 'Familles: l'honneur et le secret', in *De la Renaissance aux Lumières*, ed. R. Chartier, p.580-617 (585-86). See also Annik Pardailhé-Galabrun, *La Naissance de l'intime: 3 000 foyers parisiens XVIIe-XVIIIe siècles* (Paris, 1988), who says that 77 per cent of Parisians were tenants and that the majority lived in furnished rooms.
11. Louis-Sébastien Mercier, 'Cabarets borgnes', in *Le Tableau de Paris*, ed. Jean-Claude Bonnet, 2 vols (Paris, 1994), vol.2, p.180-81.
12. Archives nationales, AD III 5, 13.
13. Archives nationales, AD III 7, 72, 12 December 1743.

many criminals in eighteenth-century France were former soldiers. This was true of Cartouche and of several of his band. It is well known that after peace treaties were concluded gangs of criminals composed of unemployed and unpaid soldiers were quick to roam the countryside. This is not surprising: accustomed to using their weaponry, soldiers were no strangers to violence and applied their experience in military discipline to organising and leading gangs.

As for the physical attractiveness of bandits, this does not really correspond to the descriptions given in the 'wanted' posters. These records were aimed at being distributed in the streets of Paris and posted on walls in order to secure the arrest of criminals, their faces often described as ugly and scarred, their bodies certainly powerful, but also deformed by the hardships of the lives they led. Here, for instance, is the description on a poster of Charles Petit, a man who managed to escape after having murdered and cut into pieces his master in December 1735:

> Le nommé Charles Petit, se disant Italien, âgé d'environ 36 à 38 ans, haut de 5 pieds 10 pouces [...] le visage rond, brun, les yeux rouges toujours enflamez, la partie supérieure du visage jusqu'à la moitié du nez & des joues remplie de poudre à canon jusques dans la prunelle des yeux, la bouche grande, le nez gros, les cheveux noirs, petits & crêpus, la barbe rousse, les jambes très grosses.[14]

Sometimes criminals were also branded. At a time when criminal records did not exist, the only way of researching the criminal past of individuals was to read their body and look for the brand on the shoulder: in France the letter V was used for thieves (*voleurs*), and the three letters GAL for convicts (*galériens*).[15]

Let us speak briefly of the system of punishment in eighteenth-century France which was much crueller than in the England at the time. Prisons in eighteenth-century Europe were not yet the places targeting penitence and redemption that they would become a century later during an age of penal reform. Usually prisoners were there only for a short time before their trial. The principal penal sanction in the judicial system of the *ancien régime* involved constraint and the infliction of bodily suffering: branding, flogging and the pillory for petty thieves who were lucky enough to escape a death sentence. Some were banished from the territory of the Parlement de Paris (which represented almost half the country in the eighteenth century) or sent to the penal colony of Marseille. Sentences of transportation were very rare. In fact, the majority of thieves were hanged. But if they had used weapons, if they were house-breakers or highwaymen, had operated at night, stolen in

14. Archives nationales, AD III 6, 22.
15. About French convicts, see André Zysberg, *Les Galériens: vies et destins de 60 000 forçats sur les galères de France, 1680-1748* (Paris, 1987).

churches or killed, they were usually tortured to death. They suffered a first kind of torture, called the 'question', consisting of clamps which squeezed their legs and arms. The 'question' was aimed at making them confess their crime and reveal the names of their accomplices. Then, generally a few hours later or the next day, they were condemned to a public execution during which they had their chest, arms and legs broken by the hangman. After that they were tied on a wheel and died slowly. The torture of the wheel (which was applied only to men) was suppressed only a few years before the French Revolution. Such terrible executions, however, occurred only from time to time. According to the Acts of Parlement gathered in the *série* AD III (some sentences are certainly missing), the average number of public tortures in Paris between 1720 and 1740 was around ten per year. But the number increased considerably when a criminal gang was arrested. Michel Forest, speaking in his chronicle of the arrest of Mandrin and his accomplices, and of their execution in Valence in 1755, writes that there were so many executions that 'De la vie on n'a vu une telle boucherie.'[16]

The criminal body was considered as a strong symbol in Old France and its practice of public torture served as an example to the crowd. The torture on the wheel was meant to teach that those who had attacked the body of the royal state must suffer in the flesh: highwaymen, for instance, because they robbed and killed travellers on the roads belonging to the king, were convicted of *crime de lèse-majesté*, which signified that they had committed a crime putting in danger the person of the king and the coherence of the state. Therefore their body had to be dismembered, a method of showing in a spectacular way the almighty power of the state.[17] At these moments the private body of the criminal became a public object.

Social links

As early as the sixteenth century, the literature of roguery insisted on the links between the criminal world and the world of vagrants. *La Vie généreuse des mercelots, gueux et bohémiens* published in 1596 describes the secret association between rogues, gypsies and pedlars.[18] Does this correspond to what we find in the judicial archives of the eighteenth century, or is it another example of the interaction between fictional representations and reality? It is true that a certain number of criminals among the toughest come from all over the country and accomplish an

16. Forest, *Chroniques*, p.40
17. See Pascal Bastien, *L'Exécution publique à Paris au XVIIIe siècle* (Seyssel, 2006) and Georges Vigarello, 'Le corps du roi', in *Histoire du corps*, ed. A. Corbin, J. J.Courtine and G. Vigarello, vol.1, p.405-406.
18. See Claudine Nédélec, 'L'argot des gueux aux XVIIe et XVIIIe siècles', *XVIIe siècle* 186 (1995), p.147-54.

impressive number of misdeeds. Often they had been branded. Some were convicts who escaped from the penal colony of Marseille. They traveled from town to town and met local criminal gangs who welcomed and protected them. Local gangs may also have operated on a vast territory. Cartouche's gang acted mainly in Paris but some of its members were highwaymen working all surrounding main roads. A few were caught in Rouen, 100 miles from Paris.

It is somewhat surprising to report that the majority of the men and women whose cases I found in the judicial archives of the Parlement de Paris led lives which were basically not different from those of ordinary people in eighteenth-century France. In his introduction to volume 3 of the *Histoire de la vie privée*, Roger Chartier highlights the 'solidarités collectives, féodales et communales' which existed in *ancien régime* France. For criminals, it was the same. Far from belonging to an underworld or an alternative society located on the fringes, they were usually living the same life as their neighbours, participating in criminal deeds from time to time and merging afterwards into the urban or rural world. There were exceptions of course: hardened criminals and recidivists whom I have already mentioned, and also gypsies who lived apart. But gypsies are more often met in novels than in judicial archives. They seem to function as a literary cliché and to belong to the *Bildungsroman* as groups of people teaching the hardships of life to innocent young men: Wilhelm Meister meets gypsies during his life as an itinerant actor; so too do Gil Blas, when he leaves his family, looking for adventures, and Cartouche.

The French criminals described in the archives belong to domestic, professional and local spheres. It is so rare to find a criminal acting on his own that the police notice it: a highwayman caught on the road to Meaux is nicknamed 'le solitaire'. Most criminals belong to gangs, and these gangs are ephemeral: gangs gather when a coup is prepared and disappear afterwards. Sébastien Pelard, for instance, was caught and hanged on the main square of Villeneuve-le-Roi, near Paris, on the 17 October 1736. He had stolen money, clothes, poultry, sheep and seeds in several farms around Villeneuve-le-Roi. His gang was composed of five people: himself, his sister, his wife, his son and his father. The trial of Cartouche's gang, by contrast, lasted two years and led to the condemnation of more than 300 people. It is likely though that the police exaggerated the importance of the gang, in order to 'make an example' at a time when the Regent was weakened by Law's bankruptcy and the social disorders which accompanied it.[19] Other large gangs operated in Paris in the years

19. On this point, see Patrice Péveri, '"Cette ville était alors comme un bois": criminalité et opinion publique à Paris dans les années qui précèdent l'affaire Cartouche 1715-1721', *Crime, histoire et sociétés* 1:2 (1997), p.51-73; and *Cartouche Mandrin et autres brigandes du XVIIIᵉ siècle*, Lise Andries ed., (Paris, 2010).

1730 and 1740: Collot's gang in the 1730s, Raffiat's in the 1740s and Nivet's whose speciality was to climb on the roofs of Parisian coaches at night (with the complicity of coachmen) in order to commit burglary. Thanks to the archives, we know precisely what kind of people belonged to these gangs and we can attempt a sociological analysis of their composition. Collot, who was eighteen when he was arrested, was a woodcarver. His gang consisted of thirty-five members, of whom twelve were condemned to death. It was composed of eight craftsmen and apprentices, three unemployed servants, three soldiers and street vendors such as criers of lottery tickets and bootblacks. In the gang were also five women, all of them married to members of the gang.

Let us now study Raffiat's gang, called 'les assommeurs', who were judged ten years later, in 1742. Armed with clubs on which they had tied weights, its members attacked, robbed and killed pedestrians at night in the streets of Paris, especially in the district of the Marais.[20] It was a time when public lighting was not yet installed and when the streets of all European capitals became dangerous areas after sunset. Though Raffiat's gang was much more violent than Collot's, it was partly composed of the same kind of people as Collot's. Raffiat was a crier of lottery tickets; there were also a tailor, a shoemaker, a joiner, a pedlar who sold herb tea, six soldiers and others belonging to more pertinently skilled professions – several silversmiths, locksmiths and receivers of stolen goods. There were eight women too. One was a fishmonger, another a seamstress. None belonged to the milieu of prostitution, another cliché often used in biographies about the mistresses of criminals. Parisian bandits were neither rootless nor living on the fringes. They came from the popular lower classes who were not destitute but for whom life was certainly never easy. Their financial situation was always tight because they earned just enough to live on and never had any money to spare. They were always potential victims of a single unlucky chance: a disease or an accident might transform them into beggars or vagrants. Because of circumstances, friendships, complicities, domestic links, they fell into crime and violence in order to supplement their income. These people were the same as those who took the Bastille in 1789: artisans, shop assistants, apprentices.

From secrecy to privacy

Although the lives of criminals were widely publicised in pamphlets, songs and novels, they also have something to do with secrecy. Their life continually swings like a pendulum between secrecy and scandal: the

---

20. AD III 7, 19-39.

scandal of their arrest, the scandal of their public condemnation but also the secrets they will or will not reveal under torture, the secrecy and clandestine nature of their deeds. Their behaviour, too, hovers between ostentation and dissimulation, light and darkness. Let us return to the appearance of their faces and bodies. Some were patently frightening, especially as described on the 'wanted' posters. But other documents describe the elegance of certain chiefs of gangs. According to the *Weekly journal*, John Sheppard was dressed in the following way when he was arrested:

> John Sheppard, the famous London thief, was equipped every way like a gentleman, having on a wig worth about six or seven guineas, a diamond ring on his finger, a watch and snuff box in his pocket, and some gold, being also dressed in a suit of black, having furnished himself therewith on Friday morning last, by breaking open a pawnbroker's shop in Drury-Lane.[21]

In the criminal biography of Cartouche, one can also read that 'Il avait toujours eu l'ambition ridicule de se distinguer de ses pareils par de meilleurs habits et par certains airs de petit maître.'[22] Such care over one's appearance might have stemmed from professional necessity: Sheppard and Cartouche had to be well dressed because both men frequented elegant assemblies in gardens and balls, in order to steal jewels and watches. But there were certainly other reasons too. In the hierarchical society of the Enlightenment, appearance and manners were crucial in the definition of *honnêteté*. For instance, in France, sartorial laws enacted in the seventeenth century prohibited the use of silk for clothes worn by common people. Since clothes were a symbol of social rank, it may have been a temptation for 'successful' bandits to show off. Cartouche's criminal biography considers that the main reason why Cartouche became a criminal was his greed and the desire to climb up the social ladder. As for Moll Flanders, the popular versions of the novel explain that it was her love of beautiful dresses and jewels which led her to crime.[23]

In a sense, public punishments, including executions, branding and flogging, belong to the same process of ostentation. Of course, the purpose of such punishments was the reverse: to destroy honour and reputation, and separate the convict from his social sphere. Women sentenced to be flogged were often transported in carts which stopped in

---

21. *The Weekly journal, or British gazeteer* (7 November 1724).
22. *Histoire de la vie et du procès du fameux Louis-Dominique Cartouche, et plusieurs de ses complices* (Troyes, n.d.), p.8.
23. Daniel Defoe's novel was published in short chapbook editions, at the same time as the complete story.

different public squares where they were flogged again. In *ancien régime* France, all sentences included a humiliating element. In Paris there were common criers, *jurés-crieurs*, whose function was to shout the names of those convicted in 'all ordinary and public places'. Moreover, most condemnations were publicised in official pamphlets distributed by pedlars, both the Acts of the Parlement and broadsheets printed by permission of the lieutenant general of police. Scandal had to be publicised so that the names of those guilty might be made known to the whole city. Moreover, branding, humiliating and torturing the body were a way of diminishing its power: the threatening power and strength of those who had chosen to live as outlaws.

Because of public humiliation, some people tried to take refuge in what little was left of their privacy. Dominique Exinard, a highwayman caught in 1731, refused for instance to give his real name to the judges, because 'il ne veut pas porter affront à sa famille'. Women condemned to death often asked the judges for permission to hide their faces under a cloth, while being led to the scaffold. For example, nobody could see the face of Marie-Françoise Lefort, an accomplice of Raffiat: 'ny moy ni personne ne put voir son visage elle l'avoit bridé avec sa cornette et rattachée avec une épingle & toutes ces miserables de la sequelle de raffia ont obtenu d'être ainsy conduites à la potence', writes Gueullette, who was a magistrate of the Parlement de Paris. He adds how disappointed he is not to catch a glimpse of Marie-Françoise Lefort's face for 'On dit que cette marie françoise lefort étoit fort jolie.'[24] Of course other criminals showed off until the last moments. Several refused to meet their confessors, saying that they were useless. Others asked for a good supper (and got it) on the night before their execution, provided they had divulged the names of their accomplices.

For criminals, privacy is often symbolised by the dissimulation of their identity. There is a constant play between false and real names, nicknames and pseudonyms: Antoine Descroix, alias 'tête de mouton', Perrault 'va de bon cœur', François Notary or 'le petit chevalier', Jean Thibault, called 'Sans regret'. At a period when the police had no real possibility of checking the identity of individuals, it was quite easy to change names and even pretend to be someone else. A criminal could leave the part of the country where his actions were notorious, go somewhere else and begin a new life. It is true, however, that the French government, as early as the 1720s, tried to control several categories of the population, especially soldiers and vagrants, by obliging them to carry passports and *sauf-conduits*. In the army, this was done systematically

24. AD III 7, 61, 28 June 1743.

in order to identify deserters. On those papers, one could find particulars which became increasingly detailed as the century advanced.[25]

Another way of protecting privacy and secrecy was the use of a secret language. Here we meet again the literature of roguery with its dictionaries of slang, the *Jargon de l'argot réformé* published in France in 1629, and the *Dictionary of the terms ancient and modern of the canting crew* in England. Slang was considered as the secret language of thieves as early as the sixteenth century, and the literature of roguery describes the many tricks of false beggars and pilgrims, mock cripples and so on with the purpose of warning and protecting the public against them; these texts also offer definitions of many slang words. It is a fact that criminals actually used this jargon. Cartouche spoke slang in his prison; thieves employed it sometimes when talking together. Even the judges themselves quoted slang words in the judicial Acts of Parlement.

Apart from the question of identity and language, the most obvious and simplest way of discovering elements about the private life of criminals is to read their confessions. On this topic, the eighteenth century is a particularly interesting period because such documents become more numerous. In French criminal biographies, however, we do not find the so-called 'deathbed speech' as often as in English biographies, where it appears regularly.[26] But, as the century progresses, there are more and more ballads and songs, and sometimes more deathbed speeches too. Apart from a few manuscript confessions, it is difficult to know whether these texts are literary forgeries. But they are interesting to study as such because they are part of the cultural trend of the French Enlightenment, leading to self-examination and a new importance given to the interior life. In a broadsheet published in 1728, we find: 'Etant au lieu du supplice, ce garçon s'est écrié, vous tous grands & petits qui estes ici presens, je vous prie d'avoir compassion de ma pauvre ame qui a cette heure va se séparer de mon corps, & comparoistre au jugement de Dieu qui sera tres facheux pour moi, n'étant pas digne d'entrer dans son royaume.'[27] Perhaps the speech was actually pronounced but the broadsheet is signed by Herault, who was the lieutenant general of police at the time. Mandrin too, just before being tortured to death, speaks to the audience: 'Voilà donc la fin que tu me préparois malheureuse passion des richesses! [...] Je rentre dans la nuit, puisse mon nom être oublié avec mes crimes!'[28] But, as we have seen

---

25. See Vincent Denis, *Une Histoire de l'identité* (Seyssel, 2008).
26. See Peter Linebaugh, 'The ordinary of Newgate and his account', in *Crime in England 1550-1800*, ed. J. S. Cockburn (London, 1977), p.246-69.
27. *Sentence de mort* [29 September 1728].
28. *Histoire de Louis Mandrin*, p.220-21.

throughout this chapter, French criminal biographies (unlike their English counterparts, which follow the judicial data more precisely) are fictional versions of the lives of famous criminals. They provide what is lacking in the dry documents of the judges: private life, psychology, rhythm, love affairs. If necessary, they invent characters and make criminals deliver speeches they have never pronounced, as if the anonymous writers had been genuine witnesses. Mainly they transform famous criminals like Cartouche or Mandrin into heroes and supermen they never were, minimising the importance of the gang and focusing on its leader.

In the second half of the eighteenth century, while French epistolary novels and real or fictional autobiographies multiplied – Rousseau's *La Nouvelle Héloïse* was published in 1761, and the *Confessions* in 1781-1788 – a few criminal biographies appeared which were presented as 'authentic' confessions. It was also the moment when the bandit became a literary character in French novels and plays. For the first time, the criminal spoke in the first person. We find for instance in 1777 the *Visions, réflexions et aveux de Derues, trouvés dans sa prison, écrits de sa propre main*. In 1798 was published a book entitled *Les Amours de Cartouche, ou Aventures singulières et galantes de cet homme trop célèbre, qui n'ont jamais été publiées, dont le manuscrit a été trouvé après la prise de la Bastille*. Obviously this text cannot be taken seriously, but it is interesting because it uses a certain number of clichés we have already met. Cartouche becomes a criminal because of greed: 'Je suis né en 1693, avec trop peu d'argent pour ne pas en désirer d'avantage.' He meets gypsies on his road and then starts both his criminal and his gallant career, encountering a great number of women, from prostitutes to noble ladies, who are all attracted by his dangerous charm.

The prison is the place where confessions are supposed to be written by the criminals themselves. In these last years of the eighteenth century, the prison tends curiously to play a similar role to the boudoirs of sentimental novels: it appears as a space for both daydreaming and penitence, and as a place where criminals remember and regret their former life. Such a literary trope will be especially developed in the nineteenth century, at a time when prisons become places of confinement. The best example is the episode during which Fabrice, the hero of Stendhal's novel *The Chartreuse de Parme*, falls in love with Clelia, the daughter of his jailer, when he is imprisoned in the Farnese fortress of Parma. In this novel, the prison becomes a place of introspection and the proper place for the birth of passion:

> Il courut aux fenêtres; la vue qu'on avait de ces fenêtres grillées était sublime.[...] Il y avait lune ce jour-là, et au moment où Fabrice entrait dans

sa prison, elle se levait majestueusement à l'horizon à droite, au-dessus de la
chaîne des Alpes, vers Trévise. [...] Sans songer autrement à son malheur,
Fabrice fut ému et ravi par ce spectacle sublime. C'est donc dans ce monde
ravissant que vit Clélia Conti! Avec son âme pensive et sérieuse, elle doit
jouir de cette vue plus qu'un autre.[29]

But this is another story.

---

29. Stendhal, *La Chartreuse de Parme* (Paris, 2000), p.399-400.

La Nouvelle Héloïse and Wolmar's project: transforming passion into 'familiarité fraternelle'

ALISON OLIVER

All of the writings of Jean-Jacques Rousseau treat in some way the relationship of the individual to society. But it is in his fiction that he scrutinises most closely the tensions and ambivalences of private space even within domestic settings. In *Julie, ou la nouvelle Héloïse* (1761), Rousseau thoroughly questions the boundaries between the public and private spaces of the eighteenth century, and most particularly with respect to the definition of the structure of the family. The linguistic and behavioural regulation of loving feelings within the domestic family is an especially crucial issue for the novel, which focuses on a single household, that of Clarens, and describes at length two versions of the family community, before and after the marriage of the heroine to her father's best friend, Wolmar. Before this marriage takes place, the passion that ties Julie and her teacher Saint-Preux acts as a disruptive force within the household until the moment when the Baron d'Etanges arranges Saint-Preux's departure. Wolmar marries Julie who becomes the mother of two children and goes on to confide in him the intimate secrets of her love affairs. As a result, Wolmar invites Saint-Preux to Clarens and attempts to integrate passionate attachment within the family sphere, subjecting it to a process of 'guérison'. Family space will become increasingly a form of social utopia. In attempting to locate within this family space the history of an erotic passion, and therefore the inversion of family space, the novel will subject to scrutiny the definition of the family as a private space. This chapter will focus on the question of the linguistic and behavioural regulation of loving feelings within the domestic family in this novel.

As all the inhabitants of Clarens share family ties, they are all implicated in Wolmar's project. But although the bonds between the members of the community have become eroticised, they tend to exclude sexuality from the newly created family. Wolmar (the architect of the 'new' Clarens) challenges the existence of a necessary connection between passionate feeling and sexual behaviour, and hopes that his curative method will enable Julie and Saint-Preux to transform their 'erotic' bond into a purely emotional attachment that will contribute to

the 'family' structure of Clarens. Passion, in other words, is proposed as a
potential substitute for the affectionate ties between individuals that are
both natural and necessary within a close-knit community such as
Clarens, and which may be found elsewhere between members of the
same family, or within the married couple.[1] In the *Confessions*, the
autobiographer details his complex relationship with Mme de Warens,
or 'Maman', who was his lover, mother, friend and sister all at once.[2]
Timorous and hesitant before their first sexual encounter, the autobiographer reports his deeply guilty state of mind afterwards: 'J'étois
comme si j'avois commis un inceste.'[3] The sexuality that the young
Jean-Jacques had found so troubling once it intruded into the constellation of roles he had to play with Mme de Warens becomes, in *La
Nouvelle Héloïse*, something to be controlled, purified and transformed
within the family sphere.

Sexual passion is a troubling force in the early part of the novel, in the
Clarens presided over by the baron d'Etange. The lover, Saint-Preux, and
the father compete destructively for the affections and possession of the
daughter. The father–daughter relationship is brought to the reader's
attention by the 'editor', who refutes Saint-Preux's contention in one of
his letters to Julie that he is her sole male correspondent: 'Il en faut, je
pense, excepter son père.'[4] In fact, the epistolary love story creates a close
association between the notion of illicit sexuality and acts of correspondence, which colours the father–daughter relationship. The connection
between eroticism and family tenderness is at its most apparent in the
scene in which Julie's father first beats and then embraces her. The
punishment causes Julie to miscarry Saint-Preux's child, and shatters her
hopes of marrying him. But the reconciliation between father and

1. See Elena Pulcini, *Amour-passion et amour conjugal: Rousseau et l'origine d'un conflit moderne*
    (Paris, 1998) for a discussion of the conjugal bond. Pulcini argues that Rousseau modifies
    the traditional opposition between love and marriage, but that the conjugal bond in *La
    Nouvelle Héloïse* is deliberately and determinedly de-eroticised: 'L'opposition entre l'amour
    et le mariage ne se limite donc plus au contraste codifié par la conception traditionelle, et
    pas seulement aristocratique, entre le sentiment et l'institution, entre l'affectivité et
    l'univers de la norme sociale; elle se définit plutôt comme une *opposition entre deux formes du
    sentiment, entre l'amour-passion et l'amour conjugal*, l'un artificiel et destructeur, l'autre naturel
    et éthique' (p.139).
2. At an early stage in the relationship, he writes: 'elle étoit pour moi plus qu'une sœur, plus
    qu'une mère, plus qu'une amie, plus même qu'une maitresse, et c'étoit pour cela qu'elle
    n'étoit pas une maitresse' (Jean-Jacques Rousseau, *Les Confessions*, in *Œuvres complètes*, ed.
    Bernard Gagnebin and Marcel Raymond, vol.1, Paris, 1959, p.1-656, 196-97; all references
    are to this edition).
3. Rousseau, *Confessions*, p.197.
4. Jean-Jacques Rousseau, *Julie, ou La Nouvelle Héloïse*, ed. Henri Coulet and Bernard Guyon,
    in *Œuvres complètes*, ed. Bernard Gagnebin and Marcel Raymond, vol.2 (Paris, 1964), p.1-
    793, part 1, letter 60, p.164. All references are to this edition (henceforward *NH*).

daughter which immediately follows was, nonetheless, hailed by one contemporary reviewer as 'le tableau le plus attendrissant de l'amour paternel & filial'.[5] While the potentially erotic nature of the father–daughter bond is perhaps most fully developed in this scene, it is hinted at throughout the novel.[6]

Saint-Preux and the baron jockey for position in Julie's affections, and claim her obedience in certain duties. Julie's marriage to her father's friend Wolmar marks his victory and initiates the transition between the two societies at Clarens. From that moment the baron disappears from the narrative, displaced by Wolmar as head of Clarens, and from this point onwards Etange becomes a kindly, almost grandfatherly figure, who can even live on friendly terms with Saint-Preux when the latter is invited back to Clarens. The baron does not need to be present in the new society because Wolmar acts as surrogate father. The timing and the location of the baron's definitive announcement of their engagement to his daughter makes this point emphatically. It is on the very morning after the beating which causes her to miscarry Saint-Preux's child that he reminds Julie of Wolmar's claims. He enters her bedroom, sits on her bed and, as Tony Tanner puts it, names its next occupant: 'after his orgasmic assault on Julie, the father reasserts his power to name his substitute, or rather surrogate.'[7] The baron has also obviously confided in Wolmar about his daughter's relationship with Saint-Preux, a confidence hidden from Julie even after six years of marriage, signifying that she is far from able to claim 'equal' adult status with her husband. The life debt that the baron owes to his friend is repaid when he allows Wolmar to live his life in his stead: marrying him to his daughter, giving him his estate, income and authority. But Wolmar will make quite a different use of this paternal authority, as we shall see from a consideration of the society he tries to build at Clarens with his wife.

5. 'Vous ne lirez pas, Monsieur, sans verser de douces larmes, le moment de la réconciliation du pere & de la fille. C'est une de ces situations, où la nature se peint sous les couleurs les plus touchantes' (Joseph de La Porte, *L'Observateur littéraire*, 1761, vol.1, p.309). Fréron also describes the baron as 'honnête', adding that he is represented as a 'galant homme, un Militaire franc, un père sensible' (*L'Année littéraire*, 1761, letter 13, vol.2, p.304). The juxtaposition of the baron's credentials as a 'galant' and a father suggests, perhaps, that Fréron was also conscious of the erotic overtones of this scene.
6. The potential connection between lover and father is established by Saint-Preux from one of his first letters, although he does so precisely in order to reassure Julie that she is safe from his sexual advances: 'Je frémirois de porter la main sur tes chastes attraits, plus que du plus vil inceste, et tu n'es pas dans une sureté plus inviolable avec ton pere qu'avec ton amant' (*NH*, part 1, letter 5, p.42). The comment takes on a new resonance when we recall it after the later scene of the paternal beating and reconciliation: Julie is not 'safe' with either man, it appears.
7. Tony Tanner, *Adultery and the novel: contract and transgression* (Baltimore, MD, and London, 1979), p.128.

Wolmar will represent a different, if no less authoritarian, version of paternal authority, as he extends his influence beyond the bounds defined by his blood family. Wolmar uses his authority, acquired according to the rules of the aristocratic, patriarchal code, to transform Clarens from a bastion of the aristocratic family into a space in which a new model family can flourish. In this new private world affection is more important than blood ties. It is for this reason that the love between Saint-Preux and Julie is valuable to Wolmar in building his version of Clarens; he recognises that the intense passionate feeling between them is fundamentally good: 'je compris qu'il regnoit entre vous des liens qu'il ne faloit point rompre; que votre mutuel attachement tenoit à tant de choses louables, qu'il faloit plutôt le regler que l'anéantir; et qu'aucun des deux ne pouvoit oublier l'autre sans perdre beaucoup de son prix.'[8] Wolmar's challenge is to redirect passion into 'familiarité fraternelle' without destroying it, but also without allowing it to overspill boundaries that he determines. His project is to 'cure' the former lovers of their disruptive sexual desires, while integrating their passionate intensity of feeling into the family sphere. In the Clarens presided over by the baron d'Etange, we have seen how strongly identified with each other the figures of Julie's father and her lover are: there is clearly an erotic presence in the family bond, but it is such that it appears not to disturb the experience of the family, either for the characters who participate in it, or for Rousseau's early readers. La Porte's enthusiastic account of the scene of 'tendresse paternelle' (a scene which I have highlighted as being a key indicator of the suppressed eroticism of the father–daughter bond) suggests that contemporary readers did not react to any disruptive or disturbing sexuality. In channelling the erotic passion Julie and Saint-Preux feel into a more familial affection, Wolmar follows a kind of logic which is not immediately apparent to the twenty-first century reader. The novel first invites the reader to recognise that eroticism can exist within the family bond (in the parallel relationships between Julie and her father, and Julie and Saint-Preux), and then explores the problem of how an illicit, if imaginary, erotic bond can be transformed into a marriage without sacrificing emotional intensity.

Wolmar's experiment is, therefore, a practical, quasi-scientific investigation into the possibility of integrating sexual passion into the family sphere when that passion pre-exists the family bond. His term for this activity is 'guérison'. Julie de Wolmar, he explains to her cousin Claire, is no longer Julie d'Etange, 'La femme d'un autre n'est point sa maitresse, la mère de deux enfans n'est plus son ancienne écoliere. [...] Il l'aime dans le

---

8.   *NH*, part 4, letter 12, p.495.

tems passé: voila le vrai mot de l'énigme.'[9] 'Guérir' is not incompatible with 'aimer' in Wolmar's usage, hence he can confide to Claire at the beginning of Saint-Preux's stay at Clarens:

> De vous dire que mes jeunes gens sont plus amoureux que jamais, ce n'est pas, sans doute, une merveille à vous apprendre. De vous assurer au contraire qu'ils sont parfaittement [*sic*] guéris; vous savez ce que peuvent la raison, la vertu, ce n'est pas là, non plus, leur plus grand miracle: mais que ces deux opposés soient vrais en même tems; qu'ils brulent plus ardemment que jamais l'un pour l'autre, et qu'il ne regne plus entre eux qu'un honnête attachement; qu'ils soient toujours amans et ne soient plus qu'amis; c'est, je pense, à quoi vous vous attendez moins, ce que vous aurez plus de peine à comprendre, et ce qui est pourtant selon l'exacte vérité.[10]

Wolmar's project at this point in the novel relates primarily to Saint-Preux: he has apparently already worked on Julie's heart in order to conserve the worthy aspects of her affection, taking care at the same time to banish 'ce qui pouvoit y rester de trop'.[11] In fact, Wolmar's project of transforming the passion of Saint-Preux and Julie corresponds with Julie's own ideas about the ideal love relationship, which she had tried to explain to Saint-Preux early in their affair.[12] The assertion that 'le véritable amour est le plus chaste de tous les liens' because it alone has the ability to 'épurer nos penchans naturels' echoes, in fact, Rousseau's concerns about his relationship with Mme de Warens as represented in the *Confessions*.

Jean Starobinski has shown the importance of 'transparence' as a feature of the ideal love relationship in Rousseau's work, particularly with respect to Julie's overarching goal. The desire to disclose every hidden feeling, however, could also be interpreted as a first step towards reconciling all types of feeling.[13] Wolmar remarks negatively on her tendency to 'tout confondre' when she tolerates his own intrusion into her relationship with Claire;[14] and Saint-Preux tells her 'Tu as voulu

---

9. *NH*, part 4, letter 14, p.509.
10. *NH*, part 4, letter 14, p.508.
11. *NH*, part 4, letter 12, p.495.
12. *NH*, part 1, letter 50, p.138. Note that this should not be taken as a suggestion that purely spiritual love should always be preferred to the physical; in the context of the letter, Julie seems to be making a point about the 'purer' physical language of sex itself, especially between herself and her lover as privileged souls, compared to the indelicate verbal language that Saint-Preux uses when he is drunk. See Judith Still, 'Rousseau's *La Nouvelle Héloïse*: passion, reserve, and the gift', *Modern language review* 91 (1996), p.40-52 (47).
13. See Jean Starobinski, *Jean-Jacques Rousseau: la transparence et l'obstacle*, 2nd edn (Paris, 1971), ch.5.
14. See *NH*, part 4, letter 7, p.431.

concilier la tendresse filiale avec l'indomptable amour; en te livrant à la fois à tous tes penchans, tu les confonds au lieu de les accorder et deviens coupable à force de vertus.'[15] Julie, it turns out, shares the inclination of the young Jean-Jacques of the *Confessions* to fetishise the ties that bind her to others: 'Que ne puis-je inventer des nœuds plus étroits encore pour unir tout ce qui m'est cher!' she exclaims.[16] After her marriage the difference will be that, instead of mixing them together, Julie, under Wolmar's guidance, will try to 'les accorder' so that they can coexist not just harmoniously, but even in unison.[17]

As the family bond is eroticised, the erotic bond is, to a certain extent, 'familiarised'. Saint-Preux, in his ecstatic letter following the second *nuit d'amour*, seems to subscribe to this idea when he tells Julie: 'j'imagine à peine quelque sorte d'attachement qui ne m'unisse pas à toi. O ma charmante maîtresse, ô mon épouse, ma sœur, ma douce amie! que j'aurai peu dit pour ce que je sens, après avoir épuisé tous les noms les plus chers au cœur de l'homme!'[18] Julie's final two letters to Saint-Preux before her accident are letters of triumph at having, she thinks, attained her goal of 'familiarité fraternelle', and she claims the right to advise her ex-lover 'comme une sœur, comme une mère'. As such, she says, he should marry Claire so that 'Dans le nœud cher et sacré qui nous unira tous, nous ne serons plus entre nous que des sœurs et des freres [...] c'est alors que nous nous aimerions tous plus parfaitement, et que nous goûterons véritablement réunis les charmes de l'amitié, de l'amour et de l'innocence.'[19] Julie claims that, by marrying Claire, he will cement his family relationship to the community and, specifically, to herself: 'vous

---

15. *NH*, part 3, letter 16, p.336. Tanner calls this desire of Julie's 'an inclination to live in a kind of emotional blur in which her feelings can only be sure of themselves when they are no longer able, or constrained, to distinguish between their objects' (*Adultery and the novel*, p.148).

16. *NH*, part 6, letter 13, p.742.

17. See Starobinski on the desirable qualities of musical unison in the novel. In the scene of the 'fête des vendanges', the workers sing 'en chœur', naturally, allowing full appreciation of the melody rather than drawing attention to themselves as interpreters: 'Rousseau professe ici un idéalisme sentimental; pour lui, la personnalité de l'interprète et la jouissance purement sensitive sont des *obstacles* interposés entre une "essence" musicale et l'âme de l'auditeur' (*La Transparence et l'obstacle*, p.111, emphasis in original). Individual voices dissolve into the group for the greater good, just as the community at Clarens will attempt to dissolve individual bonds into overlapping collective relationships.

18. *NH*, part 1, letter 55, p.149. Saint-Preux, like Rousseau in the *Confessions*, experiences a failure of language to encompass all that he feels; the experience of a lack forces him to accumulate terms in the hope of reaching a level of intensity that still falls short of what he means to express.

19. *NH*, part 6, letter 6, p.664, 665, 671.

ne m'appartiendrez jamais de trop près; ce n'est pas même assés que vous soyez mon cousin; ah! je voudrois que vous fussiez mon frère!'[20]

In the light of her revelatory posthumous letter to him, Julie's steadfast promotion of the marriage, and her keenness to integrate Saint-Preux officially into her family by marrying him to Claire, could be read as a subconscious recognition of her need to accumulate moral obstacles to her buried passion for him, and to safeguard herself from any adulterous temptation. Rousseau's contemporaries certainly found this particular aspect strange. The generally favourable review in the *Journal encyclopédique* picked out Julie's promotion of the marriage as a defect of *vraisemblance*: 'Une femme qui brûle en secret, plus que jamais peut-être, pour cet ancien Amant, est bien aise que son Amie l'épouse.'[21] Adopting a psychoanalytical approach to the character, we could sur-mise that her wish that her lover really be her brother reflects her need to remind herself that he is out of bounds. She admits to Claire that 'j'en serai plus sûre de mes propres sentimens quand je ne pourrai plus les distinguer entre vous.'[22] In her final letter to Saint-Preux, she reveals her persistent passion and the extent of her delusion in her married life so far, and continues to exhort him to marry Claire. It cannot now be a matter of wishing to put him morally out of reach so that they can all live happily together at Clarens. We can, however, suggest an alternative explanation by examining the relationship between Julie and her cousin Claire.

The friendship between Claire and Julie is the one bond that is represented as constant and unchanging. From the start Claire mediates the love relationship between Julie and Saint-Preux by making it possible for them to meet and even to kiss. Claire's relationship with Julie goes far beyond that of the traditional confidante required by the epistolary form: she is no passive observer of events, nor simply the archivist of Julie's letters.[23] Their friendship and family bond give them the privi-leged relationship which Starobinski sees as a 'zone de transparence centrale'.[24] Indeed, this transparency is not just tolerated, but authorised by Wolmar: he rejects Julie's offer to allow him to read her letters to Claire – an offer that in turn provokes Claire's anger:

20. *NH*, part 6, letter 8, p.691.
21. *Journal encyclopédique*, vol.11, p.233 (15 March 1761, p.65).
22. *NH*, part 5, letter 13, p.634. A remark that calls into question the nature of the relationship between Julie and Claire – see further discussion below.
23. Janet Altman, *Epistolarity: approaches to a form* (Columbus, OH, 1982), p.72.
24. Starobinski, *La Transparence et l'obstacle*, p.105. Starobinski remarks that the name Claire (and indeed Clarens) is suggestive of the clarity of the communication between the two friends.

J'ai peine à comprendre comment la seule idée d'admettre un tiers dans les secrets caquetages de deux femmes ne t'a pas révoltée! [...] si je savois que l'œil d'un homme eut jamais fureté mes lettres, je n'aurois plus de plaisir à t'écrire; insensiblement la froideur s'introduiroit entre nous avec la reserve, et nous ne nous aimerions plus que comme deux autres femmes.[25]

The eroticism in the bond between Claire and Julie is closer to the surface than in the father–daughter relationship owing to the 'transparence' of communication in the cousins' letters. In the early volumes of the novel, Claire declares to Julie that 'je n'aime parfaitement que toi seule'; even her daughter, in the later volumes, is considered an extension of Claire herself, a conduit for the love between the cousins, rather than necessarily an object to be loved in her own right. Claire alone seems fully to understand Julie's conception of 'véritable amour' which would unify two souls as one, independent of gender: 'Di-moi, mon enfant, l'ame a-t-elle un sexe?' she asks Julie. 'En vérité, je ne le sens guere à la mienne.'[26] It is noticeable too that, while Wolmar (characteristically) watches Julie on her deathbed, it is Claire who actually shares it, and holds Julie at the moment of death when Wolmar has been sent away from the bedroom. Wolmar finds them clasped together, one dead, the other unconscious in a kind of *Liebestod*, fantasised about – but never enacted – by Saint-Preux.[27]

Saint-Preux is the habitual observer of the affection between the two cousins, and in a letter to Julie had noted both his pleasure in the spectacle and his jealousy at his exclusion from it: 'J'étois jaloux d'une amitié si tendre; *je lui trouvois je ne sais quoi de plus intéressant qu'à l'amour même*.'[28] The intensely physical nature of their intimacy, and the fact that it inspires jealousy in the lover of one of the participants, invites the reader to affiliate the cousin relationship with other expressions of passion and sensuality. In fact, Saint-Preux's enjoyment of the scene corresponds to the reader's pleasure in other expressions of family love in the novel: La Porte's enthusiasm for the scene of *tendresse paternelle* between Julie and her father (which has definite sexual overtones) also comes to mind. Both Saint-Preux, as an observer, and La Porte, as a reader imagining a 'tableau', take pleasure from the spectacle of *sensibilité* within the family bond. It seems to offer a guarantee of safety. Participants can enjoy and observers can approve of a sensual experience that is

25. *NH*, part 4, letter 8, p.432.
26. *NH*, part 2, letter 5, p.206.
27. *NH*, part 6, letter 11, p.733. Saint-Preux's fantasy of dying with Julie recurs several times, the most memorable being at the time of the boat trip to Meillerie: 'je fus violemment tenté de la précipiter avec moi dans les flots, et d'y finir dans ses bras ma vie et mes longs tourmens' (*NH*, part 4, letter 17, p.521).
28. *NH*, part 1, letter 38, p.115 (emphasis added).

presumed to be safe because it does not threaten the social stability of the family structure.

But the bond between Claire and Julie goes beyond eroticism: they are so closely linked that they seem to share a single identity. Though not physically alike,[29] their mutual identification virtually achieves the unity that proves unattainable for the lovers in the novel. As Claire tells her friend, 'La premiere chose que j'ai faite a été de t'aimer. Dès nos premiers ans mon cœur s'absorba dans le tien. Toute tendre et sensible que j'eusse été, je ne sus plus aimer ni sentir par moi-même. Tous mes sentimens me vinrent de toi; toi seule me tins lieu de tout, et je ne vécus que pour être ton amie.'[30] All her other connections are subordinated to this relationship. In her sole letter to her lover, later her husband, Orbe, she tells him plainly that Julie is more important to her than he is – she admits to 'bizarrerie' in placing more weight on 'amitié' than 'amour', subverting the terms she uses by reversing their usual intensity.[31] Moreover, her identification with her cousin allows her even to experience some of Julie's feelings for Saint-Preux on her own account: 'je m'attache tellement à tout ce qui lui est cher, que son amant et vous, êtes à peu près dans mon cœur en même degré, quoique de différentes manieres.'[32] When Julie is tempted by Edouard's offer of a home for herself and Saint-Preux in England, Claire declares without hesitation that she will follow Julie to her refuge and renounce Orbe: 'quel que soit ton destin je suis déterminée à le partager. [...] ton sort doit être le mien, et puisque nous fumes inséparables dès l'enfance, ma Julie, il faut l'être jusqu'au tombeau.'[33] Saint-Preux calls the cousins 'les inséparables'; while they are clearly often spatially separated (hence the many letters between them), they claim that their souls are one, with Claire telling Julie: 'Tien mon ame à couvert dans la tienne, que sert aux inséparables d'en avoir deux?'[34] The idea of a shared soul is extended to that of a shared body to complete the identity between the cousins. Claire even complains after Julie's death that 'son cercueil ne la contient pas toute entiere... il attend le reste de sa proye... il ne l'attendra pas longtems'.[35] This final, complete

---

29. Rousseau's notes on the illustrative plates signal that Julie is blonde and Claire brunette. See *NH*, appendix 2, 'Sujets d'estampes', p.762.

30. *NH*, part 6, letter 2, p.640.

31. 'Quand je vous dis que ma Julie m'est plus chere que vous, vous n'en faites que rire, et cependant rien n'est plus vrai' (*NH*, part 1, letter 64, p.179).

32. 'Je n'ai pour lui que de l'amitié, mais elle est plus vive; je crois sentir un peu d'amour pour vous, mais, il est plus posé' (*NH*, part 1, letter 64, p.179).

33. *NH*, part 2, letter 5, p.206.

34. *NH*, part 6, letter 2, p.647.

35. *NH*, part 2, letter 5, p.206; part 6, letter 13, p.745.

identification of the cousins in a shared death is the arresting idea on which the novel ends.

The identification between Claire and Julie is especially apparent once Claire is widowed, and no longer has to devote herself to her duties as a wife, and can cede even her maternal role to Julie. By planning the marriage between her daughter and Julie's son, Claire not only conspires to unite the two families, but enacts the desire for union with Julie through their proxies. Henriette, by virtue of being brought up at Clarens by Julie and with Julie's sons, becomes Julie's daughter as well as her prospective daughter-in-law – something that may well point to future problems for the planned marriage in the next generation. After all, Henriette habitually refers to Julie as 'la petite maman', and Saint-Preux remarks that outsiders, unable to discern whose daughter she is, tend to assume that she is Julie's. But if, in the future of the novel, Henriette is to marry Mali, she will have to marry 'le fils de ma mère'; the very thing that Claire proclaims herself unable to do in relation to Saint-Preux. 'Je fis mon frère de ton ami, tu le sais: l'amant de mon amie me fut comme le fils de ma mère.'[36]

The shared (or rather doubled) motherhood of Claire and Julie in relation to the three children is, of course, part of Julie's fantasy of bringing everything together, but it is also another way in which the boundaries between the respective identities of the two cousins are dissolved. They actively encourage the mistake made by outsiders that Henriette is Julie's daughter; curiously, though Julie is so adamant that a father must know that his children are his own,[37] it does not seem to matter so much whether her children are able to exactly distinguish between their mothers – presumably because Claire is Julie just as Julie is Claire.

Julie's desire to marry Claire to Saint-Preux also rests on this identification with her cousin, and the continuation within the couple of the feelings that had previously been shared between the trio. Saint-Preux has already told Claire: 'Vous m'êtes toutes deux plus cheres que jamais; mais mon cœur ne distingue plus l'une de l'autre, et ne sépare point les inséparables.'[38] Saint-Preux, substituting himself for Julie, addresses

---

36. *NH*, part 6, letter 2, p.640. Claire's rejection of marriage is not based purely on the argument of the incest taboo, as will be discussed later.

37. 'N'est-ce donc faire aucun mal, à votre avis,' she writes to Saint-Preux, 'que d'anéantir ou troubler par un sang étranger cette union naturelle, et d'altérer dans son principe l'affection mutuelle qui doit lier entre eux tous les membres d'une famille?' (*NH*, part 3, letter 18, p.360).

38. In the same letter in which he has emphasised the substitution of Julie for her mother: *NH*, part 5, letter 9, p.619.

Claire as 'Cousine', who in turn calls him 'mon ami', as does Julie.[39] Claire points out to Julie that since the latter's marriage, Saint-Preux is equally dear to both of them, a remark that Saint-Preux also makes.[40] And to complete the relationships within the trio, Julie tells Claire that she and Saint-Preux 'se confondent depuis si longtems dans [mon cœur]. Qu'ils s'y confondent mieux encore, s'il est possible; ne soyez plus qu'un pour vous et pour moi.'[41] The fantasy, whether delusion or not, is that all three are bound together by reciprocal and equivalent love which, given the history of the affair between Saint-Preux and Julie, calls into question the presence of desire, and the potential for disruption, in the relationship between Claire and Julie and that between Claire and Saint-Preux.

This potential is partially acknowledged by Julie's project to marry her cousin to her former lover. She tries to persuade Saint-Preux that Claire will be her proxy in the marriage, allowing him to enjoy Julie through Claire (and maybe even to allow Claire to enjoy Julie through Saint-Preux): 'N'est-ce pas aussi Julie que je vous donne? n'aurez-vous pas la meilleure partie de moi-même, et n'en serez-vous pas plus cher à l'autre?'[42] Her pleasure in the marriage will be vicarious as well as voyeuristic. Just as she can tell Claire, 'Je sens que je jouïs doublement des caresses de mon petit Marcellin quand je te les vois partager', Saint-Preux's marriage to Claire would allow her to enjoy the conjugal embrace that they would share.[43] Saint-Preux will not be split between them, but doubled, a point which Julie's deathbed letter also makes:

> Songez qu'il vous reste une autre Julie et n'oubliez pas ce que vous lui devez. Chacun de vous va perdre la moitié de sa vie; unissez-vous pour conserver l'autre; c'est le seul moyen qui vous reste à tous deux de me survivre, en servant ma famille et mes enfans. *Que ne puis-je inventer des nœuds plus étroits encore pour unir tout ce qui m'est cher!* [...] Julie et Claire seront si bien confondues qu'il ne sera plus possible à votre cœur de les séparer. Le sien vous rendra tout ce que vous aurez senti pour son amie, elle en sera la confidente et l'objet: vous serez heureux par celle qui vous restera, sans cesser d'être fidelle à celle que vous aurez perdue.[44]

---

39. 'A l'imitation de Julie, il l'appelloit, ma Cousine; et à l'imitation de Julie, Claire l'appelloit, mon ami' (*NH*, part 2, letter 10, p.217n.).

40. Claire to Julie: 'A présent que tes affections ont changé d'espece, crois qu'il ne m'est pas moins cher qu'à toi' (*NH*, part 4, letter 2, p.410); Saint-Preux to Claire: 'elle regne dans ce cœur infortuné comme dans le votre' (*NH*, part 4, letter 3, p.415).

41. *NH*, part 5, letter 13, p.634.

42. *NH*, part 6, letter 6, p.670.

43. *NH*, part 4, letter 1, p.400.

44. *NH*, part 6, letter 13, p.742 (emphasis added). One contemporary review suggested that a sequel could be established on the back of this marriage project, but this does not seem to have been an overwhelming response to the novel. The reviewer describes Claire's 'inclination secrete' for Saint-Preux, adding hopefully, 'Ce dernier incident, qui donne

While this merging of Julie and Claire operates via the model of female friendship, the male characters also undergo a series of transformations and substitutions that produce a network of family-oriented equivalencies. The identification of Wolmar with his friend and father-in-law, the baron, has already been discussed. But Wolmar also establishes a bond between himself and Saint-Preux, which he hopes will modify the liaison between Saint-Preux and Julie. On welcoming Saint-Preux to Clarens, he immediately adopts a paternal and authoritative tone, and introduces Julie to him as 'votre sœur et votre amie'.[45] But Julie is not just a sister figure to Saint-Preux now, she is also the wife of Saint-Preux's new substitute father, layering another incest taboo over the fraternal relationship that is in the process of forming. The bond created between Wolmar and Saint-Preux, whether as father and son or, as he suggests when Saint-Preux finally 'graduates' from his method, as brothers, will now always intrude when he looks at Julie: 'A la place de sa maitresse je le force de voir toujours l'épouse d'un honnête homme et la mere de mes enfans: j'efface un tableau par un autre, et couvre le passé du présent.'[46] This 'effacement' represents the ideal outcome of Wolmar's experiment to transform disruptive passion into a constructive force. By changing the language which describes the relationship between the former lovers, Wolmar seems to be invoking the added moral guarantee of the incest taboo. In other words, by inviting Julie and Saint-Preux to call each other brother and sister, he is simultaneously reminding them that they are forbidden to call themselves lovers any more. He is hoping to retain the virtuous elements of their attachment, while rendering their wayward sexual feelings for each other literally inconceivable by effacing the linguistic space in which it is possible to imagine a sexual relationship.

The reward for Saint-Preux's acceptance of these new family configurations is to take his own place as an adult by being granted a quasi-paternal authority over the Wolmar children, whom he is to educate. Wolmar establishes a parallel between his own marital rights over Julie ('usurped' from Saint-Preux) and the paternal rights over the children of the marriage: by resigning the latter to Saint-Preux, he is compensating him for the loss of the former. Just as Julie was a substitute for her father in the relationship between Wolmar and the baron, Julie's children are substitutes for their mother in the relationship between Wolmar and Saint-Preux. But before Saint-Preux can return from his travels with

---

un nouveau dégré d'intérêt à la fortune de Saint-Preux, est peut-être une pierre d'attente pour une continuation de l'Ouvrage' (*Affiches, annonces, et avis divers*, neuvième feuille, 4 March 1761 [p.33-34]).

45. *NH*, part 4, letter 6, p.424.
46. *NH*, part 4, letter 14, p.511.

Edouard to re-enter Clarens in triumph and take up his place as an adult there, the society itself is destroyed by Julie's death, a catastrophic event which reveals the extent of the illusion on which it had been built.

It is Julie's dying realisation that she has not been 'cured' of her love for Saint-Preux, expressed in her deathbed letter to him, and not her death itself that marks the final failure of Wolmar's project. Though the cracks had been appearing before Julie's accident (her insistence that Saint-Preux marry Claire, their reluctance, the sense of foreboding linked to Saint-Preux's dream), the project was in no way doomed to failure from the start. In fact, logically, it works very well: Wolmar's ideas are based on gathering data from the various emotional entanglements (familial and non-familial) at Clarens, where he is at first a peripheral figure – his letters are not included in the collection until his marriage. Finding common emotional ground in the different relationships that he observes, and using this observation to transmute one type of passion into another is all very well as discourse – but insufficient when it comes to reality. Wolmar's faith is in rational systems and logical extrapolations, but he has insufficient experience in passion to understand that emotion, in Rousseau's world, surpasses logic. Sexual passion resists Wolmar's hyper-rational attempts to turn it into something else through the use of language.

Although the novel finally acknowledges sexual passion as something that lies beyond other types of emotion, Wolmar's experiment never-theless opens up intriguing possibilities. If the first part of the novel sets up the terms in which the reader is invited to consider types of feeling, much of the second is devoted to the ways in which they are experienced, analysed and manipulated. Though the experiment provides a useful way of viewing these explorations, it should be borne in mind that the explorations are Rousseau's and the experiment Wolmar's. The ultimate failure of the experiment does not imply that the exploration of feelings is invalid: in fact, it adds another dimension by showing the difficulties inherent in the very discussion of emotion. Discourse is shown to fail in the novel when it attempts to contain and even to express passionate feelings.

But it would be misleading to attribute the blame for the failure of the Clarens community solely to Wolmar. Its members, who are prepared to think of themselves in terms of a series of overlapping and interlocking trios, in fact endorse his experiment. Although there is evidence from the *Confessions* to suggest that Rousseau in theory prefers these configur-ations to that of the couple as an emotional unit, the fact is that plural relationships are no more successful in fiction than in the autobiogra-pher's version of his 'life'. At Clarens, these trios are supposed to diffuse the intensity of the passionate bond by distributing it among more people, rather than eradicating it altogether. When the various trios (bound together by family affection, eroticism and often both at the same time) as well as the substitutions, equivalencies and multiple and shared identities are mapped onto each other, it becomes clear that the patterns of relationships at Clarens really do seem to enact Julie's fantasy of 'tout confondre'. Yet the overlaying of family bonds and eroticism results in the implosion of the community, rather than neutralising each other into a healthy type and degree of emotion. The very process of trying to unify all types of affective bond creates, after Julie's death, an anti-community, a group of celibate loners. Julie recognises on her deathbed that 'cette réunion n'étoit pas bonne': by its excess, *sensibilité* has dissolved all bonds and rendered them liquid and flexible, cancelling out both sexuality and family. If everything is erotic, nothing is really erotic any more.

The failure of the system is recognised by all the remaining partici-pants at Clarens. Claire acts in defiance of her friend's dying wish when she refuses absolutely to marry Saint-Preux, a refusal that effectively puts an end to the fiction of substitution and doubling of identities previously fantasised. Wolmar himself, still the source of authority at Clarens, seems belatedly to recognise the problems raised by perpetuating the fiction of shared and multiple identities: he puts an end to the role-playing game indulged in by Claire and her daughter, in which Henriette represents the dead Julie: 'Dès ce moment, je résolus de supprimer tous ces jeux, qui pouvoient allumer son imagination au point qu'on n'en seroit plus maitre. Comme on guérit plus aisément de l'affliction que de la folie, il vaut mieux la laisser souffrir davantage, et ne pas exposer sa raison.'[47] Though he is talking here about Claire, he might be thinking of the game that he has been playing with Saint-Preux and Julie. Julie's death has demonstrated the failure of role-playing, and, once again, the unattain-able goal of total transparency within the family.

In fact, after Julie's death, there can be no real family at Clarens. The society of Clarens at the end of the novel is atomised: Claire the *sensible* is at odds with Wolmar's 'froide tristesse', the baron is dying, the children are in the background. Saint-Preux is absent, prostrate with grief, we learn at second hand, but expected imminently. Just how he will fit into the remnants of the society is unclear, except we know that he will not marry Claire and will be charged with the education of Julie's sons. Claire's imminent death, which is announced if not depicted at the end of the novel, would leave a community made up of celibate males and three young children.[48] The projected marriage of Henriette and Mali, if

47. *NH*, part 6, letter 11, p.739-40.
48. For a discussion of the phallocentric ending, see René Démoris, 'De Marivaux à *La Nouvelle*

it takes place, is still far in the future, and will presumably turn the carefully cultivated fraternal feelings between the cousins into a passion-less conjugal bond on the Wolmar model, renewing Clarens for another generation without revitalising it.

The most interesting feature of Wolmar's experiment is not, in fact, that it fails, but that it could be attempted at all. In Rousseau's novel, the focus is on the role played by the characters in bringing about the conditions of their own downfall: destiny cannot be blamed for the failure of their relationships. Wolmar's hubris lies in thinking he can control and direct human relationships. But the passions are volatile and thwart outcomes predicted on the basis of either careful observation or previous experience because no two human situations are ever the same. Rousseau's novel ends with the reassertion of instinct, and sexual passion, as something which lies beyond human attempts to control, exploit and even explain it.

Héloïse: intertexte et contre-texte, entre fantasme et théorie', in L'Amour dans La Nouvelle Héloïse: texte et intertexte, ed. Jacques Berchtold and François Rosset, Annales de la société Jean-Jacques Rousseau 44 (Geneva, 2002), p.317-39. After the systematic elimination of the female characters, 'On se retrouve entre hommes au dénouement' (p.335).

Private life, personal liberty and sexual crime in eighteenth-century Venice: the case of Gaetano Franceschini

LARRY WOLFF

'I am a free man, living by myself without family relations.'[1] This affirmation was central to the legal defence of Gaetano Franceschini, who faced charges in Venice in 1785 before the blasphemy tribunal, the Bestemmia. He was accused of causing scandal after an eight-year-old girl spent one night in bed with him. When Franceschini, age sixty, said that he was 'free', he meant, precisely, legally, that there were no family bonds and obligations that he violated or offended by the conduct of his private life. In a contrasting instance, the marquis de Sade was a married man in the 1770s, and the father of young children, at the time when he was presiding over orgies at La Coste (in which his wife actually participated). It was thus a family matter for his mother-in-law to seek the royal *lettre de cachet* by which Sade was arrested, locked up and prevented from bringing further dishonour to his family. The abduction of young girls was a criminal offence in itself, but it was ultimately Sade's family relations that made it impossible for him to evade the intervention of the law and turned his private sexual conduct into a public matter. Franceschini, on the other hand, had no wife and no children who could be implicated in the scandal of his conduct, and he had separated himself from his respectable family in Vicenza to come and live alone in Venice. He was a free man, and therefore answerable only to himself in the conduct of his private life.

Yet freedom was a word with many implications in the Age of Enlightenment, in the decade after the American Revolution, in the decade before the French Revolution. 'Man is born free, and he is everywhere in chains', wrote Rousseau in the *Social contract*. Rousseau, of course, was not thinking particularly about old men accused of seeking sex with young girls, but Franceschini in the chains of prison might also have had reason to reflect on the philosophical, political and social implications of freedom. It was only a short etymological leap from

---

1. Archivio di Stato di Venezia, *Esecutori contro la Bestemmia*, Busta 40: *Processi: 1784-1785*, the case of Gaetano Franceschini; all subsequent citations from the documents of the case refer to this same archival citation.

the *uomo libero* to the *uomo libertino*, and then, as Sade recognised, it took only another little twist for the libertine free from prejudice to become the criminal free from scruple. 'Io sono uomo libero', declared Franceschini in 1785. Don Giovanni in 1787 sang out, 'Viva la libertà!' Mozart's librettist was the Venetian Lorenzo Da Ponte.[2]

As Franceschini presented his defence, a formal 'allegation' (*allegazione*) that he prepared with legal assistance, he remained in chains. The rhetorical thrust of the introduction to his deposition was a lament for the loss of his freedom:

> Most Wise Lords, Most Grave Magistrature, if ever false and arbitrary zeal and the force of unfounded deductions have been able to sacrifice innocent victims upon the altars of justice, and if ever an obscuring of the truth of the facts by means of the most inconclusive and audacious suppositions has been able to cast the simulated appearances of guilt and culpability upon the most indifferent actions, the origin of this trial and the actual situation in which I present myself – I most unfortunate Gaetano Franceschini, in the dolorous Iliad that envelops me – submit to you the most pitiable and fatal example. Sixty years of irreproachable conduct were not in fact sufficient to spare me this fatal destiny, and unfounded rumours sufficed, illegal defamation, arbitrary deductions, to destroy in one moment that which cost me the long course of a life formed in the principles of virtue, and lived according to the paths of reputation and honour.[3]

With astute legal counsel Franceschini stood prepared to demonstrate that the evidence against him was completely insubstantial. He was determined to transform a case in which he had been cast as the monstrous scourge of an innocent victim into its mirror opposite, with himself as the innocent victim of monstrous injustice. For rhetorical purposes, he donned the heroic mantle of an honourable man condemned to suffer the vicissitudes of Homeric misfortune. Above all, however, he represented himself as a victim in the violation of his privacy, and invoked the 'always respectable silence of the domestic walls'. From the beginning, the case against Franceschini was dependent

2. Larry Wolff, 'Depraved inclinations: libertines and children in Casanova's Venice', *Eighteenth-century studies* 38:3 (2005), p.417-40.
3. 'Se mai l'arbitrio, il falso zelo, e la forza d'infondate deduzioni ha potuto Sapientissimi Signori Gravissimo Magistrato immolare sugl'altari della Giustizia vittime innocenti, e ottenebrando nel mezzo alli piu inconcludenti temerari supposti la verita dei fatti ha potuto con simulate apparenze spargere di reità e di colpa l'istesse azioni piu indifferenti, l'origine di questo processo, l'attuale situazione in cui mi presento io sfortunatissimo Gaetano Franceschini vi assoggetta appunto nell'illiade dolorosa che mi circonda l'esempio piu compassionevole e fatale. Sessant'anni d'irreprensibile condotta non furono infatti sufficienti a sottrarmi dal piu fatale destino, e bastarono sole voci infondate, diffamazione illegale, arbitrarie deduzioni per distruggere in un momento ciò che mi costava il lungo giro d'una vita educata nei prinicipii d'onestà, consumata dietro le traccie di riputazione e di onore.'

upon discovering the secrets of his private life, determining what took place inside his apartment and, even more privately, inside his bedroom. Making the affirmation of his domestic privacy into the central principle of his defence, Franceschini insisted on a sharp distinction between the spheres of private sexuality and public culpability. Sade, in his porno-graphic fiction, argued philosophically for the right of the libertine to find satisfaction for his sexual tastes. Franceschini, in his legal defence, argued for the right to privacy that began at his bedroom door. Ad-dressing the relation between public and private life, he articulated a modern conception of what it meant to be a free man in the late eighteenth century.

Franceschini recognised that the principal charge against him, the crime that brought him under the jurisdiction of the Bestemmia, was simply causing scandal.[4] His defence therefore commenced by discussing legally, and even philosophically, the nature of scandal, and the ways in which it was constituted at the intersection of private and public life. 'Scandal is a deduction made by some concerning the operations of others', declared the defence. 'In order to establish someone's account-able action as a scandal, however, the judgment of others is not suf-ficient.' A man could not be convicted of scandal just because others said he behaved scandalously. Rather, it remained to be demonstrated that his conduct could plausibly be considered the 'legitimate cause' of scandal.

Though Cesare Beccaria's *Crimes and punishments*, published in 1764, did not address the subject of scandal, Franceschini's lawyer must have been familiar with the author's enlightened style of analysis, the rational application of sense to traditional categories of criminality, such as adultery, homosexuality and infanticide. The peculiar illogicality of scandal was that it might exist without reference to any actual basis in fact. If Franceschini himself was the subject of the scandal, but not its cause, then he should not be held responsible for unfounded defa-mations of his character. It was not enough to show that the scandal existed, unless it could also be demonstrated that the subject had actually committed the stipulated scandalous acts. Yet, if those acts were not criminal in themselves, then could the scandal alone be logically con-sidered to be criminal? The Bestemmia seemed to assume the plausibility

4.   Gaetano Cozzi, 'Religione, moralità, e giustizia a Venezia: Vicende della Magistratura degli Esecutori contro la Bestemmia (secoli XVI-XVII)', *Ateneo Veneto* 178/179:29 (1991), p.7-95; G. Cozzi, 'Note su tribunali e procedure penali a Venezia nel '700', *Rivista Storica Italiana* 77:4 (1965), p.931-52; Giovanni Scarabello, *Esecutori contro la Bestemmia: un processo per rapimento, stupro, e lenocinio nella Venezia popolare del secondo Settecento* (Venice, 1991); Guido Ruggiero, *The Boundaries of eros: sex crime and sexuality in Renaissance Venice* (Oxford, 1989).

of a 'don't-ask-don't-tell' scenario in which private misconduct was reserved for divine justice unless it became the subject of public scandal. Yet it was the tribunal's own investigative machinery that cracked open the protective casings of privacy. In a case like that of Franceschini the prosecution had to pursue a paradoxical procedure: the secret investigation of a public scandal. Within that framework there was always the possibility that the investigation was actually creating the very scandal that it sought to uncover, rendering notorious what had previously been private.

Scandal was inevitably a human construction, and subject to the inflections of human fallibility and human malice. 'In fact, the most indifferent actions, the most innocent operations, may acquire in the spirit of a slanderous man this most fatal interpretation', according to the defence. Franceschini's scandal derived from the accusation that he had sex with the eight-year-old Paolina Lozaro, the daughter of a poor Friulian laundress in Venice, Maria Lozaro. He believed that he had been maliciously slandered by a neighbour, who could have put in motion the legal prosecution that charged him with scandal. In fact, his neighbour seems to have stepped out of the pages of Carlo Goldoni's comedy *The Coffee house* (*La Bottega del caffè*, 1750), and could just as well have been Don Marzio, the incorrigible gossip. Franceschini himself lived just upstairs from the coffee house in Calle della Cortesia where neighbourhood gossip was brewed, and sweetened, and stirred all day long. Goldoni himself clearly appreciated the casual relation between malicious gossip and public scandal, and the distinction between them was not always necessarily clear. Franceschini's defence characterised the charge of scandal as mere 'defamation', as 'chimerical, imaginary deduction' and therefore unfounded in criminal fact. Not only did the defence refuse to admit Franceschini's guilt, but it rejected the whole category of crime with which he was being charged. Scandal always existed in the minds of others, and was therefore fundamentally susceptible to chimerical and imaginary insinuations.

'Now I understand', said Franceschini at his first appearance before the tribunal. 'There has been formed a most atrocious calumny against me.' Ten years before, in 1775, Beaumarchais first introduced the character of Figaro to the European public in the drama *The Barber of Seville*. In one of the celebrated speeches of the play, the crafty music master Don Bazile recommended 'calumny' as the infallible method for assaulting an enemy. 'There is no malice, no horrors, no absurd tale, that one can not get accepted by the idle people of a great city', he confidently declared. The course of calumny was narrated as a kind of music lesson with marked dynamics: 'D'abord un bruit léger, rasant le sol comme hirondelle avant l'orage, *pianissino* murmure et file, et sème en courant le trait empoisonné. Telle bouche le recueille et *piano, piano* nous le glisse en l'oreille adroitement. Le mal est fait, il germe, il rampe, il chemine, et *rinforzanto* de bouche en bouche il va le diable.' So the calumny finally culminates in '*crescendo* public, un *chorus* universel de haine et de pro-scription!'.[5] This enlightened appreciation of the power of calumny, and its capacity to create public scandal out of nothing at all but malice, was clearly fundamental for Franceschini's defence in 1785.

In the eighteenth century, public scandal was also regarded as a literary staple of the publishing business, and scandalous accounts were consumed by avid readers all over Europe, especially in France. Such accounts were prominent, as Robert Darnton has demonstrated, among the 'forbidden best-sellers' of the *ancien régime*. Alongside the 'philosophical' pornography of a work like *Thérèse philosophe*, there were also extremely popular works, usually semi-fictional and sometimes semi-pornographic, called *libelles*, or libels, which purported to reveal the secret scandalous truth about notable figures of the French royal court. *Anecdotes of Mme Du Barry* was a best-seller of 1775, while the *Annals of Louis XV* appeared in 1782, full of scandalous revelations about the recently deceased king. These writings fed the hunger of the reading public for scandalous sex in combination with criticism of the monarchy, and thus played a part in the evolution of political consciousness in the public sphere.[6]

By far the most potent French scandal of the *ancien régime*, however, erupted in 1785, the year of Franceschini's trial in Venice, and permitted the public of Europe to contemplate the cultural and legal implications of scandal in general. This was the Diamond Necklace Affair, which destroyed the reputation of Marie-Antoinette and undermined the credibility and legitimacy of the French monarchy in the period immediately preceding the French Revolution. In this scandal a scheming adventuress, Mme de La Motte, manipulated an ambitious cardinal, Louis de Rohan, and arranged for him a nocturnal meeting in the gardens of Versailles with a prostitute who impersonated the queen, Marie-Antoinette. Cardinal Rohan then undertook to purchase, suppos-edly in the queen's name, an immensely valuable diamond necklace, which the queen never received. The cardinal was arrested on 15 August at Versailles, a few weeks before Franceschini's September arrest in Venice, and the case received tremendous publicity in the Paris news

5. Beaumarchais, *Le Barbier de Séville* in Œuvres, ed. Pierre Larthomas (Paris, 1988), p. 310 (act 2.ix).
6. Robert Darnton, *The Forbidden best-sellers of pre-Revolutionary France* (New York, 1995); L. Wolff, 'The fantasy of Catherine in the fiction of the Enlightenment: from baron Munchausen to the marquis de Sade', in *Eros and pornography in Russian culture*, ed. Marcus Levitt and Andrei Toporkov (Moscow, 1999), p.249-61.

chronicles, all the more since the actual involvement of the queen, if any, remained fascinatingly uncertain.

The Diamond Necklace Affair of 1785 focused hostile attention on the French court, but also allowed for reflection on the nature of scandal itself, on its plausibility, dissemination and sometimes pernicious consequences, the same issues that Franceschini raised with regard to the allegedly chimerical and imaginary aspects of the case against himself. One French chronicle reported on 18 August 1785, concerning the Diamond Necklace Affair, that 'although the story is very improbable, it is so widely spread about, and sworn to by people so well placed and so trustworthy, that it is very difficult not to believe it.' The scandal fed upon the public trial of Rohan before the Parlement of Paris, and Sarah Maza, who has analysed the case in her book on *Private lives and public affairs* in eighteenth-century France, concludes that 'within the nascent oppositional public sphere of the eighteenth century, private and public experience were not sharply distinct categories, but were located along a continuum so that the one shaded off into the other.'[7] Franceschini's case revealed an analogous confusion of public and private matters under the different circumstances of secret justice in Venice. At exactly the same time that witnesses were being secretly summoned by the Bestemmia to testify about Franceschini, the customers in the coffee houses of Venice would have been reading in the gazettes about the Diamond Necklace Affair in France. Franceschini's defence was sufficiently attuned to current concerns about the equivocal nature of scandal to challenge its fundamental construction as a category of criminal conduct.

In his refutation, Franceschini focused on the circular reasoning of the indictment, which explained his character by the scandal, and the scandal by his character, while neither was a subject susceptible to proof by concrete facts.

> Everything is arbitrary, everything is deduction, there is not any real fact, there is not valid proof that can offer true and real results. Regarding the accusation in the vague aspect that includes the odious character of sensuality attributed to me, there are only reckless deductions presented. Regarding the alleged scandal, malice is absolutely apparent, rather than an innocent and legitimate scandal. In order to establish a guilty depraved custom the most occult directions have not been neglected, and it has been allowed that the testimony that was supposed to argue and prove the deductions, may wander freely and capriciously, interpreting in its fashion, defining in its fashion, circumstantiating in its fashion the things that it enunciates.[8]

7. Sarah Maza, *Private lives and public affairs: the causes célèbres of prerevolutionary France* (Berkeley, CA, 1993), p.188, 320.
8. 'Tutto è arbitrio, tutta è deduzione, non vi è fatto reale, non vi è sussistente prova, che porger possa una vera reale risultanza. O si consideri l'accusa nel generico, ch'essa

Franceschini's defence seemed almost to echo the speech of Don Bazile in *The Barber of Seville*, a study in the dynamics of calumny as it was translated into testimony: creeping and tramping from mouth to mouth and ear to ear, arbitrarily wandering and interpreting in its own arbitrary fashion, moving from the occult whispering of malice, *pianissimo*, to a public *crescendo* of condemnation. The alleged scandal was not 'innocent and legitimate', because it was maliciously concocted, and the legal indictment was similarly illegitimate because the testimony was capriciously construed. Above all, the defence insisted upon the legal and philosophical sloppiness that characterised the case, in which such elusive concepts as scandal and character were defined and interpreted with complete freedom to suit the prosecution.

According to the defence, the testimony against Franceschini was too exclusively focused on sex. Though the tribunal had attributed to Franceschini a 'guilty depraved custom' in sexual matters, sex was not the only significant aspect of character and custom. 'There was no one who introduced, who exposed, who represented me as an irreligious man, as a blasphemer', Franceschini noted. Yet the name and commission of the tribunal implied that blasphemy and impiety would be inevitably commingled with the other vices of an evil Venetian. Boldly, the defence challenged the assumption that a man's private sex life was necessarily an essential aspect of his public reputation: 'A man can be infamous in the face of society, without being sensual, and can enjoy the prerogatives of an optimal reputation even in spite of sensuality.' Sensuality, after all, could exercise its effect in private, within the domestic walls, within the bedroom chamber, without becoming the cause of scandal.

'Si on m'appelle sensuel on aura tort,' wrote Casanova, in the introduction to his memoirs, 'car la force de mes sens ne m'a jamais arraché à mes devoirs, quand j'en ai eu.'[9] Franceschini, like Casanova, affirmed that sex did not definitively compromise character, and that sexual relations were not the crucial determinant of social reputations. The hypocrisy of society, then as now, permitted perfunctory piety and pervasive impropriety to coexist. According to Franceschini's defence, however, it was

---

comprende nell'adossatomi odioso carattere di sensualità, e non sono che temerarie deduzioni quelle, che si presentano. O si consideri il reclamato scandalo, e la malignità assolutamente comparisse piuttosto che uno scandalo innocente e legittima. Per stabilire un reo depravato costume non si sono neglette le direzioni piu occulte, e si è lasciato che il testimonio, che render doveva ragione ragione vera delle deduzioni, libero a capriccio vagasse interpretando a suo modo, a suo modo definendo, a suo modo circonstanziando le cose da lui ennunziate.'

9. Giacomo Girolamo Casanova de Seingalt, *Histoire de ma vie*, 12 vols (Wiesbaden, 1960-1962), vol.1, p.xv.

not actually hypocritical but perfectly proper for a man to enjoy an optimal reputation in spite of his sexual activity; character was not simply a matter of sex, and the public conception of character was rightly separate from what occurred within the 'always respectable silence of the domestic walls'. He was a free man, and he dared to regard his libertinism as a prerogative of his freedom.

Indeed Franceschini offered himself as proof that a free man with a freely cultivated private life might possess an optimal reputation. 'I have always been received in whatever civil, virtuous, noble society', he announced, and it was one of the few points of his entire defence for which he summoned witnesses to corroborate his account. Anzolo Zorzi, living in the neighbourhood of Santa Maria Formosa, testified concerning Franceschini, 'I have known him for four or five years on account of circumstances that draw him into that society which I also customarily frequent.' The Zorzi were one of the grand patrician families of Venice, and this scion of the clan testified to seeing Franceschini received 'in every civil, virtuous, and noble circle', mentioning particularly casinos and theatre boxes. Since Franceschini supposedly settled in Venice only two years before, he must have been visiting the city regularly for some years before that to enjoy its social diversions. Carlo Foncel, also of Santa Maria Formosa, had known Franceschini for two years from another venue: 'the coffee house at the Ponte dell'Angelo, which I customarily frequent'. This referred, very probably, to the same coffee house beneath Franceschini's apartment. Foncel also claimed to have seen Franceschini received 'in the most virtuous and noble society'. Foncel was apparently of non-noble but privileged 'civil' birth, a citizen, his status comparable to that of Franceschini himself. Felice Sartori was a lawyer who had known Franceschini as a client for about two years, but once encountered him also in a casino. 'Was he received in noble and virtuous society?' the tribunal asked. 'I saw him well received in that casino,' replied Sartori, 'and I saw him with the most noble and virtuous persons.'

Paolo Valmarana belonged to one of the great noble families of Vicenza, the family for which Palladio built the Villa Valmarana in the sixteenth century, but, like Franceschini, Valmarana had moved to Venice and was living in the neighbourhood of Sant'Angelo. He testified that he had seen Franceschini 'well received among virtuous and noble families'. Francesco Panizzon was another transplanted native of Vicenza, living in Venice for ten years, and serving as a public official. 'I have known him very well from my earliest years,' he said of Franceschini, 'since he too is from Vicenza.' In Venice they continued to move in the same society: 'I have certainly seen him at the coffee house at the Ponte dell'Angelo, where he dealt with the best gentlemen.' Thus a sampling of respectable society, from Venice and Vicenza, patricians and citizens, testified to the point that Franceschini was well received in their own circles. The defence sought to establish that Franceschini, as a man of good reputation, could not be considered the cause of scandal but must be the victim of arbitrary and malicious defamation. Such testimony must also have made clear to the patrician judges of the Bestemmia that Franceschini belonged to circles not so far from their own, that he was someone they might have encountered at the casino, in the theatre, even at the coffee house. Franceschini's character witnesses simply certified for the judges what must anyway have been evident from the start: namely, that he stood far closer to their own social world than did the poor laundress Maria Lozaro and her eight-year-old daughter.

Valmarana and Panizzon, as natives of Vicenza, were further questioned concerning Franceschini's status as a 'free man', without family obligations. 'Does Franceschini have any family relations?' Valmarana was asked. 'His family lives in Vicenza', was the reply. 'He has separated from his family, and has been living by himself, not being married, as far as I know and is universally known.' Panizzon replied similarly to the same question: 'For many years he has been living separated from his entire family, which lives in Vicenza, and not being married he has therefore no relations.' Well received in Venetian society, embedded in respectable social circumstances and connections, a man without family relations or obligations susceptible to indiscretion or violation, Franceschini, in the view of the defence, was incapable of causing scandal. He was a free man, and whatever conduct he pursued in private concerned only himself.

Though free from family relations, Franceschini did not hesitate to invoke his respectable family in decrying the indictment against him. He even invoked the name of God, as if to demonstrate that there was nothing incongruous, let alone blasphemous, in a libertine's expression of religious sentiment. 'Good God! what a weak foundation supported the absolute ruin of the good name, the honour, the reputation, of a sixty-year-old man.' Like Beccaria, he seemed to object to a system of secret justice in which testimony was 'covered with the odious darkness of the most false suppositions'. Franceschini invoked the 'moving spectacle' of himself, an old man, who was now, in December 1785, entering into his fourth month of imprisonment. He called upon the tribunal to reflect on what he had lost, 'the irretrievable, demonstrable sacrifice of honour'. While the indictment argued that it was his character and reputation that created scandal and made him culpable, Franceschini replied that it was the case itself that defamed his character, destroyed his reputation, and sacrificed his honour. The honour of a libertine was not merely a cynical expression: Casanova in Poland in the 1760s fought a famous duel when he was called a 'Venetian coward', and Mozart and

Da Ponte's Don Giovanni audaciously confronted his own damnation when he invited the ghostly statue to dine with him as a point of honour.

The indictment against Franceschini had been divided into two parts, focusing first on the scandalous consequences of his 'sensual dissoluteness', and second on his proclivity for 'pushing it still further' by pursuing young girls. Correspondingly, the defence replied on both counts and, after having addressed the general issues of sensuality and scandal, proceeded to refute the particular charges that made the case so remarkable. 'Concerning the accusation of procuring girls of tender age as the objects of my alleged sensuality,' wrote Franceschini, 'I have heard the reproach, in addition to some particular circumstances, that I was also in the habit of introducing into my apartment girls of tender age.' Yet bringing girls into his apartment was not in itself a criminal act: 'The most indifferent actions were clothed in the most odious appearances of doubt and uncertainty. It has been attempted to attribute to these actions the agitation of a culpable intention.' He therefore asserted a sharp distinction between indifferent actions, like bringing a girl into his apartment, and guilty intentions, like procuring her for sex. 'If the simple fact of girls coming into my apartment is not a crime, to construct it as such, one needs the proof of a guilty intention.' Just as scandal and character were shown to be dependent upon intangible factors, susceptible to manipulation, so Franceschini's ultimate intentions, in the argument of the defence, were represented as fundamentally unprovable.

There were two witnesses who claimed to have heard Franceschini assert that he wanted a girl in his bed because he believed that the warmth of her body would be medically restorative for him. He was not told the identity of those witnesses, but he rightly recognised the importance of that remark for the attribution of a 'guilty intention'. He simply claimed that he was joking:

> This expression certainly cannot appear to an enlightened judge as either a legal proof of fact, and not even as a reasonable index of a concealed intention. Woe indeed, if such expressions in the course of pleasant conversations, playfully enunciated, could form the proof of a criminal question! Woe, if in order to decide about volition, and about intention, which has always been an object concealed from the mind of man, which law and reason have set apart from the judge since it is recognised as the impenetrable work of Divine Providence, removing this from the penetration of men and reserving to itself the judgement, woe if one can be convinced by the trifle of a vain expression![10]

10. 'Quest'espressione. . . non puo certamente comparire ad un Giudice illuminato non solo come prova legale d'un fatto sussistente, ma neppure un'indizio ragionevole d'un'occulta

Franceschini pleaded his own jocularity in pleasant conversation; perhaps the expression was tasteless, the joke unfunny, but, he asserted, it could not be convincingly construed as the evidence for criminal intention.

In demanding a rigorous standard of proof Franceschini appealed to a sense of 'enlightened' jurisprudence, aligning himself with legal critics like Beccaria who had emphasised the arbitrariness of justice under the *ancien régime* in Europe. The problem of intention was relevant to every criminal case, but particularly relevant to one in which the charge was confused and the deed even more elusive. His 'playful' expression about sleeping with the girl could hardly be taken as a 'proof of fact', a proof of any sexual act with the child, for the crucial fact of the case was that the girl's virginity was not violated. A surgeon had examined the girl and testified to her virginity, but also claimed to see some evidence of genital irritation that might be attributable to Franceschini's sexual molestation. Guido Ruggiero, writing about sex crime in Renaissance Venice, has noted that penalties were particularly severe in cases where the victim was a pre-pubescent girl, not yet menstruating and therefore not yet ready for marriage. The violation was supposed to make her less marriageable, and the punishment of the violator might include a fine to pay for the girl's eventual dowry.[11] Franceschini himself would ultimately be required to pay a fine.

Eighteenth-century Venetian legal texts by Benedetto Pasqualigo and Lorenzo Priori noted that the rape of a virgin could be punishable by death, that sex with a virgin was often presumed to be rape and that even attempts to have sex with young girls were considered criminal. Priori's treatise thus observed that the death penalty could, in theory, be applied to the man 'who deflowered or attempted to deflower a little virgin of less than ten years approximately, not fit to receive a man' – but that, for merely attempted defloration, judges preferred not to apply such an extreme penalty.[12] Any accusation of 'attempted' sex would inevitably become a matter of intention. The indictment of Franceschini – which

---

intenzione. Quai infatti se l'espressioni dette nel mezzo a discorsi piacevoli giocosamente annunziate formar potessero quindi la prova d'una criminale questione! Guai se per decidere di quella volontà, e di quell'intenzione, che fu sempre un'oggetto occulto alla mente dell'uomo, che la Legge e la ragione allontanò dal Giudice poiche la conobbe impenetrabile opera della divina Providenza, che togliendola alla penetrazione degl'uomini ha solamente a se stessa riservato il Giudizio, potesse esser convinta nell'inezia d'un'inutile espressione.'

11. Ruggiero, *The Boundaries of eros*, p.96-98, 148-52.
12. Benedetto Pasqualigo, *Della giurisprudenza criminale, teorica e pratica*, vol.1 (Venice, Stefano Orlandini, 1731); Lorenzo Priori, *Pratica criminale secondo le leggi della Serenissima Repubblica di Venezia* (Venice, Gasparo Girardi, 1738), p.162-63.

had to exclude the charge of defloration – therefore depended upon establishing his depraved intention, in order to make plausible the implication that depraved acts, short of intercourse, could have occurred during the night that Paolina Lozaro spent in his bed. Yet intention, as Franceschini insisted, was the aspect of a criminal case most inaccessible to the eye of merely human justice.

The defence was obliged to comment on the testimony of the girls themselves: Paolina Lozaro had spoken of pinching, and another girl had mentioned an attempt to touch her breasts. Surely such testimony gave some clue to Franceschini's 'guilty intention'. Yet the defence simply rejected the testimony of the girls as 'unreliable' (*inattendibile*), and suggested that such girls, offered employment as servants at a young age, often resented having to do their work, and therefore ended up inventing excuses for not wanting to remain in service. Little girls would naturally have regretted 'the sacrifice of a liberty enjoyed up until that moment', and would have had to make up some story to tell their parents about why they found serving Franceschini to be oppressive. That was how and why the lazy little girls themselves invented the tale of his sexual attentions to them, and, after that, the *crescendo* dynamics of calumny proceeded from the first *pianissimo* murmuring. The question of why Franceschini had brought Paolina Lozaro into his apartment was there-fore easy to answer: he employed her as a servant. Yet the tribunal insisted on twisting his intentions: 'Not for the motive of personal service, but for a wicked sensuality, it is alleged that I procured the girl's coming into my apartment. Vague disseminations constitute the basis of this deduction which, penetrating into the hidden darkness of a concealed intention, attempt to show clearly a different contested motive.' Franceschini rejected such speculative probing into his personal motives. He affirmed not only the domestic privacy of his apartment, but also the personal privacy of his inner self, arguing that they were both off limits to the investigation of the tribunal, and that nothing legally convincing could be known about what was hidden within his home and himself.

In Franceschini's case, the elaborate defence of his domestic and personal privacy was specifically related to matters of sex. He was arguing that both his sexual activity, within his home, and his sexual thoughts, within himself, were off limits to the law and belonged to him alone. The argument of the defence suggested that not only was the tribunal wrongly encroaching upon his privacy as a free man, but also that it was anyway virtually impossible for the law to penetrate into his private life to obtain legally meaningful evidence. In these respects, Franceschini's defence did indeed reflect the most modern legal criti-cism of the Enlightenment, as summed up by Beccaria in his discussion of 'crimes difficult to prove'. The crimes that Beccaria especially cited were adultery and homosexuality, noting that in such matters 'the tyrannical presumptions of the nearly proofs and half-proofs are admitted', in the absence of more rigorous legal evidence, 'as if a man could be half-innocent or half-guilty.'[13] Beccaria deplored such sloppy justice by halves, and it was just this sort of sloppiness that Franceschini's defence undertook to demonstrate in the case of his supposed scandals.

Beccaria, however, went further, in discussing adultery at least, and criticised the whole concept of sex as a subject of criminal justice: 'Adultery arises from the abuse of a constant and universal need in all mankind, a need antecedent to and, indeed, foundational of society itself, whereas other socially destructive crimes result from transitory emotions rather than natural need.'[14] Thus, the eighteenth century already adumbrated the enlightened idea that sex crime was legally problematic, founded as it was on human libido. Beccaria did not explicitly state the same argument for homosexuality, but an astute reader might have been able to make the connection. Sade's Mme Delbène offered the radically and outrageously extreme extension of this argument when she confided in Juliette: 'si je voyais qu'il n'y eût de possibilité pour moi d'être heureuse que dans l'excès des crimes les plus atroces, je les commettrais tous à l'instant, sans frémir.'[15] Like Beccaria, Sade respected the compelling nature of the sexual impulse, and critically questioned the classification of certain sexual acts as crimes.

In the twentieth century Michel Foucault attempted to describe the emergence of a modern notion of sexuality in the eighteenth and nineteenth centuries through a 'discursive explosion' of writing about sex. Foucault argued that this was the historical epoch that witnessed 'the setting apart of the "unnatural" as a specific dimension in the field of sexuality', that general prohibitions concerning sex fragmented into particular taboos: 'to marry a close relative or practice sodomy, to seduce a nun or engage in sadism, to deceive one's wife or violate cadavers, became things that were essentially different.' Though he did not name them, Foucault surely had in mind both Casanova and Sade, the legendary seducer of nuns and the notorious patron of sadism. Furthermore, though the enumeration of unnatural practices did not strictly follow Leporello's catalogue, Foucault clearly recognised the importance of Don Giovanni.

Here we have a likely reason, among others, for the prestige of Don Juan, which three centuries have not erased. Underneath the great violator of the

13. Cesare Beccaria, *On crimes and punishments and other writings*, ed. Richard Bellamy, trans. Richard Davies (Cambridge, 1995), p.79-80.
14. Beccaria, *On crimes and punishments*, p.80.
15. Marquis de Sade, *L'Histoire de Juliette*, in *Œuvres*, ed. Michel Delon, 3 vols (Paris, 1998), vol.3, p.270.

rules of marriage – stealer of wives, seducer of virgins, the shame of families, and an insult to husbands and fathers – another personage can be glimpsed: the individual driven, in spite of himself, by the somber madness of sex. Underneath the libertine, the pervert.[16]

In the shadow of Don Giovanni, Gaetano Franceschini. With a philosophical defence focused on his personal interior privacy, defiantly affirming that no external testimony could ever discover his concealed intentions, Franceschini appears as a sort of spokesman for the mystery of modern sexual identity. Foucault found an epochal distinction between the traditional concept of sex, understood as the commission of sexual acts, and a modern idea of sexuality, understood as a person's essential sense of self. The nineteenth century was, for Foucault, the great age of emerging sexual identities: 'Homosexuality appeared as one of the forms of sexuality when it was transposed from the practice of sodomy onto a kind of interior androgyny, a hermaphrodism of the soul. The sodomite had been a temporary aberration; the homosexual was now a species. So too were all those minor perverts whom nineteenth-century psychiatrists entomologized by giving them strange baptismal names.' Foucault mentioned, for instance, Krafft-Ebing's 'zoophiles' and 'zooerasts', the minor perverts who found love and sexual satisfaction with animals, but there were a multitude of such eccentric identities constituting the modern sexual taxonomy of the nineteenth century. Foucault argued that such identities were psychiatrically assigned to individuals, and thus 'implanted in bodies, slipped in beneath modes of conduct, made into a principle of classification and intelligibility'.[17] It was this fitting of a category of sexual identity to each characteristic mode of sexual conduct that produced the modern notion of sexuality. While Gaetano Franceschini in the eighteenth century may have considered himself a free man, engaging without prejudice in different forms of libertine sexual relations, Krafft-Ebing in the nineteenth century might have 'entomologised' him in the category of 'erotic paedophilia'.

As he defended his 'character' from 'chimerical' and 'imaginary' imputations, as he shielded his innermost 'intentions' from the presumption of the law which sought to interpret them as the evidence of a libidinous identity, Gaetano Franceschini stood at the historical crossroads where sex was already being overtaken by the ideological principle of sexuality. In the modern sexual universe, according to Foucault:

> it is through sex – in fact, an imaginary point determined by the deployment
> of sexuality – that each individual has to pass in order to have access to his

---

16. Michel Foucault, *The History of sexuality: an introduction* (New York, 1980), p.39.
17. Foucault, *The History of sexuality*, p.43-44.

own intelligibility (seeing that it is both the hidden aspect and the generative principle of meaning), to the whole of his body (since it is a real and threatened part of it, while symbolically constituting the whole), to his identity.[18]

Casanova, to be sure, discovered the intelligibility of his life in a discursive explosion of endless writing about his sexual adventures, and when he summed himself up in 1797, at the age of seventy-two, he proudly recognised the pervert behind the libertine:

> J'ai aimé les mets au haut goût: le pâté de macaroni fait par un bon cuisinier napolitain, l'Ogliapotrida, la morue de Terre-Neuve bien gluante, le gibier au fumet qui confine, et les fromages dont la perfection se manifeste quand les petits êtres qui les habitent commencent à se rendre visibles. Pour ce qui regarde les femmes, j'ai toujours trouvé que celle qu'j'aimais sentait bon, et plus sa transpiration était forte plus elle me semblait suave.
> Quel goût dépravé! Quelle honte de se le reconnaître, et de ne pas en rougir! Ce critique m'excite à rire. En grâce de mes gros goûts, je suis assez effronté pour me croire plus heureux qu'un autre, d'abord que je me trouve convaincu que mes goûts, me rendent susceptible de plus de plaisir.[19]

Casanova unabashedly celebrated his own tastes for the extravagant and the extreme; like Don Giovanni he had broad interests, and sampled women of every form and every age, but he recognised that his more unusual tastes more aromatically summed up the unique nature of his identity. In Russia in 1765 Casanova purchased a thirteen-year-old girl and regarded her as his sexual slave.[20]

The libertine was a free man, who enjoyed the freedom to explore and cultivate personal tastes and preferences, even individual perversions. Franceschini declared himself 'a free man without family relations', and therefore a man who could not give offence to society or the state by his private sexual conduct. 'There is nothing strange even in the alleged sensuality', he noted in his defence. For his libertine freedom encompassed the prerogative of sensuality, as something essential, neither strange nor extraneous, to the life of a free man. The Venetian expression 'niente di estraneo' ('nothing strange') might be read as the slogan of a libertinism diversely indulged, including an interest in little girls which was only just beginning to seem notably strange and problematically criminal, though not yet taxonomically perverse, according to the libertine values of the Enlightenment.

---

18. Foucault, *The History of sexuality*, p.155-56.
19. Casanova, *Histoire de ma vie*, vol.1, p.xv-xvi.
20. L. Wolff, *Inventing Eastern Europe: the map of civilization on the mind of the Enlightenment* (Stanford, CA, 1994), p.50-62.

Handling sin in eighteenth-century Russia

VIKTOR ZHIVOV

The private self and Russian salvation

Virtue can be exhibited and paraded. Sin, by contrast, tends to be concealed. Sins when recognised as sins belong to the order of intimate things and are kept in the privacy of the self. They hardly can be kept absolutely private, however, because then they are unconfessed sins; unconfessed sins lead the sinner into hell or, if they are minor, into purgatory. A Christian has to confess his or her sins, that is to make them at least to some extent public, to receive salvation. Confession can be regarded as one of the most potent technologies of the self that produces the self-representation of the individual in Christian cultural traditions.[1] The whole sphere of avowal, penance and absolution is permeated by the interaction between private and public. It is hardly accidental that in the Catholic West the radical growth of the importance of privacy coincided in time with the development of a new penitential discipline and the appearance of the confessional as a specially designated space where public and private confronted each other.

Russian sins and Russian salvation were different from their Western counterparts. There was no purgatory in the East. Confessional discipline was considerably more lax than in the West. Whereas in the West the decree of the Fourth Lateran Council of 1215 ordered the annual confession for lay Christians of both sexes, Russians during their Middle Ages usually did not confess regularly; many of them 'delayed their repentance' to the last moment 'to get absolution from the sins committed during their whole life'; they set 'their hopes on the absolute redemptive power of the last deathbed repentance'.[2]

Penitential practices are tightly connected with the representations of

---

1. See M. Foucault, *Histoire de la sexualité*, vol.1: *La Volonté de savoir* (Paris, 1976), p.25-49, and Michel Foucault, 'Technologies of the self', in *Technologies of the self: a seminar with Michel Foucault*, ed. L. H. Martin, H. Gutman and P. M. Hutton (Amherst, 1988), p.16-49.

2. V. Zhmakin, 'Mitropolit Daniil i ego sochineniia', *Chteniia v Imp. Obshchestve istorii i drevnostei rossiiskikh* 2 (1881), p. 257-762 (639-40): 'откладывали свое покаяние […], желая пред смертью […] получить прощение во грехах, сделанных в течение всей своей жизни [...], надеясь на всеискупляющее действие последнего, предсмертного покаяния.' All translations are my own unless otherwise noted.

the world to come that are current in the society in question. It may be assumed that the information about the other world that served as guidance for Russian medieval Christians was rather optimistic, at least in comparison with the West; this fact naturally explains the lack of rigour in the labours of repentance. Though descriptions of infernal torments were rather popular in medieval Russia, a sinner could nevertheless rely on God's mercifulness and hope not to enter the gates of hell; this hope existed irrespective of the quantity and gravity of unrepented sins. Divine clemency was limitless and irrational.

Russian medieval writings contain many stories about sinners who were miraculously saved without any special efforts on their part; it may be assumed that the medieval oral tradition was even richer in this respect. In one late medieval story, a monk who sinned gravely was taken to the other world. There he saw the eternal torments that he deserved for his sins. But the merciful Lord gave him three commandments with which he could save his soul: 'to abstain from the impurity (i.e. fornication), not to drink wine nor to smoke tobacco'.[3] After a certain time the monk relapsed into the same sins and was punished by a mortal wound. He did not die and go into the fire of hell, however, but was healed thanks to the intercession of the miracle-working icon of the Mother of God from Nerekhta. As can be seen, the sins do not block the way to salvation. On the contrary, sins seem to incite the display of divine mercy. The author quotes the Apostle Paul to substantiate his claim ascribing a peculiar (but probably not unusual in the Russian context) meaning to the following verse: 'But where sin abounded, grace did much more abound' (Romans 5.20).

This type of salvation, which I call 'illicit', could be obtained through the intercession of the saints, or the divine energies of a wonder-working icon, or by the action of relics or sacred fonts, or by other miraculous means. In accordance with the Eastern tradition, these uninstitutionalised sources of the holy were more important for salvation than regular 'institutionalised' penitential discipline, including sacramental confession and absolution given by the ministers of the Church.[4] In such circumstances, the fear of eternal damnation could not be very strong and penitential hardships could be perceived as optional for salvation.[5]

---

3. A. V. Pigin, 'K izucheniiu Povesti Nikodima Tipikarisa Solovetskogo o nekoem inoke', in *Knizhnye tsentry Drevnei Rusi. Solovetskii monastyr'*, ed. S. A. Semiachko (St Petersburg, 2001), p.303-10: 'prestani ot nechistoty i ne piti vina i tabaka' (p.307).
4. See Peter Brown, *Society and the holy in late antiquity* (Berkeley, CA, 1982).
5. See V. M. Zhivov, 'Imperator Traian, devitsa Fal'konilla i provoniavshii monakh: ikh prikliucheniia v Rossii XVIII veka', in *Fakty i znaki: Issledovaniia po semiotike istorii*, ed. B. A. and F. B. Uspenskii, (Moscow, 2008-), vol.1, p.245-68, on the story of a Kievan monk who

This fearlessness was grounded in a certain set of soteriological notions. Salvation when it was reflected upon was understood as entirely unconnected with human efforts, with the moral behaviour or the discipline of the Christian community. Salvation relates to the community of the Orthodox as a whole and comes by itself. It consists in a gradual transfiguration of this world into the Kingdom of Heaven and proceeds not by moral improvement but rather as an expansion of the liturgical cosmos into the outer world. The proliferation of the deified state of the world, that is its salvation, does not demand human efforts, so that a religious community has only to maintain the liturgical activity in its purity and continuity. This soteriology is the basis of the so-called Russian 'placing faith in rituals' (*obriadoverie*).

This was the background of the process of religious and social disciplining that started in Russia in the seventeenth century. Similar processes had innumerable repercussions for the culture and social psychology of post-Tridentine Europe. They gained some force in Russia only much later and were characterised by a number of peculiarities that seriously affected their results. In particular, it may be assumed that confession in Russia never played a role identical to its role in the West, that individual piety was based on different rituals and institutions, and that, consequently, the formation of the self followed there a different path.

Religious disciplining as Church and state policy in early modern Russia

The seventeenth century in Russia was a century of transition. It started with the trauma of the Time of Troubles; in the subsequent decades various sectors of society tried to find means to heal the wound of internecine war and moral degradation, but these efforts only aggravated the situation and led to further estrangement and hostility among different groups of the population. Reformist activities, started by the so-called 'zealots of piety' (*bogoliubtsy*) and rather modest in the reign of Michael Romanov, were greatly intensified during the next reign; various groups of reformers had different agendas, different purposes and different plans. At the beginning, these differences seemed to be rec-oncilable but, very soon, different interests came into conflict and, in the absence of any established institutions of compromise, led the parties

---

concealed his sins from his spiritual father but was saved after death thanks to the promise that God gave to St Anthony, the founder of the monastery, that every person who would be buried in the monastery would be pardoned. Such cases of 'illicit' salvation are not mentioned in non-East Slavic descriptions of the afterlife.

involved into insurmountable hostility. The results were disastrous: the schism of Old Believers and the transformation of the Church–state relationships into a battleground on which tsars and patriarchs, with varying success, tried to gain more power than they traditionally had.

The main weapon in these endless strivings was control over the population, its social and religious practices. When young Aleksei Mikhailovich ascended the throne in 1645, it looked as though he would implement the reformist programme of the zealots of piety; one of the representatives of this group, archpriest Stephan Vonifatiev, was his confessor. On the eve of Lent in 1647, the tsar made Patriarch Joseph issue an encyclical instigating the clergy to pray piously and to live in purity and sobriety. Then the tsar himself published a sabbatarian decree ordering his subjects to attend church on Sundays and requiring the closure of inns and shops. On 5 December 1648, the tsar, bypassing the patriarch's authority, published another decree that was to be read on Sundays in all churches. The decree ordered the people to abstain from impious and devilish deeds. They were not to listen to the mockery of itinerant minstrels, nor bait bears or dance with dogs, nor sing diabolical songs. Popular musical instruments were to be confiscated and burnt.[6] The first steps on the path of moral regeneration undertaken by the tsar corresponded exactly to those with which such zealots of piety as Ioann Neronov and Avvakum had started their reformist careers; the difference lay in the fact that now these measures were carried out on the state level. Even the state, however, did not have adequate power at that time to enforce religious discipline of this sort.

Though the Russian case demonstrates a number of peculiarities connected with specific traits of Russian soteriology, many aspects of religious disciplining of this period were typical for all policies of institutionalised bodies against charismatic, spontaneous, unrestrained religiosity. Social and religious disciplining is typically intertwined with the centralisation and consolidation of authority to the detriment of local traditions and provincial leaderships. All these elements were present in the developments of the second half of the seventeenth century. The authorities made efforts to regularise monastic life; itinerant monks were regarded as particularly suspicious and in need of constant control; special rules were formulated for this purpose at the councils of 1666 and 1667.[7] Unruly holy men and especially fools in Christ became the object of vigilant supervision; the authorities tended to suppress any disruptions of the ecclesiastical decorum and to rep-

6. Philip Longworth, *Alexis, tsar of all the Russias* (London, 1984), p.54.
7. *Materialy dlia istorii raskola za pervoe vremia ego sushchestvovaniia*, ed. N. I. Subbotin, 9 vols (Moscow, 1875-1890), vol.2, p.140-41, 256-60, 365.

resent new fools in Christ and new charismatic ascetics (naked, dirty, with long hair, in iron chains) as deviations from the models canonised in the Orthodox tradition (such as Andrew the Fool in Christ or Symeon of Emessa).[8] Various local shrines and holy fonts, wonder-working icons and supposedly spurious relics, which created the texture of religious life in an Orthodox community and constituted the basis of its local religious identity, were gradually drawn into the orbit of official inspection, re-evaluation and, from time to time, repression.

In his book *At War with the Church* Georg Michels claims that the Old Believers movement was to a large extent a reaction against the disciplining and suppression of local traditions by the central authority, whereas the correction of books and ritual innovations by Patriarch Nikon were secondary justifications of a broader protest. He claims that 'it appears that the Russian Schism resulted from official church policies. By suddenly and drastically intruding into age-long local and personal autonomies, the church generated popular opposition to its reforms. Rejection of the Nikonian reforms was therefore largely a response by communities as well as individuals to the church's insistence on controlling the religious affairs of Muscovy's hinterlands.'[9] This view is only partly justifiable, although it has the advantage of bringing together various processes of social and religious disciplining, heterogeneous negative reactions and subsequent confessionalisation of the Old Belief.

It is important from our perspective that regularisation of the penitential discipline was an integral part of the policies of secular and ecclesiastical authorities that have been described above. Regular confession had to serve as an instrument of religious and social control. Already in the encyclical issued by Metropolitan Iona of Rostov in August 1652, it was prescribed to monks and laymen 'to take communion and go to confession three times a year'.[10] This prescription was an element of a larger programme that included other injunctions: the decorous officiating of the liturgy, pious behaviour of parishioners in the Church, sobriety and knowledge of the basic elements of the Orthodox doctrine. A similar programme can be discovered in several documents issued by the tsar.[11] These parallel efforts to regulate religious life meant not only the co-operation of the two powers, spiritual and secular, but

8. *Materialy dlia istorii*, vol.2, p.137-38, 262-63; compare S. A. Ivanov, *Holy fools in Byzantium and beyond*, trans. Simon Franklin (Oxford and New York, 2006).
9. G. B. Michels, *At war with the Church: religious dissent in seventeenth-century Russia* (Stanford, CA, 1999), p.220.
10. Michels, *At war*, p.107.
11. See Michels, *At war*, p.189; *Polnoe sobranie zakonov Rossiiskoi imperii* [Sobranie 1-e] (henceforward *PSZR*), 45 vols (St Petersburg, 1830), vol.1, no.47, p.246.

also their tacit competition: those who give orders have supreme power in the sphere to which the relevant orders belong.

It is difficult to define what the success was of these efforts to introduce stricter rules for regular confession and communion. Nevertheless, symbolic efforts to enforce more rigid penitential discipline figured quite prominently in the activities of the clergy after the councils of 1666-1667. The councils promulgated several rules concerning the frequency of confession and relationships between spiritual fathers and their flock. In the eleventh act of the council of 1666 we read:

> The priests must teach their parishioners, men and women and their children, to go frequently to their spiritual fathers for confession, especially during the four holy fasts and not to deprive themselves of the taking of the Holy Mysteries [...] If somebody remains without confession over the whole year not by any necessity or because of travels and his hour has struck he should not be buried in the church yard and there should not be any funeral service for him since he himself during his lifetime retreated from the divine church.[12]

Priests were ordered not to accept as spiritual children persons who did not have a manumission letter from their previous spiritual fathers;[13] although this injunction is usual in Russian penitential texts of the preceding period, it certainly brings in an additional emphasis on the rigidity of the new regulations.[14]

Already at this time regular confession and communion began to be used as instruments of discovering and persecuting religious dissenters, first of all Old Believers. 'In 1682, for example, Metropolitan Kornilii of Novgorod instructed the new archimandrite of Solovki to discipline residents of the monastery's hinterlands: [...] Priests must be strictly ordered to see to it that their male and female parishioners and children over twelve attend Mass during the Lenten season, fast, go to confession and, if worthy, take communion.'[15] It is important to note that confessional lists came into existence as early as the 1680s and 1690s, and the initiative belonged to the bishops.[16] Patriarch Adrian tried to make

---

12. *Materialy dlia istorii*, vol.2, p.132-33: 'Ксему же научати прихожан, чтобы ко отцем духовным на исповедание, мужи и жены и их дети, приходили почасту, паче же в четыре святыя посты, и по разсуждению отцев духовных Пречистых Таин прията, тела и крове Христовы, себя не лишали. [...] Аще кто пребудет целой год без исповедания, кроме путешествий и нужных случаев, а случится ему смертный час, и такова у церкви не погребати и последования усопших христианъ над таковым не пети: зане таковый, живъ сый, удалил есть себе божественныя церкви.'

13. *Materialy dlia istorii*, vol.2, p.141.

14. S. I. Smirnov, *Drevne-russkii dukhovnik. Issledovanie po istorii tserkovnogo byta, Chteniia v Imp. Obshchestve istorii i drevnostei rossiiskikh* 2 (1914), p.50-63.

15. Michels, *At war*, p.116.

16. Michels, *At war*, p.293, n.6.

this practice obligatory in his instructions to the priests' elders.[17] Confessional lists were by no means a peculiar invention of Russian hierarchs. The same practice was characteristic of Counter-Reformation Europe. It is possible that Russian bishops had some information about this Catholic practice, though records of this type were indispensable for any control by superior institutions and they could be introduced independently of any similar measures in other countries.[18]

Patriarch Adrian's instruction was the last effort of the ecclesiastical hierarchy as an autonomous body to enforce stricter rules of penitential discipline and, in general, to suppress deviant phenomena of popular spirituality and to promote institutionalised forms of religious life. In 1700 Patriarch Adrian died and the Church entered a period of ruin and disarray. Peter the Great did not even pretend to be a pious Orthodox monarch. Until the middle of the 1710s, Peter's Church policy was essentially destructive. Nobody could seriously care about the religious disciplining of society in general and about the strictness of confessional practices in particular.

Around 1716 Peter changed his Church policy.[19] One of the first signs of this change was the decree of January 1716 that supplemented with a number of new articles the hierarchical vow which was recited and signed by each member of the higher order of the clergy at his installation.[20] In the additional articles the bishop promised to be circumspect and not to overstep the boundaries of his spiritual power, not to interfere in secular 'affairs and rites' (*obriady*), not to give permission to build new churches without absolute necessity and not to consecrate priests in excessive numbers. These articles were manifestations of Peter's anti-clerical policy aiming at the restriction of the clerical influence and the possibilities for the clergy of getting involved in political activities. There were, however, two other articles the purpose of which was different. In one of these articles the bishop promised to keep watch over monks and to prohibit them from wandering from one monastery to another. In the other article the bishop gave an oath to visit his parishes regularly, to control the priests and to suppress any schisms, superstitions and false worship; the bishops had to ban any veneration of unauthorised relics, of charismatic holy men walking about with matted

---

17. *PSZR*, vol.3, n.1612, p.413-25 (26 December 1697).
18. 'After the Council of Trent, diocesan and provincial synods began to order pastors to keep records of parish events such as births, deaths, and baptisms, and of those who fulfilled their Easter obligations' (W. D. Myers, *'Poor, sinning folk': confession and conscience in Counter-Reformation Germany*, Ithaca, NY, 1996, p.116).
19. V. M. Zhivov, *Iz tserkovnoi istorii vremen Petra Velikogo: Issledovaniia i materialy* (Moscow, 2004), p.48-53.
20. P. V. Verkhovskvoi, *Uchrezhdenie Dukhovnoi Kollegii i Dukhovnyi Reglament*, 2 vols (Rostov-on-Don, 1916), vol.2, p.109-13.

hair, or barefooted, or in single shirts and to prohibit idolisation of holy icons. Although the rhetoric of these articles was humiliating for the clergy, they were directed towards another goal, towards religious and social disciplining that had to be executed by the humiliated and subjugated clergy. This disciplining was part of a larger programme of building the 'regular' state.

The decree of 8 February 1716 can be regarded as a continuation of the same policy.[21] The decree obligated Old Believers to get 'inscribed into the schism' (*zapisyvat'sia v raskol*); they had to register their confessional deviance and to pay double tax. The measure was by and large fiscal; it belonged to a heterogeneous set of government enactments aimed at raising state revenues; it had much larger repercussions, however. It meant a *sui generis* limited legalisation of the Old Belief and was an incentive in its confessionalisation. Confessionalisation of the Old Belief automatically generated a similar process among the rest of the Orthodox population that recognised the official Church; confessionalisation was accompanied by religious disciplining.[22]

Old Believers preferred to evade the double taxation, so that there arose a task to discover covert Old Believers. In pursuance of this goal, Peter issued the decree of 17 February 1718 and a series of its later elaborations. The decree ordered:

> men of various ranks, urban residents and peasants to attend the church on the Lord's feasts and Sundays [...] and go to confession every year. It must be controlled on the parish level by the priests and by the stewards and by the priests' elders, depending on circumstances. They must have books with annual lists of those who confessed and of those who did not confess, and these books must be sent to the ecclesiastical chancellery in every bishopric. And parish priests have to collect fines from those who did not confess according to these books.[23]

Annual confession and its registration in confession books were an instrument that enabled the authorities to separate Old Believers from the adherents of official Orthodoxy and to exclude the possibility of evading the double taxation. It was the beginning of the long cat-and-mouse game in which one side developed more and more elaborate

---

21. *PSZR*, vol.5, no.2991, p.196.
22. A. Lavrov, *Koldovstvo i religiia v Rossii, 1700-1740gg.* (Moscow, 2000), p.60-74.
23. *Zakonodatel'stvo Petra I*, ed. A. A. Preobrazhenskii and T. I. Novitskaia (Moscow, 1997), p.538-39: 'все вышеписанные люди ['разночинцы и посадники и поселяня'] в господские праздники и в воскресные дни ходили в церковь Божию к вечерни, к завтрене, а паче же ко святои литургии [...] и по вся б годы исповедывались. И то надзирать в приходех самим священником и прикащиком, и старостам, где случитца. И кто будет исповедыватца и не исповедыватца, тому всему иметь книги погодно и присылать их по епархиям в духовные приказы, и кто по тем книгам явитца без исповеди, и с таких править тех приходов священником штрафы.'

techniques of detection and the other side responded by designing more and more elaborate methods of concealment. The nature of the evidence at our disposal makes it impossible to judge who the winner was in this contest.

It is tempting to treat the decree of 17 February 1718 as a purely fiscal measure introduced without any intention of changing the religious attitudes of the population. Under more thorough examination, however, such treatment seems inappropriate. The decree has too much in common with other measures of social disciplining. In the propagation of all these measures, the clergy played an important role. They announced these new regulations during their Sunday church service and they were entrusted with the registrar's office. This was the source of the ambiguity in Peter's attitudes towards the clerical estate. He could dislike and despise them, but he, as all his successors in the eighteenth century, could not communicate with society at large without their help. State bureaucracy was underdeveloped and its short arms reached only a small part of the population; the clergy were much more numerous and effective as state agents, and Peter could not help using them in this function.[24] Irrespective of what the initial purpose of the annual confession could be, this measure, the introduction of which was entrusted to the clergy, inevitably acquired religious meaning and was perceived as yet another step in the enforcement of religious discipline.

It is not likely that Peter envisaged any improvement in the religious standards of his subjects or that he cared about the salvation of their souls. Control and discipline were his favourite ideas and regular confession was a disciplining procedure.[25] In this respect Peter's decrees were different from similar efforts of ecclesiastical reformers (zealots of piety, patriarchs of the seventeenth century, participants of the Moscow Council of 1666-1667). Ecclesiastical reformers intended to create a new piety, more firmly connected with the institutionalised Church than the traditional one. Peter was indifferent or hostile to piety of any sort.

This attitude had many important repercussions. They may be seen with particular clarity when Russian development is compared with similar processes in Counter-Reformation Europe. In the sixteenth and seventeenth centuries in such areas as Bavaria or Austria, the policy of religious disciplining was also widely practised and this policy included the emphasis on regular and frequent confession. There were many differences in the conceptualisation of confession and its relation to salvation between East and West; among other things, Russian authorities in the seventeenth and eighteenth centuries were satisfied with

24. Lavrov, *Koldovstvo i religiia*, p.346.
25. Compare Lavrov, *Koldovstvo i religiia*, p.346.

annual confession, whereas Catholic reformers were much more ambitious in that they regarded annual confession as a 'mere compliance
with Church law' that 'implied religious indifference or worse' and they
understood frequent confession as monthly or even weekly.[26] The process of enforcement as such produced a number of at least superficial
similarities: coercive practices in which secular authorities played a
prominent or even the main role led to an emphasis on formal observ-
ance that temporarily pushed aside the idea of the new piety. Nevertheless, this idea was not forgotten, and remained a long-term goal that was
cherished and promoted by influential Catholic ecclesiastical bodies. In
the second half of the seventeenth and in the eighteenth century the new
piety won the day; there was no more need of coercion to maintain it. Its
coming into existence had numerous consequences for the religious life
and religious aspirations of Catholic societies.

Notwithstanding some superfluous similarities, Russian development
was quite different. Religious disciplining was carried out by the eighteenth-century Russian rulers for the sake of disciplining, not with the
idea of spiritual regeneration. There was no interest in the increased
frequency of confession or its greater role in the religious life of the
society. Annual confession remained the common practice of the Orthodox Christians who were devout supporters of the official Church
during the entire eighteenth century. New piety favouring more frequent confession appeared later and from a source (monastic revival)
that was not influenced by government policies or connected with social
disciplining.

Religious disciplining and private piety

It is very difficult to define what the effect of the disciplining religious
policies was on individual piety in the eighteenth century. The state, as
has been noted above, was not interested in piety. The clergy, it may be
assumed, entertained at least some notions of what Orthodox piety
should be and from time to time tried to impress these notions on the
population. Whereas the secular administration (in co-operation with
the Church hierarchy) strove to discipline the behaviour of the population, ecclesiastical leaders also tried, so to speak, to discipline the
Weltanschauung of their flock. They aspired to instil in the faithful an
Orthodox doctrine more true to the patristic tradition, more rational
and more scholarly (more true and more scholarly from their point of
view) than the variety of the Orthodox teaching that was accepted by the
majority of the population.

26. Myers, *'Poor, sinning folk'*, p.187, 188-201.

This attitude can be illustrated by the *Order of the Service of Penitence* (*Posledovanie o ispovedanii*) written by Gavriil Buzhinskii and published in 1723. The book is based on the traditional liturgical prescriptions for the sacrament of penitence and preserves the traditional structure of this service, but it contains a newly organised list of questions that the confessor should address to the penitent.[27] This list is written 'in the vulgar language so that the most dull-witted person could understand it';[28] this part of the book is in fact written in a colloquial Russian, whereas the rest of the text is in Church Slavonic; this was a serious innovation. Not less serious were the innovations in the structuring and choice of confessional questions. Instead of traditional order or, more exactly, traditional disorder, the questions are arranged in ten rubrics titled according to the Ten Commandments. This order is well known from Latin penitential texts; it is characteristic of *summae confessorum*.[29] Though Buzhinskii was by no means an admirer of Catholic institutions, he could not find a better model for a systematic exposition of human sinfulness and a manual of moral discipline.

The policy of religious disciplining is more than manifest in this text; there are many unequivocal parallels to the decree of January 1716 and the *Spiritual regulation* (*Dukhovnyi reglament*) of 1721; there is no doubt that these sources were used by Buzhinskii as instructions for action. There is a passage on the improper veneration of icons (as a transgression against the Second Commandment) and on the sinfulness of relying on icons as though they were God.[30] There is also a passage on the impiety of announcing fictitious miracles produced by icons, or of false visions of saints who ordered the penitents to address the faithful.[31] Possessed women (*klikushi*) are condemned and the belief in the Holy Fridays is strongly censured.[32] Particularly illuminating is a passage on the saints; those people are reproved who revere the saints with the same honours as God (a transgression against the First Commandment) and have reliance on them 'in all his or her good things in this world and in the world to come'.[33] It is evident that in the overall plan of religious disciplining Buzhinskii specially emphasises the impossibility of salvation

27. See P. P. Pekarskii, *Nauka i literature pri Petre Velikom*, 2 vols (St Petersburg, 1862), vol.2, p.592.

28. Gavriil Buzhinskii, *Posledovanie o ispovedanii* (Moscow, Moskovskaia tipografiia, 1723), f.32*v*: 'Сие написалось просторечно, да бы самое скудоумнейшее лице могло выразуметь.'

29. P. Michaud-Quantin, *Sommes de casuistique et manuels de confession au Moyen Age (XII-XVI siècles)* (Louvain, 1962).

30. Buzhinskii, *Posledovanie*, f.12*r*-12*v*.

31. Buzhinskii, *Posledovanie*, f.14*r*-14*v*.

32. Buzhinskii, *Posledovanie*, f.14*v*, 16.

33. Buzhinskii, *Posledovanie*, f.11: 'и на них во всяком своем добре здешном и будущем надеетца'.

by various irregular (or illicit) ways – through the intervention of holy
men, wonder-working icons and other intermediaries. He characterises
the hope in such irregular salvation as superstitious; this was a manifest
breach with Russian medieval notions of salvation discussed above.
Instead, Buzhinskii insisted on salvation through ecclesiastical institutions, first of all through regular (annual) sacramental confession;
those who neglect this duty and do not confess annually out of sloth
are condemned as sinners who think nothing of their salvation.

This opposition between the institutionalised salvation through the
agency of regular clergy and 'illicit' salvation through the improper
intervention of saints or through miraculous actions of unauthorised
holy men or wonder-working icons came to the fore in the discussion
around the preparation of a new edition of the hagiographical collection
of St Dimitrii of Rostov (*Chetii Minei*) in 1755-1756. The editors revised
the original editions of 1689 and 1711 and decided to exclude from the
new edition several passages from the life of St Thecla. These passages
were used by Dimitrii to prove the omnipotence of the intercessory
powers of the saints in bringing salvation not only to the living but also to
the dead. This was exactly the thesis that could not be accepted by the
Church leadership in the middle of the eighteenth century. They
regarded it as recognition of 'illicit' salvation, a recognition that could
not help being detrimental to the authority of the institutionalised
Church and institutionalised penitential discipline. This reasoning led
the Holy Synod to expunge the seductive story.[34]

There is no doubt that the policy of religious disciplining brought only
very limited results, mostly of an external nature. Though secular and
spiritual authorities suppressed many manifestations of popular religiosity, they were unable to suppress the beliefs as such. They continued to
play a much more important role in popular religiosity than
institutionalised forms of piety prescribed by the authorities. It should
be noted that 'popular' in this context does not apply only to lower layers
of society but to the population at large, with the exclusion of a tiny
group of Europeanised nobility and scholarly clergy. This meant among
other things that the impact of the policy of disciplining on the real
penitential practices and the perception of institutionalised methods of
penance was rather negligible. The majority of people continued to have
traditional notions of piety; they continued to believe in their fools in
Christ, in miraculous events, in sacred wells and other 'superstitious'
things; they continued to rely on them as important instruments of their

---

34. Buzhinskii, *Posledovanie*, f.6. See Zhivov, 'Imperator Traian', and *Opisanie dokumentov i del,
    khraniashchikhsia v archive Sviateishego Pravitel'stvuiushchego Sinoda* (henceforward *ODDS*), 49
    vols (St Petersburg, 1869-1914), vol.20, no.587/18, col.641-46.

salvation and pay only minor attention to regular confession and regular communion.

The evidence is mostly negative, but it is indicative nevertheless. In the numerous memoirs and diaries of the eighteenth century, authors almost never mention their experience of confession and communion. Gavriil Derzhavin, for example, was a religious person, he probably confessed once a year and he was not reticent in writing about his religious feelings, such as his ecstatic state when he composed the ode 'God'. Neither confession nor communion, however, figures even a single time in his autobiography (*Zapiski*), which is otherwise detailed and at times introspective.

In this context the diaries of Ivan Tolchenov are rather an exception. Their exceptional nature is evidently connected with the social status of their author – a merchant from Dmitrov. The diaries cover the period from 1770 to 1812, and record what the author did during the day. Tolchenov was a very pious man; his church attendance was exemplary: when he was not occupied with business trips he went to church practically daily.[35] He was not only pious but also interested in religion, and he had strong religious feelings. Describing his visit to the Tikhvin monastery, he wrote: 'After dinner we went to the monastery for another time to pray to the Mother of God; and there involuntarily I shed tears from joy and sorrow that there was no hope of being once again in this holy place.'[36] Though only part of the diary has been published, these records provide a glimpse of Tolchenov's piety and the role of penitential discipline in it.

It appears that Tolchenov confessed and took communion once a year, usually during Lent. How rigorously he obeyed this rule is not clear. There is no mention of a confession or communion for several years. It seems that Tolchenov did not confess and take communion in the years 1791 and 1812. Only deathbed confessions are of special importance.[37] Tolchenov confessed during a dangerous illness in 1777 and several times called a priest to give communion to his dangerously ill children.[38] It may be assumed that Tolchenov's attitude towards confession was by and large quite traditional. It was only superficially influenced by the

---

35. Statistical data demonstrating this pastime are given in the supplement to the edition in I. A. Tolchenov, *Zhurnal ili zapiska zhizni i prikliuchenii Ivana Alekseevich Tolchenov*, ed. A. I. Kopanev and V. Kh. Bodisko (Moscow, 1974), p.434-37.
36. Tolchenov, *Zhurnal*, p.377: 'После обеда ходили еще в монастырь помолиться пресвятей Богородице и тут слезы полились невольно от радости и скорби, что впредь уже нет надежды быть в сем святом месте.'
37. For accounts of confession and/or communion for the years 1776, 1778, 1779, 1782, 1805, see Tolchenov, *Zhurnal*, p.74, 110, 144-45, 172, 368.
38. Tolchenov, *Zhurnal*, p.93, 127, 214, 215.

disciplining policies of the Church administration so that institutionalised penance played a very small role in his piety.

Frequency of confession: evasion of the confessional 'duty' in various sectors of society

It could be surmised that external behaviour of the believers would have
been more easy to analyse. At least, there is a lot of statistical evidence for
the eighteenth century. Though we do not have comparable statistical
data for the preceding centuries we can assume that there was a
substantial increase in the number of those who made confession
annually. All parish priests were obliged to send penitential registers
to the chief priests of the district (*popovskie starosty*); combined registers
were made at this local level and then sent to diocese chancelleries; from
the dioceses, statistical data were dispatched to the Holy Synod.[39] Until
1742 exact copies of the entire lists of parishioners, divided into three
parts (for those who confessed and took communion, for those who
confessed but did not take communion, and for those who did not
confess and did not take communion), were dispatched to the Synod;
after that date only excerpts were dispatched, whereas the full lists were
kept in the parishes (see below). Not only were general figures counted
but there was also a breakdown across a range of social groups; there
were special sub-divisions for nobility (*shliakhetstvo*); officers (*ober i under
ofitsery*); secretaries and chancellery officials; Church officials; urban
dwellers (*posadskie*); monastery servants; coachmen; soldiers, dragoons,
artillerymen; sailors; peasants; beggars and so on.[40] Some of these record
books are extant, so that it seems to be possible, at first glance, to
represent at least the development of external observances in figures and
to have an 'objective view' of the dynamics of religious disciplining for
various social groups.

These figures, however, have only limited validity. They are fraudulent
because they were obtained by deceit, practised above all by the unlucky
priests who submitted the primary data. Deceit was practised on a
relatively large scale, but we do not know what corrections in the
available statistical data would be appropriate. The following example
can serve as an illustration. In 1725 Anthony, the metropolitan of
Tobol'sk, sent to the Synod a register showing the number of non-
confessants from 1718 to 1723 (he summarised the lists sent to him by
parish priests). According to this register, the number of non-confessants

39. I. K. Smolich, *Istoriia russkoi tserkvi*, 2 vols (Moscow, 1996-1997), p.63.
40. See the form of the confessional book for the year 1725: *ODDS*, vol.8, p.xcic-cx; for the
    year 1737: *PSZR*, vol.10, no.7226, p.119-25.

grew from year to year: there were 4,909 persons in the register in 1718 but 7,900 in 1723.[41] There is no reason to believe that the population of the metropolitanate of Tobol'sk became morally degraded during these years. It is more likely that Anthony brought pressure to bear on his clergy, and they became more cautious in registering their non-confessants as confessants (or, alternatively, they took bigger bribes for false registration and part of their parishioners could not pay). We cannot trust the figure for 1718 as well as the figure for 1723. The real number of non-confessants was probably much greater but we do not know what adjustments could be made to get a more realistic picture.

It is evident that there should have been a correlation between the strictness of control and the number of reported non-confessants: the stricter the control the greater the number. This general principle defines the differences in the validity of available statistical data. The strictness of control varied in different periods; there were periods of comparative severity (for instance, the reign of Empress Anna) and periods of comparative indulgence (for instance, the early years of the reign of Elizabeth). No less important was the factor of locality; for various reasons some areas were monitored more rigidly than others. Last but not least, social status also played an important role: some social groups were treated with more suspicion than others. It is impossible to estimate numerically the influence of all these factors on any concrete set of statistical data. That is why it is all but impossible to describe the development of penitential discipline through 'objective' statistics. It is better to deal with individual examples in the context of our knowledge of what was made manifest and what was concealed. As a source of individual examples I have used the published volumes of *Opisanie dokumentov i del Sviateishego Pravitel'stvuiushchego Sinoda* and *Polnoe sobranie postanovlenii i rasporiazhenii po vedomstvu pravoslavnogo ispovedaniia*, which as a whole provide sufficient information on the religious life of the eighteenth century, at least in those aspects that are connected with official policies and religious disciplining.

We have only very limited trustworthy information on the penitential discipline among the culturally most important social group, the nobility. Non-confessants from the nobility are not registered in confession books in considerable numbers. This fact is not easy to interpret. The decree on annual confession of 1718 (as well as its numerous elaborations) was originally directed against Old Believers. From the 1710s, Old Belief was a non-noble confession; those few Old Believers who belonged to the upper strata of Muscovite society lost their nobility and no new converts appeared among the nobles until the twentieth century. Old

41. *ODDS*, vol.2.2, no.807/583, col.39.

Belief became a religion of the lower classes. Consequently, the motivation to discover Old Believers did not apply to the nobility and
administrative control in their case was particularly lax. At the same
time noble landowners usually were the most influential people in their
rural parishes: a priest could feel himself obliged to register them as
confessants without reference to their actual behaviour. The literary
characters in Prostakova and Skotinin could be pious enough to make
their yearly confession, but they could just as well order their priests to
register them in the confessional books without ever appearing in the
church. According to the reports of parish priests from six Moscow
districts (*sorok*), there were only 124 non-confessants in 1716; when in
1718 the priests were ordered to sign a commitment to submit true
information on pain of being defrocked, they counted 7,594 non-
confessants, among them an unspecified number of officers and gentry
(*dvoriane*).[42]

We have some examples demonstrating that nobles could live without
confession for several years. In the Synod files for the year 1754 there is a
report from Kostroma provincial chancellery concerning a landowner
(hence, a noble), Aleksei Skripitsyn. The chancellery declines to turn
Skripitsyn over to local Church authorities for investigation and punishment. Kostroma consistory accused the gentleman of impiety and
insubordination, namely, that he swiped his cane at the local bishop and
had not confessed for the last three years.[43] The consistory's attack was
clearly instigated by the offended bishop who demanded a punishment
for the disrespectful behaviour of Skripitsyn. This confrontation made
the consistory check Skripitsyn's confessional records (which otherwise
would not have drawn anybody's attention), discover his delinquency
and request an investigation from Skripitsyn's superiors. It is characteristic that these superiors refused to comply.

Perusal of eighteenth-century documents creates an impression that
nobles could evade the obligation to confess annually with impunity at
least for several years running (compare the fines of 9 roubles that had to
be paid by senior officers, their wives and children when avoiding
confession for more than three years).[44] There had to be something
extraordinary in their circumstances to attract attention to their religious behaviour. It could happen when ecclesiastical authorities had
some reason to get suspicious about their orthodoxy. In the bishopric of
Smolensk, for instance, spiritual powers were constantly afraid of possible Catholic subversions. In 1745 the archbishop received an instruction

---

42. *ODDS*, vol.1, no.761/2, col.771-72.
43. *ODDS*, vol.34, no.378/368, col.319.
44. *Polnoe sobranie postanovlenii i rasporiazhenii po vedomstvu pravoslavnogo ispovedaniia Rossiiskoi
    Imperii* (henceforward *PSPR*) (Sankt Peterburg, 1869-1915), Catherine, I, no.265, p.310.

from the Synod to look with particular attention to the converts from Roman Catholicism. In furtherance of this instruction, he issued an order in accordance with which those nobles (*shliakhetstvo*) of Smolensk who previously had been Roman Catholics had to confess and to take communion in the Dormition Cathedral of Smolensk, that is under the archbishop's direct supervision. At the same time he complained that only a few of the nobles came to the cathedral to confess; the consistory of Smolensk demanded from the provincial chancellery that the recalcitrant nobility be sent to the ecclesiastical authorities for investigation, but the chancellery did not provide any help.[45] As early as 1722 a Smolensk noble, Denis Potemkin, was denounced to the Synod as a convert to Roman Catholicism; during the investigation Potemkin testified that until 1720 he had confessed and had taken communion annually, though in 1721 and 1722 he had not gone to confession because he had been too busy with his official duties, 'both important and unimportant', though he could not remember what they were exactly. It is evident that if there had been no denunciation (probably calumniatory) he would not have had any trouble.[46]

In the special circumstances of potential apostasy, annual confession was used as an instrument of police control. The results, however, were very unlike the Old Believer pattern: the nobility as a privileged estate had enough influence to withstand the attacks of the clerical discipliners and, it seems likely, to continue to neglect annual confession. If it was possible in the Smolensk diocese, where a religious confrontation between Orthodoxy and Catholicism made clerical authorities especially vigilant, it was all the more possible in other areas where nobody suspected noble parishioners of any sort of apostasy. The confessional duty was not strictly enforced in the case of the nobility, so that a religiously indifferent *honnête homme* (that was a common phenomenon in the eighteenth and nineteenth centuries) could live for years without worrying about his sins, confession and absolution. One may remember the story of Konstantin Levin from Tolstoi's *Anna Karenina*: before marrying Kitty he had to confess and take communion; he was entirely unaccustomed to this and had not confessed since his adolescence. It is possible that penitential discipline was more rigorous even for the gentry in the eighteenth century, but Levin's experience certainly had many precedents in the past. The nobility definitely did not develop a special piety of the confessional.

The situation with lower layers of society was different. Merchants, city dwellers, peasants, coachmen, even chancellery workers were under

---

45. *ODDS*, vol.19, no.320/375, col.452-53.
46. *ODDS*, vol.9, no.365/274, col.518; vol.32, no.145/179, col.320-80; vol.29, no.8/307, col.17-25.

constant suspicion of being secret schismatics (known as Old Believers). If they did not confess regularly and did not take communion out of traditional negligence, they were nevertheless in danger of being accused of religious deviance. They could try to prove the opposite, to call as a witness a priest who had confessed them if not in the last year then in the recent past, to refer to their church attendance (even if it was far from regular), to claim that they were visited by local clergy with some celebratory rituals. The problem was that the same tactics were used by Old Believers who tried to conceal their breach with the official Church. Covert Old Believers bribed parish priests to make them conceal their deviance or represent it as negligence in case of investigation. We do not know how successful this tactic was. The extant documents naturally reflect mainly failures when the conspiracy was discovered and the deceivers punished. We may suspect that in the majority of cases the efforts of Old Believers were successful, but these successes are not reflected in any documents. The documents at our disposal are deceptive and the growing rigour of official control made them only more deceitful; documentation became part of the vicious circle of deceit.

When the enforcement of religious discipline became the government's business the administration started to use its usual bureaucratic means of coercion. Government officials constantly discovered new stratagems by which Old Believers (and probably not only they) managed to evade annual confession and communion. They introduced new measures of control to exclude these possibilities and by these acts forced the recalcitrant population to invent new methods of deceit. For instance, Church officials and parishioners were instructed to denounce a priest who listed some persons among loyal confessants even though nobody saw them in the process of confession. The fear of denunciation was a strong factor that could dissuade the priest from illegal acts, but it was not difficult to find a countermeasure. A parishioner declared that he or she was ill and had called the priest for a confession *in extremis*; then they recovered, but the priest had legal ground to insert the name in the list of confessants. The government learnt about this stratagem and issued a decree requiring that there should be a witness at deathbed confessions.[47] The result was predictable: an Old Believer had to pay not only the priest but also the witness. Strokes and counterstrokes of this type could continue endlessly.

A popular method of evading confession was to claim that the person in question had confessed and taken communion elsewhere, outside his or her parish. It was not uncommon from the earliest time to have spiritual fathers (confessors) who were not parish priests. In the eight-

47. *PSZR*, vol.6, no.4022, art.15; Smirnov, *Drevne-russkii dukhovnik*, p.238.

eenth century usually some sort of certificate had to be produced, issued by the priest who acted as confessor. This possibility, the legality of which was supported by tradition, could be used as a loophole: it was not difficult to find a priest who would give the certificate for certain compensation. Already in 1721 it was decreed that those who confessed and took communion not in their parish had to prove that their absence from the parish was necessitated by their business and to produce the certificate issued by a priest from the place to which they travelled.[48] In 1743 these regulations were supplemented by an instruction prescribing that those who wanted to confess outside their parish must firstly justify their desire, secondly get written permission from their parish priest and, thirdly, receive a certificate from their confessors authenticated by a Church seal; if they did not comply with these regulations, they could not get their passports (i.e. documents necessary for any travel).[49]

Many Old Believers did not refuse to confess, but they did not take communion. It was probably a compromise based on a different perception of the two sacraments. Communion was a sacrament par excellence. A considerable number of Old Believers seemingly assumed that a false confession was a much lesser sin than a false communion. At any rate, making confession but not taking communion was a well-established and widespread practice in the eighteenth and nineteenth centuries. Besides spiritual reasons, this practice could be boosted by financial consideration: those who followed this pattern did not pay non-confession fines. In the confessional books that had to be compiled by parish priests, there was a special column in the tables for the number of those who confessed but did not take communion (alongside a column with the number of those who did not confess and did not take communion and a column with the number of those who fulfilled both obligations).[50]

There is evidence that this type of behaviour was more common than the unconditional refusal to confess, at least among the undeclared Old Believers.[51] It is possible that not all persons who behaved in this way

---

48. *ODDS*, vol.2.1, no.139/608, col.161-64; *PSPR*, series 2, no.721, p.409-10; series 9, no.3073, p.460-61.

49. *ODDS*, vol.23, no.50/343, col.78-79.

50. See the decree of 16 April 1737 with sample forms: *PSZR*, vol.10, no.7226, p.114-25. There is evidence that this type of behaviour was more common than the unconditional refusal to confess, at least among the undeclared Old Believers.

51. Thus in Astrakhan in 1725, there were 696 non-confessants and 1293 persons who confessed but did not take communion (*PSPR*, vol.5, no.1597, p.130; *ODDS*, vol.5, no.177/225, col.317-18). In the diocese of Ustiug in 1728, there were 2666 non-confessants and 29,231 persons who confessed but did not take communion (*ODDS*, vol.9, no.480/280, col.660-61; *PSPR*, vol.6, no.2270, p.408). In Novgorod in 1739, there were 112 non-confessants 'out of negligence' and 970 persons who confessed but did not take communion; these two categories comprised approximately 10 per cent of the entire population (*ODDS*, vol.19, no.594, col.668).

were Old Believers, acting on grounds that have been discussed above. Some people belonging to the official Church could be afraid to go to communion because they thought they were unworthy and liable to bring down judgement on themselves. In some cases a spiritual father could suspend a penitent from communion until he or she carried through the prescribed penance. By comparison there is also an interesting story of a Siberian peasant Artemii Sakalov who wrote a detailed list of his sins but did not go to confession (he confessed only three times during his life and never went to communion); Sakalov was not an Old Believer; his behaviour, according to Nikolai Pokrovskii, was motivated by the perception of his magical practices as incompatible with regular penance and communion.[52] Statistically, however, such cases hardly amount to a perceptible fraction of the total.[53]

In August 1722 Anthony, metropolitan of Tobol'sk, reported to the Synod that some covert schismatics in his diocese came to confession and made an avowal of the gravest sins of Sodom and Gomorrah or the like; the confessors were embarrassed, not knowing whether to permit them to take communion or not.[54] The embarrassment was produced by the fact that the canonical punishment for such grave sins included non-admission to communion for a period of up to fifteen years. The confessors suspected that this long excommunication was the main goal of their penitents in making these false avowals. They faced a difficult decision: to grant permission to commune meant to ignore the avowal of a mortal sin; to deny permission to commune meant to succumb to the stratagem of the schismatics. They complained about this difficulty to the metropolitan, and Anthony sent a letter of enquiry to the Synod. The Synod decided that in these circumstances the excommunication was tantamount to the condoning of the schismatics' plan 'to hurl back the communion of the Holy Eucharist'. They were ordered to admit these people to communion 'exigently' (*bezotlozhno*), in the conviction that God would exercise His judgement.[55] In this conviction they were not afraid of the sacrilege of giving communion to an unrepentant sinner; they were too busy with discovering and destroying the loopholes

---

52. N. N. Pokrovskii, 'Ispoved' altaiskogo krest'ianina,' in *Pamiatniki kul'tury. Novye otkrytiia. Pis'mennost', iskusstvo, arkheologiia. Ezhegodnik 1978* (Leningrad, 1979), p.49-57.

53. Some Old Believers used another method of avoiding the communion. They took communion and then spat out the Elements. When discovered, this act was treated as a case of abominable sacrilege and perpetrators were severely punished (see *PSPR*, vol.4, no.1393, p.251, 252; *ODDS*, vol.15, no.184/387, col.213-21; vol.16, no.324/275, col.396; vol.23, no.176/421, col.247-52). We certainly do not know how often it remained undiscovered.

54. *ODDS*, vol.2, no.917/1233, col.159.

55. *ODDS*, vol.2, no.917/1233, col.160, 163-64; see also *PSPR*, series 2, no.454, p.104, 107; series 3, no.1117, p.195-96: 'дабы тако отбиться от причастия святыя евхаристии.'

used by Old Believers. The cat-and-mouse game was more engrossing than consideration of traditional piety.

With this dialectic of deceit in action, it is impossible to define how many members of the official Church disregarded their duty of annual confession out of negligence. The existence of such cases was freely admitted by the ecclesiastical authorities. In most cases, however, they suspected the schism and tried to investigate them with this idea in mind. Sometimes they succeeded; sometimes they were unable to prove that Old Belief was involved. The evidence is scarce and we can only surmise with greater or lesser probability that the investigators did not find anything because there was nothing to find.

Several typical stories can be cited. For instance, in 1722 Feofan Prokopovich, at that time archbishop of Pskov, requested an enquiry into the life of an old chancellery worker, Dementii Davydov. A rumour reached Feofan that Davydov was a schismatic and did not confess and go to communion together with his wife, son and daughter-in-law. The investigation demonstrated, however, that Davydov never was an Old Believer, that from time to time he went to confession and communion with his family, though he did not do it on a yearly basis.[56] In the same year princesses Anna and Elisabeth, then in their adolescence, sent a petition to the Chancellery of Church Affairs asking to exempt the royal baker Ivan Sakulin from paying the non-confessant fine. The petition was dismissed, but we know from this source that Sakulin, by all probabilities not an Old Believer, ignored the confessional duty for several years.[57] In 1724 lieutenant Ivan Rozhnov, who had been sent to the diocese of Novgorod to deal with schismatics, asked the Synod about the amount of money he had to take as non-confession fines from church servitors, attendants, choristers, dragoons, soldiers and other groups of population; all these church servitors who had to pay non-confession fines definitely were not Old Believers.[58] Such examples can be multiplied. They demonstrate that penitential discipline was not particularly rigorous, especially among ordinary believers who did not lead a particularly religious life.

It is important to bear in mind that many possibilities of ignoring the obligation to confess existed in eighteenth-century Russia. Though there was some progress in Weberian bureaucratisation from the beginning to the end of the eighteenth century, the resources remained inadequate. The Synod tried to reach to the local level and demanded annual reports

56. *ODDS*, vol.1, no.472/274, col.547-48.
57. *ODDS*, vol.2.1, no.691/1143, col.1052-53. See also the story of Artemii Sakalov above and a story from 1732 about Danila Kobelev, in *ODDS*, vol.12, no.107/206, col.87-188.
58. *ODDS*, vol.4, no.324/191, col.308-10; see also about non-confessants from the clerical estate in 1784: *PSPR*, vol.2, no.1172, p.500.

from parish priests, but the priests were often unable to satisfy these demands in time and in many cases they were unwilling to do so. The Synod several times returned to the problem that was regularly raised by the parish clergy: they complained that the burden of chancellery work was too heavy for them and that they could not help neglecting their priestly duties.[59]

The Synod could do nothing to solve these problems, though the bishops might look with sympathy on priestly difficulties. The Synod was held responsible by the state for religious disciplining of society and for the registration and correction of any religious deviance. This was its sphere of action and the justification for its special position in the state apparatus. The Synod could not help, but nor could it turn a blind eye to the imperfections of confessional books. An important step in this direction was made when in 1742 the Synod decided not to require the full copies of the confession books but only short summaries with numerical data. The reasons for this innovation were explained in a letter to the empress: 'the shortage of chancellery workers, the delay of important business, great expenditure of paper, expenses for binding and postage; besides, in the future there will not be enough space in the Synod building since the Moscow *dikasterium* [church administration] alone sends five thousand booklets per year and thirteen hundred or more come annually from each other diocese.'[60] The Synod acknowledges that it cannot handle all the incoming information, that it is able to provide only selective control and that the disciplining cannot be more rigorous than the current resources support.

This attitude gave ordinary people many chances to not confess and to evade detection. The enforcement of religious discipline turned into a set of police measures, unpleasant and burdensome for practically all participants. They did not have the support of parishioners who, irrespective of their piety, regarded them as external coercion and did not associate them with interiorisation of Christian teaching. For priests, it was again a tiresome duty that was not sanctified by tradition, but remained a function delegated by the state; even if they were conscientious spiritual fathers, the duty of registering and reporting confessants

---

59. Compare a petition of Moscow priests' elders in 1728 in *ODDS*, vol.8, no.321/645, col.314-15; of priests and staff of St Petersburg churches in 1738 and 1742 in *ODDS*, vol.20, no.41/436, col.45-50, 57-59; a report by Arsenii (Matseevich), metropolitan of Tobol'sk in *ODDS*, vol.20, no.41/436, col.56-57; *ODDS*, vol.21, no.698/630, col.505-11.

60. *ODDS*, vol.21, no.698/630, col.503-504; *PSPR*, vol.1, no.90, p.101-102: 'недостаток канцелярских служителей, остановка важных дел, большой расход бумаги, траты на переплет и переесылку, да впредь и мест для их помещения в Св. Синоде не будет, ибо по одной Московской духовной дикастерии за один год до 5000 тетрадей будет и из других епархий по 1300 тетрадей и более.'

and non-confessants was a heavy burden that had no religious justification. The bishops had to control their subordinate priests, punish
them in cases of delinquency and take care of their parishes when they
were under arrest. Secular bureaucracy and various representatives of
lay society were not supportive because lengthy investigations of those
who were under suspicion of the schism, their arrests and fines were
disruptive for ordinary business and state service.

Conflicts between secular authorities who defended their people and
clergy that often had no other choice but to denounce and persecute
potential schismatics were numerous. In 1729 Lavrentii, the bishop of
Ustiug, complained to the Synod that there were many non-confessants
in his diocese, although neither town magistrates nor local (*voevoda*)
chancelleries had collected the fines and forced the people to confess
annually but acted with indulgence and countenance (*chiniat im
poslablenie i ponorovku*); the Synod complained to the Senate but without
much success.[61] We have already discussed various cases when secular
institutions refused to give up noble non-confessants, justifying their
refusal by the needs of service and the like.

Conclusions

The introduction of the obligatory annual confession was originally an
element of religious disciplining of society, a policy that gained momen-
tum in Russia in the second half of the seventeenth century. In the reign
of Peter the Great, this policy was appropriated by the state. Annual
confession, compilation and maintenance of confessional books came
under control of the state and were used as a tool in the persecution of
the Old Believers. After the introduction of the double taxation of the
Old Believers, the goals of this persecution were mixed; they included
simultaneously the extermination or at least containment of the 'heresy'
and the increase of state revenues. Religious disciplining was almost
universally perceived as external coercion in response to which various
sectors of the population used various methods of evasion. The secular
and ecclesiastical administration introduced stricter and stricter forms
of control, and society invented more and more intricate stratagems to
deceive the administration.

Due to the deceptive nature of available evidence, it is very difficult to
define who the winner in this struggle was. The concomitant results were
by far more important than achievements in the policing of Orthodox
society. Since confession turned into an act of political loyalty and

---

61. *ODDS*, vol.9, no.480/280, col.660-61; for similar stories, see for instance: *ODDS*, vol.3,
no.233/384, col.240; *PSPR*, vol.2, no.918, p.644-45; vol.2, no.939, p.661-62; *PSPR*, vol.3,
no.1064, p.100-101; *PSPR*, vol.5, no.1564, p.101-102.

administrative docility, it ceased to be an act of individual piety. It may be argued that the measure of religious devotion pertaining to confession was in reverse proportion to the measure of official coercion. Confession could hardly be simultaneously a revelation of a suffering soul and an act of officially enforced obedience.[62]

The enforcement of religious discipline probably contributed to the growth of church attendance and the regularity of confession. In the middle of the nineteenth century the relation of those Orthodox who confessed and took communion and those who did not confess because of negligence (*po neradeniiu*) was approximately ten to one; this proportion remained stable for a long period.[63] It seems probable that this proportion came to exist already in the reign of Catherine the Great. Though it looks likely that the proportion of non-confessants in this period was much lower than in the Middle Ages, it was not the result of the growth of religious zeal. With the development of administrative apparatus and tightening of bureaucratic control, it became increasingly troublesome to evade confession.

At the same time Russian modernisation, however imperfect, was accompanied by secularisation (as in other European societies). In these circumstances the enforced confession became more and more formal. At this late stage it did not help much that the fines for non-confession were abandoned and religious policy was liberated from financial convoy.[64] With the emergence of relative tolerance, priests started to persuade their parishioners to confess and to show repentance rather than to intimidate them into a formal avowal of their sins. It was too late and did not change the general situation: confession and penitence did not become important elements of Russian Orthodox piety.

One of the factors that made the Orthodox believers so unreceptive to

62. This effect is probably universal. David Myers writes in his study of the penitential discipline in Counter-Reformation Germany: 'Curiously, despite all the discussion of motivation in confession, sincerity seems not to have been an issue here. The judicial machinery of state and church demanded obedience rather than contrition, and less thought was given to purity of intent and disposition than to affirming and displaying the spiritual authority of the Church' (*'Poor, sinning folk'*, p.123).

63. See data for 1835 (confessants *c.*27.5 million; negligent non-confessors *c.*2.7 million): Rossiiskii gosudarstvennyi istoricheskii arkhiv, f.797, opis' 97, no.555; for 1836 (confessants *c.*28.2 million; negligent non-confessors *c.*2.8 million): RGIA, f.797, opis' 97, no.557; for 1865 (confessants *c.*35.4 million; negligent non-confessors *c.*3.9 million): RGIA, f.797, opis' 97, no.608. I am greatly indebted to my colleague and friend Professor Victoria Frede who kindly shared with me the results of her archival work. For similar data for 1858, see Smolich, *Istoriia russkoi*, vol.2, n.243, p.398-99.

64. See the decree of 18 January 1801, *PSZR*, vol.26, no.19,743; *PSPR*, Paul, no.547, p.680-81; compare Smolich, *Istoriia russkoi*, vol.2, n.243, p.398-99; N. Rozanov, *Istoriia Moskovskogo eparkhal'nogo upravleniia so vremeni uchrezhdeniia Sviateishego Sinoda, 1721-1821*, 3 vols (Moscow, 1869-1871), vol.3, part 1, p.245.

the benefits of a rigorous penitential discipline, frequent confession and a certain assuredness in future salvation resulting from it was the specificity of their soteriological beliefs, namely, their reliance on uninstitutionalised ways of salvation. Salvation could be attained through the instrumentality of holy men, wonder-working icons, sacred wells and so on. Granting the availability of these means, the believer could hardly be tempted by strict penitential rules and the tiresome process of institutionalised absolution. Some efforts to condemn this 'illicit' salvation were made in the eighteenth century. It is particularly indicative that these efforts brought results so negligible. For the majority of the population an obscure wonder-working icon or a shady fool in Christ remained a much more effective and reliable means of evading the eternal torments than an avowal of vaguely understandable transgressions to a parish priest. Popular religiosity continued to be traditional; it had numerous repercussions both for the religious life of Russian society and for the patterns of its cultural behaviour.

First of all, the notion of individual sin remained vague and of secondary importance; sin was perceived much more as an existential parameter of human life rather than a personal guilt. Characteristically, in Russia of the eighteenth and nineteenth centuries, criminals were the objects of popular pity and compassion; they were looked upon as victims – not so much of the state system as of the human condition in this world of sorrows. Their sufferings were not regarded as atonement for their wickedness but rather as the highest manifestation of the misery of terrestrial existence. Dostoevsky probably reworked these popular ideas when, in the *Brothers Karamazov*, he introduced a notion of universal sin or universal guilt. Zosima claims that 'each of us is guilty before everyone, for everyone and everything' or, with liturgical connotations, 'on behalf of all and for all'.[65] All sins are sins of all. All sins become not an individual but a common property; as a result, salvation also turns to be communal; it can be shared by the righteous with their sinful brethren. Sinners can be saved even after death, which definitely is a heterodox idea reminiscent of the salvation of the unrepentant sinner by St Anthony of the Caves Monastery.[66]

It is tempting to connect with these or similar ideas the emergence of the practice of communal confession (*obshchaia ispoved'*) introduced by St Ioann of Kronstadt. Father Ioann was immensely popular as a preacher,

---

65. F. Dostoevsky, *Polnoe sobranie sochinenii*, 30 vols (Leningrad, 1972-1990), vol.14, p.262, 290: 'всякий из нас пред всеми во всем виноват'; 'за всех и за вся виноват.'

66. See Sergei Hackel, 'The religious dimension: vision or evasion? Zosima's discourse in *The Brothers Karamazov*', in *New essays on Dostoevsky*, ed. M. V. Jones and G. M. Terry (Cambridge, 1983), p.139-68, and n.1 above.

spiritual father and miracle worker. In the words of Thomas Tentler, his 'popularity as a charismatic pastor of souls led to the dramatic aberration of shouted confessions of sins followed by his public, mass absolution. [...] What passed for charismatic spirituality in Russia in the twentieth century would have been branded centuries before in the West as rogue pastoral practice.'[67] It seems that these practices were tolerated precisely because they were in agreement with a centuries-old traditional religiosity.

It was claimed at the beginning of this chapter that confession produced a nuclear biographical narrative and this narrative was one of the main instruments in the construction of the self. The laxity of penitential discipline in Russia could not help generating a self characterised by certain commonality, a certain indeterminacy in the distinction between the individual and the communal. In the seventeenth and eighteenth centuries there were some efforts of religious disciplining. They were appropriated by the state, acquired a direction different from Western analogues and, in consequence, did not bring the results comparable with those which became the foundation of Western modernity. The notion of privacy was to a large extent born in the privacy of the confessional. Since Russians did not go to confession very often and when they went tended to do it formally, they had only a vague notion of privacy. Consequently, the opposition of the public and private spheres as applied to the Russian case should be problematised. Undoubtedly, private life was not unknown in Russia, but it is by no means clear what the boundaries are that circumscribe this sphere and make it distinct from other spheres of social behaviour.

67. T. N. Tentler, 'Epilogue: a view from the West', in *Orthodox Russia: belief and practice under the tsars*, ed. V. A. Kivelson and R. H. Greene (University Park, PA, 2003), p.274-75.

Writing, ranks and the eighteenth-century Russian gentry experience

IRINA REYFMAN

For European elites, challenged by changes in the idea of what makes an aristocrat, writing became a new technology of self-fashioning through which they shaped their public and private identities. Jonathan Dewald has observed that one purpose of writing for the seventeenth-century French nobility was to separate 'themselves from their surroundings, establishing themselves as individuals and freeing themselves from a variety of constraints. At the same time, with writing they entered a new kind of relationship with the society around them [...] The circulation of writing, like that of money, challenged the principles of a hierarchical society.'[1]

Unlike their contemporaries in the West, nobles in pre-Petrine Russia as a rule did not practise any types of writing – indeed, many were illiterate.[2] Writing, for both belletristic and administrative purposes, was mainly the preserve of the clergy and, later, the state bureaucrats. A substantial aim of the Petrine reforms was to educate nobles.[3] As a result, in the eighteenth century, newly literate Russian elites turned to writing in search of modern modes of existence. They also became active producers of literature and, by the second half of the eighteenth century, began to dominate the literary sphere.

The swiftness with which the nobility created a literary field is the more remarkable in that it happened under the patronage system dominant in Russia in the eighteenth century.[4] Writers of noble status

1. Jonathan Dewald, *Aristocratic experience and the origins of modern culture: France, 1570-1715* (Berkeley, CA, 1993), p.174-75.
2. For estimates of literacy rates in seventeenth-century Muscovy, see Gary Marker, 'Literacy and literacy texts in Muscovy: a reconsideration', *Slavic review* 49 (1990), p.74-89. Marker concludes that the most optimistic estimates suggest that 'rudimentary literacy rates [...] were well below 10 per cent for the entire population', with the number of those who could write at about 3 per cent. Less optimistic estimates give 3 to 5 and 1 to 2 per cent respectively (p.89).
3. See Marc Raeff, *Origins of the Russian intelligentsia: the eighteenth-century nobility* (New York, 1966), esp. chapter 'Home and school'; Brenda Meehan-Waters, *Autocracy and aristocracy: the Russian service elite of 1730* (New Brunswick, NJ, 1982), p.39-47.
4. See William Mills Todd III, *Fiction and society in the age of Pushkin: ideology, institutions, and narrative* (Cambridge, MA, 1986), p.51-52.

employed different strategies in dealing with it: some resisted it, unhappy about its inherent inequality; others ignored it; yet others participated in it fully, using it to their advantage – especially if the patron happened to be the monarch. The nascent market system was another factor that complicated the situation for noblemen reluctant to participate directly in the sale of the fruits of their literary labours. Both factors made eighteenth-century writers of noble rank ambivalent about their literary pursuits; therefore they often preferred to publish anonymously if at all.[5]

Although this ambivalence about professional writing and publishing persisted among Russian nobles well into the nineteenth century, it did not hinder their partaking in the production of literature. In contrast, in arts other than literature (painting, sculpture, music and theatre), nobles did not participate professionally in any significant numbers until the second half of the nineteenth century. Thus literature was the only art nobles did not consider beneath their dignity to acknowledge publicly as their professional occupation.[6] Moreover, as Gareth Jones points out, beginning with the second half of the eighteenth century 'literary accomplishments were considered to be one of the clearest indications of nobility'.[7]

At the same time, in post-Petrine Russia writing was not the only – or even the main – tool of self-fashioning for nobles: service to the state and the monarch offered a surer means of establishing and maintaining one's noble status. The Table of Ranks, a list of positions in the military, civil and court services introduced by Peter the Great in 1722, was a powerful means of forging a new noble class that was to replace the Muscovite elites. It defined the nobility as a service class, obliging every noble to serve, offering tangible evidence of career progress, and, at the same time, providing a way for gifted commoners to enter the noble estate. It also introduced a new hierarchy within the noble class: every service category contained ranks from one to fourteen, in decreasing order of importance. Military service was given preference over the other two (hereditary nobility, for example, was granted to commoners in the military beginning with the fourteenth rank, while in the civil service it

---

5. See, for example, Joachim Klein, 'Poet-samokhval: "Pamiatnik" Derzhavina i status poeta v russkoi kul'ture XVIII veka', in *Puti kul'turnogo importa: Trudy po russkoi literature XVIII veka* (Moscow, 2005), p.498-520.

6. See Viktor Zhivov, 'Pervye russkie literaturnye biografii kak sotsial'noe iavlenie: Trediakovskii, Lomonosov, Sumarokov', *Novoe literaturnoe obozrenie* 25 (1997), p.24-83 (55). Zhivov quotes statistical data on the participation of the nobility in literature provided in Vladimir Nahirny, *The Russian intelligentsia: from torment to silence* (New Brunswick, NJ, 1983), p.28.

7. W. Gareth Jones, 'The Russian language as a definer of nobility', in *A Window on Russia: papers from the V International Conference of the Study Group on Eighteenth-Century Russia, Gargnano, 1994*, ed. Maria Di Salvo and Lindsey Hughes (Rome, 1996), p.293-98 (297).

began with the eighth rank).[8] The Table of Ranks thus determined a post-Petrine Russian nobleman's status vis-à-vis his counterparts.

This chapter explores how the circumstances I have described affected writers of noble status, particularly their authorial self-image. I will pay special attention to the way participation in the service and rank system (which was compulsory until 1762, and after that remained customary and, for many, highly desirable) complicated their view of writing as simultaneously a private and a public activity. The aim is to determine what strategies of authorial behaviour they worked out as they dealt with the complex and often contradictory hierarchies in which they were forced to participate. I will also briefly consider the relevance of these models for subsequent generations of Russian writers.

Three comparable, though distinctive, figures serve as case studies. The first, Aleksandr Sumarokov, remained in the service as long as he could, despite significant pressure to retire. At the same time, he continued to write and publish, and worked hard to establish a view of writing as service to the state and to be acknowledged as a servitor in good standing based on his status as a writer. The second, Andrei Bolotov, left service as soon as he could and used writing, which was his everyday occupation throughout his life, to forge his private identity as a nobleman. Writing – in every genre imaginable – shaped Bolotov's daily existence but was not a status-building activity for him. The third, Ippolit Bogdanovich, was the first Russian writer to construct a public persona of himself as a dilettante writing for pleasure in the privacy of his home, a servant to the Muses, not a servitor to the state. At the same time, paradoxically, he built on the success of his best-received narrative poem *Dushen'ka* (*Psyche*, 1783) not only to earn the patronage of Catherine the Great but also to repair and advance his service career.[9]

Aleksandr Petrovich Sumarokov (1717-1777), the well-educated scion of a respectable family of servitors that became prominent in seventeenth-century Muscovy, was in many ways representative of the new post-Petrine nobility. His father, a supporter of Peter the Great's reforms, had a long and successful service career, retiring in 1762 in the rank of actual privy councillor (second class). Sumarokov graduated from the newly established Noble Infantry Cadet Corps, the first educational institution for children of the nobility, in 1740; and began his service as a member of the staffs of several important statesmen, includ-

---

8. See Table of Ranks, paragraphs 11 and 15, in *Zakonodatel'stvo Petra I* (Moscow, 1997), p.398 and 400.

9. I have chosen to put aside the case of Gavrila Derzhavin, as the most idiosyncratic of all and thus requiring a separate treatment. On some aspects of this topic, see Anna Lisa Crone, *The Daring of Deržavin: the moral and aesthetic independence of the poet in Russia* (Bloomington, IN, 2001), esp. ch.9.

ing Aleksei Razumovsky (1709-1771), Empress Elizabeth's favourite (perhaps her morganatic husband) and the head of the *Leib* Company, the guards regiment that helped Elizabeth ascend the throne in 1741. In his capacity as Razumovsky's aide-de-camp, Sumarokov ran the regiment's affairs. In 1755, he was promoted to the rank of brigadier (fifth class).

Parallel to fulfilling his military duties, Sumarokov built up a formidable literary career, actively producing in all genres and vying for the place of Russia's foremost author with two other prominent writers of the time, Vasily Trediakovsky and Mikhail Lomonosov. Despite his success as a writer, the idea of leaving the service never occurred to Sumarokov. Moreover, when, in 1756, he was appointed director (manager) of the first Russian public theatre (which officially became a court theatre in 1759), he retained his military rank as brigadier.

Sumarokov is often regarded as the first professional writer in Russian literary history and, whether one agrees with this view or not (Sumarokov never sold his literary works directly to publishers and felt uneasy about the very idea), he undoubtedly saw his literary activities as the centre of his life.[10] It is surprising, in this context, to observe how much importance Sumarokov gave to his place in the service hierarchy. When his service career came to a halt following his appointment as theatre director, he complained bitterly and repeatedly that he was being 'passed over' for promotion ('menia obkhodiat'). In a letter of 15 November 1759 to Ivan Shuvalov (Elizabeth's favourite and the overseer of several Russian cultural institutions, including theatre), Sumarokov writes, 'I never took part in a war and perhaps never will, but I labour as much in time of peace as I would have in time of war, but they pass me over.' The labour he has in mind is managing the theatre and writing plays and poems. Furthermore, Sumarokov believes that this labour qualifies him for a military rank. Asking in the same letter to be appointed to the Academy of Sciences, he insists that as a member of the Academy he would have the right to remain in the military service: 'I don't want a civil rank, since I am a senior brigadier, and I am not inclined to take off voluntarily the military uniform I have worn for twenty-eight years; and nothing prevents me from being in both the Academy Chancellery and the Conference.'[11]

---

10. For a discussion of the view of Sumarokov as the first professional writer, see Marcus Levitt, 'The illegal staging of Sumarokov's *Sinav i Truvor* in 1770 and the problem of authorial status in eighteenth-century Russia', *Slavic and East European journal* 43 (1999), p.299-323 (299-300).

11. 'Я на войне не бывал и, может быть, и не буду, и столько же тружуся и в мирное время, сколько в военное, а меня обходят' and 'Я штатского чина не хочу, ибо я старший бригадир, да и мундира добровольно, который я двадцать восемь лет ношу, скинуть не намерен; а в академической Канцелярии и в Конференции мне ничто быть не препятствует'. *Pis'ma russkikh pisatelei*, ed. G. P. Makogonenko (Leningrad, 1980),

Sumarokov was 'relieved of his duties' (*uvolen*) as theatre director by Elizabeth's decree of 13 June 1761. In anticipation of this event, he vigorously campaigned for promotion ('My memory tells me that upon retirement everyone gets promoted, even if he has been in his current rank for only a year. And I have been senior brigadier and a most unhappy man for six years') or, at least, for keeping his military rank. In his letter of 24 April 1761 to Shuvalov, he writes, obviously not quite sincerely:

> Have mercy on me [...] and dismiss me. I just do not want a civil rank, since, having worn a military uniform and boots all my life, it will not be easy for me to learn to wear shoes. After all, I am retiring, not going into the civil service, and I would rather be a captain [ninth class] than receive a higher civil rank.[12]

When, in September 1762, the newly enthroned Catherine conferred on Sumarokov the civil rank of actual state councillor (fourth class), following his request for promotion and as a sign of her benevolence, Sumarokov was not satisfied in the least: he felt that he had not gained anything, arguing that a military rank was in fact equivalent not to the civil rank with which it shared a line on the Table of Ranks but to the civil rank one slot above it. Having been promoted from the military rank of fifth class to the civil rank of fourth class meant, effectively, that he had not risen in the hierarchy of ranks. Sumarokov summarises his grievances in his letter of 3 May 1764 to the empress:

> After the general promotion that took place before the [1756-1763 Seven Years] War, I was second or third brigadier, and not only have all brigadiers [fifth class], colonels [sixth class] and lieutenant-colonels [seventh class] overtaken me, but many of those below the seventh class; and now even those who in the time of Your Majesty's reign were promoted from lieutenant-colonels are my seniors in military rank, and I was never in civilian service.[13]

---

p.86 and 87. The Chancellery was the general assembly of all academicians and adjuncts, and the Conference was the assembly of all Academy members with collegiate ranks; see V. P. Stepanov's commentary to Sumarokov's letters, in *Pis'ma*, p.193, n.10. Obviously, Sumarokov implies that his superior rank as a brigadier gives him the right to join the Academy without leaving the military service for the civil one. Here and throughout the article translations are my own, unless indicated otherwise.

12. 'Помнится мне, что при отставке даются чины всем, хотя бы кто год только в чину своем был настоящем. А я шесть лет старший бригадир и несчастнейший человек...' and 'Помилуйте меня [...] и сделайте мне отставку. Я только не хочу штатского чина; ибо я, нося во весь век мой мундир и сапоги, башмаки носить не скоро выучуся, да я ж иду в отставку, а не к штатским делам, и лучше пойду в капитаны, нежели с произвождением во штатский чин'. *Pis'ma*, p.91, 92.

13. 'Я по генеральном произвождении, которое еще до войны было, был второй или третий бригадир, и обошли меня не только все бригадиры, полковники и

Rejecting the rank conferred on him by the empress, Sumarokov concludes his letter with a plea: 'I ask only to learn what I am: am I in service and in which one? Otherwise, retire me properly, as all good people are retired, with a proper rank.'[14] He is asking for what, in his view, is his due: to be promoted to the next rank upon retirement, as a servitor in good standing. His requests were never satisfied: he died in 1777 in the rank of actual state councillor.

It can be argued that service was Sumarokov's main source of income, the way he supported himself and his family. True, his requests for promotion were often accompanied by requests for money, usually back pay. These requests were satisfied for the most part, even if not always immediately. Furthermore, after Sumarokov's retirement from the position of theatre director, an arrangement was made to continue to pay him his allowances both as brigadier and as theatre director.[15] Once she was in power, Catherine in her turn forgave his considerable debts to the Academy press and granted him the 'lifetime privilege of having all his works printed at her cost'.[16] Even in the 1770s, when Catherine's benevolence faded (and Sumarokov's financial situation drastically worsened from 1767 owing to a family quarrel that deprived him of much of his inheritance), the empress occasionally granted the writer monetary support. All this suggests that, for Sumarokov, anxiety over rank was a separate issue from anxiety over his financial situation.

Furthermore, the option of publishing for money was available to Sumarokov, and he considered taking it, if half-heartedly, as is evident from his letter to Catherine of 31 January 1773:

Perhaps, having worked for fame, I should undertake the writing of novels, which could bring me a good income, because Moscow likes this kind of writing. Now, is it really becoming for me to write novels, especially in the reign of the wise Catherine, who, I am sure, doesn't have a single novel in her entire library? When Augustus rules, then Virgils and Ovids write, and

---

подполковники, но многие и обер-офицеры, да и ныне все те, которые уже во время в. в. владения из полковников жалуются, берут у меня по военному чину старшинство, а я в штатских делах не бывал никогда'. *Pis'ma*, p.96. It is not quite clear what Sumarokov meant by 'second or third brigadier': there were no classes within the rank. It is possible that Sumarokov means the order of promotion to the rank of brigadier, that is, that only one or two people were promoted to this rank earlier than he.

14. '...прошу только по крайней мере о том, чтоб я знал, что я: в службе ли и в какой? Или отставьте меня надлежащим порядком, как все добрые люди отставляются, с надлежащим при отставке чином....' *Pis'ma*, p.97.

15. For Elizabeth's decree see *F. G. Volkov i russkii teatr ego vremeni: sbornik materialov* (Moscow, 1953), p.144-45.

16. Marcus Levitt, 'Aleksandr Petrovich Sumarokov', in *Dictionary of literary biography*, vol.150: *Early modern Russian writers, late seventeenth and eighteenth centuries*, ed. Marcus Levitt (Detroit, MI, 1995), p.370-81 (376-77).

Aeneids are held in respect, not *Bovas the king's sons*.[17] I, however, wouldn't dishonour myself even if I wrote a *Bova*, although I wouldn't gain much honour either.[18]

What is remarkable in this passage is the mixture of contradictory views of the writer: as a client writing to laud a powerful patron (Virgil lauds Augustus, and Sumarokov, Catherine), as a producer of saleable goods (an identity that Sumarokov tries on hesitantly and reluctantly) and as a nobleman serving the state (evident in Sumarokov's use of the vocabulary of honour).[19]

It was Sumarokov's position as servitor to the state that helped him resist the patronage system.[20] Even though at times he accepted the role of a client of powerful patrons, such as Shuvalov and, later, Catherine's favourites Grigory Orlov and Grigory Potemkin as well as Catherine herself, at other times he attempted to reject it.[21] He writes in a letter of 10 June 1758 to Shuvalov:

> [I]n all truth, I haven't asked for a present, which I have never done and will never do, but requested from your cabinet a loan for the theatre, and it was not any kind of political game on my part. I would sooner become a beggar and be exposed to various misfortunes than be among those who seek patrons in order to profit from them.[22]

His view of his writing as a fulfilment of service duties helped him justify his protestations.

Sumarokov consistently presents his writing as the fulfilment of service duties. In October 1758 he complains to Elizabeth that he has not been paid for nine months and lists his managing the theatre and his writing as service: 'I [...] must live on what I have thanks to my rank and

---

17. *Bova the king's son* is one of the chivalric romances adapted in Muscovite Russia and extremely popular among lowbrow eighteenth-century readers. These romances were despised by Russian classicists, Sumarokov in particular.

18. 'Разве мне, поработав ради славы, приняться за сочинение романов, которые мне дохода довольно принести могут, ибо Москва до таких сочинений охотница. Но мне романы ли писати пристойно, а особливо во дни царствования премудрый Екатерины, у которой, я чаю, ни единого романа во всей ее библиотеке не сыщется. Когда владеет Август, тогда пишут Виргилии и Овидии, и в почтении тогда «Энеиды», а не «Бовы королевичи». А я и «Бовою», выданным от себя, не обесчещуся, хотя и не много чести присовокуплю.' *Pis'ma*, p.163.

19. See Levitt, 'The illegal staging', p.317, for his analysis of the place the notion of honour played in Sumarokov's view of authorship.

20. See Zhivov, 'Pervye russkie literaturnye biografii', p.58.

21. On Sumarokov's participation in the patronage system, see Todd, *Fiction and society*, p.53-55.

22. 'я истинно не подарка просил, чего я никогда не делал и не сделаю, а требовал от комнат ваших взаймы для театра, и моей политики никакой тут не было. Я лучше по миру пойду и всякому подвергнусь несчастью, нежели быть в числе тех, которые ищут патронов для того, чтобы пощечиться.' *Pis'ma*. p.79

my labours, labouring as hard as I can in versification and theatre'[23]. He goes on to compare his literary efforts to his service as Razumovsky's aide-de-camp. Arguing in his letter of 15 November 1759 to Shuvalov that he deserves promotion, Sumarokov again insists that his writing is comparable in importance to other types of service: 'My [literary] exercises do not have the slightest similarity with either court or civil duties, and therefore I do not impede anyone's progress, but my labours are no smaller that anyone else's, and they are of some use, if literature is considered useful in this world'[24]. Continuing his fight for promotion in a letter to Shuvalov of 24 April 1761, Sumarokov directly calls his achievements in literature service to the state and the empress: 'I have served exactly thirty years, and tomorrow it will be twenty years that I have served h[er] m[ajesty] [i.e. Elizabeth]'[25].

Sumarokov uses the same argument in his letters of complaint to Catherine. In August 1762 he writes that he has been 'passed over': 'And I am offended more than anyone, because, without any fault on my part, having laboured both in fulfilment of my duties as well as beyond them in literature, I have been left behind everyone, not only behind my peers, but also behind those who were much junior to me in rank'.[26] According to Sumarokov's reasoning, writing was additional service on his part and should have particularly qualified him for promotion. Sumarokov ends up asserting the superiority of literary activity over other types of service. In his letter of 4 March 1770 to Catherine, he declares: 'Sophocle, le prince des poètes tragiques qui était en même temps le général des Athéniens et camarade de Periclès, est encore plus connu sous le nom de poète qu'en qualité de général'[27]. Thus, gradually, Sumarokov comes to see his literary activities as not just comparable to, but superior to the types of services legitimised by Peter in the Table of Ranks. What astonishes in his position is the trouble he has assigning value to himself as writer outside the rank system. He needs a rank to confirm the significance of his writing activities, both in the eyes of the public and his

---

23. 'должен жить только тем, что я своим чином и трудами имею, трудяся сколько сил моих есть по стихотворству и театру'. *Pis'ma*, p.83.
24. 'Мои упражнения ни со придворными, ни со штатскими ни малейшей сходства не имеют; и ради того я ни у кого не стою в дороге, а труды мои ничьих не меньше, и некоторую пользу приносят, ежели словесные науки на свете пользою называются'. *Pis'ma*, p.86.
25. 'Взавтре двадцать лет, как я служу е. в., а всей моей службы тридцать лет уже прошло'. *Pis'ma*, p.92.
26. 'А я паче всех изобижен; ибо я без малейшей моей прослуги, трудяся и по моей должности, и сверх моей должности во словесных науках, ото всех, не только от моих товарищей, но и от тех, которые чинами меня гораздо были ниже, остался'. *Pis'ma*, p.94.
27. *Pis'ma*, p.139.

own eyes. This explains Sumarokov's reluctance to retire and his insistence on his right to be promoted.

While interpreting his writing as service to the state, Sumarokov sometimes mentions the Muses. Curiously, however, these references are consistently placed in the context of service. At least once Sumarokov directly calls his relations with the Muses 'service'[28]. On another occasion, he reports to Catherine about a rare period of harmony in his life as a playwright: 'The Muses, the local governor-general, the chief of the police, the impresarios, and the actors are in total agreement with me'[29]. Characteristically, Sumarokov never complains that his service to the state interferes with his service to the Muses, but does explain his failure to succeed in his service career by his devotion to them: 'The main reason for all of this is my love for poetry, because, having relied on it and literature, I cared not so much for rank and possessions as for my Muse'[30].

Crucially, the idea of literature as a private pursuit is absent from Sumarokov's view of himself as a writer. Only once does Sumarokov seem to express a desire for a 'Parnassian refuge' ('parnasskoe ubezhishche', p.118), but even then he justifies his wish for a retreat by his eagerness to be useful to the state. He writes to Catherine in February 1769: 'In my letter to the count [G. A. Orlov], I also asked for a small humble estate. I need it only to have a Parnassian refuge there, and it would bring more profit in the form of verses and other compositions than it gives grain to the state treasury'[31]. Once he received the desired 'Parnassian refuge', it did not figure in his representations of his authorial pursuits at all. Clearly, Sumarokov viewed writing as a public activity, as a fulfilment of his service duty to the state and the monarch, its success to be reflected by his place in the system of ranks.

Certain expressions in Sumarokov's letters suggest that for him rank not only indicated his place in the service hierarchy but defined who he was as a human being. This is clearly evident in his question to Catherine in his letter of 3 May 1764: 'What am I?' ('chto ia?'). The expression also crops up earlier in the same letter, with a similar anguished overtone: 'I, by the way, don't have a place or position. I am not in the military, not in

---

28. *Pis'ma*, p.91.
29. '… Музы, наместник здешний, полицеймейстер, антрепренеры и актеры со мною в крайнем согласии'. *Pis'ma*, 125.
30. 'Всему сему главная причина любление мое ко стихотворству; ибо я, на него полагался и на словесные науки, не столько о чинах и об имении рачил, как о своей музе'. *Pis'ma*, p.174.
31. 'Еще я ко графу в письме о малой деревнишке просил. Она мне только на то надобна, чтобы я в оной имел парнасское убежище, и принесла бы она больше дохода стихами и прочими сочинениями, нежели хлебом казенного доходу'. *Pis'ma*, p.118; compare p.116.

the civil service, not at court, not in the Academy, and not retired. I dare
to submit my request to Your Imperial Majesty, so that something might
be done with me in order for me to know what I am.'[32] Sumarokov
obviously had trouble conceiving himself outside the service hierarchy,
and his writing (which, as Lomonosov caustically claimed in his letter of
19 January 1761 to Ivan Shuvalov, Sumarokov put 'above all human
knowledge') was not quite enough for him to define his identity.[33] It is
noteworthy that when Sumarokov wants to claim his status as poet, he
does so by adding a third component to the formula 'an officer and a
gentleman'. He uses it in this form twice in his correspondence, in
Russian ('Дворянин и офицер, и стихотворец сверх того', that is, 'I am
[...] a gentleman and an officer, and a poet to boot', p.73) and in French
('poète, gentilhomme et officier')[34].

In contrast, Andrei Bolotov (1738-1833), arguably the most prolific
Russian writer ever, viewed writing as primarily an activity of private self-
fashioning. As a teenager, he amused and educated himself by copying his
favourite books, both translations of European fiction and traditional
Russian literature, such as saints' lives. As a young officer stationed in
Königsberg during the Seven Years War, he discovered 'the pleasures of
letter writing', initiating a correspondence with the navy officer N. E.
Tulub'ev.[35] In 1789, when Bolotov began his formidable writing enterprise, the memoir *The Life and adventures of Andrei Bolotov, depicted by himself
for his descendents*, he adopted an epistolary form, addressing entries to an
imaginary intimate 'Dear friend'. In addition to the *Life and adventures* (on
which he worked until the late 1820s, eventually penning thirty-seven
manuscript volumes that covered his life from the year he was born to the
early nineteenth century), Bolotov also kept several diaries and various
kinds of journals, minutely documenting his life and circumstances. He
also wrote prolifically in other genres, including poetry, drama, literary
criticism, books for children and treatises on economy, agriculture,
philosophy and religion. Bolotov continued writing well into his eighties,
eventually producing, in Thomas Newlin's estimation, 'the equivalent of

---

32. 'Я в прочем не имею никакого места и должности. Я ни при военных, ни при
штатских, ни при придворных, ни при академических делах, ни в отставке. Я приемлю
дерзновение в. и. в. принести мою просьбу, дабы мне было учинено что-нибудь,
чтобы я знал, что я'. *Pis'ma*, p.96. Thomas Newlin detects 'existential panic' in these
formulations; see his *The Voice in the garden: Andrei Bolotov and the anxieties of Russian pastoral,
1738-1833* (Evanston, IL, 2001), p.223, n.13.

33. 'выше всего человеческого знания ставит'. M. V. Lomonosov, *Polnoe sobranie sochinenii*,
10 vols (Moscow and Leningrad, 1957), vol.10, p.545.

34. *Pis'ma*, p.78.

35. T. Newlin, 'Andrei Timofeevich Bolotov', in *Early modern Russian writers*, ed. M. Levitt, p.36-
42 (38).

some 350 volumes of written material'.[36] As Newlin suggests, the purpose of Bolotov's lifelong writing activity was, in significant part, to create a model of Russian private gentry experience that lacked precedents in the life of the eighteenth-century service-bound nobility.[37]

Like every eighteenth-century Russian nobleman before 1762, Bolotov was obliged to serve: at the age of ten he was enlisted in the regiment of which his father was commander. Even though his service was nominal and his time mostly occupied with schooling and partly spent away from the regiment, he was promoted twice, first to corporal, and then to sergeant. Bolotov began actual service at the age of seventeen, still in the rank of sergeant, and was made a commissioned officer in 1757.

Bolotov's career shaped up reasonably well, but he disliked service, viewing it as a hindrance to his private pursuits (which, like Sumarokov, he often calls 'exercises'). His resentment of his service duties is often mentioned in his memoir. In 'letter' 61, for example, he complains that his clerical duties as an officer stationed in Königsberg are difficult and boring and describes how he rejoiced when, having cleared up a backlog of paperwork, he was able to free himself for more interesting occupations:

> Now, continuing my story, I will tell you that as this life was for me at the beginning somewhat difficult and boring, so afterwards it became pleasant and merry. [...] [W]hen I finished up this difficult work, there was much less writing left for me to do, and finally there was so little that I had hardly one page a day to write. Therefore I could finish this small work in half an hour, and I not only did not have to go to the office in the afternoon, but sometimes even in the morning I did not have any work and could, with the permission of my little old man, absent myself and sometimes even spend the entire day at home.
>
> This circumstance, which allowed me more leisure and free time [...], pleased me, because I could devote a longer time to my exercises and live as I wished, without any concern that I would be sent to perform some company duties or appointed to guard detail.[38]

---

36. Newlin, 'Andrei Timofeevich Bolotov', p.37.
37. Newlin, *The Voice in the garden*, p.8-10 and esp. ch.2.
38. 'Теперь, продолжая повествование мое далее, скажу, что колико жизнь сия была мне сначала трудновата и скучна, толико сделалась потом приятна и весела. [...] [К]ак я сию трудную работу совершил, то письма мне было гораздо меньше и, наконец, сделалось столь мало, что мне и в целый день не доставалось написать по странице. Следовательно, небольшую сию работу мог я в полчаса оканчивать, и мне не только уже не было нужды ходить после обеда в камору, но я и по утрам иногда совсем дела не имел и мог, с дозволения старичка моего советника, отлучаться, а иногда и целый день оставаться дома.
   Сие обстоятельство, доставлявшее мне более досуга и свободного времени [...], было мне [...] приятно тем, что я множайшее время мог посвящать на собственные мои упражнения и жить по своему произволу, не заботясь ни о чем и не опасаясь,

Later, when Bolotov's knowledge of German landed him a job in the
governor's chancellery as a translator and interpreter, he again became
upset by the large volume of boring paperwork. Even the governor's
benevolence did not quite console him:

> But when, on the other hand, I recalled the difficult and tedious translations
> that bored me silly in a single day, when I pictured how I would be obliged to
> go to the chancellery every day and to spent the entire day toiling incessantly
> over them and be deprived completely of all the freedom so pleasant to me,
> these thoughts diminished my delight [at being accepted in the governor's
> house] and concerned me indescribably. Most of all I grieved that I would be
> tied down [by my duties] and would not have a minute, so to speak, of free
> time for myself, time that I could use for my own interesting exercises.[39]

Only in retrospect does Bolotov acknowledge that his busyness kept him
out of trouble, crediting his new duties and his association with col-
leagues in the chancellery as good for his education.[40]

   In describing his subsequent service in St Petersburg, Bolotov continues to complain that it is a tedious hindrance to his private occupations. He therefore chose to retire as soon as he could, right after Peter
III granted the Russian nobility freedom from obligatory service with his
decree of 1762. Bolotov writes in his memoir how ecstatic he felt on the
day his retirement became official: 'Finally, said date of 14 June, the most
memorable day in my life, arrived, and I received my so passionately
desired dismissal. [...] In such a way on that day my fourteen-year military
service came to an end, and, having received my dismissal, I became a
free and independent man forever.'[41] Having retired at the age of

---

чтоб послали меня куда в команду или в караул…'. A. T. Bolotov, *Zhizn' i prikliucheniia
Andreia Bolotova, opisannye samim im dlia svoikh potomkov*, 3 vols (Moscow, 1993), vol.1, p.399-
400. Bolotov calls his commander 'the little old man' ('starichok').

39. 'Но когда, с другой стороны, приходили мне на память трудные и скучные мои
    переводы, которые мне и в один уже тот день как горькая редька надоели, когда
    воображал я себе, что я всякий день должен буду ходить в канцелярию и с утра до
    вечера сидеть беспрестанно над ними, и лишиться совершенно всей прежней и толь
    милой для меня вольности, то сии мысли уменьшали много моего удовольствия и
    озабочивали меня несказанно. Пуще всего горевал я о том, что через то связан я буду
    по рукам и по ногам и не буду иметь ни минуты, так сказать, свободного для себя и
    такого времени, которое б мог употребить я на собственные свои любопытные
    упражнения'. A. T. Bolotov, *Жизнь и приключения*, letter 63, accessed from http://
    az.lib.ru/b/bolotow_a_t/text_0080.shtml on 19 May 2010.
40. Bolotov, *Zhizn' i prikliucheniia*, letter 64, accessed from http://az.lib.ru/b/bolotow_a_t/
    text_0110.shtml on 19 May 2010.
41. 'Наконец настало помянутое 14-е число июня, день, наидостопамятнейший в моей
    жизни; и я получил свой с толиким вожделением желаемый абшид. […] Таким
    образом кончилась в сей день вся моя 14 лет продолжавшаяся военная служба, и я,
    получив абшид, сделался свободным и вольным навсегда человеком'. Bolotov, *Zhizn' i
    prikliucheniia*, letter 64, accessed from http://az.lib.ru/b/bolotow_a_t/text_0110.shtml on 19
    May 2010.

twenty-three with the rank of army captain (ninth class), Bolotov
returned to civil service between 1774 and 1797 and eventually retired
with the rank of collegiate assessor (sixth class). He took great care,
however, not to let his service interfere with his private pursuits.

Bolotov arrived on his estate in September 1762. When the autumn
weather put a stop to the first necessary improvements (which happened
to be planting his first garden), he turned to reading and writing in order
to fill his lonely leisure.[42] Soon he realised that it was precisely these
occupations that made his life in the country meaningful and pleasur-
able: 'In a word, the effect my learned exercises produced was that,
instead of boredom, I was beginning even then to perceive all the
pleasure of country life, free and independent, unconstrained and
tranquil; and I was not burdened in the least either by [free] time, or
by my solitude.'[43]

Intellectual pursuits were so important for Bolotov that, in looking for
a bride, he sought a partner with similar interests. Unfortunately, soon
after the wedding, he realised that he had not succeeded: 'I did not find
and could not notice in her even the slightest inclination toward reading
books or to anything concerning learning.'[44] He hoped that with time his
young wife would develop these interests so central to his own existence
but, to his disappointment, this never happened. He was lucky enough,
however, to find a kindred soul in his mother-in-law. His ideal of private
gentry existence was thus complete: he had his independence, plenty of
time to read and write, and a person with whom to share his intellectual
interests. Later his son Pavel became his 'best friend and dear comrade
and interlocutor'.[45]

Bolotov's literary pursuits were largely private: he published almost
exclusively in non-literary and non-autobiographical genres, such as
pedagogy, philosophy, science, gardening and economics, the one excep-

---

42. Newlin comments on the correspondence between gardening and writing for Bolotov –
    his two favourite occupations while in the country. See Newlin, *The Voice in the garden*,
    p.115 and 231-32, n.38. On Bolotov's gardening projects, see Andreas Schönle, *The Ruler in
    the garden: politics and landscape design in imperial Russia* (Oxford, 2007), ch.2. Schönle also
    comments on analogy between Bolotov's gardening activities and his writing, p.124.
43. 'Словом, ученые мои упражнения произвели то, что я вместо скуки начинал и тогда
    уже чувствовать всю приятность свободной и ни от кого не зависимой,
    непринужденной и спокойной деревенской жизни, и не скучал нимало ни временем,
    ни одиночеством своим'. Bolotov, *Zhizn' i prikliucheniia*, vol.2, p.214.
44. 'Не находил и не примечал я также в ней ни малейшей склонности и охоты к
    читанию книг и ко всему, до наук относящемуся. Не видно было и того, чтоб она и к
    садам могла быть когда-нибудь охотница И чтоб ее и в них что-нибудь особливое
    веселило, но она смотрела на все с равнодушием совершенным'. Bolotov, *Zhizn' i
    prikliucheniia*, vol.2, p.303.
45. 'наиличшего друга и любезного моего сотоварища и собеседника'. Bolotov, *Zhizn' i
    prikliucheniia*, vol.3, p.470.

tion being his drama *The Unfortunate orphans*. Neither his poetry nor his memoirs and diaries went to print in his lifetime. It was not for the public that he wrote in these genres, but to give shape to his pastoral existence in the privacy of his estate. In this, he followed a literary tradition that imagined life in the country as necessarily including intellectual activities, such as reading and writing.[46] Based on Horace's Second Epode, this pastoral ideal was first formulated for Russians by Antiokh Kantemir in his satire 'On true happiness' (1738) and survived at least until 1834, when Pushkin sketched his unfinished poem 'It's time, my friend, it's time'. It is crucial, however, that Bolotov not only wrote prolifically about a life in the country that was independent and full of intellectual pursuits, but also succeeded in implementing this literary topos in real life.

My third case, Ippolit Bogdanovich (1743-1802), worked on his narrative poem *Dushen'ka (Psyche)* during a time in his service career that was filled with uncertainty as well as activity. Firstly, his civil service career faltered: in March 1779 he was transferred from the Foreign College, where he served as a translator in the rank of collegiate assessor (eighth class), to the Office of Heraldry, but the new appointment was without pay. Bogdanovich could not afford to serve without compensation and had to resign. He was able to return to service (to the newly established State Archive) only in October of 1780. Bogdanovich also experienced difficulties in his parallel career as editor of several state-sponsored periodicals published by the Academy of Sciences, including the official newspaper *St Petersburg news*. In July 1782 the Academy Conference, its secretariat, accused him of printing articles in *St Petersburg news* that were 'poorly chosen and often childish'.[47] In August, more accusations followed. As a result, in December 1782, Bogdanovich was forced to resign his position as editor, and Catherine was informed of his alleged blunders. No doubt, in the late 1770s and the early 1780s, Bogdanovich must have been both overwhelmed by the volume of his duties and distressed by his bad luck in his service career.

Curiously, Bogdanovich's service woes did not affect the persona that he developed as a writer. *Dushen'ka*, which was composed during roughly the same years (canto 1 appeared in print in 1778 and the entire poem in 1783), fostered in the minds of both Bogdanovich's contemporaries and posterity a very different image of its author: not that of a busy impecunious servitor whose career was being threatened, but that of 'a carefree Bohemian' writing in his (seemingly abundant) spare time. As Thomas Barran states in his biography of Bogdanovich, '[T]his persona

---

46. Newlin, *The Voice in the garden*, p.29-32.
47. 'худо выбранных и нередко детских'. Quoted in N. D. Kochetkova, 'Ippolit Fedorovich Bogdanovich', in *Slovar' russkikh pisatelei XVIII veka*, vol.1: *A–I*, ed. N. D. Kochetkova et al. (Leningrad, 1988), p.104-109 (106).

does not agree with the biographical facts. Bogdanovich adopted an authorial pose in the preface to *Dushen'ka* that may have provided the impetus for the rewriting of his biography.'[48] Indeed, the first sentence in Bogdanovich's introduction to the 1783 edition reads: 'To entertain myself in hours of idleness was my only motivation when I began writing *Dushen'ka*.' He goes on to claim that he did not even plan to publish it until the praise of his friends compelled him to do so. Bogdanovich concludes his introduction with an assertion of his dilettante status as a writer: 'I am [...] not from among the established writers.'[49]

Dushen'ka was hugely successful. Most importantly, it gained Bogdanovich Catherine's patronage: in March 1783 the entire print run of the poem was acquired by the Academy of Sciences and, in November 1783, the poet was elected to the Russian Academy (created the same year to emulate the Académie française). The Empress herself encouraged Bogdanovich in his literary pursuits, and he produced several plays for the Hermitage Theatre, beginning with the 1786 adaptation of *Dushen'ka* for the stage. His labours as a court playwright were rewarded with substantial sums of money and a diamond ring. More importantly, the poem also allowed Bogdanovich to relaunch his service career. In March 1784 he was promoted to the rank of court councillor (seventh class) and, in 1788, he received the rank of collegiate councillor (sixth class) and became the head of the State Archive. His literary activities gradually came to an end after this appointment. He retired in 1795.[50]

The image of Bogdanovich as an idle and carefree poet creating his poem in the privacy of his home to amuse himself in his spare time was amplified and consolidated by N. M. Karamzin in his 1803 article 'On Bogdanovich and his works'. Claiming that the image of the author can be discerned from the poem itself, Karamzin writes: 'He lived at the time on Vasil'evsky Island, in a quiet, isolated little home, devoting his time to music and verse in happy insouciance and freedom; [...] he loved to go out on occasion, but he loved even more to return to where the Muse awaited him with new ideas and colours.'[51]

48. Thomas Barran, 'Ippolit Fedorovich Bogdanovich', in *Early modern Russian writers*, ed. M. Levitt, p.29-35 (33).

49. 'Собственная забава в праздные часы была единственным моим побуждением, когда я начал писать «Душеньку»' and 'Я же, не будучи из числа учрежденных писателей...'. I. F. Bogdanovich, *Stikhotvoreniia i poemy, Biblioteka poeta, Bol'shaia seriia* (Leningrad, 1957), p.45.

50. See Kochetkova, 'Ippolit Fedorovich Bogdanovich', p.106-108; J. Klein, 'Bogdanovich i ego "Dushen'ka"', in *Puti kul'turnogo importa*, p.459-77 (476-77).

51. 'Он жил тогда на Васильевском острову, в тихом, уединенном домике, занимаясь музыкою и стихами, в счастливой беспечности и свободе; [...] любил иногда выезжать, но еще более возвращаться домой, где муза ожидала его с новыми идеями и цветами...'. N. M. Karamzin, 'O Bogdanoviche i ego sochineniiakh', in *Izbrannye stat'i i pis'ma* (Moscow, 1982), p.113-36 (118). I quote Barran's translation, 'Ippolit Fedorovich Bogdanovich', p.33.

The legend of Bogdanovich as the carefree creator of the charming *Dushen'ka* not only ignored the realities of his early struggles as a poorly paid bureaucrat but also completely disregarded his destitute and unhappy post-retirement life. It also overlooked his desperate and unsuccessful attempts to return both to service and to the literary scene in the early 1800s. In June 1801 Bogdanovich petitioned the Russian Academy for help in publishing his ode on the coronation of Alexander I and his collected works, but his petition was rejected. On several occasions in 1802 he sent his works to the Academy for publication, but they were rejected as well. In his accompanying letters Bogdanovich wrote of his utter poverty, which had forced him to sell his library. It is noteworthy that in his letters this self-proclaimed dilettante also begged for an opportunity to return to service or at least to be rewarded 'either with a rank, or with a cross, or with any other state decoration, but not with [...] a small one-time monetary allowance, which humiliates the spirit and extinguishes zeal in a nobleman'.[52] These requests were also ignored, and Bogdanovich died soon thereafter.

Nineteenth-century Russian writers inherited from eighteenth-century literati of noble status several models of authorial behaviour that negotiated between the public and private spheres. One type is exemplified by Sumarokov, who strove to cast away the patronage system and placed his literary activities in the context of state service. He believed that rank, a public criterion of his standing within the service hierarchy, was needed to give value to his writing. Thus writing was not a private activity for him: in his formulation, 'service to the Muses' suspiciously resembles service to the state. At the same time, Sumarokov rejected publishing for money as an activity that would dishonour him as author and nobleman. Sumarokov's view of writing as state service was aimed at elevating the status of literature in the eyes of his contemporaries. Even though Sumarokov's attempts were not quite successful during his lifetime, they proved essential for the eventual construction of the image of the Russian writer as an influential public figure.[53]

A second model is exemplified by Bolotov. Engrossed in his lifelong writing activity, Bolotov did not regard it as service, was not interested in service ranks and did not look for patrons. Furthermore, as Newlin puts it, 'throughout his life Bolotov remained oddly ambivalent about the whole business of being published.'[54] Perhaps not so oddly: unlike

52. '...хоть чином, хотя крестом, хотя другим каким государским отличием, только б не [...] малою единовременною денежною выдачею, какая унижает дух и погашает дворянское усердие'. Quoted in Kochetkova, 'Ippolit Fedorovich Bogdanovich', p.108-109.

53. See Zhivov, 'Pervye russkie literaturnye biografii', p.54-55.

54. Newlin, 'Andrei Timofeevich Bolotov', p.40.

Sumarokov, who insisted that his writing was valuable service to the state, Bolotov saw his writing as a private activity that defined personal, even intimate, space for him – the space he perceived as suitable for gentry existence. Bolotov's experiment in creating an authorial identity entirely independent of the idea of service and the Table of Ranks remained without consequence in his own time, at least in part because his authorial reticence kept his literary pursuits private. It is safe to assume that it did not affect the public view of writers in any significant way. Furthermore, it is not even clear whether Russians, who, during the late-eighteenth and nineteenth centuries, grew to expect a writer to be a public figure, would ever have approved of this kind of love of privacy in a writer. As I have pointed out, Nikolai Karamzin, who was looking for ways to declare authorial independence, chose a different model. Even after the publication of Bolotov's *Life and adventures*, in the 1870s, Russians, while acknowledging his importance as a memoirist, did not warm to the description of writerly existence that he offered. Perhaps it was not public enough and thus not heroic enough for the Russian taste. A century later Aleksandr Blok, the pre-eminent poet of the 1910s, devoted his undergraduate thesis to comparing Bolotov and the writer and publisher Nikolai Novikov, and confirms the durability of this attitude: Blok hails Nikolai Novikov, a highly visible public figure, and presents Bolotov, with his subdued authorial aspirations and love of privacy, as a philistine, a man without 'citizenry interests' ('obshchestv[enykh] interesov').[55]

Unlike Sumarokov and Bolotov, Bogdanovich eagerly participated both in the service hierarchy and in the patronage system. At the same time, in his introduction to *Dushen'ka*, he attempted to present writing as a private activity, that of a dilettante who indulges in it in his free time and for his own pleasure. Unlike Bolotov, Bogdanovich's authorial self-image had no basis in reality. Nevertheless, it took root and, once developed further by Karamzin, fully supplanted his true biography as a writer. Bogdanovich's (quite public) image as the carefree and inde-pendent author of the charming *Dushen'ka* was used by Karamzin to forge the idea of writing as a private occupation separate from service to the state. Later in the nineteenth century, Bogdanovich's self-constructed persona of a dilettante writing in the privacy of his home and publishing only when pressed by his friends proved useful for other Russian writers, including Pushkin, in working out the idea of writing as both a private and a public activity.

---

55. I. Vladimirova [Irina Reyfman], M. Grigor'ev [Mark Altshuller] and K. Kumpan, 'A. A. Blok i russkaia kul'tura XVIII veka', *Blokovskii sbornik*, ed. D. E. Maksimov et al., vol.4 (Tartu, 1980), p.27-115 (84).

Largely illiterate until the eighteenth century, Russian nobles took to writing with a vengeance in the post-Petrine era. Like their European counterparts, some used writing to define their private sphere of existence or to formulate an authorial position that made them, at least nominally, independent of the state and its hierarchies. At the same time, obligatory or, later in the century, expected service to the state made any non-service activity suspect, forcing Russian noblemen to justify their right to write. Moreover, because they had trouble imagining themselves outside the service hierarchy institutionalised in the Tables of Ranks, they attempted to elevate writing to the status of state service. Paradoxically, their strategy helped establish writing, and writing literature in particular, as a highly regarded public activity in Russia.

Private walks and public gazes: Enlightenment and the use of gardens in eighteenth-century Russia

ANDREAS SCHÖNLE

The well-travelled Heinrich von Storch, a political economist from Riga, was called as a young man to St Petersburg in 1789 to teach in the School of Cadets. His study of the capital, *Gemälde von St Petersburg* (1794), subsequently brought him notoriety. It was translated into English in 1801, and has been regarded as a reliable source. He describes among other things the striking absence of venues for public entertainment in the capital by comparison with other European cities:

> The establishments for public recreation are here neither so numerous nor so sumptuous, as I have frequently found them in towns of far less pretentions. The reason of this singular phaenomenon is neither in the indisposition of the public nor in the want of undertakers; but in the prevailing fashion which is averse to a public and unlimited participation. In all the capital towns that I have visited, the contrary is so much so case, that it is by this very peculiarity that they differ from places of inferior conse-quence. At Paris, London, Berlin and Vienna those entertainments are particularly preferred in which every person, without exception, may par-ticipate. Almost all kinds of entertainment are public, that is, under certain conditions, are open to all. The enjoyment of them may be had at a comparatively very small expense, and is even much enhanced by the participation of a great concourse of persons. The company of ladies is indispensably necessary at all entertainments, softening by their presence the harsh or rude manners into which even the best selected companies of men are liable to fall. In St Petersburg we see almost entirely the reverse of this. What is called good company contracts itself into family-parties, circles of acquaintance, clubs, &c. to which a stranger, without especial recommen-dation can with difficulty gain access, and whose manners, for want of a proper mixture with a variety of characters and conditions are apt to acquire a dull and formal stamp. It is held unbecoming to frequent public houses; people of any consequence, heads of families, placemen, wealthy merchants never enter a coffee-house. Ladies can only visit public places, at any time, under extremely severe restrictions; from most of them they are absolutely excluded by the laws and customs of society. Hence it arises that houses opened for public entertainment here scarcely ever succeed, even though fitted up with great expense and taste and countenanced by the patronage of some person of rank and fashion.[1]

1. Henry Storch, *Picture of Petersburg* (London, 1801), p.421-22.

Storch laments the absence of opportunities for the various social classes and two sexes to mingle. He posits that 'the participation of a great concourse of persons' not only enhances the pleasures afforded by public sociability, but also generates a beneficial flexibility and smoothness in manners that will be absent when access is narrowly restricted by gender and class.

My purpose here is to explore the role of gardens as a place of limited public sociability in St Petersburg, its vicinity and further afield in the Russian Empire. Did gardens in Russia afford opportunities for spontaneous interaction across social and gender barriers that did not exist elsewhere? Did they soften and refine manners, facilitate social mobility, enable erotic pursuits, foster the exchange of information and ideas, or promote exploration with identity? In short did they allow the emergence of a public sphere otherwise sorely lacking in Russian cities? Or were gardens just as socially restrictive and hierarchically stratified as other public venues of the capital, such as theatres, clubs, coffee houses and so on? We do not need to agree fully with Storch in all respects – and he himself goes on to describe a few exceptions to his general observation – to accept the premise that, in comparison with other European cities, the development of a public sphere in St Petersburg was hampered in part by the absence of open and inclusive sites of sociability. It becomes then all the more important to look at the role gardens might have played in this regard.

Much has been written about the design and symbolic import of gardens, but very little on their 'consumption' – the role they play in the everyday life of their visitors, the way they are used and enjoyed – and it is to the pragmatics of gardens, rather than to their semantics, that I wish to turn. Sources for this undertaking are fairly abundant in the nineteenth century, but much scarcer in the eighteenth, and part of my work will require piecing together scraps of available evidence. By gardens I mean what in Russian goes under the label of 'sady i parki', that is everything from the grand imperial parks created in the eighteenth century, such as Tsarskoe Selo and Peterhof, to the modest patches designed by noblemen of middling rank on their country estates. I shall consider primarily the period between the 1750s and 1825 – in other words, the second half of the long eighteenth century.

Genuine public gardens did not exist yet in St Petersburg. Only avenues and streets could serve the purpose of public strolling. And even then their enjoyment was hampered by the clouds of dust raised by carriages racing along and by the absence of sidewalks. On 24 May 1756 Elizabeth issued the edict 'On access to the imperial gardens on Thursdays and Sundays for walks' which codified criteria for admission to the First and Second Summer Gardens – the Third Garden was kept mostly for herself, although exceptions were made.[2] A select group of dignitaries and officials, including some named personally in the edict, as well as ladies and gentlemen of the court, obtained unrestricted access to the gardens. In addition, entrance would be granted on Thursdays and, in Elizabeth's absence from St Petersburg, also on Sundays, to carefully defined categories of people:

> foreign ministers, as well as generals, non-commissioned officers of the Life-Company [Elizabeth's personal guard, composed of the company which assisted her in overthrowing her predecessor Anna Ioanovna], the corporals and grenadiers of the Life-Guards and of army regiments, the staff officers and high officers of the corps of cadets, of engineers, and of the artillery and of the fleet; and among the civil ranks, those equivalent to officers, and the entire nobility, as well as elite Russian and foreign merchants with their families, the skippers of foreign ships, but not the sailors, as well as common people in livery and with their masters.[3]

It is interesting that this fairly inclusive list identifies various groups of people rather than adopting a more blanket definition of the society authorised to enjoy Elizabeth's gardens. Indeed, the list is not socially homogenous – non-commissioned officers of the Life-Company were allowed, but only higher officers of the fleet. Nor is the listing organised in the order of descending rank, even though the sequencing of categories was clearly thought out meticulously. The company closest to the empress – her personal guard – trumps almost every other social group except generals and foreign ambassadors. Access to the gardens is a privilege granted according to complex and sometimes conflicting parameters, reflective of a highly structured and hierarchical society in which the ruler's preferences can still override the logic of the social order. Curiously, the instruction given to the police a year earlier was less

2. The 1756 decree was preceded by other edicts and instructions, starting in 1750, which all aimed to define access to the gardens on various days and for various categories of people. See Paul Keenan, 'Creating a "public" in St Petersburg, 1703-1761', doctoral dissertation, SSEES/UCL, 2006, p.151-58. For a summary of these developments, see P. Keenan, 'The question of access to the Summer Gardens in St Petersburg in the first half of the eighteenth century', *Newsletter of the study group on eighteenth-century Russia* 34 (2006), p.17-22.

3. '[…] как иностранных Министров, так и здешний Генералитет, Лейб-Компании унтер-офицеров, капралов и гренадер Лейб-Гвардии и армейских полков, Кадетского Инженерного и Артиллерийского корпусов и Морского флота Штаб и Обер-Оффицеров, а из штатских чинов, состоящих в рангах Офицерских и все Дворянство, також Российское и иностранное знатное купечество, с их фамилиями и иностранных кораблей шкиперов, кроме матросов, також и господских, ливрейных и подлого народа'. 'O propuske dlia gulian'ia v Pridvornye sady po Chetvergam i Voskresen'iam', in *Polnoe sobranie zakonov rossiiskoi imperii s 1649 goda, Pervoe sobranie*, vol.14 (St Petersburg, 1830), no.10.560 (14 May 1756), p.573. Translations here and elsewhere in this chapter are mine.

restrictive, allowing access on Thursdays to people of 'all ranks', provided
they fulfil certain dress requirements, with the exception of 'liveried
servants by themselves' (i.e. without their masters), suggesting that the
empress may have had second thoughts about ill-defined openness.[4]

The 1756 edict stipulated a detailed sartorial code: 'those whose hair is
unkempt, who have scarves on their necks, or are in boots, as well as in a
grey caftan and bearded merchants, women in the Russian dress, in a
bonnet or wearing other similar simple clothes are not to be admitted.'[5]
The garden is set off from its environment. Its relative inclusiveness
comes at a cost: merchants are permitted entry only to the extent that
they do not look like Russian merchants, and likewise women cannot
resemble common Russian women. In short, as much else at court, the
gardens demand a certain degree of formality or even theatricality. In
this respect, although more inclusive, they are hardly different from
other official settings of court life, bearing out the observation of the
historian Carsten Goehrke that the nobility lived in an 'entertainment
ghetto'.[6] Yet, despite all these restrictions, the gardens offered an opportunity for unstructured if stately sociability, which is, in itself, a
novelty. It is important that they were intended to be enjoyed even when
the empress was absent, since in her munificence she afforded her
subjects this opportunity for relaxation on her grounds. A narrower
group consisting of foreign ambassadors with their suite and the first two
ranks of the *Generalitet* was allowed to these gardens on any day, regardless of the presence of the empress.

During the reign of Peter the Great the Summer Garden had been
used primarily for the purpose of collective and obligatory festivities
hosted by the emperor, which included forced drinking, dancing and
fireworks. At these times, the gates to the garden were closed so that no
one could slip away before the end.[7] Such festivities served the incul-
cation of courtly manners and provided exposure to classical artefacts. A
statue of Venus prominently displayed – and vigilantly guarded –
welcomed the guests, a provocative gesture on Peter's behalf given the
Orthodox prohibition against sculpture.[8] The first elephant to be seen in
Russia resided in the garden. Upon his death he was briefly replaced by

4. *Kamer-fur'erskii zhurnal* (St Petersburg, 1755), p.54-55.
5. '[…] а кои будут неопрятны, то есть: волосы не убраны, платки на шеи и в сапогах,
    также в серых кафтанах и из купцов с бородами, а женщин в Русском платье, в
    чепчиках и в прочих тому подобных простых платьях отнюдь не пущать', p.573-74.
6. Carsten Goehrke, *Russischer Alltag: eine Geschichte in neun Zeitbildern vom Frühmittelalter bis zur
    Gegenwart*, vol.2: *Auf dem Weg in die Moderne* (Zurich, 2003), p.109.
7. See S. N. Shubinskii, *Ocherki iz zhizni i byta proshlogo vremeni* (St Petersburg, 1888), p.6-8. On
    the use of gardens in the first half of the eighteenth century, see T. V. Dubiago, *Russkie
    reguliarnye sady i parki* (Leningrad, 1963), p.34-35.
8. M. I. Pyliaev, *Staryi Peterburg* (Moscow, 1997), p.66.

the Great Gottorp Globe, one of the first planetariums – both were testimony to Peter's scientific interests.[9] Venus and the elephant are two sides of the same coin, a deliberate attempt initiated by the ruler to use the garden in order to jolt his subjects out of their premodern worldview.

In contrast with this didactic and ruler-directed exploitation of the Summer Garden, Elizabeth's policies thus initiated something closer to the leisurely enjoyment of nature, albeit within clear temporal and social limits. The evidence suggests that access to the Summer Garden in the 1740s had been tightly restricted, prompting complaints from the Austrian ambassador in 1750.[10] The empress' readiness to open her gardens to the noble public may have been inspired by the example set by foreign courts. Versailles, for example, had long been an attraction for travellers. Beginning in the 1670s, guidebooks and descriptions of Versailles began to appear, including by such writers as Charles Perrault, Jean de La Fontaine and Madeleine de Scudéry.[11] Louis XIV famously wrote a text called *Manière de montrer les jardins de Versailles*, which, historians assume, was designed as a directive for garden *intendants* on how to exhibit the grounds to foreign monarchs and high dignitaries in the absence of the king.[12]

The edict triggered the partial opening of other gardens. A year later, in 1757, the *St Petersburg news* announced the opening of the garden of the Corps of Land Cadets daily except on Thursdays and Sundays, from 6pm to 10pm, 'to people of all ranks and conditions, except peasants and those dressed in vile clothes. Servants in livery attending nobles of both sexes or other ladies are to be let in, but those in livery without their masters shall not be admitted.'[13] The criteria here are more implicit and less legalistic than in Elizabeth's edict, though in the end they encompass a group quite similar to the one she had singled out. What is curious, however, is the schedule: the garden closes precisely when the Summer Garden is open. In all likelihood, it would have been pointless to provide an alternative venue on days when society was invited to stroll in the imperial gardens. This assumption speaks volumes about the function of the garden in the life of society. The garden was intended to be a site where society could meet itself as a group and act in a fairly homo-geneous fashion, rather than for individuals to engage in a private

9.   Shubinskii, *Ocherki*, p.4.

10. Keenan, 'Creating a "Public"', p.153.

11. See Robert W. Berger, *In the garden of the Sun King: studies on the park of Versailles under Louis XIV* (Washington, DC, 1985), p.29-40.

12. Louis XIV, *Manière de montrer les jardins de Versailles*, ed. Simone Hoog (Paris, 1982), p.14.

13. '[…] всякого звания и достоинства людям, от 6 до 10 часов по полудни кроме крестьянства и одетых в гнусное платье. Господские служители в ливрее за знатными обоего пола особами, и за прочими дамами впусканы быть имеют, а в ливрее без господ впусканы не будут'. *Sanktpeterburgskie vedomosti* 59 (1757).

pursuit of pleasure.[14] The swings in the garden of the Land Cadets enabled pupils to display their skill in front of the empress and the court. In fact, as a nineteenth-century historian of the Corps of Cadets maintained, this elite institution 'formed part of the court of the Empress'.[15]

Two years later the Corps of Cadets decided further to open its garden to the noble public. This time the garden was open all day long on Thursdays and Sundays, but to a narrower segment of the urban population, as it specifically excluded servants and people dressed in common attire. This new restrictiveness may be explained by the fact that the garden now featured a summer house where various Russian and foreign newspapers and journals were made available. In addition, refreshments (tea, coffee, lemonade, candy, fruits and ice cream) could be purchased, as well as full-fledged meals ordered in advance.[16] It is unclear whether this new timetable superseded the opening hours announced for the summer of 1757, or whether it added to them.

The garden fostered the sense of participating in a collective choreography, one in which the participants are at once actors and spectators: 'On the two Whitsun holidays, all elegant and fashionable people parade [the Summer Garden's] walks in state', Storch noted about the nobility during Catherine's age, continuing:

> How much or how little of this honour may be ascribed to an affection for the beauties of nature, it is not my duty to inquire; but certain it is, that many ladies of great quality leave their beautiful villas, in order, on these days, to shove about among the crowd of well-dressed citizens, and that, except in the grand walk, where all appear to see and be seen, only a few unfashionable walkers are found.[17]

Decades later, writers still bemoaned the aristocracy's propensity to display their eminence in the garden. Writing in 1826, A. Glebov commended the empress mother's name-day celebration, as one

> didn't notice there the vainglory, which usually transpires in the movements of people of highest ranks, who look to distinguish themselves from others; on the contrary, here everyone seemed fully to embrace the feeling of

---

14. Overstating her point somewhat, N. V. Sipovskaia maintains that noble festivities remained ritualistic and lacked the element of individual entertainment well into the nineteenth century: 'Prazdnik v russkoi kul'ture XVIII veka', in *Razvlekatel'naia kul'tura Rossii XVIII-XIX vv.* (St Petersburg, 2000), p.28-42.

15. 'состовлял часть Двора Ее'. Aleksandr Viskovatov, *Kratkaia istoriia pervogo kadetskogo korpusa* (St Petersburg, 1832), p.29.

16. *Prazdnoe vremia v pol'zu upotreblennoe* 1 (1759), p.365-66.

17. Storch, *Picture*, p.432-33. On the same festivity in the early 1800s, see Pavel Svin'in, quoted in A. I. Uspenskii, *Imperatorskie dvortsy*, 2 vols (Moscow, 1913), vol.1, p.264.

pleasure and to be absorbed by the beauty of the place where they were; the line dividing the highest class from the rest appeared to have vanished.[18]

Praising the unique democratic nature of this celebration, Glebov suggests that, on other occasions, rank still very much defined the experience of gardens.

The sense of collective identity fostered by the aristocratic enjoyment of gardens also appears in the design of the country seats granted to the nobility. Families at the highest echelon of society were given estates on the so-called 'Peterhof road', the track that led from St Petersburg to the imperial palace at Peterhof in the west of the city. By order of Elizabeth, these estates, which followed one after the other in a continuous sequence, were to be outfitted 'for the enhanced beauty of these houses and the sublime glory of the entire sea shore [...] with a single exquisite railing, in one line, as if it was a unique large elongated settlement'.[19]

Access to gardens expanded during the reign of Catherine the Great. To judge from Johann Georgi, Catherine ordered the daily opening of the original Summer Garden to all people 'properly dressed'. The garden in his account was highly popular among people 'who drink juices', suggesting that alcohol consumption was prohibited.[20] Storch noted that the garden 'is visited with much satisfaction' – all the more so as during the reign of Catherine and up to 1812 an ensemble of the court *chasseurs* played music on Sundays.[21] Yet Catherine closed the Second Summer Garden, which was destined 'solely for the walks of the Empress' and contained a small hermitage with a good collection of paintings as well as hot houses for the imperial kitchen.[22]

During Catherine's reign, grandees close to the empress opened their gardens for selective public access on certain days. This practice, initiated probably at various times in the 1770s and 1780s, provided a

---

18. 'Я не заметил здесь того тщеславия, которое обыкновенно на публичных гуляньях проглядывает сквозь все движения людей высшего звания, ищущих отличиться от других; напротив, каждый, казалось, вполне предавался чувству наслаждений и был занят только красотами того места, где он был; черта, разделявшая высший класс от низшего, казалось, изчезла'. A. Glebov, 'Poezdka v Petergof 22 Iiulia', *Novosti literatury* 26 (May 1826), p.76.

19. '[…] для лучшей красоты оных домов, также и для высокой славы всего приморского берега [...] оные приморские домы украсить одною решедчетою преискусною городбою, под одну линею, так, как бы одна некая великая простирающаяся была украшена слобода'. A. I. Bogdanov, *Opisanie Sanktpeterburga 1749-1751* (St Petersburg, 1997), p.226-27.

20. I. G. Georgi, *Opisanie rossiisko-imperatorskogo stolichnogo goroda Sankt-Peterburga i dostopamiatnostei v okrestnostiakh onogo, 1974-1796g.* (St Petersburg, 1996), p.82.

21. *Putevoditel' po S.-Peterburgu* (St Petersburg, 1903), p.74. The music was played by a group of horns, each capable of playing at one pitch only, producing an effect not unlike the organ. Similar ensembles existed on a few aristocratic estates.

22. 'Он определен единственно для прогулки ИМПЕРАТРИЦЫ'. Georgi, *Opisanie*, p.105.

different sort of entertainment, as the master often played host to his visitors and entertained them in various ways, which often required that he be retired from service. It is not clear if subtle differentiations existed as to the inclusiveness of such festivities. Descriptions of these gardens by Storch and Georgi refer to the requirement that visitors be of 'decent appearance', but also emphasise their cross-social appeal.[23] Storch implies that the gardens on the islands attracted rather the lower classes, while the estates on the Peterhof road were more select.[24] Georgi explicitly argues that the Elagin garden qualified as a public garden[25] and also called it an 'almost open popular garden'.[26] Yet when Georgi states that on a nice summer day the paths of such gardens are full of 'people of all classes', he probably means the nobility and merchants.[27] Not only the dress code, but also problems of physical access would have prevented other city dwellers from joining the festivities. In his customary sceptical tone, Storch claims that gardens 'are but little frequented. The short summer, the dirty or dusty streets and the wide extent of the town, render the keeping of a carriage almost indispensably necessary to the enjoyment of this recreation; and the opulent part of the inhabitants usually pass the fine season of the year at their country-seats.'[28] Yet he also effusively recommends the enjoyment of such gardens, in particular as an entertaining scene of social mixing: 'This noble hospitality is by no means unenjoyed; the concourse of persons of all descriptions, from the star and ribband to the plain well-dressed burgher, forms such a party-coloured collection and sometimes groupes are so humourously contrasted, that for this reason alone it is well worth the pains of partaking once in the amusement.'[29]

The invitation and access restrictions were often exhibited on a plaque at the entrance to the grounds. At the estates of the brothers Naryshkin, for example, such invitation was issued in four different languages, indicating the cosmopolitan aspirations of the estate. The Naryshkins went so far as expressly to enjoin inhabitants of St Petersburg to savour the fresh air and undertake a walk in the garden for the sake of good health and 'to dispel thoughts'.[30] Such rhetoric evokes the views of

23. Storch, *Picture*, p.440.
24. With regard to the Elagin estate he maintains that 'On Sundays and holidays are seen a great confluence of citizens of the lower classes, taking their pleasure unmolested' (Storch, *Picture*, p.439).
25. Georgi, *Opisanie*, p.139.
26. '[...] соделался неким образом почти открытым садом'. Georgi, *Opisanie*, p.456.
27. 'В прекрасные летние дни многочисленные дорожки в саду прогуливающимися всех классов [...] покрыты'. Georgi, *Opisanie*, p.457.
28. Storch, *Picture*, p.430.
29. Storch, *Picture*, p.441.
30. 'для рассыпания мыслей'. Georgi, *Opisanie*, p.458.

Catherine, who looked kindly upon the gardening of her grandsons[31] – which she presumably welcomed as a way to promote fitness and to eschew the temptations of melancholy – and whose concern for public health is well documented.[32]

This practice was likewise adopted in Moscow. Aleksandr Voeikov noted that, as they retired, 'Orlov-Chesmenskii, Dolgorukii-Krymskii, Eropkin, Panin, Sheremetev [...] organised parties for the people and extended hospitality to the noblemen in order to earn their love and benediction.'[33] The distinction between the two social groups is interesting. Indeed, at his estate Kuskovo, Count Petr Borisovich Sheremetev ended the festivity by inviting the nobility to dinner while treating the people to fireworks. Regardless of their inclusiveness and the 'exemplary liberality' of their tenants, gardens preserved the basic social demarcations of society.[34] In fact, gazing at the well-dressed lower nobility or third estate contributed to the aristocracy's recreation. Sipovskaia presents evidence suggesting that, in some instances, the 'people' were framed as a spectacle destined to the enjoyment of the aristocratic guests.[35] And, surely, the reverse was true as well. The hope of brushing against a grandee in the garden must have been intrinsic to the thrill of such events for the 'decent' commoner.

The gardens of the grandees offered not only enjoyment of nature, but also music, theatrical performances, dance shows, occasional fireworks, balls, a sometime fishery, swings, a bowling green, boating on the lakes, places for rest, including some outfitted with sofas and chairs for 'sedate conversation',[36] taverns and so on. Storch refers to the existence of a proper vauxhall on the Elagin and Krestovskii islands. Outside the fisheries, the entertainment and refreshments, often handed out by servants in livery, were free, and offered as a magnanimous gesture on behalf of the grandee, who normally adopted a visible role in the goings-on: 'M. Yelaghin himself usually takes part in the amusements he so liberally dispenses to others, and his daughters at times open the ball with some gentleman present. That the enjoyment of all these amuse-ments is free of expense to the visitants scarcely needs to be

31. *Sbornik imperatorskogo rossiiskogo istoricheskogo obshchestva*, vol.23 (St Petersburg, 1878), p.273.
32. W. Bruce Lincoln, *Sunlight at midnight: St Petersburg and the rise of modern Russia* (New York, 2000), p.68-69.
33. 'Орлов-Чесменский, Долгорукий-Крымсий, Еропкин, Панин, Шереметев [...] старались, праздниками для народа и хлебосольством для дворян, заслужить их любовь и благословение.' A. A. Voeikov, 'Progulka v sele Kuskove', *Novosti literatury* 27 (1826), p.103. For a more detailed discussion of the festivities at Kuskovo, see Sipovskaia, 'Prazdnik v russkoi kul'ture', p.30-33.
34. Storch, *Picture*, p.439.
35. Sipovskaia, 'Prazdnik v russkoi kul'ture', p.32, 35-36.
36. Storch, *Picture*, p.441.

mentioned.'[37] According to M. I. Pyliaev, the steward at Elagin's garden was under strict orders to 'treat all who wanted to a lunch and dinner'.[38] Generous hosting was part of the patriarchal 'contract' that underpinned absolutist society, and such gestures of goodwill reinforced the emotional bond that tied the lower to the upper class and exemplified the personal nature of power in court society.[39] Country squires understood this well and so they regularly arranged festivities for their serfs on their estates. Although aristocratic gardens enabled a degree of social intermingling, they also legitimised social differences by exemplifying the 'benefits' of a patriarchal society, exhibiting the patronising duty of care assumed by the upper class vis-à-vis the rest of the polity, which blurred the line between the private and the public, and enlisted private life in support of the public order. In this regard the plans created by N. A. L'vov for Count A. A. Bezborodko's estate in Moscow seem unusual because L'vov, who was always concerned to make external form fit inner purpose, planned to section off a part of the garden for public use, with separate access through gates opening directly onto the street. The aim was to create a sort of fair, where visitors could purchase various trinkets and refreshments.[40] The introduction of monetary exchange into the park inserted a distance between the landowner and the visitors and objectified their relationship. Had this project been implemented, it would have created a more genuinely public urban garden, since its visitors would have been less explicitly cast in the role of grateful guest than in other gardens.

Attempts to open gardens to the entire urban public were hardly successful. The most notorious case is the festivity thrown by tax farmer Longinov in the winter of 1778 to thank the people for the fortune he amassed in the four years he sold them spirits. William Coxe, who gave an extended first-hand account of the event held in the Summer Garden, describes how about 40,000 people, who had been invited by leaflets distributed through town, congregated in the gardens to enjoy the games and refreshments provided:

> A large semicircular table was covered with all kinds of provision, piled in different shapes, and in the greatest profusion. Large slices of bread and caviare [*sic*], dried sturgeon, carp, and other fish, were ranged to a great height, in the form of pent-houses and pyramids, and garnished with crawfish, onions, and pickles. In different parts of the grounds were rows

37. Storch, *Picture*, p.439-40, 441.
38. 'угощать всех желающих обедом и ужином'. Pyliaev, *Staryi Peterburg*, p.408.
39. See A. Schönle, 'The scare of the self: sentimentalism, privacy, and private life in Russian culture, 1780-1820', *Slavic review* 57:4 (1998), p.723-46 (727-28).
40. G. G. Grimm, 'Proekt parka Bezborodko v Moskve (Materialy k izucheniiu tvorchestva N.A. L'vova)', *Soobshcheniia instituta istorii iskusstv* 4-5 (1954), p.107-135 (122).

of casks full of spirituous liquors and still larger vessels of wine, beer, and quass. Among the decorations I observed representations of an immense whale in pasteboard, covered with cloth and gold or silver brocade, and filled in the inside with bread, dried fish, and other provisions.[41]

After some time devoted to the usual amusements – swings, slides, pole climbing – a fire rocket signalled the beginning of the libations. A second signal meant to invite the people to partake of food was hardly necessary as the masses threw themselves on the displays after their first gulp of alcohol and went on a rampage. The whale became the primary focus of the people's pent-up greed:

> The whale was the chief object of contention: within the space of a few minutes he was entirely divested of his gaudy trappings, which became the spoils of his successful invaders. They had no sooner flead off his drapery, and secured the fragments of rich brocade; than they rent him into thousand pieces, to seize the provisions with which his inside was stored. The remaining people, who were too numerous to be all engaged in contending about the whale, were employed in uncovering the pent-houses, and pulling down the pyramids.[42]

In popular belief the whale is a demonic being. As a distinguished inhabitant of the seas against which Petersburg contended, it might well have represented in the minds of many people the elemental force of water that had swept through the city in the great flood of 1777, just a year earlier. The sea is both the enemy and the livelihood of the city, and tearing the whale apart could have evoked the intensely ambivalent feelings it must have raised among Petersburg dwellers. Richly decked out in the fabrics of the aristocracy, the whale – its incongruous dimensions perhaps symbolising the inflated ego of the host or his insatiable appetite for riches – also inspired social resentment. It was either stupendously naive or savagely ironic on the part of the designers of this celebration to set off revengeful destructive impulses in a population, which was after all enduring miserable conditions and incurring many losses for the sake of building a magnificent city primarily designed for the benefit of the court and aristocracy. If there is something carnivalesque in this scene, in which the flensing of a whale marks a reversal of hierarchies, it is a carnival run amok. Coxe can hardly conceal the social violence inherent in the behaviour of the carousers, who also made liberal use of the alcohol dispensed in unlimited quantities and consumed by 'great wooden ladles'. Meanwhile the host, who had been enriched by holding a monopoly on the sale of alcohol, was savouring

41. William Coxe, *Travels in Poland, Russia, Sweden and Denmark*, 5th edn, vol.2 (London, 1802), p.224.
42. Coxe, *Travels*, p.226.

fine wines with some noblemen in a pavilion of the garden. 'The confusion and riot, which soon succeeded, is better conceived than described; and we thought it expedient to retire', Coxe concluded,[43] and rightly so, for on the next day he found out not only that many drunken merrymakers froze to death on the streets, but also that others had died during quarrels or were robbed and murdered as they were retiring to their distant homes. In his estimation, on this 'melancholy occasion' more than 400 people fell victim to this unfortunate, and perhaps somewhat cynical, attempt to thank the people.

It is not for nothing that fairgrounds providing recreation for the people were mostly confined to the outskirts of the city. Along with the usual sets of swings, these also featured mechanical contraptions and freak shows.[44] Baron Vanzhura, the deputy director of the imperial theatres, attempted to draw on this style of entertainment when he organised a vauxhall in the Naryshkin garden in St Petersburg. Concerts, pantomimes, theatrical productions, balls, masquerades, fireworks and folk dances were given on Wednesdays and Sundays in the evening, while various musicians, actors, dancers, acrobats and showmen produced small acts in the gardens, including freak shows and the exhibition of rare wild animals. The cost of entrance was one rouble per person, and two roubles were charged for the theatrical shows. While not explicitly reserved to the upper class, the entrance fee would have turned away some. According to Pyliaev, despite its initial success, the vauxhall soon folded its operations, suggesting perhaps that Russian society was not ready yet for commercial forms of entertainment.[45]

Imperial estates in the vicinity of St Petersburg also offered opportunities for public conviviality. During the reign of Elizabeth, access to Tsarskoe Selo, which she conceived primarily as a place for intimate gatherings, was strictly limited. In 1746 she ordered that 'no one be allowed in the gardens and to place guards. If someone by force or obstinacy nevertheless enters, then to shoot such obdurate ones with dry peas.'[46] Tired of pupils straying in her garden, she also ordered in 1750 that a neighbouring school be moved to another settlement.[47] In the same vein, access to the road leading to Tsarskoe Selo was limited. An edict issued in 1755 instructed the Office for the Construction of State

43. Coxe, *Travels*, p.226.
44. See Goehrke, *Russischer Alltag*, p.107-108.
45. Pyliaev, *Staryi Peterburg*, p.407.
46. '[…] в сад никого не пускать и поставить караул; ежели же кто силой и упрямством пойдет, в таких упрямых стрелять из ружья горохом'. Aleskandr Benua [Benois], *Tsarskoe selo v tsarstvovanie Imperatritsy Elizavety Petrovny* (St Petersburg, 1910), p.233. My thanks to Simon Dixon, who kindly supplied me with this quote as well as other valuable suggestions for this article.
47. Benua, *Tsarskoe selo*, p.234.

Roads that 'since on this road her Majesty always deigns to travel to Tsarskoe and St Petersburg, no unauthorised person is to be allowed to use it, especially peasants, with the exception of noble persons in Berlins who have received a pass from the Office.'[48] During Catherine's reign, many accounts concur that it was surprisingly easy to gain access to the grounds at Tsarskoe Selo, where Catherine resided most of the summer. Alexander Pushkin's depiction in his historical novel *The Captain's daughter* (1835) of Masha Mironova's early-morning visit to the gardens at Tsarskoe Selo, where she chanced upon the empress in her morning attire, is not entirely unlikely. Similar evidence exists in memoirs. Thus M. N. Nikoleva relates how her uncle had asked his servant to bring his two sons to St Petersburg in order to secure their admission to an elite educational establishment. At a loss about what to do, the servant was advised to take the children to the gardens at Tsarskoe Selo in the hope of bringing them to the attention of the empress, which surely enough happened without delay.[49] Although this account seems too literary to be entirely reliable, it belongs to a widespread type of anecdote about people stalking the ruler in a garden in order to plead some cause, which all presume the openness of imperial gardens. We know for a fact that Catherine was in the habit of taking early morning strolls through the grounds, usually all by herself.[50]

Nevertheless, it is likely that a form of dress control was in effect. Guards were manning the entrance to the grounds and, although writers make a point of asserting that they were not stopped, a commonly dressed individual arriving on foot might have been turned back. A visitor to Pavlovsk in 1815, where the empress mother Mariia Fedorovna resided, wrote that:

> we proceeded along an excellent and calm road to the gates of Pavlovsk. They are open to everyone: no interrogation stops the visitors. Police are nowhere to be seen in this town. They only cater to the enjoyment of visitors and don't even suspect, it seems, that anyone might have other designs than to bow to the Mother and to take delight in life.[51]

48. '[...] потому что по сей дороге ее Величество всегда изволит ездить в Царское и Петербург, и никому из посторонних, а особливо крестьянам, непозволено по ней ездить, кроме знатных особ в берлинах, и получающим из Конторы билет для проезда по ней'. Il'ia Iakovkin, *Istoriia sela tsarskogo*, vol.2 (St Petersburg, 1829), p.188.

49. 'Cherty starinnogo dvorianskogo byta. Vospominaniia Mar'i Sergeevny Nikolevoi', *Russkii arkhiv* 9 (1893), p.111-12.

50. *An English lady at the court of Catherine the Great*, ed. Anthony Cross (Cambridge, 1989), p.56.

51. '[...] мы по прекрасной и покойной дороге непременно очутились у Павловской заставы. Она открыта для всякого: никакие распросы не останавливают въезжающих. Полиция не видна в сем городе. Она заботится только об удовольствии посетителей. Она не подозревает, кажется, чтобы мог кто войти в оной с иным намерением как поклониться Матушке, и насладиться жизнию'. 'Vecher i utro, provedennye v Pavlovsk', *Syn otechestva* 24:34 (1815), p.41-55 (44).

Yet one later finds out in the account of this traveller that most structures in the garden were protected by 'retired' soldiers.[52] Similarly,
Count Choiseul commented that the gardens at Tsarskoe Selo were
open day and night to visitors, even when Alexander I was in residence,
yet sentinels guarded the palace.[53] When a peasant arrived at Tsarskoe
Selo to express his gratitude to Alexander II for emancipating the serfs,
he was presented to one of the tsar's aides-de-camp, who chaperoned
him through the park and eventually presented him to the tsar.[54] It
would have been unthinkable, it seems, to allow the peasant to lurk in the
garden on his own.

The rhetoric of openness belongs in part to sentimentalist discourse
about universal human values. Pavlovsk served as the model of an estate
made attractive 'to the most diverse visitors' without undue profligacy.[55]
True to the exemplary function of imperial estate architecture, Pavlovsk
was deemed to pursue a didactic aim, that of teaching proper stylistic
inclusiveness in matters of design. From the outset, in the account of the
above-quoted traveller in 1815, the estate addressed itself to socially
diverse visitors. Incidentally, Pavlovsk also impressed upon the mind 'the
obligations [of the landowner] in regard to the peasants entrusted by
God and by the laws of fatherland to his care'.[56] Tourists could actually
venture so far as the front steps of the palace, from where one could
catch sight of the empress, seated at the dinner table in 'country garb'.
'Only a door, and an open one at that, separated us from the empress',
the visitor noted with astonishment.[57] The next day, in the absence of
Mariia Fedorovna, he and his party easily gained permission to visit the
palace, including her bedroom, where representations of her beloved
parents, children and grandchildren composed an idyllic image of family
life. In Paul's study, a collection of books on botany highlighted the
deceased emperor's commitment to the Enlightenment, which led our
author to ask coyly if 'there exists another kingdom in which the home of
the king would contain as much Enlightenment'.[58] The use of this term
was anything but innocent, at a time when in the wake of the Napoleonic
wars the philosophy of the Enlightenment was seen to be thoroughly
compromised by the behaviour of the French army in Moscow. The Rose

52. 'Vecher i utro', p.52.
53. Uspenskii, *Imperatorskie dvortsy*, vol.2, p.279.
54. Uspenskii, *Imperatorskie dvortsy*, vol.2, p.290-92.
55. 'Vecher i utro', p.41.
56. '[...] почерпнуть уроки обязанностей его, относительно доверенных ему Богом и
    законами его Отечества поселян.' 'Vecher i utro', p.42.
57. 'Одна только, и то открытая дверь стала отделять нас от Государыни'. 'Vecher i utro',
    p.46.
58. 'Было ли, есть ли хотя одно царство, где бы дом Царский имел столько просвещения,
    как у нас?' 'Vecher i utro', p.49.

Pavilion, in which an album encouraged visitors to consign their feelings to paper, indicated that 'virtue has dedicated this summer house to freedom'.[59] Thus the narrative of this visit to Pavlovsk leaps resolutely into cultural wars, advocating an Enlightenment-informed vision of individual freedoms and a kind of social openness and inclusiveness. More importantly, it indicates that Pavlovsk intentionally and visibly blurred the line between the private and public spheres. In an attempt to delineate an idyllic image of simplicity and innocence, it exhibited the family life of the empress to the gaze of complete strangers. The empress' very bedroom was showcased as a monument to sentimentalist virtue. Considerations of theatrical stylisation have invaded the private sphere.

The historian Nikolai Karamzin, who lived for many years at Tsarskoe Selo while writing his *History of the Russian state*, very much endorsed this vision of an essentialising garden, augmenting it with the Rousseau-inspired notion that gardens enable the exercise of a kind of interiority that is otherwise hampered by the bustle of society. About Pavlovsk he wrote:

> I thank the August Landlady of this country house [...] Here, in peace, in the silence of passions, oblivious to the magnificence of the court and to the artificial demands of society, she can be a human being in the embrace of Nature and family, converse with the creator and her conscience, and derive happiness from her memories of the past and her intentions to do good works [...]. In a country house one believes in the truth which emanates from the heart [...]. I do not like the court, but I like tsars and tsarinas when they adorn their conscience with their inner qualities and love country houses.[60]

The notion of nature-rooted authenticity Karamzin posits in this passage looms large in Russian culture.[61] It underpins the nineteenth-century myth of the Russian country estate as well as its recent resurgence.[62]

---

59. 'Она свидетельствует, что сию беседку добродетель посвятила свободе.' 'Vecher i utro', p.51.

60. 'Благодарю Августейшую Хозяйку сельского домика [...] Здесь в тишине, в безмолвии страстей, забывая искуственное веление света и пышность Царскую, Она может быть человеком в объятиях Природы и семейства, беседовать с творцом и совестью, счастливая в минувшем — воспоминанием, а в будущем — намерением блага [...] В сельском домике верят истине, которая изливается из сердца [...] я не люблю Двора, но люблю Царей и Цариц, когда они украшают человечество своими внутренними достоинствами и любят сель-ские домики'. 'Mysli v sadu Pavlovskom', in *Neizdannye sochineniia i perepiska Nikolaia Mikhailovicha Karamzina*, part 1 (St Petersburg, 1862), p.185-86. In the early 1800s, the contrast between reflective Pavlovsk and agitated Tsarskoe Selo becomes a cultural stereotype. See the correspondence of Aleksandr Turgenev, quoted in E. F. Gollerbakh, *Gorod muz: Tsarskoe Selo v poezii* (St Petersburg, 1993), p.80-81 (23 July 1818; 5 August 1819).

61. See A. Schönle, *Authenticity and fiction in the Russian literary journey, 1790-1840* (Cambridge, MA, 2000).

62. See Schönle, *The Ruler in the garden*, p.305-57.

Why did the garden have such high value in the self-presentation of the imperial family and of its noble subjects? It skilfully concealed the traces of deliberate agency. In its emphasis on spontaneous biological growth, on slow unnoticeable change, on the universality of processes, on their stubborn commonness – in its reliance on nature, in short – the garden seemingly eluded the marks of design and distinction that otherwise defined the life of the nobility. To a certain degree the garden naturalises the choreography that unfolds on its grounds.

Countess Varvara Golovina reported in her memoirs that Catherine used her gardens at Tsarskoe Selo to stage games, which contributed to an atmosphere in which 'it seemed that everybody fell into the illusions that are so destructive for young people. This majestic court, this palace, these gardens, and these terraces fragrant with flowers, instilled chivalrous ideas and quickened the imagination.'[63] Unlike Peter, Catherine preferred not to participate in these games, but instead to watch over them indulgently. Casting herself as the spectator of amicable court life, Catherine seemed at once to enjoy the fruits of her 'enlightened' reign and to conceal the power relations inherent in it. In part, these games were designed to turn the court into a simulacrum of idyllic country life, something Princess Ekaterina Dashkova called 'obnoxious sham' ('gnusnoe pritvorstvo').[64] Inevitably they led to non-trivial consequences. According to Golovina, they fostered a kind of erotic dallying that threatened propriety. Thus she relates the case of Platon Zubov, who used these events as an opportunity to court Elizabeth, the wife of the future Alexander I, in a way that endangered the reputation of the grand duchess and the honour of the grand duke.[65] Whether it served rulers to instil a notion of polite conduct, as Peter attempted, or to bask in the role of the emperor benevolently presiding over courtiers allowed, or rather ordered, to behave spontaneously, as Catherine preferred, the garden fostered the strengthening of the bond between monarch and subject. Aristocrats often modelled their manners on the demeanour of the ruler. Emulation is visible in such matters as the aesthetics and use of gardens. Aleksandr Voeikov claimed in his poetic description of Russian gardens:

> The example of the court is holy to grandees and richmen
> And in all of them was born an exquisite passion for gardens.[66]

63. 'Казалось, все предавались столь пагубным для юности иллюзиям. Этот величественный двор, этот дворец, эти сады, эти благоухающие цветами террасы, внушали рыцарские идеи и возбуждали воображение'. 'Zapiski grafini V. N. Golovinoi', *Istoricheskii vestnik* 75 (1899), p.801.
64. Letter to A. B. Kurakin of 28 May 1774, *Arkhiv kniazia F. A. Kurakina* 7 (1898), p.304.
65. Uspenskii, *Imperatorskie dvortsy*, vol.2, p.253-55.
66. 'Пример Двора священ вельможам, богачам; / Во всех родилась страсть изящная к садам'. A. A. Voeikov, 'Opisanie russkikh sadov', *Vestnik Evropy* 68 (1813), p.193.

Indeed, gardens in country estates strengthened social cohesion, as they provided venues for the festivities the landowner organised for his serfs and the formal events for the neighbouring nobility and visitors from further afield. Gardens in many instances showcased the wealth, taste, cultural orientation, political allegiances and even sentimental life of the proprietors.[67] And it was considered proper for a nobleman or woman to call on an estate and ask to visit the grounds even if one did not know the landowners.[68] Visitors then were often asked to stay overnight, if not longer. Indeed, many a nineteenth-century memoirist complained that on such occasion one would often be expected to stay for a week.[69] Ostentatious and coercive hospitality was the norm, and it conferred the estate and its gardens a semi-public dimension. Visits by the monarch were considered so important that they would often lead to the erection of a memorial to this event.

At the same time, country gardens were also perceived as a site in which the strictures of polite society were relaxed, allowing for more spontaneous forms of behaviour, including courtship, as well as fraternising with the lower class. In gardens, landowners and their guests could give freer rein to their inner life and cultivate forms of interiority, such as moral reflection, reading, daydreaming, intimate chatting and so on. Yet upon closer inspection it becomes clear that the garden is never immune to public scrutiny, nor is it fully removed from the logic of representation and ostentation that characterises much of the life of the nobility. Thus it would be a mistake to align it firmly with the private sphere, despite the suggestions of much of the country estate mythology developed in the second half of the nineteenth century and recently revived.

I have written at length on the social and cultural status of country estate gardens elsewhere.[70] In order to illustrate the ambivalent role of gardens in the provinces, it will be sufficient here to evoke a humorous fictional reflection of the public exhibition of private life so characteristic of the way estate gardens are used. The story 'Artemii Semenovich Bervenkovskii' by A. K. Tolstoi, first published in 1845, captures what can only be called the exhibitionist streak of a landowner's enjoyment of his

---

67. For an example of the latter, see Schönle, *The Ruler in the garden*, p.164-217.

68. For the narrative of such a visit at Robsha, the estate where Peter III was murdered, see Moscow, Russian State Library, 'Voyage de Robcha par une société des gens de lettres', f.64 (Viazemskii), 81.10.

69. To mention a few: N. V. Davydov, 'V Spasskom', in *Iz proshlogo*, 2 vols (Moscow, 1913) vol.1, p.203-250 (220, 228); N. Makarov, *Moi semidesiatiletniia vospominaniia i s tem vmeste moia polnaia predsmertnaia ispoved'*, vol.1 (St Petersburg, 1881), p.7, 12; 'Vospominaniia M. K. Arnol'da (1819-1833)', *Golos minuvshego* 2 (1917), p.194-224 (196).

70. Schönle, *The Ruler in the garden*, p.305-34.

gardens.[71] As the narrator's carriage breaks down, he is forced to call on
an estate, where he is taken to a reception room, from which, as he
discovers, he has unimpeded view on the landowner, jogging naked in his
garden, but in his wig and shoes. As he catches sight of his guest, the
proprietor winks at him, yet continues to do his rounds, merely covering
his intimate parts with a sunflower. Following his fitness routine, he
produces a loud cleansing shriek, timing it with his watch. And only then
does he go to meet his visitor, with whom he immediately strikes a note
of familiarity, as if they were long-standing friends. The scene captures
both the eccentricity that the estate garden enables and the ostentatious
nature of this exercise of individual freedom. Despite his nudity,
Bervenkovskii continues to display trappings of his class through his
wig. His strictly timed routine parodies the stylisation of country living
that many a landowner observed during the second half of the eighteenth century and beyond. And his unconcealed enjoyment at being
watched reveals the theatricality inherent in the nobility's everyday life.
Not only does Bervenkovskii give his guest a tour of the gardens, he
detains him for several days for this purpose, as quick fixes to the
technical contraptions he displays on his estate require a renewed visit
day after day. Improvements to the grounds become a pretext to prevent
his guest from leaving. In the end, Bervenkovskii tries to trap the
narrator in his garden labyrinth, a metaphor of the coerced and self-
serving hospitality he dispenses.

The evidence reviewed here indicates the role gardens played in the
second half of the eighteenth century and beyond as a place of sociability, including to some degree across social barriers. Even when this
sociability seems unstructured and spontaneous, it in fact underpins if
not reinforces the social hierarchy, as the pastoral setting only thinly
disguises differences in power and prestige among the social groups
sharing the use of a garden. Even the countryside gardens that seemed to
suspend social etiquette remain enmeshed in considerations of public
representation that compromise their privacy. Thus both city and
country gardens ultimately draw their distinctiveness and their social
potency from the peculiar entanglement of public and private they
evidence. As such, they represent an intrinsic part of the personalisation
of power rampant in court society at all levels.

The extent to which gardens enabled the formation of public opinion
independent from the state is difficult to fathom. This chapter takes as a
premise the notion that, if gardens were perceived as places preserved
from public, in particular state, scrutiny, they could possibly be con-

71. A. K. Tolstoi, 'Artemii Semenovich Bervenkovskii', in *Sobranie sochinenii*, vol.3 (Moscow,
    1964), p.130-39.

ducive to the unimpeded articulation and exchange of political messages. Yet the record suggests that gardens functioned as sites of intensified public gazing as the contemplation of nature often yielded to prurient attention to the activities of fellow human beings. While a few gardens displayed the heterodox political views of their owners, these were few and far between.[72] At once actors and audience of a collective spectacle that seemed often to naturalise social differences and power relations, garden strollers participated, often unwittingly, in the legitimation of a political order that prevented the crystallisation of a genuine private life, thus discouraging the emergence of liberal individuality. The prince de Ligne, himself an enthusiastic gardener, as well as quintessential social animal, knew it well: 'There is no virtue that I do not attribute to him who loves to talk of, and to create, gardens. Absorbed by his passion, which is the only one that augments with age, the gardener daily loses all those other passions that disturb the soul and shake the social order.'[73]

72. I. V. Lopukhin's gardens at Savinskoe and N. I. Novikov's at Avdot'ino-Tikhvinskoe encoded the Masonic views of their owners, for example. See V. I. Novikov, 'Masonskie usad'by Podmoskov'ia', *Russkaia usad'ba* 5:21 (1999), p.225-39. A. B. Kurakin used his gardens to express his stance in court politics, in particular his allegiance to Paul. See Schönle, *The Ruler in the garden*, p.164-217.
73. Charles-Joseph de Ligne, *Coup d'œil at Belœil and a great number of European gardens* (Berkeley, CA, 1991), p.153.

Embracing and escaping the material: genre painting, objects and private life in eighteenth-century France

MARK LEDBURY

That nebulous and ill-defined thing called 'genre painting' (or, more precisely at the time, 'bambochade', 'peinture de petits sujets', 'peinture de mœurs', etc.)[1] has some claim to being the most direct vehicle for the representation of the private and the intimate in the visual culture of the eighteenth century (in France, at any rate, and it is on French art that I will dwell). That we cannot see genre painting as in any way a transparent window on to physical, material life in the eighteenth century or any other century is now so universally held a belief as to be a cliché, and all students are warned off taking it literally. The iconological mindset which is part of art history's claim to seriousness cannot consider a cabbage or a poker without pondering its latent content; at the same time the post-structural wing of art history as a discipline, deeply influenced by trends in literary studies, is deeply suspicious of anything that might be labelled 'the reality effect' and links it firmly and usually negatively with philosophical shallowness or, worse, pernicious and dishonest bourgeois ideology.[2] Nevertheless, when large exhibitions assemble genre paintings in any kind of survey, one cannot fail to be struck by the fact that at the heart of the genre's dynamic anonymous, domestic space is given imaginative life and populated with objects, gestures and spaces recognisable to their contemporary audiences (and sometimes fascinating to the imaginations of later viewers).[3]

1. On the contemporary terms in which genre painting was described see Colin B. Bailey, 'Surveying genre in eighteenth-century French painting', in *The Age of Watteau, Chardin and Fragonard: masterpieces of French genre painting*, ed. Philip Conisbee, Colin Bailey and Thomas Gaehtgens (Ottawa, Washington and Berlin, 2003-2004), p.2-40.
2. For cabbages in Boucher, see Colin Bailey, 'Details that surreptitiously explain: Boucher as a genre painter', in *Rethinking Boucher*, ed. Melissa Hyde and Mark Ledbury (Los Angeles, 2006), p.39-60. For a range of views on Dutch seventeenth-century genre painting which is where the genre painting debates about realism first raged in modern scholarship, see *Looking at seventeenth-century Dutch art: realism reconsidered*, ed. Wayne Franits (Cambridge, 1997). For more post-structural musings on genre painting, see Norman Bryson, *Word and image: French painting of the ancien regime* (Cambridge, 1984) and N. Bryson, *Looking at the overlooked: four essays on still life painting* (London, 2004).
3. See Conisbee, Bailey and Gaehtgens, *Age of Watteau*.

In the context of a collective volume on private lives, I thus want to ask the question: in what way, if any, do we profit by exploring the objects, spaces and processes depicted in genre painting in eighteenth-century France? And might we map these representations in any way onto what we have learnt about the worlds of domestic space, object ownership and relations of people to things in the eighteenth century from historians of the world of consumption and of private life such as Daniel Roche and Annik Pardailhé-Galabrun,[4] and from cultural historians of the object like Carolyn Sargentson, Michael Kwass and others?[5] Specifically, I want to propose that awareness of the spatial, material and decorative realities of intimate existence is crucial to the appeal of a mid-century wave of genre painting which celebrated painting's circulation in the world of goods in its delighted *mise-en-scène* of ownership and the occupation of private, domestic space. I want to go on to suggest that some of the most celebrated of later eighteenth-century genre paintings deliberately refuse such a task.

Daniel Roche and Annik Pardailhé-Galabrun's respective research teams opened up, via the *inventaire après décès*, a vision of what domestic and private life was in terms of its physical structures. In different ways each argued for a progressive move throughout the century towards what Daniel Roche called *confort*. That is to say the acquisition of commodities and greater ease in the living of everyday life, among a wide spectrum of income groups, or what Pardailhé-Galabrun described thus: 'En personnalisant [...] leur demeure par différents moyens, leurs occupants contribuent à l'adapter à leurs propres besoins, et à réaliser, à leur manière, leurs aspirations à l'intimité et au mieux-être.'[6] Whether cooking standing up or making alterations to the room spaces of their dwellings, the argument is that there were physical, bodily and visual markers of a change in the space of private life which went with an aspiration to an enhanced space of intimacy. Moreover, Pardailhé-Galabrun makes it clear in her study that physical and visual embellishment of space by the purchase and display of images (whether oil paintings, prints or other) was also widespread across the spectrum of

4.   Daniel Roche, *Le Peuple de Paris* (1981; Paris, 1998); D. Roche, *Histoire des choses banales: naissance de la société de consommation, XVIIIe-XIXe siècle* (Paris, 1997); Pardailhé-Galabrun, *Naissance*; C. Fairchilds, 'The production and marketing of populuxe goods in eighteenth-century Paris', in *Consumption and the world of goods*, ed. John Brewer and Roy Porter (London and New York, 1993), p.228-48.

5.   Carolyn Sargentson, *Merchants and luxury markets: the marchands merciers of eighteenth-century Paris* (London and Los Angeles, 1996); Michael Kwass, 'Consumption and the world of ideas: consumer revolution and the moral economy of the marquis de Mirabeau', *Eighteenth-century studies* 37:2 (2004), p.187-213.

6.   Pardailhé-Galabrun, *Naissance*, p.270.

incomes. A total of 66.5 per cent of all the inventories her team surveyed mentioned paintings or prints as decoration of private spaces, and 71.5 per cent for the period after 1750.[7] The visual image is, then, profoundly and inextricably bound up in this process of the spread of *confort*.

It is equally clear from the work of Sargentson and others that painting was absolutely and utterly a part of a world of consumption, finely graded, complex, growing and linked to the wider circulation of luxury and decorative objects for the domestic interior.

From Gersaint – who is best known through his association with Watteau as a picture dealer but in fact, as his business card shows (see Figure 1), was a dealer in a range of luxury commodities for the home[8] – to the wide range of *marchands-merciers* whom Sargentson (and before her Courajod) surveyed, painting took its place very consciously in a world of high *luxe* (or 'populuxe' goods), and was understood as a commodity in circulation.[9] My reflections in this chapter, proceeding via some very well-known genre paintings and painters, concern the way that genre painting in France acknowledges or refuses its place within these social and cultural currents, and what might be speculatively said about the objects and spaces of these paintings in relation to a wider history of private life.[10]

I will start with a painter, decorator, collector and supplier of a visual vocabulary to a generation, François Boucher. Boucher's genre work is less well known than other aspects of his oeuvre, but for a period in the 1730s and 1740s he created works which show a finely tuned awareness of both the new world of goods and the developments in domestic space. This is unsurprising in Boucher's case, as this ambitious son of artisans quickly established himself as purveyor of decoration and embellishment

7. Pardailhé-Galabrun, *Naissance*, p.377. She can talk about 'l'omniprésence de l'image dans la majorité des foyers parisiens'. For some extraordinary statistics about the flood of paintings in seventeenth- and eighteenth-century Europe, see Hans J. Van Miegroet, 'Recycling Netherlandish paintings in eighteenth-century France', in *Collectioner dans les Flandres et la France du nord au XVIIIᵉ siècle*, ed. Sophie Raux (Villeneuve d'Ascq, 2005), p.251-88; H. J. Van Miegroet and Neil de Marchi, *Mapping markets for paintings in early modern Europe 1450-1750* (Turnhout, 2006).

8. On Gersaint, see Andrew McLellan, 'Watteau's dealer: Gersaint and the marketing of art in eighteenth-century Paris', *The Art bulletin* 78:3 (1996), p.439-53.

9. Sargentson, *Marchands merciers*; *Livre-journal de Lazare Duvaux, marchand-bijoutier ordinaire du roy, 1748-1758*, ed. Louis Courajod (Paris, 1873).

10. My thoughts in this chapter accord in certain ways with the work of Denise Amy Baxter on Jean-François de Troy, whose *tableaux de mode* she has explored convincingly in the context of post-Law consumerism. there is much in her thinking that overlaps with my own. See especially her excellent 'Fashions of sociability in Jean-François de Troy's tableaux de mode, 1725-1738', in *Performing the 'everyday': the culture of genre in the eighteenth century*, ed. Alden Cavanaugh (Newark, DE, 2007), p.27-46.

Figure 1: 3686.1.56.103; François Boucher; *Trade card of Edme Gersaint, a jeweller, A la Pagode* [1740], Waddeston, The Rothschild Collection (the National Trust). Image: University of Central England Digital Services, © The National Trust, Waddeston Manor.

in many ways from book illustration to tapestry cartoons to theatre and porcelain designs.[11] Boucher's *The Milliner: morning* (see fig.2, p.192) is one of the most striking of his genre paintings, produced in response to a commission from Queen Louise Ulrike of Sweden.[12]

The series was envisioned thus:

> Morning will be a woman who has finished with her hairdresser, but is still in her peignoir, enjoying examining knickknacks displayed by a milliner. Midday, an encounter in the Palais Royal between a lady and a wit reading her some dreadful poem calculated to bore her, so that she indicates the time by her watch. The sundial showing noon in the background. After dinner, or the evening, gives us the most difficulty – either notes brought to arrange a rendezvous, or mantles, gloves, etc., being given by the lady's maid to her mistress wishing to pay calls. Night can be shown by some giddy young women in ball gowns, making fun of someone who is already asleep.[13]

But the fact that this was due to be part of a very worldly, urban, consumerist, intimate reworking of the (mythological or pastoral) times of day tradition is perhaps less important here than the fact that François Boucher, enemy of truth in the view of Diderot, clearly demonstrates a keen awareness of the material realities, circumstances and social habits of the class who patronised his work. More than this though, Boucher's chronicling of material culture of private life for this elite group is playfully conscious of his, and painting's, own role in this circuit.

If we examine *The Milliner: morning* we find that this 'fabrication' is a kind of celebration of fabric and of material exchange, and indeed a celebration of the status and knowledge of those purveyors of luxury. Milliners were not here sellers of hats (the French is 'marchande de modes'), but transformers of fabric into a range of goods from caps to gloves to ribbons, sashes, gowns and other accoutrements.[14] Predominantly women, the expert sellers were both salespeople and trusted advisers, whose adept transformation of imported and well-sourced fabric into elegant accessories made them a specialised, sought-after and elevated kind of merchant. Here the interest is surely in the sense of the complicity – complicity between women whose

11. On Boucher, see especially the exhibition catalogue, *François Boucher*, ed. Alastair Laing (Paris, 1986-1987); Melissa Hyde, *Making up the rococo: François Boucher and his critics* (Los Angeles, 2006); Jo Hedley, *François Boucher: seductive visions* (London, 2006).

12. For the complete circumstances of the commission, see Laing, *François Boucher*, p.224-29. For recent discussion of the painting, see especially Conisbee, Bailey and Gaehtgens, *Age of Watteau*, p.116-19; *Intimate encounters: love and domesticity in eighteenth-century France*, ed. Richard Rand (Hanover, NH, 1997).

13. Cited from Laing, *François Boucher*, p.224-25.

14. See Kimberley Krisman Campbell, 'The face of fashion: milliners in eighteenth-century visual culture', *British journal for eighteenth-century studies* 25:2 (2002), p.157-71.

Figure 2: François Boucher, *The Milliner: morning* (1746). © Nationalmuseum, Stockholm.

equality in elegance is thematised by the play of blue satins and the mass of fabric which joins the women in a material union, creating a material space of intimacy and understanding as well as suggesting negotiation, measurement and even judgement. The space itself is made both boutique and boudoir. The polyvalent space of most artisanal dwellings is perhaps ironically displaced up the income and social bracket in this visit, in which the luxury-service trades enter the space of greatest intimacy, the bedroom. The comfortable chairs, themselves high fashion, are subtly given prominence by the witty conceit that the *marchande* has to kneel because the cat has taken up its unmovable position on the chair that otherwise might have been used in the business. A beautiful visual play allows the rectilinear lines of the *marchande*'s box of wares, round and out of which curl the fabrics to echo the architectural space out of and around which are wrapped the fabrics of the women's dresses, the wall coverings and the table coverings. All these details lead us to the sense of a painter perfectly in tune with both the interiors of aristocratic and noble dwellings of fashion and the underlying economy of luxury and display developing in Paris in mid-century. But there is deliberate complicity on the part of the painter, an absolute understanding of his own place in this economy that is signalled by his signing of the painting on the box of goods. As Melissa Hyde argues, Boucher seems pleased to associate himself with the 'embellishments and *agréments* that the critics held in so much contempt'.[15] Moreover, he aligns himself with the commerce and with the position of the *marchande*; this very picture was the product of an interaction with a royal lady of fashion and education (Crown Princess Louisa Ulrike of Sweden) and Boucher's equal but supplicant *marchande* is a good natured self-portrait of the artist as purveyor of decoration and embellishment and participant in a privileged economy of circulation of luxury goods. By sneaking himself into the boudoirs of the fashionable, he becomes witness to and part of the new patterns of consumption and display which shaped a certain Parisian private life at mid-century.

We next turn to a painting owned and cherished by the broker of the Louisa Ulrike commission, Count Carl Gustav Tessin, the crown princess' envoy in France: the *Lady fastening her garter* (see fig.3, p.194). This painting has far more of a sense of a *grivois* narrative running through it, and thematises the import trades and their sway over Parisian fashion (by enclosing the pair of women within a kind of lacquer box formed out of screens and folds, all in *chinoiserie* taste).[16] There is a sense of what might

---

15. Hyde, *Making up the rococo*, p.53.
16. See Laing, *François Boucher*, p.195-96; Conisbee, Bailey and Gaehtgens, *Age of Watteau*, p.222-23.

Figure 3: François Boucher, *Lady fastening her garter* (*La Toilette*) (1742). Museo Thyssen-Bornemisza, Madrid.

be called 'wrapping' here in the painting. The garter tie, the powdering mantle, the dangling ribbons all seem to hesitate between lascivious narrative drive and a strange celebration of the cluttered spaces of intimacy together with the gestures of complicity that define privileged relationships in private life. And again, the odd rhyming of the two women, their *mouches*, their angles and the elevation of the servant vis-à-vis the lady, speaks to a certain kind of complicity, equality even, created by the very fabric and space. All of this may ultimately be in the service of voyeuristic pleasure, and the male presence is signalled in the assemblage of fire implements which are also painterly stand-ins arranged above the signature. These inscribe Boucher's complicity, his presence in this economy of goods and gestures, his awareness of his own place in both the celebration of and, in a sense, the creation of the aesthetics of private life for an elite patron class.[17] Once again, while it is possible to insert this painting into both times-of-day and seasons traditions, we must recognise its transformation of these 'natural' cycles into interior space, far from the light of day or any vocabulary of the natural world. In doing so, Boucher celebrates, in however ironic a way, the fact that the world, the very identity of the fashionable young woman, is in fact created out of the artifice of objects and interiors, and links this artifice with the skill of the craftsman, and with painterly artifice and skill.[18] There is 'excess', here, too, as if Boucher were himself creating a visual inventory of objects as a counter-narrative or parallel cultural narrative to the possible 'novelistic' intrigues hinted at by the letter on the mantelpiece, the door left ajar and the complicit glance.

Another painting of this type has as its very subject, I believe, elite consumerist sensibility. This is Boucher's *Lady on a day bed*, often referred to without any real evidence as a 'portrait of the artist's wife' (see fig.4, p.197). This painting is a 'sleeping spinner' for the consumer generation: it creates a material frame, almost a box, for its subject, out of which she, like much else, protrudes, drips, dangles or flaps in the painting as if to defy the rectilinear and escape its frame. This creates an atmosphere of defiant conquest of moral and social constraint facilitated by access to luxury and economic power, made apparent in the fabric and compo-

---

17. It is impossible to deny the painting's participation in circuits of scopophilia, explored in relation to certain pornographic images in eighteenth-century French visual culture by Mary Bellhouse and others. See Mary Bellhouse, 'Erotic "remedy" prints and the fall of aristocracy in eighteenth-century France', *Political theory* 25:5 (1997), p.680-715; On Boucher, voyeurism and the gaze, see also Candace Clements, 'The Academy and the other', *Eighteenth-century studies* 25:4 (1992), p.469-94, and Hyde, *Making up the rococo*.

18. Again the best overall discussion of Boucher's involvement with the 'feminine' world of make up is Hyde, *Making up the rococo*.

sition of the painting itself. Can one go as far as to say that Boucher's genre moment is a sophisticated attempt to both render that new confident process of identity formation which Michael Kwass has called 'the reflective self, which consciously pursues the project of its own construction'[19] and hitch his own painting to this project?

All these paintings are, I think, the product of an artist deeply attuned to the material processes of his moment. But they are also a response to artistic trends. Boucher's work seems to draw some inspiration from the richly object-filled, ludic and bafflingly complex productions of English 'modern-life painting' in Hogarth's idiom.[20] But they are also to be understood as a response to another way of figuring material realities of French life, as developed by Chardin, who is predominantly known as a still-life painter but created genre paintings (paintings of human figures in domestic activities and spaces) between 1735 and 1748. Scholarship finds itself confounded and overwhelmed by Chardin's 'magic', or attempts a moralising ideas-based interpretation derived from iconological approaches developed by de Jongh and others for Dutch genre painting.[21] But, despite the magic and the stillness that can inspire philosophical reflection, we should be aware that Chardin's still-life and genre work are both attentive to and indeed preoccupied with objects and the spaces of intimacy; moreover, the interaction between people and objects in domestic space is the constant theme of his painting. Work by Marie-Laure de Rochebrune and others has made the connection between the actual disposition of Chardin's home, the objects he owned and those depicted in his paintings.[22] But more interestingly Chardin is, in his way, as attuned as Boucher to the changes in the manufacture and ownership of goods and their circulation and 'transfer'. His attention to tin-glazed earthenware, for example, reveals a consciousness of its movement into bourgeois interiors in the first third of the eighteenth

19. Michael Kwass, 'Big hair: a wig history of consumption in eighteenth-century France', *American historical review* 3:3 (2006), accessed from www.historycooperative.org/journals/ ahr/111.3/kwass.html on 17 March 2010, para. 51.

20. On relationships between Hogarth's painting and French thought and art, see especially Robin Simon, *Hogarth, France and British art* (London, 2007).

21. For the 'magic' interpretation, see especially the entries on the genre paintings in the latest catalogue by Pierre Rosenberg, *Chardin* (London, 2000); for the 'moral' interpretation, see Ella Snoop-Reitsma, 'Chardin and the bourgeois ideals of his time', *Nederlands Kunsthistorisch Jaarboek* 24 (1973), p.147-243. For a brilliant and concise discussion of the more recent Chardin literature, see Frédéric Ogée, 'Chardin's time: reflections on the tercentenary exhibition and twenty years of scholarship', *Eighteenth-century studies* 33:3 (2000), p.431-50.

22. Marie-Laure de Rochebrune, 'Ceramics and glass in Chardin's paintings', in *Chardin*, ed. P. Rosenberg (2000), p.37-53.

Figure 4: François Boucher, *Lady on a day bed*, presumed portrait of Mme Boucher (1743). © The Frick Collection.

century, which is attested to by the inventories catalogued and analysed by Pardailhé-Galabrun.[23] More specifically, Chardin seems to choose objects that are 'freshly minted', part of the manufacturing explosion in *objets de confort*, an important part of French cultural self-assertion in the early and mid-century – specifically those from the Chantilly porcelain factory founded by the prince de Condé in 1730.[24] In a sense, these highly contemporary, 'of the moment', material presences might be seen to contradict the oft-remarked on 'timelessness' or 'suspended' quality of Chardin's painting. They are chronicles of a specific moment in the history of objects and their circulation, of the organisation of domestic space as current and as attuned to the new world of objects as those of Boucher, but intended for the sphere of the 'third estate' who famously were supposed to recognise themselves in Chardin's work.[25] In fact, we might cheekily compare Chardin's *Domestic pleasures* (see fig.5, p.199) with Boucher's *Lady on a day bed*.

After all, Chardin's painting was a commission by the very same Crown Princess Ulrike who so prized François Boucher. In Chardin's painting, whatever its air of modest bourgeois gravitas, the objects tell a tale not too dissimilar, if more subtly told, of the increase in *confort* made available by the circulation of goods (often imported and hybridised) and of the activities that form part of the new networks of leisure and comfort – reading and reflecting, relaxing in comfort. Here the bourgeois well-run home is the space of both luxury and thrift, both industry and leisurely idleness – what might even be called the space of the reflective self. In this picture, the model is much more likely to be Chardin's wife than the model of the *Lady on a day bed* is to be Mme Boucher, but other details too are domestic – the elegant corner cupboard for instance, which was part of Chardin's own domestic decor, is conspicuous. More interestingly, the porcelain (Japanese or Chinese) jar, probably placed in a silver mount of French origin, is a classic piece of contemporary decor. It is the product of the particular cannibalising and combining traits of *marchand-mercier* trade described in detail by Carolyn Sargentson.[26] This is a fluid and to an extent hybrid scene – leisure, industry, luxury, decorum, the signs of all of these flow in layers through the painting. Chardin's stress and tone are of course different from Boucher's, but are, arguably, a similar chronicle of the movement of what Lisa Jardine called 'worldly goods', together with a sense in which lives, behaviour, times and spaces are shaped by the commerce and

---

23. See Pardailhé-Galabrun, *Naissance*.
24. Rochebrune, 'Ceramics and glass', p.43-44.
25. See below for full citation.
26. See Sargentson, *Marchands merciers*, p.66-70.

Figure 5: Jean-Baptiste-Siméon Chardin, *Domestic pleasures* (1746). © Nationalmuseum, Stockholm.

presence of objects.[27] It is, of course, almost a heresy to compare Chardin and Boucher, after the powerful and long-lasting interventions of Diderot.[28] In fact, their preoccupations with the nature of domestic interior space and how the rhythms of private lives are shaped by the material and commercial environment of their moment link them as clearly as their shared elite patron class.[29]

Chardin, too, seemed to acknowledge the role of painting and the painter in the circuits of consumption. His attitude to the painter's role, though, is markedly different, however. Let us examine one of the most compelling and beautiful of Chardin's genre paintings, *Les Aliments de la convalescence* (see fig.6, p.201), in which a woman servant, acting as nursemaid, peels an egg which is going to be part of a cure, we assume, for an unseen convalescent (the intended object of the meal remains totally unknown apart from the title).

But what we see apart from a glorious exercise in white tones is a collection of objects and furniture which convey a narrative of quotidian processes. We assume that the egg has emerged from its boiling at the fireplace in the long-handled pan, still steaming, that it has been removed and cooled in the earthenware pot and is going to join its already prepared companion as part of a meal for a sick charge. There is a recognition of the ways in which the rhythms of life are dictated by elements (fire, water, air) by the tools and materials and configurations of domesticity. But beyond this there is a deliberate conflation of the materials of painting and the materials and objects depicted. By the use of flecks of raw paint to depict the peelings of shell, by the use of paint glazes in a kind of game with the glazing on the various implements, there is a recognition of painting itself as a chemical, material process, painstaking and not to be hurried. And if not for the first time, then probably for the last, Chardin, whose working methods were notoriously slow and patient, here allies not only himself with domestic labour but his art with the very materials and stuff of the domestic sphere. This is something he seems to have done explicitly in other paintings or pairs of paintings. For instance, one painting he returned to repeatedly was the *Young student drawing* (see fig.7, p.203), in which the

---

27. Lisa Jardine, *Worldly goods: a new history of the Renaissance* (London, 1996).
28. On these see M. Hyde, 'Introduction', in *Making up the rococo*; Hyde and Ledbury, *Rethinking Boucher*.
29. I am not the first to wish to compare Boucher and Chardin's genre works of the 1730s and 1740s more closely – Colin Bailey said as much in his 'Anglo-Saxon attitudes: recent writings on Chardin', in *Chardin*, ed. P. Rosenberg (2000), p.91-92, though our angles of comparison are very different. Since the writing of this chapter, a catalogue has appeared whose insights more closely parallel my own ideas. See Anne Dulau, Christoph Vogtherr and Ann Eatwell, *Boucher and Chardin, masters of modern manners* (London, 2008).

Figure 6: Jean-Baptiste-Siméon Chardin, *The Attentive nurse* (*c*.1738). Samuel H. Kress Collection, image courtesy National Gallery of Art, Washington.

young man in his outdoor clothes is hunched over a task not traditionally carried out in such a physical position (indeed, other pictures of young draftsmen, such as that by Nicolas-Bernard Lépicié, show drawing as an altogether less arduous labour).

There is a real sense, from the bold impasto flecks, the canvas and palette knife, that actually we are watching the physical training labour not just of a young draftsman but of a would-be painter, and that the academic drawing of a male (oddly placed on the wall and not on any kind of support), is a kind of 'master', a figure of the Academy, or other authority in the studio.[30] Thus the trainee artist, who we assume is cold because his coat, hat and boots remain on indoors, becomes an impecunious servant figure, placed in a hierarchy. Chardin's own narrative of becoming a painter reflects this sense of arduous work.[31] Painting and servitude thus become linked in this image, so often repeated that it seems of particular poignancy for Chardin. An opposite movement which reinforces the link between the artist and servant occurs in those works in which Chardin, when dealing with servant figures or women involved in domestic labour, chose particularly painterly ways of casting their work. One such is the *Embroiderer* (see fig.8, p.204) which, it seems, was on at least one occasion displayed as a pendant to the *Young student drawing*.[32] In the *Embroiderer* the colours of the balls of wool in the box, together with the tilted yardstick, echo – if not explicitly conjure – the painter's apparatus (palette and easel).

And in the near contemporary [Kitchen Maid] (see fig.9, p.205) Chardin uses raw paint flecks in a pointed way to associate paint with peelings of discarded vegetable and the act of painting with the quotidian and servile act of peeling. There is, I would argue, in Chardin's genre painting a conscious identification of painter, and painting, with the patient and laborious spaces of the maid, servant and hired hand of one kind or another. If Boucher figures the painter as *marchand-mercier*, Chardin's parallel is with the servant.

This is a much less subtle discussion of Chardin's self-identification with the subjects of his painting than that to be found in Rene Démoris's

---

30. For a moving discussion of the *Young student drawing* in a different, religious context, but which also stresses the relationship between paint and blood, between material reality and painted representation, see Thomas Crow, 'Chardin at the edge of belief: overlooked issues of religion and dissent in eighteenth-century French painting', *Studies in the history of art* 72 (2007), p.91-103.

31. Cited by Diderot in his *Salon de 1765*, ed. Else-Marie Bukdahl and Annette Laurenceau (Paris, 1984), p.25.

32. See *Chardin, 1699-1779*, ed. Pierre Rosenberg (Paris, 1979), p.225-28; and *Chardin*, ed. Pierre Rosenberg (2000), p.196-97.

Figure 7: Jean-Baptiste-Siméon Chardin, *Young student drawing* (*c.*1733-1738). Kimbell Art Museum, Fort Worth. © image@RMN / Art Resource NY.

Figure 8: Jean-Baptiste-Siméon Chardin, *Embroiderer* (1733-1734). © Nationalmuseum, Stockholm.

Figure 9: Jean-Baptiste-Siméon Chardin, *The Kitchen maid* (1738). Samuel H. Kress Collection, image courtesy National Gallery of Art, Washington.

work, of course.[33] But I take issue with his claim in his complex essay on Jansenism, pictorial theory and Chardin that 'Chardin tends to de-socialise the object he is representing, to cut it off from anything that could connect it to a history and a culture',[34] a point which seems to tie his views to Thomas Crow's argument that 'Middle-class life evidently held no great interest [for him]' and discussion of Chardin's 'careful exclusion of all but the most minimal references to the contemporary world beyond his interiors, of sexual and power relations among adults'.[35]

My aim in pointing out just how much objects matter in their creation of the conditions of private life in Chardin is to nuance these 'asocial', dematerialised histories of Chardin but also to counter the tendency of much of the most sophisticated commentary on Chardin. There is a consensus on the inadequacy of simply showing how Chardin transforms Dutch precedents and is rightly suspicious of moralising interpretations of the paintings – and so for that reason insists on establishing his 'magic' absolutely outside subject matter, and in claiming that these paintings are 'timeless', have 'no particular subject' and 'defy all interpretation'.[36] Their subjects are objects and processes, the structures of quotidian gesture and the place of objects in private lives, and these can surely be mapped onto the new cultural historical paradigms of consumption. While one cannot take it as a transparent summary of the contemporary viewers' experience, the striking terms of one commentary on Chardin's figure subjects does remind us that a social and material explanation of these pictures was not far from contemporary viewers' minds: 'C'est toujours de la Bourgeoisie qu'il met en jeu. Il ne vient pas là une Femme du tiers-état qui ne croie que c'est une idée de sa figure, qui n'y voie son train domestique, ses manières rondes, ses occupations journalières, sa morale, l'humeur de ses enfants, son ameublement, sa garde-robe.'[37] I

33. R. Démoris, *Chardin, la chair et l'objet* (1991; Paris, 1999), and R. Démoris, 'Chardin and the far side of illusion', in *Chardin*, ed. Pierre Rosenberg (2000), p.99-109.
34. Démoris, 'Chardin and the far side of illusion', p.103.
35. T. Crow, *Painters and public life in eighteenth-century Paris* (New Haven, CT, and London, 1985), p.137.
36. For Chardin defying interpretation, see for example the subtle, phenomenological account of four of Chardin's figure paintings in Gabriel Josipovici's *Touch* (New Haven, CT, and London, 1996); for timelessness see (among many others) entries by Pierre Rosenberg in, for example, *Chardin*, ed. P. Rosenberg (2000), p.206, 228. For Baxandall's comments about Chardin's banal or unimportant subject matter, see his wonderful pages on the *Young student drawing* in *Shadows and Enlightenment* (New Haven, CT, and London, 1995), p.139-42.
37. *Lettre à Monsieur de Poiresson-Chamarade lieutenant-général au baillage et siège présidial de Chaumont en Bassigny au sujet des tableaux exposés au Salon du Louvre* (Paris, 1741, Deloynes, no. 14), p.33. In Crow's analysis of this text, *Painters and public life*, he points out that this is the only time that a salon critic makes the explicit link between the 'third estate' and painting (p.100).

think then that we might want to consider how Chardin and Boucher interrogate or celebrate the place of the object in private life, the movement of goods, the materials of existence, in the light of research which points to a historical moment in the life of France (broadly, from the rise and fall of Law, to Fleury and to the late 1740s) in which trade and wealth increased, the flow of objects gathered pace, growth rates in exports and imports accelerated and a number of luxury industries flourished. This is what Colin Jones, referring to the period from 1743 to 1756 but discussing a period from the Treaty of Utrecht to the outbreak of the Seven Years War, called 'the unsuspected golden years'.[38] To map their work onto the contemporary inventories (not only theirs but those of a representative sample of merchants, nobles, bourgeois and artists) is to realise with what insistence both Boucher and Chardin chronicle the birth of a certain kind of intimacy which can be cross-referenced with these material studies.

I want now to turn, however, to a genre painter whose career began shortly before the outbreak of the Seven Years War, and in whose work we witness what I am going to argue is a progressive and fascinating rejection of the object as material presence and whose own vision of private life moves away from space, place and object into a different conception of genre painting in which kinship is determinedly stripped of its material circumstances and played out in a world where objects are assigned very different kinds of role. Jean-Baptiste Greuze worked in a period in which the pace of acquisition among all classes increased, colonial trade 'boomed prodigiously' and domestic consumption rose.[39] But what we seem to see in Greuze's work is in fact a diminution of recognisability, a decreasing emphasis on markers that allow contemporaries (and historians) to register or distinguish classes and recognise interiors. I want to spend my final section of this chapter speculating somewhat on the reasons for this change.

Of course, Greuze, just as much as Boucher, is a victim of his appropriation by Diderot. But, undeniably, one of the shifts between the mid-1740s heyday of Chardin and Boucher's genre painting and the high

---

38. See C. Jones, *The Great nation: France from Louis XV to Napoleon* (Harmondsworth, 2002), esp. p.159-69.

39. See Pardaihlé-Galabrun, *Naissance*; *Consumers and luxury: consumer culture in Europe, 1650-1850*, ed. M. Berg and Helen Clifford (Manchester, 1999); and *Luxury in the eighteenth century: debates, desires, and delectable goods*, ed. M. Berg and Elizabeth Eger (Houndmills, 2003); D. Roche, *The Culture of clothing: dress and fashion in the ancien régime*, trans. Jean Birrell (Cambridge, 1994); M. Jones, *Sexing la mode: gender, fashion and commercial culture in old regime France* (Oxford, 2004); Michael Kwass, 'Ordering the world of goods: consumer revolution and the classification of objects in eighteenth-century France', *Representations* 82 (2003), p.87-116.

points of Greuze's career is the well-known aesthetic intervention of
Diderot's dramatic theory and (abortive) practice, in which emphasis was
oddly split between the fascination of the object and a new focus on the
domestic space as a space of a certain kind of fantasy of virtue and the
family in which the dramas of kinship could be played out.[40] That
transition is nicely evident in the opening scene of the *Fils naturel*, in
which Diderot gives us 'un salon: on y voit un clavecin, des chaises, des
tables de jeu; sur une de ces tables un trictrac; sur une autre quelques
brochures; d'un côté un métier à tapisserie', familiar accoutrements
inventoried in the comfortable bourgeois homes of the period. He then
cannot decide, however, how to animate the scene. His character, Dorval,
moves violently around the stage, shifting restlessly between objects in
the most 'un-Chardinian' manner. It is his inner state, his crisis of virtue,
that must draw our attention: the character competes with the objects
rather than interacts with them, and they prove to be the foil to an inner
state rather than the real matter of the scene.[41] We might see that
'tableau' moment as emblematic of a certain set of tensions in the
aesthetics of bourgeois genres. Diderot needs a locatable, recognisable
interior of the household, as aesthetic lure but also as social and cultural
signifier. But Dorval is torn apart by vast and 'generalised' conflicts of a
purportedly universal interiority (love, duty, morals, desire) and no
harmony is possible.

As Greuze's paintings have been exhaustively analysed in comparison
to Diderot's aesthetics, I will not dwell on the ways in which these
canvases too create a fantasy space of virtue.[42] My focus here will be
on the representation of private space and the domestic object in the
large, ambitious, multi-figure paintings of the 1760s. I will mostly be
concerned with the large-scale multi-figure canvases which cemented
and perpetuated Greuze's fame but, in order to make the comparison
with Chardin and Boucher, it may be instructive to introduce a well-
known single-figure painting – the Getty Museum *Laundress* from 1761
(see fig.10, p.209).

40. On Diderot's dramatic theory, see especially Alain Ménil, *Diderot et le drame* (Paris, 1995);
    Derek Connon, *Innovation and renewal: a study of the theatrical works of Diderot*, SVEC 258
    (1989); for the performance history of the two dramas, see Anne-Marie Chouillet, 'Dossier
    du *Fils naturel* et du *Père de famille*', SVEC 208 (1982), p.75-166; on Diderot's aesthetic theory
    see especially the essays and entries in *Diderot et l'art de Boucher à David* (Paris, 1984).

41. Diderot, *Le Fils naturel*, in *Théâtre du dix-huitième siècle*, ed. Jacques Truchet, 2 vols (Paris,
    1974), vol.1, p.6, I.i.

42. See for example Mark Ledbury, *Sedaine, Greuze and the boundaries of genre*, SVEC 380 (2000),
    p.143-59; Emma Barker, *Greuze and the painting of sentiment* (Cambridge, 2004); Régis Michel,
    'Diderot et la modernité', in *Diderot et l'art de Boucher à David* (Paris, 1984), p.110-21; *Diderot
    et Greuze: actes du colloque de Clermont-Ferrand, 16 novembre 1984*, ed. Antoinette Ehrard (Arles,
    1986); Pierre Frantz, *L'Esthétique du tableau dans le théâtre du dix-huitième siècle* (Paris, 1998).

Figure 10: Jean-Baptiste Greuze, *The Laundress* (1761). © The J. Paul Getty Museum, Los Angeles.

   Here, a figure is involved in domestic duties, but all is not what it might
be in the world of objects. Apart from the fact that the social historians
tell us that, for reasons connected with water supply, laundry work was
normally given out to the laundresses who worked by the Seine,[43] we
have other specific issues to ponder. We can leave aside the coquetry and
even the provocation of the fixed gaze and the hands that enjoy the
sensuousness of the water rather than seem to work the washing. What
matters has to do with the play of objects as signifiers and as materials. As
Colin Bailey has pointed out, the beech beetle used to bash out the dirt of
the washing is relegated to a compositional corner, but, more than this,
the earthenware basin and pewter *marabout* are manifestly inadequate to
the task at hand, nowhere near capacious enough to supply the water or
the space to achieve the required level of cleanliness for the amount of
laundry which envelops the laundress. This is not a naive point, since the
very fact that Greuze grew up knowing Chardin (and it has been
suggested that the very pewter water pot is a homage to a similar one
used in Chardin's *The Morning toilette*) means that to deploy objects in a
different way was a strategy, part of a set of changed priorities for genre
painting. We know that Greuze was a capable, indeed a brilliant, painter
of objects and decor from a number of his paintings – think of the *Boy
with a lesson book* of 1757 (National Galleries of Scotland), for example.
Under certain circumstances he was able to chronicle new fashions and
new tastes with specificity, as in his portrait of Auge-Laurent de Lalive de
Jully (1759, National Gallery of Art, Washington) surrounded by his
avant-garde furniture *à la grecque*.[44] The discarded basher and the
prominent mule in the painting, however, deliberately confound any
recognisability outside a certain fictional play. This is Greuze in a ludic
mood, seemingly providing us with perfectly created space. In fact, he is
taking on board the indelicate 'mass' of the washerwoman (pro-
portionally to her surroundings), the awkwardness of her entire posture.
We see immediately that any resemblance to the aesthetic of Chardin is
superficial, and we are witness to a different kind of relation to the
object: indebted to genre painting traditions, but also to popular lore
and custom. The water running through the hands of the laundress
makes her a kind of parody of a water nymph as well as itself using purity
as a vehicle of seduction. Given Greuze's massive ambition and cussed-
ness, the absolute lack of absorption here might be one more element of

---

43. For a discussion of the laundress in eighteeenth-century Paris in the context of this
    painting see Colin B. Bailey, *Greuze: the laundress* (Los Angeles, 2000).
44. On this painting, see especially Svend Eriksen, 'La Live de Jully's furniture *à la grecque*', *The
    Burlington magazine* 103:701 (1961), p.338-47; and *Jean-Baptiste Greuze*, ed. Edgar Munhall
    (Hartford, 1978), English edition.

what could be a parody of Chardin rather than homage. Greuze's earlier works, including the works produced and exhibited during and just after his Roman sojourn, as well as the *Laundress*, bear witness to the genre painter not as *marchand* or servant but as parodist and pedlar of popular jest and fable.

If Greuze's relationship to his elders in the genre-painting tradition and to the labours of the third estate is filtered through ironies, we know too that Greuze felt moved on occasion to 'spoil his manners' in high society. When asked to paint the portrait of the dauphine to accompany his portrait of the dauphin, he is reported to have said, 'je ne saurais pas peindre de pareilles tetes.' As the outraged Mariette reports in his *Abecédario*, 'il voulait critiquer le rouge qui défiguroit les joues de la princesse; mais était-il permis de manquer d'une manière si ignoble au respect et aux convenances? [...] chacun haussa les épaules et regardoit le peintre en pitié.'[45] It would be easy yet perhaps a little naive to associate this outburst with a political programme, but what it might more clearly show is how far Greuze's vision of the relationship of the painter to 'artifice' had shifted – no joyous self-identification with 'make-up' here, and certainly none of Boucher's admiration for the project of the reflective self. Often there is a parodic lack of complicity. Yet at the same time there is an ambition to storytelling on a vast scale, an epic dimension to the multi-figure paintings, which stage the domestic decor not as part of a reflection on the material facts of the domestic sphere but as ambitious commentary on vast social and psychological themes.

Greuze's two genre scenes of the early 1760s, which made his reputation at the Salon, were *Un Mariage* (now often called *The Village bride* but better called *The Marriage contract*) of 1761 (see fig.11, p.212) and *Un Paralytique soigné par ses enfants* (see fig.12, p.215) of 1763.

These canvases have been much analysed of late. I want to add only a few reflections on some material details of their domestic interiors.[46] I have often puzzled over certain aspects of the decor of *Un Mariage*. Where precisely is it set? As Diderot noticed, the scene is not precisely locatable in the social topography of the era. He reports:

Une femme de beaucoup d'esprit a remarqué que ce tableau était composé de deux natures: elle prétend que le père, le fiancé et le tabellion sont bien des paysans, des gens de campagne, mais que la mère, la fiancée et toutes les

---

45. P.-J. Mariette, *Abecédario de P. J. Mariette et autres notes inédites de cet amateur sur les arts et les artistes*, ed. Anatole de Montaiglon and Philippe de Chennevières, 6 vols (Paris, 1851-1860), vol.2, p.331.

46. See especially Barker, *Greuze and the painting of sentiment*, but also Kevin Chua, 'Painting paralysis: "filial piety" in 1763', *Studies in the history of art* 72 (2007), p.152-77, and the many discussions of Greuze in P. Conisbee (ed.), *French genre painting in the eighteenth century* (New Haven, CT, and London, 2007).

Figure 11: Jean-Baptiste Greuze, *Un Mariage (L'Accordée de village)* (1761). Louvre, Paris. © image@RMN / Art Resource NY.

autres figures sont de la halle de Paris. La mère est une grosse marchande de fruits ou de poissons, la fille est une jolie bouquetière.[47]

The location needs to be explained by reference to different, mixed, social strata because the occasion is a bizarre hybrid of private and public, where multiple and compressed parts of a public and private narrative happen simultaneously.[48] Its details, however, are also revealing. If we examine the furniture, we cannot help but notice the differences within the scene where different 'orders' of furniture coexist, and think about the space in the wake of *La Naissance de l'intime* and its stratification of different types of interior. Is this space a rustic village interior or a large prosperous farm building? The improvised safety rail on the stone step, the chipped stone walls suggest modest and aged solidity, but other architectural details (is there the hint of a pilaster?) would argue for something grander, and the strange assembly of the group in a room which serves as salon and food-preparation space would argue for a more modest milieu. The fact that we get to see the stores of bread is, as Emma Barker points out, a nod to the ideally organised farming family and thus to physiocratic ideals of the *laboureur*.[49] They are set far too high, however, and, if we are to believe the economic historians, there are too many to be a perishable comestible for family consumption. Should we therefore infer that this is bread for sale?[50] If so, I would like to contrast this bread bulimia with the anorexic purse, which is supposed to represent the dowry handed over by the father of the bride to the son-in-law. Are we to believe that, in the notarised age of *rentes*, annuities, land-based loans and so on, this bag literally contains the wealth handed over with the daughter? Surely it is a deliberately shrunken symbol, somewhere between a metaphor and a metonymy, but one which speaks of a kind of disguise, a downplay of the complexity and significance of money (and of the economy of exchange) which together with the belaboured references to natural maternal care and tender human emotion (the stock-in-trade of 'affective' genre painting) might be argued to speak to a fantasy of abundance without commerce, of material comfort without goods and trade – a strange utopia? Compare this anaemic, apologetic symbol to the purse dangling from the fire guard in Boucher's *Lady fastening her garter* twenty years earlier, a perfectly

47. Diderot, *Salon de 1761*, ed. Jacques Chouillet (Paris, 1984), p.169-70.
48. Ledbury, *Boundaries of genre*, p.145-46.
49. Barker, *Greuze and the painting of sentiment*, p.58-60.
50. For the average bread consumption rates (a disputed matter) in later eighteenth-century rural France, see the exchange between G. W. Grantham, 'Divisions of labour: agricultural productivity and occupational specialization in pre-industrial France', *Economic history review* 46:3 (1993), p.478-502 and J.-C. Toutain, 'Food rations in France in the eighteenth and early nineteenth centuries: a comment', *Economic history review* 48:4 (2005), p.769-73.

believable material object as well as part of the *grivois* ensemble which mischievously refers to the male presence heavily implied in the scene. We know from the complexity of Greuze's contracts with engravers and his numerous legal proceedings that he was as worldly an artist as any of his generation.[51] So perhaps we should conclude that one of the great efforts of Greuze's genre painting is in the opposite direction to that of Chardin and Boucher, that is, a wilful attempt to deny painting's material nature, its fundamental situation as part of the economy of surplus value goods and services, its place in the world of consumption. But this does not mean a neglect of the task of depiction of goods. In *Un Mariage* we have very simple earthenware on display for the most part – the showy stuff is both seen and not seen, tidily arranged in the modest cupboard. This move to downplay commerce and materiality might easily be explained as part of that aspiration to universality on behalf of his painting which formed part of Greuze's claim to be equal in merit to a history painter, or as the kind of naturalising disguise that Marxist cultural historians have identified as part of the crucial work of bourgeois ideology.[52] Whatever the explanation, the evacuation of material life from the space of representation operates in many of Greuze's major and complex figure paintings thereafter.

Un Paralytique soigné par ses enfants (see fig.12, p.215), presented at the next Salon, shows a paralytic tended in equally unlikely circumstances, in a setting which recalls *Un Mariage* in its structure and hybridity, in its mixture now of ages, with the aged patriarch conferring with his son-in-law and daughter in their twenties, a *mélange* again noticed by commentators along with the fundamental impossibility of knowing precisely what was going on in the scene.[53] Once again I see a confusion of registers of material well-being here. There is a tension between the way that fabric (clothing, sheets, furnishings) is used to indicate a certain wealth, comfort and status and the restrained use of objects in this space. Together with a classicising elongation of both figures and structures, this again seems to cast us into a 'limbo' and transforms recognisability into exemplarity or universality. Here again an exchange takes place which seems significant: the son (or son-in-law) is supposedly feeding the

---

51. The complexities of Greuze's financial dealings with engravers and marital difficulties are explored in Françoise Arquié-Bruley, 'Documents notoriés sur Greuze', *Bulletin de la Société de l'histoire de l'art français* 1981 (1983), p.125-54. The great irony remains that, on the death of Marigny, *Un Mariage* became the object of a heated and secretly discussed bidding war between France and Russia, and was bought for a phenomenally high price by the French crown. See Ledbury, *Boundaries of genre*, p.260.

52. For an elegant summary of the Marxist and post-Marxist concept of ideology, see Terry Eagleton, *Ideology: an introduction* (1991; London, 2007).

53. See Conisbee, Bailey and Gaehtgens, *Age of Watteau*, p.266.

Figure 12: Jean-Baptiste Greuze, *Un Paralytique soigné par ses enfants* (1763). Hermitage Museum, St Petersburg. © image@RMN / Art Resource NY.

father (from a spoon which shines like silver and what seems like a tin-glazed earthenware bowl), but in fact points the spoon towards himself as if the flow of wise words from the possibly moribund figure will nourish his heart. This gestural reversal of the flow of material help – we see not the scene of the provisioning of the ailing father but that of the paralytic imparting wisdom – is another, subtler denial of material realities. It says, 'I give more than I take, even in this helpless physical state.' While we can compare the painting easily to Enlightenment discourses and ideals of care for the elderly, no contemporary commentator recognises or locates the scene as representing conditions that actually pertain as they had done with Chardin. Indeed, the scene as depicted would fit ill with the actual material conditions of the elderly infirm as chronicled by the investigations of Troyansky and others, particularly in provincial France.[54] At the same time the apparently 'charming' gesture of the little boy, presumably a grandchild too young to know, who offers a bird to his grandfather, pushes us further away from the material. The goldfinch is a knowingly symbolic offering, as it figures extensively in a multiplicity of symbolic ways in the history of art – from ward against the plague and as a cure for illness, to figure of the Passion, and symbol of forbearance.[55] Thus what we can read in Greuze is a conscious effort to remove his painting from the material register as well as an open debt to the genre painting traditions that gave him an idiom in which to work. The draw of particularity versus the aspiration to universality; the profusion of moral sentiment versus the lure of the object: these tensions are, I contend, one of the reasons for the uneasy, disconcerting aspect of Greuze's genre painting.

I would like to argue that the examples I have discussed all point to genre painting being in some way inevitably conditioned by the world of goods, and by the growth of private life as the sphere of material exchange and consumption. Devoid of any true theoretic grounding and living in a kind of theoretical limbo, the choices for genre painters might seem to be either an enthusiastic or meditative acceptance of this fact or a complex and multi-layered effort of self-conscious denial – neither of which, one might argue, can be sustained for a lengthy period, which is maybe why Chardin abandoned genre painting and Greuze began to try to escape from it into the loftier realms of history painting almost as soon as the Salon of 1763 was over.[56] And the same dilemma

54. David Troyansky, *Old age in the Old Regime: image and experience in eighteenth-century France* (Ithaca, NY, 1989).

55. See Herbert Friedmann, *The Symbolic goldfinch: its history and significance in European devotional art* (New York, 1946).

56. Of course, Greuze continued to exploit the commercial appeal of his genre paintings and return to complex, non-historical pictures throughout his career after 1763. I would

still faces all of us who try to analyse it: we weave from the material to the symbolic, from idea to object, all the time not quite certain what genre painting is or what it does. This chapter is just one more contribution to this general perplexity but, as we think through how private life is represented in eighteenth-century Europe, I do believe we have to return to fundamental questions of the status and purpose of genre painting in order to create any kind of coherent theory of the relation between private life and its visual representation in the epoch.[57] To do this we must learn more directly from those thick cultural histories of similar visualities, such as Svetlana Alpers' work on seventeenth-century Holland, and from the material and economic histories of painting that have been pioneered by Hans Van Miegroet and others.[58] We must also be prepared to do what has seemed naive or wrong-headed to recent commentators, which is to start to take seriously the objects depicted in genre painting, and to dare to project a self-conscious understanding of the place of the painter and painting in the world of goods as a frame of understanding of the paintings themselves.

---

argue, however, that in the late complex genre paintings the tendency to tension between 'epic'-scale storytelling and material recognisability is heightened even further.

57. Recent collections of thoughts on genre painting include Conisbee, *French genre painting*; A. Cavanaugh, *Performing the 'everyday': the culture of genre in the eighteenth century*.

58. Svetlana Alpers, *The Art of describing: Dutch art of the seventeenth century* (Chicago, 1984).

Eccentricity and the self: private character in English public portraiture

SHEARER WEST

Philippe Ariès and Roger Chartier's magisterial *History of private life* provides a compelling taxonomy of privacy in the Enlightenment, embracing literacy, devotional practices, solitude, the domestic interior, food, friendship and many other characteristics of daily living in late-eighteenth-century Europe. Ariès sums up the history of private life as 'a change in the forms of sociability; from the anonymous social life of the street, castle court, square or village to a more restricted sociability centred on the family or even the individual'.[1] Private life, therefore, is what is carried out at the surface, and is explicitly not about interiority, identity or the self. As Chartier puts it, 'To be sure, the history of private life should not be confused with the constitution of the individual as subject, whether in the philosophical, psychological, or political sense.'[2] Such a conception of private life locates portraiture in an indefinite position. In eighteenth-century England, portraiture was by far the most prevalent art genre, offering a livelihood to the majority of professional artists. Portraiture was a relentlessly public art in both its display and its form. Portraits were exhibited at the Royal Academy and other communal venues; they were made into prints and circulated widely, even among those who were not personally known to the sitter; in private houses they were designed to be seen by visitors.[3] Because they were so ostentatiously displayed and reproduced, portraits seemed to be largely about how people wished to be seen in public, a conspiracy between artist and sitter to fashion an image that would gain positive notoriety for both. Thus portraits were dominated by signs of status and masquerade: military men with their uniforms; families posing before their

1. Philippe Ariès, 'Introduction', in *Passions of the Renaissance*, ed. R. Chartier, p.1-12 (9).
2. Roger Chartier, 'Introduction to "The forms of privatisation"', in *Passions of the Renaissance*, ed. R. Chartier, p.163-67 (165).
3. See, for example, Mark Hallett, 'Reading the walls: pictorial dialogue at the eighteenth-century Royal Academy', *Eighteenth-century studies* 37:4 (2004), p.581-604; Shearer West, 'The public nature of private life: the conversation piece and the fragmented family', *British journal for eighteenth-century studies* 18:2 (1995), p.153-72; and Kate Retford, *The Art of domestic life: family portraiture in eighteenth-century England* (New Haven, CT, and London, 2006).

country estate; women garbed as goddesses; children dressing up as Henry VIII. Portraiture, however, was also a representation of individuals, 'the self *as* art and the self *in* art', as Marcia Pointon so succinctly proposes.[4] In both its public nature and its focus on the individual subject, portraiture therefore appears to lie outside Ariès and Chartier's conception of private life in the Enlightenment.

The exact parameters of 'private life' in the Enlightenment, however, are less self-evident than they might appear. Habermas, writing from a sociological perspective, necessarily confines the private sphere to the 'realm of commodity exchange and social labour', omitting consideration of the Enlightenment discourse of individualism – arguably a philosophical and psychological notion, rather than a sociological one.[5] Although Ariès, like Habermas, located privacy solely in the social sphere, I would argue that privacy is as much about the hidden life and character of an individual as it is about the way that individual behaves in an intimate society. It is equally legitimate, therefore, to consider how the 'self' functioned in private life, quite apart from the commercial and familial relations that concerned Habermas and Ariès. If this is accepted, portraiture, like biography, can be used as a thermometer to test the way in which private character is conceived of and represented in specific historical periods. Turning to England in the late eighteenth century, an increasing scrutiny of individual personality and behaviour entered the public domain through a diversity of print media from intimate and scurrilous biographies to portraits and caricatures. This constellation of activity has been used by sociologists, philosophers, literature specialists and historians as evidence of a fundamental paradigm shift from the individual as a social agent, acting communally in a civic society, to a unique, interiorised and atomised 'self', chasing private concerns at the expense of public good.[6] Various explanations for this transformation have been given, but many scholars concur with the view that political ideology in the wake of revolutions in America and France precipitated the change.[7] A parallel argument has occurred in histories of portraiture.

4. Marcia Pointon, *Hanging the head: portraiture and social formation in eighteenth-century England* (New Haven, CT, and London, 1993), p.1.
5. Habermas, *The Structural transformation* (Cambridge, 1989), p.30. See Frederick Rider, *The Dialectic of selfhood in Montaigne* (Stanford, CA, 1973), p.6, who refers to individualism as 'put[ting] distance between the self and the social world'.
6. Most obviously, see Richard Sennett, *The Fall of public man* (London, 2002); and Habermas, *The Structural transformation*. Habermas' ideas of the public sphere were adapted to the history of eighteenth-century art by David Solkin, *Painting for money: the visual arts and the public sphere in eighteenth-century England* (New Haven, CT, and London, 1993). Solkin notably ends his discussion with the foundation of the Royal Academy in 1768.
7. See Charles Taylor, *Sources of the self: the making of modern identity* (Cambridge, 1989); Michael

While Jonathan Richardson in the early eighteenth century claimed that 'A Portrait is a sort of General history of the Life of the Person it represents',[8] William Hazlitt by 1814 would counter that portraiture is the 'biography of the pencil'.[9] Recognising this shift in perception from Richardson to Hazlitt, David Piper, Richard Wendorf and Nadia Tscherny, among others, have identified a change in the visual rhetoric of the late eighteenth century from Grand Manner idealism to Romantic specificity, with portraitists probing increasingly intimate aspects of individual character.[10] While extremely valuable, such studies tend to seek an ur-moment of modern identity, viewing the Enlightenment as a harbinger of our own notions of selfhood. Even those scholars who examine a *longue durée* do not always acknowledge that selfhood, interiority and individuality have been variously 'discovered' in the Middle Ages, the Renaissance and the seventeenth century.[11] I would therefore like to consider eighteenth-century portraiture, selfhood and individuality archaeologically, rather than diachronically, excavating some contemporaneous circumstances that help convey why English portraiture strained against its public limits from the 1770s until the early years of the nineteenth century. Examining portraiture and selfhood in terms of a discourse on privacy allows a somewhat different take on this ostensible birth of modern identity and reinforces our understanding of portraiture in this complex period. I will tackle two neologisms – celebrity and eccentricity – and two fashions – physiognomy and caricature – that coincidentally came together to threaten portraiture's traditional public role, and will conclude with the case study of Joshua Reynolds' portraits of his 'Club' circle, including those at

---

Mascuch, *Origins of the individualist self* (Cambridge, 1997); and Dror Wahrman, *The Making of modern self: identity and culture in eighteenth-century England* (New Haven, CT, and London, 2004).Wahrman argues that after the American War of Independence an increasingly essentialised and individualised view of self emerged. Wahrman posits 'the shift from mutability to essence, from imaginable fluidity to fixity, from the potential for individual deviation from general identity categories to an individual identity stamped indelibly on each and every person' (p.128).

8. Jonathan Richardson, *Two discourses: an essay on the whole art of criticism as it relates to painting* (London, W. Churchill, 1719), p.1-45.

9. William Hazlitt, 'On the imitation of nature', *The Champion* (25 December 1814), in *The Complete works of William Hazlitt*, vol.18: *Art and dramatic criticism*, ed. P. P. Howe (London and Toronto, 1932), p.74-75.

10. See David Piper, *The English face* (London, 1992); D. Piper, *Personality and the portrait* (London, 1973); Richard Wendorf, *The Elements of life: biography and portrait painting in Stuart and Georgian England* (Oxford, 1990); and Nadia Tscherny, 'Likeness in early Romantic portraiture', *Art journal* 46:3 (1987), p.193-99.

11. See John Martin, *Myths of Renaissance individualism* (Basingstoke, 2004). For another source on pre-Enlightenment selfhood, see also Rider, *The Dialectic of selfhood*.

the Thrale Library at Streatham, where privacy, individuality and selfhood converged in an unsettling and ultimately unstable combination.

I will begin, paradoxically perhaps, with celebrity, which is usually considered a product of public life. 'Celebrity' as a noun signifying a person was a new concept in the Enlightenment, and its semantic connotations distinguished it from a lasting notion of fame.[12] Celebrity as a temporary state, based more on actions than on birth, was fuelled by the prolific growth in print culture and publicly exhibited art in the eighteenth century – a phenomenon that was hugely beneficial to portraitists.[13]

Heinrich Ramberg's print of the 1787 exhibition at the Royal Academy (see fig.13, p.223) gives a potent flavour of the way in which portraiture dominated the annual exhibition, where artists competed with each other for the largest, most ostentatious display of newsworthy public characters, whether they were the actress Sarah Siddons, the prostitute Kitty Fisher, Charles James Fox, the prince of Wales or the duchess of Devonshire. While the public roles of celebrated individuals were discussed, admired or abjured, increasing curiosity about their private lives and character was apparent in such publications as the prurient *Town and country magazine* and an unprecedented array of ephemeral publications that flooded from London booksellers. The duchess of Kingston, whose public life was beset by scandal, summed up the effect of this relentless surveillance: 'This is an age when the prying eye of curiosity penetrates the privacy of every distinguished person [...] The most trivial pursuits of the one [living], and the table-talk of the other [dead] are exposed and narrated.'[14] Leo Braudy, Chris Rojek and Joseph Roach have recognised that the growth of a celebrity culture brought with it a fascination for the unique, the singular and the unusual; it equally fuelled a desire to unpeel the layers of a renowned individual's public facade.[15] While the generic and extrinsic qualities of public figures had long been sufficient fodder for curiosity, surveillance of an ever-more intrusive sort

---

12. See the OED, which cites 'A person of celebrity; a celebrated person: a public character' as the final definition of the word, using examples from the nineteenth century. Published books and pamphlets also began employing the term regularly in this way from the 1790s onwards.

13. See *Joshua Reynolds: the creation of celebrity*, ed. Martin Postle (London, 2005); and *Theatre and celebrity in Britain, 1660-2000*, ed. Mary Luckhurst and Jane Moody (New York and Basingstoke, 2005).

14. *An Authentic detail of particulars relative to the late duchess of Kingston*, new edn (London, G. Kearsley, 1788), p.1.

15. See Leo Braudy, *The Frenzy of renown: fame and its history* (New York, 1997), p.380; Chris Rojek, *Celebrity* (London, 2001), p.9; and Joseph Roach, *It* (Ann Arbor, MI, 2007).

Figure 13: Johann Heinrich Ramberg, *The Exhibition of the Royal Academy* (1787), etching. British Museum, London.

became the norm by the 1790s.[16] Since portraits inevitably represented those members of society who were so severely exposed by scandal sheets and pamphlet literature, one should then ask how, if at all, this new curiosity about both the distinctive and the hermetic attributes of public figures was realised through portraits.

A symptom as well as a catalyst for this wholesale invasion of privacy was the publication of Johann Caspar Lavater's *Physiognomische Fragmente*, which first appeared between 1775 and 1778 and was translated into English from 1789, with at least twenty more English editions published by 1810.[17] It was Lavater who gave portrait painters the tools and the excuse to expose the private characters of their sitters to the public gaze. The subscription list of this lavish edition was vast, and included both portraitists and commissioners of portraits from among the elite. Lavater himself was an obsessive collector of engraved portraits, seeing portraits as a synonym for living faces,[18] and he claimed that 'The most natural, manly, useful, noble, and, however apparently easy, the most difficult of arts is portrait painting [...] Each perfect portrait is an important painting, since it displays the human mind with the peculiarities of personal character.'[19] Lavater's idiosyncratic Noncon-formist perspective led him to an obsessive concern with the minute particularities of his own emotional and moral state, exemplified in the publication of his 'secret journals' in the 1790s, in which he catalogued sudden minor pains in his tooth, his lazy inability to rise from bed to pray each morning and his guilty fixation with writing endlessly in his diary instead of fulfilling his family duties.[20] He justified the revelation of such intimate thoughts and actions by claiming that:

> I should think myself very much obliged to every person who would com-
> municate to me such a *genuine* history of his life, and his heart, interspersed
> with so many trifling incidents, and enriched with such an accurate account
> of bad, good, and indifferent actions and sentiments. [...] Do not all philo-
> sophical historians complain that, as yet, the history of man has afforded so

16. John Barrell, *The Spirit of despotism: invasions of privacy in the 1790s* (Oxford, 2006).
17. See Erik Shookman, 'Pseudo-science, social fad, literary wonder: Johann Caspar Lavater and the art of physiognomy', in *The Faces of physiognomy: interdisciplinary approaches to Johann Caspar Lavater*, ed. E. Shookman (Columbia, SC, 1993), p.1-24 (2).
18. Lavater's collection of portraits is catalogued and discussed in *Das Kunstkabinett des Johann Caspar Lavater*, ed. Gerda Mraz and Uwe Schögl (Vienna, 1999). See also Joan K. Stemmler, 'The physiognomical portraits of Johann Caspar Lavater', *Art bulletin* 75:1 (1993), p.151-68 (167).
19. Johann Caspar Lavater, *Essays on physiognomy*, 3 vols (London, John Murray, 1789-1798), vol.2, p.73-76.
20. J. C. Lavater, *Secret journal of a self-observer, or Confessions and familiar letters of the Rev. J. C. Lavater*, 2 vols (London, T. Cadell, 1795).

little moral advantage, because one knows so very little of their private history, and the detail of their life?[21]

With the lack of 'private histories' to go on, Lavater advocated the study of portraiture as a sort of spy-glass to detect those qualities of individuals that they elected to hide from the public gaze.

Although Lavater was highly critical of the inaccuracy of much portraiture, his extensive analyses of how the exterior reveals the interior was so consistent in method, while inconsistent in detail, that it was, in principle, easily adaptable to the portraitist's art. Thomas Lawrence's judgement of Byron's face is typical of how Lavater's voyeuristic approach to the human countenance could be evoked:

> Lavater's system never asserted its truth more forcibly than in Byron's Countenance, in which you see all the character. Its keen and rapid genius – its pale intelligence – its profligacy, and its bitterness, its original symmetry distorted by the Passions [...] the brow boldly prominent, the Eyes bright and *dissimilar*, – the Nose finely cut [...] the Mouth well-form'd, but wide, and contemptuous even in its smile, falling singularly at the corners.[22]

Lawrence himself, however, did not paint Byron, and it is notable that attempts to realise Byron's insouciance, such as Thomas Phillips' famous portrait of the poet (see fig.14, p.226) eschew the physiognomic signs of cruelty in favour of a more idealised image.

Indeed, Lavater's semiotic approach to the human face potentially gave a new vocabulary to artists and sitters alike, but the implications of his method constrained artists from representing actual features that may have been construed as signs of venality, criminality or cruelty.[23] To counter this, Lavater's facial observations were mercurial enough to resist reduction to a formula, and he himself admitted that physiognomic study was an infinite and elusive science. Despite this check on the specific application of Lavater, his wildly popular volumes fuelled a desire to look closely at physical features for a sign of hidden character. This in itself fostered a more probing approach to the viewing of portraiture.

If celebrity was the impetus for a fascination with the private lives of individuals, and if Lavater provided the tool-kit and incentive for portraitists and spectators to explore the hidden depths of the character

---

21. *Secret journal*, vol.2, p.xx-xxi.
22. *Sir Thomas Lawrence's letter-bag*, ed. George Somes Layard (London, 1906), p.94-95. See also John Clubbe, *Byron, Sully, and the power of portraiture* (Aldershot, 2005).
23. For Lavater as a semiotician, see Christoph Siegrist, '"Letters of the divine alphabet": Lavater's concept of physiognomy', in *The Faces of physiognomy*, ed. E. Shookman, p.25-39, and Carsten Zelle, 'Soul semiology: on Lavater's physiognomic principles', in *The Faces of physiognomy*, ed. E. Shookman, p.40-59.

Figure 14: Thomas Phillips, *George Gordon, Lord Byron* (1835), replica of 1813 oil painting. © National Portrait Gallery, London.

of these celebrities, caricature operated as visual challenge for the portraitist. Although scholars like Vic Gattrell interpret caricature as a personalised form of visual satire, both artists and writers in the late Georgian period saw caricature and portraiture as generically related.[24] Lavater argued that many works of art that were called portraits were actually caricatures, because they distorted the truth, rather than embodying it.[25] This distortion could take the form of grotesquerie or idealisation, but neither, according to Lavater, had the fidelity to the original that portraiture required. This idea was echoed by Hazlitt, whose 1814 essay 'On the imitation of nature' labelled Grand Manner portraits as 'merely *caricature* transposed; that is, as the caricaturist makes a mouth wider than it really is, so the painter of *flattering likeness* (as they are termed) makes it not so wide, by a process just as mechanical, and more insipid.'[26] Within the Royal Academy the artist John Opie called portraiture 'a more respectable kind of caricature'.[27] Caricature was specifically designed to unmask the darker side of public figures by means of metaphor and association.[28] The methods for doing this were restricted to external signs: exaggerated bodies and normally private behaviours such as defecation or sexual intercourse.

Gillray, whose caricatures combined brutally intimate scenes with uncannily familiar exaggerations of the faces and bodies of popular celebrities, began his career as a portraitist. In 1789, for instance, Gillray was among several artists in London who produced a portrait engraving of William Pitt the younger, at a particularly victorious moment in Pitt's political career when the House of Commons passed the Regency Bill (see fig.15, p.228).

At the time, Gillray was advertising himself in London as a 'portrait painter', and this print was intended to capitalise on the contemporary celebrity of the young prime minister in order to enhance Gillray's reputation. It was not intended to be a caricature. To Gillray's dismay, however, his publisher Samuel Fores found much to complain about in this interpretation of Pitt. Gillray's exasperated response is revealing:

> with regard to altering ye Nose, Mouth, Hair, Eyes, Chin &c.&c.&c. which you seemd to think unlike, I must observe, that I have had again two opportunities for examining every particular feature of ye face of ye original – and

24. Vic Gatrell, *City of laughter: sex and satire in eighteenth-century London* (London, 2006).
25. Lavater, *Essays on physiognomy*, vol.1, p.108.
26. Hazlitt, 'Imitation of nature', p.75.
27. John Opie, *Lectures on painting delivered at the Royal Academy of Arts* (London, 1809), lecture 1, p.34.
28. Amelia Rauser's forthcoming work on caricature's ability to 'unmask' is discussed in Wahrman, *Making of the modern self*, p.302-305.

Painted & Engraved by James Gillray.

THE RIGHT HONORABLE   WILLIAM PITT,

Chancellor of the Exchequer.   first Lord of the Treasury, &c.

Figure 15: James Gillray, *The Right Honorable William Pitt* (1789), etching. British Museum, London. © Trustees of the British Museum. All rights reserved.

am convincd that my likeness is a striking one therefore, I will not alter an Iota for any Mans opinion upon Earth.[29]

Fores must have seen Gillray's portrait of Pitt as an exaggeration: Pitt's emaciated frame gawky rather than elegant; his nose curled contemptuously rather than nobly aquiline; his chin feeble; his neck giraffe-like. Gillray, on the other hand, insisted that he had studied Pitt 'from the life' and was offering an accurate representation. Gillray's engraved portrait of Pitt opens up the problem for portraitists who wanted to express the uniqueness of their sitters' physiognomies, employing Lavater's theory if not his method, but had to take care not to exaggerate that distinctiveness and thereby overlay the portrait with the tinge of caricature.

Art historians have interpreted the growing popularity of caricature from the 1770s as a turning away from an emblematic tradition of popular prints and thereby a signal of the transformation to an increasingly individualist society, thus reinforcing the argument that the Enlightenment ushered in modern notions of selfhood and identity.[30] Looking at the allure of caricature from a different perspective, however, this fascination with the deformities and imperfections of the body was a signifier of aspects of private life which generally absent from portraiture. Caricatures served a parallel purpose to Lavater's physiognomy: while Lavater provided a means of reading the face, caricatures ruthlessly exposed the most intimate aspects of the body. Whereas portraiture conventionally was intended to evade disabilities and imperfections, both Lavater's studies of physiognomy and the art of caricature drew attention to these very things. Portraiture, like caricature, was confined to exterior signs, but these were the only reliable signifiers of what was hidden beneath the public facades of celebrated individuals.[31] The outré, the exaggerated and the extremes of the body –

29. Christiane Banerji and Diana Donald, *Gillray observed: the earliest account of his caricatures in London and Paris* (Cambridge, 1999), p.263-64.

30. See, for example, Diana Donald, *The Age of caricature: satirical prints in the reign of George III* (New Haven, CT, and London, 1997); Amelia Rauser, 'Embodied liberty: why Hogarth's caricature of John Wilkes backfired', in *The Other Hogarth: aesthetics of difference*, ed. Bernadette Fort and Angela Rosenthal (Princeton, NJ, 2001), p.240-57; and Wahrman, *Making of modern self*. Although these arguments are part of a recent historiographical tendency, they have been visited in the past. See, for example, Robert L. Patten, 'Conventions of Georgian caricature', *Art journal* 41:4 (1983), p.331-38.

31. See Lisa Freeman's persuasive argument for the way in which dramatists and actors negotiated the new concerns with private character: *Character's theatre: genre and identity on the eighteenth-century English stage* (Philadelphia, PA, 2002): 'we find a medium [drama] obsessed not with the tensions between interiority and exteriority [...] In contrast to the novel [...] the stage offers us a medium in which public exteriors were taken not merely as symptomatic of an interior, but rather as the *only* basis upon which judgments about character could be formed' (p.27).

the hallmarks of caricature – began to creep into popular forms of portraiture, such as frontispieces to biographies of lower-class individuals noted for unusual physical features.[32] Thus the anonymous print of the orotund John Love, bookseller at Weymouth, known for his vast girth, was not unlike Gillray's *A Sphere projecting against a plane* of 1792 which represented Albinia, countess of Buckinghamshire, as a grossly fat woman (see fig.16, p.232 and fig.17, p.233).

The many representations of disabled beggars (see fig.18, p.234 and fig.19, p.235) that accompanied quotidian biographies of the 1770s onwards were no doubt appropriated from representations such as Gillray's ostensible self-portrait caricature of John Bull as a blind man with a peg leg.

These slippages between portraiture and caricature naturally rely on the body as a conveyor of meaning, just as Lavater was to do for the face, but, in both cases, these fashions provided artists with methods with which to probe, unlock and unmask the unique qualities of individuals that were hitherto felt to be outside the realm of the portraitist's art.

Explicit connections between more intimate qualities of the body and of character that in the past had been deliberately overlooked or coyly avoided were encapsulated in another Enlightenment neologism, 'eccentric'. The term 'eccentric' surfaced in a version of its present-day usage only in published writing from the 1780s.[33] While occasionally appearing in metaphysical poetry of the seventeenth century in reference to individuals, 'eccentric' at that time retained connotations of Ptolemaic astronomy – of planets out of line with the orbit of the earth; or geometry – of circles without a common centre.[34] By the 1780s and

32. Such extremes of behaviour and appearance had conventionally been associated with biographies of criminals and other figures on the fringes of polite society. See Lincoln B. Fuller, *Turned to account: the forms and functions of criminal biography in late seventeenth- and early eighteenth-century England* (Cambridge, 1987); Hal Gladfelder, *Criminality and narrative in eighteenth-century England: beyond the law* (Baltimore, MD, 2001); and Cheryl Wanko, *Roles of authority: thespian biography and celebrity in eighteenth-century Britain* (Lubbock, TX, 2003).

33. David Weeks and Kate Ward suggest that the number of eccentrics peaked in the late Georgian and Regency period, but their fascinating discussion fails to take into account how the invention of the term fuelled its discursive usage in print. It was therefore the term itself and its usage, rather than the actual existence of eccentrics, that peaked in this period. See David Joseph Weeks and Kate Ward, *Eccentrics: the scientific investigation* (Stirling, 1985). The only really serious study of eccentricity in this period is *L'Excentricité en Grand-Bretagne au 18e siècle*, ed. Michèle Plaisant (Lille, 1976).

34. Eighteenth-century dictionaries define 'eccentric' and 'eccentricity' almost solely in their geometrical and astronomical sense, using 'singularity' and 'particularity' to refer to odd and distinctive individuals. The OED dates the earliest usage of 'excentric' – in the sense of an odd individual – to 1685, but these earlier uses retain their metaphorical associations with mathematics and astronomy. See, for example, Samuel Johnson, *A Dictionary of the English language*, 2nd edn (London, J. Knapton, 1760); Frederick Barlow, *The Complete English dictionary* (London, the author, [1772-1773]); and John Ash, *The New and complete*

1790s, however, 'eccentric' had lost these associations and began to replace the concept of 'singularity' in referring to oddity or whimsicality. Initially, this oddity could be anything, from the quack James Graham's *Eccentric lecture on the art of propagating the human species* of 1783, to G. M. Woodward's *Eccentric excursions* of 1796, where the 'eccentricity' characterised the distinctiveness of geography and culture, as well as people. But by 1791, when the art critic Anthony Pasquin published the *Eccentricities of John Edwin* (an exceedingly lengthy discourse on an obscure actor's trials and adventures), eccentricity had come to connote odd individuals, and thus broke away from the more generic implications of 'singularity'.[35] Unlike the modern psychological usage of the word, eccentricity in this period had a very wide and sometimes indiscriminate set of connotations, referring to anomaly or difference in all its forms – both behavioural and physical.[36]

Eccentricity, like caricature, was inextricably linked with portraiture and, like caricature, it encompassed details of character and behaviour that normally would have been consigned to the private sphere.[37] The association of the term 'eccentric' with both physical and behavioural characteristics owes something to James Granger's *Biographical history of England* of 1775, which organised biographies and accompanying portraits into twelve classes. The first eleven of these were based on status and profession, with only the lowest class relating to behaviour and appearance. This final class was designated: 'Persons of both Sexes, chiefly of the lowest order of the People, remarkable from only one

dictionary of the English language, 2nd edn (London, Vernor and Hood, 1795). Despite the fact that his *Dictionary* did not adopt this usage of the term, it is notable that to my knowledge Johnson used the word 'eccentricity' twice outside his own *Dictionary* – once in reference to the 'eccentrick talents' of Bet Flint, a prostitute who asked him to write a preface for her collection of poems; and another instance in his *Life of Akenside*, where he associates eccentricity with Akenside's obsession with liberty. James Boswell, *Life of Johnson* (Oxford, 1980), p.1144; and S. Johnson, *The Lives of the English poets*, 3 vols (Dublin, William Wilson, 1780-1781), vol.3, p.329.

35. James Graham, *Eccentric lecture on the art of propagating the human species* (London, A. Roger *et al.*, 1783); G. W. Woodward, *Eccentric excursions, or Literary & pictorial sketches of countenance, character and country* (London, Allen and West, 1796); and John Williams [Anthony Pasquin], *The Eccentricities of John Edwin, comedian* (London, 1791).

36. See Felicity Nussbaum's definition of 'anomaly'as 'a variety of irregularities or deviations from that which is presumed to be the natural order of things. The applications include a range of disabilities (for example, being mute, blind, lame) and of physical and mental oddities (for example, dark skin, pock-marked complexion, eunuchism, giantism) occurring naturally or caused by accident' (*The Limits of the human: fictions of anomaly, race and gender in the long eighteenth century*, Cambridge, 2003, p.1). See also *'Defects': engendering the modern body*, ed. Helen Deutsch and Felicity Nussbaum (Ann Arbor, MI, 2000).

37. Lavater himself was labelled an eccentric by the English editor of his secret diaries (Lavater, *Secret journal*, p.vii).

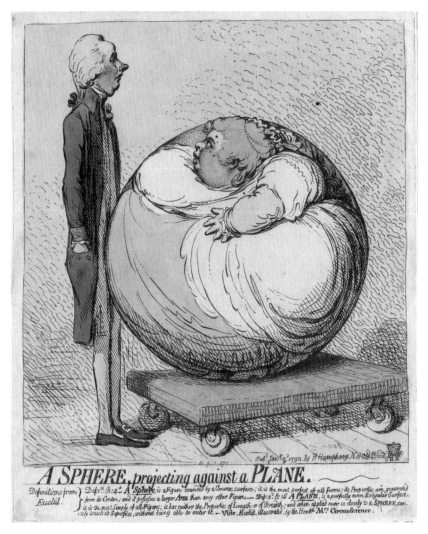

Figure 16: James Gillray, *A Sphere projecting against a plane* (1792), etching. British Museum, London.

Mr IOHN LOVE, BOOKSELLER, of WEYMOUTH,
The Fatest & Heaviest Man ever known in England.

Figure 17: Anonymous, *John Love, bookseller of Weymouth* (n.d.). Author's private collection.

Figure 18: James Gillray, *John Bull and his dog Faithful* (1796), etching. British Museum, London. © Trustees of the British Museum. All rights reserved.

Circumstance in their Lives; namely, such as lived to a great Age, deformed Persons, Convicts &c.'[38] Granger was particularly interested in this bottom class, and argued that penetrating the private selves of all his classes would have a levelling result: 'A skilful anatomist would find little or no difference, in dissecting the body of a King and that of the meanest of his subjects, and a judicious philosopher would discover a surprising conformity, in discussing the nature and quality of their minds.'[39] Granger's categories were adopted by, among others, Henry Bromley, whose *Catalogue of engraved British portraits* matches Granger's character types with existing images.[40]

Although monarchs, nobility, poets and artists did not fall within Granger's category 12, by the beginning of the nineteenth century, Granger-like compendia and extra-illustrated editions of portraits and biographies included all classes of society under the label 'eccentric'.[41] These collections concentrated on extremes of both behaviour and body type. Included among the eccentrics was a man who ate and defecated rocks; rich men who acted poor, such as the merchant farmer who starved his animals; or poor men who pretended to be powerful. People who exhibited criminal behaviour, such as pyromaniacs or murderers, were included in the same category as publicans, actors, prostitutes, authors, tightrope walkers and recluses. Giantism and genius were both subject to scrutiny. A celebrated individual such as Alexander the Great could appear in the same collection as the obscure 'Dirty Dick' who lived in squalor in Leadenhall Street.[42] A physical impairment, such as loss of a limb, was just as prone to be given the eccentric label as exceptional behaviour, and indeed the physical and behavioural were frequently conjoined. In effect, eccentricity in these grangerised collections meant singularity and difference in all its manifestations. Much of the eccentric compendia were concerned with the private lives of individuals – what they ate; how they behaved when in select company; and their daily

38. Rev. James Granger, *A Biographical history of England from Egbert the Great to the Revolution*, 4 vols (London, T. Davies, 1775).

39. *A Biographical history*, p.356.

40. Henry Bromley, *Catalogue of engraved British portraits from Egbert the Great to the present time* (London, T. Payne, 1793).

41. Granger's category 12 became the basis for James Caulfield's collections of the 1790s, including *Blackguardiana* and *Caulfield's remarkable characters*. From 1800 the term 'eccentric' was used universally for these types of illustrated collections, including *An Account of remarkable and eccentric characters* (1800) *Eccentric biography* (1801), the *Eccentric magazine* (1812) and the *Eccentric mirror* (1813). One of the fullest collections of these eccentric compendia is available in the Hope Collection, Ashmolean Museum, Oxford, which includes William Granger's *The New wonderful museum and extraordinary magazine* [1804] and *Kirby's wonderful and eccentric museum* [1803-1820], among others.

42. Granger, *The New wonderful museum*.

habits. Such biographies therefore tended to probe into the minutiae of their subjects' lives. The engraved portraits which accompanied them, however, were subject to limitations. The anonymous and often second-rate engravers who supplied portraits for such eccentric biographies were searching for the signifiers that would satisfy public curiosity, but were unable to do more than nod to the methods of Lavater or the caricaturists.

My argument so far has been that the relationship between Enlightenment portraiture and privacy can be seen as part of a matrix of novelties – celebrity, physiognomy, caricature and eccentricity. While celebrity was the impetus for public curiosity about the private lives of individuals, physiognomic theory provided a method for probing that inner life, caricature offered an unrestrained model for representing the body, and eccentricity encapsulated the growing interest in the odd and often trivial details of individual character. It is worth asking whether this dizzying array of innovations had any substantial or lasting effect on portraiture. Here I would like to turn to the earliest part of my chosen period – the 1770s – and reconsider the unusual and significant portraits that Joshua Reynolds painted of Samuel Johnson and his other friends in the 'Club', including those designed for the Thrale Library at Streatham. Reynolds' portraits were contemporaneous with the fashions I have just analysed, and they are therefore another manifestation of growing fascination with private character, rather than a cause or an effect. These works are symptomatic, I believe, of a skilful portraitist's attempt – against his own public pronouncements – to find a means to unlock the private character of his sitters. The struggle Reynolds had with these portraits, and the brilliant, yet problematic results, reveal both the limitations of the portraitist's art and the ambivalence about representing the exterior signs of character that signalled eccentricity.

Reynolds' assertions about portraiture in his *Discourses* were discussed widely during the last decades of the eighteenth century. The portrait painter should improve the 'lower' style by 'borrowing from the grand', and use generalised facial features, historically ambiguous dress, poses borrowed from the best old masters and vague settings in order to ensure that portraits carried the same authority as history paintings.[43] Although both likeness and general character must be retained in a portrait, Reynolds felt that detail should be avoided. This included both bodily anomaly and idiosyncrasy: 'Peculiarities in the works of art, are like those in the human figure; it is by them that we are cognizable and dis-

---

43. Joshua Reynolds, *Sir Joshua Reynolds: discourses on art*, ed. Robert Wark (New Haven, CT, and London, 1959), discourse 4, p.72.

tinguished one from another, but they are always so many blemishes.'[44]
As many scholars have noted, however, contradictions abound between
Reynolds' theory and his practice and, while he provided a theoretical
foundation for his contemporaries, he did not always practise what he
preached. Indeed, what his admirers often valued in Reynolds' portraits
was their ability to get beneath the surface. For example, William
Combe's poetical epistle to Reynolds' claims that the 'addition of character' is what prevents his portraits from being the mere 'Trash and
Lumber' that consigned most modern portraits to obscurity.[45] Hazlitt
later highlighted this quality in Reynolds' work, but confined his praise to
those 'intimate acquaintances' of Reynolds – Johnson, Garrick, Goldsmith, Baretti, Burney – whose portraits Reynolds painted ostensibly for
his own pleasure, rather than for public consumption:

> Their traits had probably sunk deep into the artist's mind [...] he painted
> them as pure studies from nature, copying the real image existing before
> him, with all its known characteristic peculiarities; and, with as much wisdom
> as good-nature, sacrificing the graces on the altar of friendship [...] What if he
> had painted them on the theory of middle forms, or pounded their features
> together in the same metaphysical mortar? Mr. Westall might just as well
> have painted them. They would have been of no more value than his own
> pictures of Mr. Tomkins, the penman, or Mrs. Robinson, who is painted with
> a hat and feather, or Mrs. Billington, who is painted as St. Cecilia [...] Would
> the artist in this case have conferred the same benefit on the public, or have
> added as much to the stock of our ideas, as by giving us *fac-similes* of the most
> interesting characters of the time.[46]

Hazlitt recognised that it was the 'characteristic peculiarities' of these
individuals that exerted the most fascination for posterity, and it was
Johnson, perhaps more than any other of Reynolds' sitters, who
exemplified these qualities. Reynolds' portraits of Johnson helped focus
and define the idea of eccentricity that emerged at the end of the
eighteenth century as both somatic and behavioural, at a time when the
details of Johnson's private life gradually became the stuff of public
consumption through Boswell's *Tour of the Hebrides* and *Life of Johnson*.

Johnson represented the ultimate eccentric character, as his behaviour, personality and physical appearance projected several categories of
difference. His intellect and conversational abilities were as well known
as his often offensive outspokenness and ready tendency to anger, his
piety, monarchism and charitable generosity. He was stricken with

44. *Sir Joshua Reynolds*, discourse 6, p.102.
45. William Combe, *A Poetical epistle to Sir Joshua Reynolds, Knt.* (London, Fielding and Walker,
    1777), n.p.
46. W. Hazlitt, 'Character of Sir Joshua Reynolds', *The Champion* (30 October and 6 November
    1814), in *Art and dramatic criticism*, ed. P. P. Howe, p.54-55.

blindness in one eye, deafness in one ear and facial scars after childhood bouts of scrofula and smallpox; and he suffered from depression, obsessive/compulsive behaviour, hypochondria and a form of Tourette's syndrome that resulted in nervous tics. Boswell's description of Johnson's physical appearance in his *Journal of the Tour to the Hebrides* gives a flavour of Johnson's physical eccentricity:

> His person was large, robust, I may say approaching to the gigantick, and grown unwieldy from corpulency. His countenance was naturally of the cast of an ancient statue, but somehow disfigured by the scars of that *evil*, which, it was formerly imagined the *royal touch* could cure. He was now in his sixty-fourth year, and was become a little dull of hearing. His sight had always been somewhat weak [...] His head, and sometimes his body, shook with a kind of motion like the effect of a palsy: he appeared to be frequently disturbed by cramps, or convulsive contractions.[47]

Hester Piozzi's remarks about Johnson were equally acute: 'his Heighth was five Foot eleven without Shoes, his Neck short, his Bones large & His Shoulders broad: his Leg & Foot eminently handsome, his hand handsome too, in spite of Dirt, & of such Deformity as perpetual picking his fingers necessarily produced.'[48]

Boswell and Piozzi's biographies were based on observations formed in private, on conversations held in intimate circumstances, and on their own voyeuristic fascination with Johnson's peculiarities and the abjection of his body. To an extent, this fascination with private life had its roots in Johnson's own theory of biography, as outlined in a *Rambler* essay written early in his career. Johnson claimed that the lessons of biography were more likely to be drawn from private life: 'The business of the biographer is often to pass slightly over those performances and incidents, which produce vulgar greatness, to lead the thoughts into domestick privacies, and display the minute details of daily life, where exterior appendages are cast aside, and men excel each other only by prudence and by virtue.'[49] Unlike Lavater, however, Johnson's focus was on those quotidian moments that unite all human beings, rather than those that distinguish them from each other.[50] In this he differed from

47. J. Boswell, *The Journal of a tour to the Hebrides*, 2nd edn (London, Henry Baldwin, 1785), p.9.
48. Hester Piozzi, *Thraliana: the diary of Mrs. Hester Lynch Thrale 1776-1809*, ed. Katherine Balderston, 2 vols (Oxford, 1951), vol.1, p.189 (entry dated December 1777).
49. S. Johnson, *The Rambler*, 6 vols (London, J. Payne, 1752), vol.2, no.60, p.211.
50. For a discussion of Johnson's view of private life in biography, see Robert Folkenflik, *Samuel Johnson biographer* (Ithaca, NY, and London, 1978), p.30: 'His work rests on the assumption that men are essentially similar and that the business of the biographer is to relate those facts which are common to human experience.' See also Martin Maner, *The Philosophical biographer: doubt and dialectic in Johnson's 'Lives of the poets'* (Athens, GA, 1988); and *Domestick privacies: Samuel Johnson and the art of biography*, ed. David Wheeler (Lexington, KY, 1987).

his own biographers, Piozzi and Boswell, whose obsessions with private life were designed to represent Johnson's uniqueness. The intimacy and specificity of their scrutiny were satirised in the outrageous *More last words of Dr Johnson* of 1787, which recognised that curiosity about private life could go too far. This pamphlet, written by the pseudonymous 'Francis, barber', Johnson's alleged wigmaker (so named to distinguish him from Francis Barber, Johnson's famous black servant), included a letter from a putative doctor who had studied Johnson's faeces. This doctor justifies his invasion of privacy in mock-medical terms: 'I have not thought it beneath me to inspect the water-closets of the learned. Such a custom may be ridiculed by the superficial, but the sensible and erudite will applaud that curiosity which looks into the *bottom* of things, and which must of course be *fundamentally* learned.'[51] The epistle further describes how the doctor spied unobserved on Johnson when he crept away to the underbrush to relieve himself:

> I plainly observed the Doctor unbutton his breeches, and if I may use the expression, stand in a sitting posture behind the hedge, for the laudable purpose of easing nature. I observed there was a great mole on the right cheek of his posteriors, which were very large; a circumstance that Mrs. Piozzi, who ought to know the fact, has neglected to make public. The sight was extremely sublime, and inspired me with emotions of awe and admiration, similar to those which I feel upon the perusal of Milton's *Il Penseroso* or the *Inferno* of Dante.[52]

This episode has overtones of the scatological excess of caricature, but equally it reveals an awareness of the inappropriate exposure of private life that characterised Johnson's circle of friends.

Like Piozzi and Boswell, Reynolds was seemingly fascinated by Johnson's private quirks but, in a written character sketch of Johnson, his ambivalence about observing them was more apparent. Attributing Johnson's alleged rudeness to a zeal for truth, Reynolds commented on the proper limits of biography:

> This caution appears to be necessary to a biographer, supposing the biography to consist in anecdotes, as in Dr. Johnson's case:–to proportion the eccentric parts of his character to the proportion of his book. A short book containing an account of all the peculiarities and absurdities of a man would leave on the reader's mind an impression of an absurd character. That Johnson was rude at times cannot be denied, but by reading any account of him you would shrink at the idea of being in his company. Every prominent part of a man's character, every eccentric action when exerted, counts for ten, like some particular cards in a game. Ten negatives amount to one

51. Francis, barber, *More last words of Dr. Johnson*, 2nd edn (London, the author, 1787), p.29.
52. *More last words*, p.48-50.

affirmation. I know of no greater inducement to uniform propriety of conduct than this consideration: how much one breach of uniformity cancels a great number of acts of a regular and comfortable consistency.[53]

Reynolds' choice of the word 'eccentric' here preserves the remnants of the term's earlier meaning – the misalignment of planetary orbits – and in appropriating this metaphorical use, he reveals discomfort with singularity. Reynolds' character sketches (which also included Goldsmith and Garrick) were never published and were apparently written towards the end of his life, after Boswell's intimate explorations of Johnson had turned the author into a public commodity. While Reynolds included observations about Johnson that he, like Boswell, had garnered through years of friendship and private conversation, he was clearly uncomfortable about the exposure of too much private detail to prurient public interest. In the same character sketch he reflected on the limitations of his own art with what could be construed as relief:

> From thirty years' intimacy with Dr. Johnson I certainly have had the means, if I had equally the ability, of giving you a true and perfect idea of the character and peculiarities of this extraordinary man. The habits of my profession unluckily extend to the consideration of so much only of character as lies on the surface, as is expressed in the lineaments of the countenance. An attempt to go deeper and investigate the peculiar colouring of his mind, as distinguished from all other minds, nothing but your earnest desire can excuse the presumption of attempting.[54]

Nevertheless, in his portraits of Johnson, Reynolds began to push against the restrictions of 'surface character' imposed by the limitations of portraiture, and was in danger of offending his own principles by overemphasising these 'eccentric parts'.

Reynolds produced his five portraits of Johnson between 1756 and 1782, the same period in which caricature, eccentricity, celebrity and physiognomy were beginning to emerge as fashionable concerns.[55] Although it has been argued – not least by Lavater himself – that Johnson's portraits exemplify the qualities of a superior mind, the portraits are dominated by close attention to Johnson's body.[56] While these portraits refer both to Johnson's literary achievements and to his

53. In *Portraits by Sir Joshua Reynolds*, ed. Frederick W. Hilles (London, 1952), p.78.
54. Hilles, *Portraits*, p.66.
55. The fullest discussion of these portraits is contained in David Mannings, *Sir Joshua Reynolds: a complete catalogue of his paintings*, 2 vols (New Haven, CT, and London, 2000), catalogue, p.280-83; and Wendorf, *Elements of life*.
56. For an example of the argument that Reynolds was trying to paint Johnson's 'mind', see Morris Brownell, *Samuel Johnson's attitude to the arts* (Oxford, 1989), p.87. For Lavater, see below.

singularities, the latter gradually take precedence over the former. The first portrait of 1756-1757 (see fig.20, p.243), produced after the early success of Johnson's *Dictionary*, is in many ways a conventional work, showing the author seated on a patterned chair, with the obvious literary accoutrements of pen and paper beside him on his desk.

Such specificity of setting was rare in Reynolds' other portraits of the same year, most of which contained generalised backgrounds or no background at all.[57] This particularity of setting is accompanied by an equally uncharacteristic observation of expression and pose. Johnson appears to be speaking to someone outside the picture, and his left hand is clenched in a decisive yet tense gesture. Reynolds also represents Johnson's large-boned stature, which was commented on by numerous observers and led to his nickname 'Gargantua'.[58]

Reynolds' next portrait of Johnson, painted in 1769 (see fig.21, p.244), was a more public work, exhibited at the Royal Academy in 1770. Here, an emphasis on Johnson's public success combines oddly with idiosyncrasy in a painting designed to reinforce Johnson's celebrity status. Lavater, who used an engraved variant of the profile portrait in his *Physiognomy* claimed that '[the] nose inclining downward, the contour of that closed mouth, the form of that chin, those half-opened eyes, that air of reflection – in a word, every feature presents, in my opinion, signs of sagacity and meditation.'[59] Reynolds chose to present Johnson in a classical profile, redolent of ancient coins and symbolic of Johnson's appointment as professor of ancient history at the Royal Academy. Such a potentially elevating range of referents is, however, countered by the awkward configuration of Johnson's features and a profile that is neither noble nor inspiring. Reynolds darkened Johnson's eye and gave it a slight cast, alluding to the partial blindness Johnson had suffered due to childhood illness. The profile pose potentially enabled Reynolds to occlude this disability, but he clearly chose not to. Furthermore, Johnson's hands are contorted in a gesture that is more spastic than oratorical, reminding the viewer of his characteristic nervous tics, or what Reynolds himself referred to as his 'strange antic gesticulations'.[60] Although this was painted well before the English translation of Lavater's *Physiognomy*, the use of the profile here anticipates the rage for silhouettes

57. For a comparison of the portraits produced in this year, see Mannings, *Reynolds*, volume of plates.
58. Giantism in late eighteenth-century English imagination was associated with 'eccentrics' such as Patrick O'Brien, who were inevitably classed by James Granger in his bottom 'category 12'.
59. Lavater, *Essays on physiognomy*, vol.1, p.193-94.
60. Hilles, *Portraits*, p.70.

Figure 20: Joshua Reynolds, *Samuel Johnson* (1756-1757), oil on canvas. © National Portrait Gallery, London.

Figure 21: James Watson after Joshua Reynolds, *Samuel Johnson* (1787), mezzotint. British Museum, London.

that Lavater initiated, in the belief that the profile offered the most unambiguous signs of private character.[61]

The symbolic trappings and allusions to Johnson's public role notably disappeared from the last three portraits Reynolds painted of his friend. The 1775 portrait for Edmond Malone (see fig.22, p.246) zooms in to a close-up of Johnson's face squinting at a book – again signalling the author's visual impairment. The half-length portrait that Reynolds produced for the Thrale Library at Streatham represents Johnson scowling and posing awkwardly as if he is experiencing the convulsive discomfort that often accompanied his conversation. The very last portrait of Johnson, which Reynolds produced in *c.*1782, is stripped to essentials – showing the author as an old man without any other notable singularities or signs of his public reputation. In this work, the visual mnemonics for Johnson's uniqueness and for his celebrity are both erased.

Despite his well-known eccentricities, Johnson himself was disdainful of the kind of singularity that ironically made him a public celebrity. While Boswell felt that 'minute particularities are frequently characteristick, and always amusing, when they relate to a distinguished man'[62] Johnson was deeply sceptical, '*Nothing odd will do long. Tristram Shandy* did not last', he told Boswell; 'Never believe extraordinary characters which you hear of people. Depend upon it, Sir, they are exaggerated.'[63] In his *Life of Swift* Johnson opposed singularity for its own sake and, if Hester Piozzi's anecdotes are to be believed, he was offended by the specificity of one of Reynolds' portraits of him:

> When Sir Joshua Reynolds had painted his portrait looking into the slit of his pen, and holding it almost close to his eye, as was his general custom, he felt displeased and told me 'he would not be known by posterity for his *defects* only, let Sir Joshua do his worst.' I said in reply that Reynolds had no such difficulties about himself, and that he might observe the picture which hung up in the room where we were talking, represented Sir Joshua holding his ear in his hand to catch the sound. 'He may paint himself as deaf if he chuses (replied Johnson); but I will not be *blinking Sam*.'[64]

The sensitivity of Johnson about his disabilities was noted by both Piozzi

---

61. Reynolds produced two other profile portraits in the same year – one equally specific portrait of Goldsmith and another more 'classical' profile of Samuel Dyer.
62. Boswell, *Life of Johnson*, p.25.
63. *Life of Johnson*, p.696.
64. H. Piozzi, *Anecdotes of the late Samuel Johnson LL.D.*, 4th edn (London, T. Cadell, 1786), p.244. There is an ongoing academic debate about which portrait Piozzi is referring to here, which is by no means conclusive or concluded. See, for example, Loren Rothschild, *Blinking Sam: the true history of Sir Joshua Reynolds's 1775 portrait of Samuel Johnson* (Los Angeles, 2002), reprinted in *Age of Johnson* 15 (2004), p.141-50.

Figure 22: John Hall after Joshua Reynolds, *Samuel Johnson* (1782), engraved frontispiece for John Hawkins' biography of Johnson. © National Portrait Gallery, London.

and Boswell, the latter of whom cautioned that it was 'necessary [...] to guard against those who were not acquainted with him, against overcharged imitations or caricatures of his manner'.[65] Piozzi observed that, despite his own singularities, Johnson's conservative inclinations led him to scorn extremes of behaviour and character, and he seemingly suffered deep embarrassment about the very traits that enhanced his fame.[66] The problem here was that bodily disability was the simplest way to characterise Johnson's difference, his individuality, his eccentricity. But it was also all too easy, as in caricature, for that difference to become a metonym for the whole person.[67]

Johnson and Reynolds, therefore, both recognised the power of singularity, or eccentricity, as signs of character, but both shied away from an exposure of such signs to public scrutiny. The singularities observed by Reynolds, Boswell and Piozzi were those gleaned through years of intimate acquaintance with Johnson: making them available for public consumption had the flavour of impropriety. The more intimate aspects of character attracted the curiosity and skill of a portraitist like Reynolds, but when the external signs were unduly extreme, they could too readily consign the sitter to a caricature. With this in mind, it is worth considering the context of Reynolds' portraits of Johnson a little more thoroughly. Four of the five portraits were private commissions – primarily from Johnson's closest circle – and even the portrait of Johnson in classical profile that was exhibited at the Royal Academy was later bought by the duke of Dorset for his library. The positioning of Johnson's portraits in the Dorset and Thrale libraries exposes the clash between public and private that these works exemplified. Hester Thrale's telling reference to the 'Streatham Worthies' reveals the legacy from the Renaissance *studiolo* of filling a library with portraits and busts of the most exemplary poets and philosophers in history, as objects of inspiration and emulation. The Thrales updated this tradition in the Streatham Library, relying solely on living 'worthies' – contemporary celebrities whose reputation had not yet stood the test of time.

The portrait series, which included playwrights, politicians, musicologists from Goldsmith and Burke to Charles Burney and Arthur Murphy, among others, were painted by Reynolds over a ten-year period from 1772. Nadia Tscherny has argued that these portraits were placed

65. Boswell, *Life of Johnson*, p.600.
66. 'Mr. Johnson was indeed unjustly supposed to be a lover of singularity. Few people had a more settled reverence for the world than he, or was less captivated by new modes of behaviour introduced.' Piozzi, *Anecdotes*, p.108.
67. For how bodily disability could serve this function in eighteenth-century imagery, see S. West, 'Wilkes's squint: synecdochic physiognomy and political identity in eighteenth-century print culture', *Eighteenth-century studies* 33:1 (1999), p.65-84.

in the library so as to appear as if they were carrying on a private conversation – thus their exemplary quality was overwhelmed by an index of private friendship.[68] I would certainly agree that there is a temporal and temporary quality about many of the Streatham worthies, who appear to be engaged in transitory activities such as reading or talking; or who are animated as if they are about to burst out of their frames. The commemorative legacy of worthies is therefore replaced by a sense of the evanescent and the fleeting, characteristics of both public celebrity and the private friendship of the sitters depicted. But the portraits also in many cases focus strongly on the singularities and imperfections of their subjects. Johnson was not the only person in Reynolds' circle whose physical disabilities were given a visual treatment. Reynolds depicted Giuseppe Baretti's myopia (see fig.23, p.249), and he played with his own deafness and failing eyesight in two self-portraits.

The Streatham portraits became the nexus of a consideration about private character, how it might be represented and what the limits of such representations might be. Reynolds' written character sketches of Johnson and Goldsmith suggest that he was bothered enough by the elusiveness and danger of dwelling on 'minute particularities' that he was still reflecting on this theme many years later. Piozzi also ruminated about the Streatham portraits, and they inspired her to write character sketches of the sitters, which she referred to as 'portraits'. Piozzi's portraits are particularly notable for their emphasis on the outré and nasty qualities of her subjects, friends though they may have been, but she justified this as a sign of objectivity: 'I once thought of writing the Characters in Verse of all the Friends whose Portraits hang round our Library [...] I will give the good and the bad of each impartially', and she included herself in her list.[69] She therefore dwells on her own 'Temper sarcastic', Arthur Murphy's 'vacant' face and Edmund Burke's tendency to 'talk Obsaenely' and live in a squalor of 'Dirt Cobwebs, Pictures and Statues'.[70] Goldsmith, who was sometimes a figure of fun among the 'Club' circle, receives a special lashing of Piozzi's sarcasm, but her focus here is revealing:

> This Lusus Naturae – Non-Descript in Wit; –
> May best be compar'd to those Anamorphóses,
> Which for Lectures to Ladies, th'Optician proposes,
> All Deformity seeming in some points of View,
> In others quite regular, uniform, true:

---

68. N. Tscherny, 'Reynolds's Streatham portraits and the art of intimate biography', *Burlington magazine* 128:944 (1986), p.7.
69. Piozzi, *Thraliana*, vol.1, p.49 (entry dated 28 May 1777).
70. *Thraliana*, vol.1, p.475.

Figure 23: Joshua Reynolds, *Giuseppe Baretti* (1773), oil on canvas. © National Portrait Gallery, London.

> Till the Student no more sees the figure that shock'd her,
> But all in his Likeness – our odd little Doctor.[71]

Such oddity and specificity, alluded to in pseudo-scientific metaphor, like Piozzi's observation of Johnson's picking at his fingers, or Reynolds' attempt to encapsulate Johnson's nervous tics in a portrait, reveal how intimacy could lead to a dangerous focus on 'eccentric parts' – a problem for portraiture designed for public display.

The Enlightenment and Romantic fascination with celebrities – with their darker sides, their eccentricities and their private lives – therefore remained a problem for portraiture. Reynolds' Streatham portraits had little progeny, with Lawrence, for example, preferring only to hint at the character hidden beneath the lavish spectacles of dress, elegant pose and beautiful features. Although Alison Conway has argued that in England portraits, like novels, were objects 'around which the public debated the idea of private interests',[72] the interiority and intersubjectivity that the novel encouraged rested uneasily with the extrinsic qualities of portraiture exhibited in public or even shown in private houses. Portraits exposed the limits of the late eighteenth-century essentialised self, and sat uncomfortably with the fascination for private character encouraged by novelties of celebrity, physiognomy, caricature and eccentricity.

---

71. *Thraliana*, vol.1, p.473.
72. Alison Conway, *Private interests: women, portraiture and visual culture in the English novel, 1709-91* (Toronto, 2001), p.4.

Friendship and materialism in the French Enlightenment

ADAM SUTCLIFFE

What is a friend? What do we owe to friends, and what do they owe to us? What are they for? Are friendships indispensable for happiness and for virtuous living, or is it possible, perhaps even preferable, to live without such potentially fickle attachments? Is friendship fundamentally an instrumental relationship, serving a selfish purpose for either party, or should an ideal friendship be grounded on selfless love? Should we accept the faults of our friends, or should we only befriend people of the highest quality, and move away from them if they do not sustain these standards? How many true friends can, or should, a person have? What is the relationship of friendship to sexual relationships, and are friendships different, or even possible, across the gender divide? Should we always grant friends preference over people we do not know? And how does the privacy of friendship relate to the wider public relationships of political solidarity, impersonal sympathy and familial or ethnic kinship?

In eighteenth-century France these questions were raised directly, in detail, and relatively often. Friendship was not explicitly a central Enlightenment concern, and this topic has not been widely studied.[1] As Naomi Tadmor has shown for eighteenth-century England, however, the nature and obligations of friendship were a subject of significant cultural reflection.[2] A lofty ideal of friendship, understood as a non-instrumental, reciprocal relationship between equals and most prominently articulated in early modern France by Montaigne, retained a potent allure for many eighteenth-century thinkers, particularly those concerned to advance a positive and theologically non-threatening analysis of the virtuous nature of human co-operation and sociability. This ideal was repeatedly challenged, however, by more socially disruptive thinkers, who drew on Epicurean, sceptical and materialist argu-

---

1. For the limited existing literature on friendship in early modern France see Maurice Aymard, 'Amitié et convivialité', in *De la Renaissance aux Lumières*, ed. R. Chartier, p.455-99; Anne Vincent-Buffault, *L'Exercice de l'amitié: pour une histoire des pratiques amicales aux XVIIIe et XIXe siècles* (Paris, 1995); Frédérick Gerson, *L'Amitié au XVIIIe siècle* (Paris, 1974); Jeffrey Merrick, 'Male friendship in prerevolutionary France', *GLQ: a journal of lesbian and gay studies* 10 (2004), p.407-32.
2. Naomi Tadmor, *Family and friends in eighteenth-century England* (Cambridge, 2001), p.237-71.

ments in order to question conventional religious and ethical assumptions. The question of the possibility of authentic friendship emerged as a complex intellectual terrain, at the intersection of multiply contested boundaries between science and theology, the individual and the social, and private and public life.

Eighteenth-century French materialist thought has long been considered a key originary source in the history of modern social and political radicalism. Georgi Plekhanov in 1893 identified Helvétius and the baron d'Holbach as crucial forerunners of Marx; and the embattled advance of materialist arguments in the second quarter of the century has been much more recently emphasised by Jonathan Israel as central to the development of the French radical Enlightenment.[3] As Ann Thomson has recently emphasised, however, early Enlightenment materialism was a complex and diverse phenomenon, articulated in a range of registers and within a mobile intellectual environment in which the opposition between orthodoxy and heterodoxy was not always clearly drawn.[4] A central difficulty for most materialist thinkers was how to accommodate an account of human ethics within their broader philosophical framework, and thereby to avoid the charge of atheistic amoralism, which only a very few extremely bold thinkers were willing in any sense to avow. In the middle decades of the eighteenth century the topic of friendship emerged as a significant focus of attempts by several thinkers to articulate the place of virtue and obligation within a broadly materialist understanding of social relations. This topic presented writers influenced by materialism with an inviting subject for social satire; but it also posed serious intellectual challenges, including the risk of a philosophical slide towards a more coldly instrumentalist vision of interpersonal intimacy than they were generally willing to fully endorse. These writings on friendship thus present a subtle testing ground for the subversive potential of radical and materialist ideas, and of attempts to circumscribe and control this potential, not only in theoretical terms but also when applied to a significant domain of social life.

Eighteenth-century considerations of friendship took place against a backdrop of profound changes in the social and cultural conditions that shaped actual friendships, and in the political freight borne by the concept. Early modern humanists almost exclusively conceived of friendship as a relationship of similarity, between male members of the social elite. Seventeenth-century French aristocrats invested considerable

---

3. George Plekhanov, *Essays in the history of materialism* (London, 1934); Jonathan Israel, *Enlightenment contested* (Oxford, 2006), p.712-21, 733-50. See also Denis Lecompte, *Marx et le baron d'Holbach* (Paris, 1983).
4. Ann Thomson, *Bodies of thought: science, religion and the soul in the early Enlightenment* (Oxford, 2008), p.17-27.

emotial energy in such relationships, which they valued, according to
Jonathan Dewald, as 'providing a private shelter from public life'.[5] In the
eighteenth century, however, notions of friendship were increasingly
mobilised as part of a political attempt to envision, at an intimate and
personal level, the possibility of solidarities that might transcend differences of gender, confession and race.[6] Reformist political discourse in
the 1780s often mobilised a language of friendship: this is apparent in
discussions of Jewish political emancipation and socio-economic ameli-
oration, and also in opposition to slavery, spearheaded in France by the
Société des amis des noirs. In the French Revolution friendship was
translated into fraternity, and in this form became a key rhetorical term.[7]
The key difference between friendship and fraternity is that the latter
was imagined as extensible, potentially to all, and thus sought to overcome the division between the public and private realms. As Peter
Fenves has pointed out, however, it ultimately makes little sense to speak
of fraternity unless this term is distinguished from something else,
designating those it excludes.[8] The tensions embedded in this Revol-
utionary attempt to politicise and universalise friendship are valuably
brought into relief by the various attempts by earlier eighteenth-century
French materialist thinkers to scrutinise friendship and bring it philosophically to heel.

Many early- and mid-eighteenth-century French Enlightenment radicals were seduced by the subversive power of materialist philosophy,
particularly in its 'sensationist' form, which, in seeking to interpret all
phenomena in unified material terms and regarding all knowledge as
derived through the human senses, readily undermined theological
doctrines such as the immortality of the soul.[9] The implications of
materialism when applied to human social relations, however, were
more troublesome, even in irreligious circles. If all aspects of human
existence could be reduced to the sensory interaction between material
bodies, impelled by nothing more than the pursuit of pleasure and the
avoidance of pain, then in what ethical terms should interpersonal

5. Dewald, *Aristocratic experience*, p.144.
6. See Adam Sutcliffe, 'Spinoza and friends: religion, philosophy and friendship in the
    Berlin Enlightenment', in *Love, friendship and faith: intimacy, idioms and institutions in early
    modern Europe*, ed. Michael Hunter, Miri Rubin and Laura Gowing (Basingstoke, 2005),
    p.197-220.
7. Marisa Linton, *The Politics of virtue in Enlightenment France* (Basingstoke, 2001), p.204-205,
    210-11.
8. Peter Fenves, 'Politics of friendship – once again', *Eighteenth-century studies* 32 (1998-1999),
    p.133-55 (140).
9. For general accounts see John Yolton, *Locke and French materialism* (Oxford, 1991); John C.
    O'Neal, *The Authority of experience: sensationist theory in the French Enlightenment* (University
    Park, PA, 1996).

relationships be understood, and what politics followed from this? Several decades before the marquis de Sade articulated his outspokenly libertine answers to these questions, earlier radicals, such as the marquis d'Argens, the marquis de Vauvenargues and Claude-Adrien Helvétius, explored amoral conceptions of human nature and advanced deflationary conceptions of friendship.[10] These positions, however, were difficult to sustain, and even more difficult to integrate with any sort of reformist politics, or with a viable ethic of friendship in lived experience. Both in theory and in practice, French Enlightenment radicals revealed in their approach to friendship a recurrent slippage from bold materialist analysis to more moderate humanist formulations in the vein of Montaigne. These slippages, which can be discerned not only in theoretical texts but also in the vivid personal correspondence from Diderot to Rousseau as their friendship dissolved into acrimony, reveal a more fluid and uncertain face of eighteenth-century materialism than is usually recognised.

Aristotle, in his *Eudemian ethics*, offers a crisp definition of friendship that served as a key point of orientation in subsequent debates: 'A man becomes a friend whenever, being loved, he loves in return.'[11] Reciprocity, for Aristotle, was of fundamental importance to true friendship, as is the associated feature of non-instrumentality, or goodwill. True friends, Aristotle believed, must love each other for themselves, and disinterestedly wish each other the best. In places, however, Aristotle seems to retreat from this claim, allowing that certain, less ideal forms of friendship are to a degree instrumental, being based not on common virtue, but on the pleasure or other benefits provided by the company of a friend. The purest friend, however, is nothing less than 'another self'. This exacting ideal was extremely influential on later writers, most notably Cicero (in his *De amicitia*) and the most significant sixteenth-century writer on friendship, Michel de Montaigne.[12]

In his famous essay 'De l'amitié' (1580) Montaigne makes frequent reference to Aristotle, Cicero and Plutarch, and follows Aristotle both in his unrestrained celebration of ideal friendship and in the sharp distinction he draws between this rare ideal and the more limited nature of most 'amitiés communes'. He endorses Aristotle's definition of ideal friendship as 'une âme en deux corps': a fusion of souls, in which there can be no instrumentalism because there is no sense of separate

---

10. On Sade in relation to his materialist antecedents, see Caroline Warman, *Sade: from materialism to pornography*, SVEC 2002:01, p.21-57.

11. Aristotle, *Eudemian ethics*, VII.ii.1236. See also his *Nichomachean ethics*, VIII.ii.1155.

12. On Aristotle and friendship see A. W. Price, *Love and friendship in Plato and Aristotle* (Oxford, 1989), p.103-61; Nancy Sherman, 'Aristotle on the shared life', in *Friendship: a philosophical reader*, ed. Neera Kapur Badhwar (Ithaca, NY, 1993), p.91-107.

interests, or even of those sentiments which imply 'division et différence', such as obligation or gratitude.[13] In such a friendship there is absolute honesty and trust. Montaigne writes that he would have more willingly trusted himself to his own lamented friend, Etienne de La Boétie, for whom this essay is a eulogy, than to himself. In most friendships, however, Montaigne acknowledges that this ideal is not attained, and caution with friends is therefore necessary. He approvingly quotes the saying that you should love your friend 'comme ayant quelque jour à le haïr'; in recognising this painful realism he again quotes Aristotle, in the saying attributed to him by Diogenes Laertius: 'Ô mes amis, il n'y a nul ami!'[14]

This dictum, to which we will return, captures the core ambiguity of the classical tradition of European thought about friendship. On one level Montaigne, like Aristotle, is attempting to distil a perfect ideal of friendship. He claims, however, that this ideal was reflected in his own friendship (a singular friendship: it is only possible, he writes, to have one friend),[15] and he also seeks to say something of relevance to the real world, in which most friendships, inevitably, are not ideal. It is in this more practical spirit that Montaigne distinguishes friendship from love. At this point Montaigne significantly differs from the Ancients, equating love with sexual passion, intense but unsteady, and oriented towards women, and defining friendship as a calmer warmth, 'toute douceur et polissure', only possible between men.[16] Love is destroyed by physical satiation; friendship, in contrast, strengthens the more it is enjoyed, and is thus an aid to self-improvement. While Montaigne here verges on offering a form of advice literature, he leaves the core of friendship shrouded in mystery. While mundane friendships may be held together by 'occasion ou commodité', true friendships cannot be rationally understood: as an explanation of his own intense friendship bond he could only offer 'parce que c'était lui; parce que c'était moi'.[17]

In this essay Montaigne's humanist optimism outweighs his sceptical analysis. His friendship ideal, however, is very sharply marked apart from the vulgar and compromised self-interest and suspicion of 'amitiés communes', about which he has little to say. For the leading French sceptic of the next generation, La Mothe Le Vayer, the balance tipped. La Mothe Le Vayer, while operating in a largely similar sceptical mode to Montaigne, took a pessimistic view of friendship. It is impossible to

13. Michel de Montaigne, 'De l'amitié', in *Œuvres complètes*, ed. Maurice Rat (Paris, 1962), p.177-93 (189).
14. Montaigne, 'De l'amitié', p.188-89.
15. Montaigne, 'De l'amitié', p.190.
16. Montaigne, 'De l'amitié', p.184.
17. Montaigne, 'De l'amitié', p.186-87.

know, he argued, that a friendship is reciprocal, claiming also that all friendships were ultimately motivated by self-interest.[18] This shift towards an emphasis on self-interest in human affairs, based on scepticism towards religious orthodoxy and seasoned with a measure of libertinism, set the tone for much commentary on friendship over the subsequent century.

The development of reasoned critical analysis in the seventeenth century did not, however, straightforwardly undermine the humanist friendship ideal. Human emotions and passions – including friendship – were taken seriously by seventeenth-century thinkers as both mental and bodily states, playing an important role, when properly managed, in the pursuit of knowledge and of happiness.[19] The distinction between mastered and unmastered passions, however, was nonetheless crucial, and nowhere more so than in Spinoza's *Ethics* (1677), in which rational, measured friendship stands in sharp juxtaposition to the potentially destabilising effects of love. Whereas love can readily be excessive, and thus disturb the balance of mind, friendship is for Spinoza unreservedly positive, because it is associated, by definition, with the supreme faculty of reason. 'The desire to establish friendship with others', he writes, is 'a desire that characterizes the man who lives by the guidance of reason.'[20] Spinoza's view of friendship is extremely idealised: only the truly rational few, he claims, are capable of establishing genuine friendship bonds. For these enlightened individuals, fully in command of their desires and their intellect, the opposition between self-interest and common interest dissolves, and it is this shared understanding that binds them together: 'Only free men are truly advantageous to one another and united by the closest bond of friendship.'[21]

Spinoza's view of friendship was, like that of Montaigne, both highly rarified and defined in stark contrast to the mundane relationships of the masses. Unlike Montaigne, however, he sought to demystify friendship, according it a prominent position in his meticulously rational geometric analysis of the ethics of self-mastery. Despite this, Spinoza's abstracted vision of perfected friendships, fully transcending both individual selfishness and the instabilities of desire, echoed the humanist tradition as much as it dissented from it. For eighteenth-century French radicals, for whom Spinoza's monist philosophy shared the transgressive appeal of materialism and was often mingled messily with it, the *Ethics*

18. Gerson, *L'Amitié*, p.35-38.
19. Susan James, *Passion and action: the emotions in seventeenth-century philosophy* (Oxford, 1997), p.85-252.
20. Spinoza, *Ethics*, IV.37, in *Complete works*, ed. Michael L. Morgan (Indianapolis, IN, 2002), p.339.
21. Spinoza, *Ethics*, IV.71, p.356.

offered an emboldening model of a fearlessly secular approach to personal and interpersonal morality. Yet this text also offers an early example of the close intertwinement of Enlightenment interpretations of human relationships with those of their humanist antecedents, although this was seldom, if ever, recognised as such.

The complexities of friendship were experienced with particular passion and intellectually explored with particular vigour in the Parisian salons, where stylised norms of social interaction and a heightened consciousness of interpersonal dynamics were conducive to an interest in the subject. A notable debate on friendship emerged in the early 1660s in the salon of the prominent Jansenist convert, the marquise de Sablé, which engaged a number of leading Jansenist figures as well as La Rochefoucauld.[22] This circle generally perpetuated a pessimistic view of the human potential for sincere friendship, in the vein of La Mothe Le Vayer, which remained influential for the remainder of the century. In the salons of the early eighteenth century, however, the tensions between idealistic and pragmatic approaches to friendship were approached with less solemnity, reflecting the rise of a lighter, more playful attitude to the strain between the countervailing poles of public etiquette and philosophical provocation. This shift can be traced in the notable conduct literature on friendship that emerged in France at the end of the seventeenth century.[23]

Early examples of this genre varied in their degree of exuberance or optimism towards friendship, but had in common a tendency to avoid abstraction, focusing instead on practical questions of how to find, improve and sustain friendships. By the 1740s, however, this conduct literature had become a site of semi-surreptitious philosophical experimentation. Critics seeking to stir the social, religious and sexual conventions of urban elite culture found a ripe target in ideals of friendship, which they regarded as ridden with psychological fancy and moral hypocrisy. From the perspective of materialist philosophy, which by this time constituted the main intellectual current of radical subversion in France, human relations, no less than human bodies and human passions, demanded analysis without reference to unexplained moral absolutes. Radical writers on friendship drew on these ideas to challenge and mock the demure moralism of the more conventional conduct literature. While inhabiting the same close social milieu of the Parisian

---

22. Benedetta Craveri, *The Age of conversation* (New York, 2005), p.97-136; John J. Conley, *The Suspicion of virtue: women philosophers in neoclassical France* (Ithaca, NY, 2002), p.20-44; Sylvie Requemora, 'L'amitié dans les "Maximes" de La Rochefoucauld', *Dix-septième siècle* 51 (1999), p.687-728.

23. For a survey of these friendship manuals see Vincent-Buffault, *Exercice de l'amitié*, p.75-134.

salons as the authors they satirised, these writers offered a contrastingly
unsentimental and at times unabashedly erotic view of the forces driving
interpersonal intimacies.

The first prominent friendship manual of the eighteenth century was
the *Traité de l'amitié* (1703) by Louis de Sacy (1654-1727), a lawyer,
academician and a close friend and regular salon attendee of the
marquise de Lambert, to whom he dedicated this text. Like Spinoza,
Sacy rejected Montaigne's view of friendship as an inexplicable rapport:
friendship, he wrote, is not 'une inclination aveugle, mais un sentiment
éclairé', requiring that friends be chosen with care.[24] He was particularly
careful in his handling of the problem of self-interest in friendships,
seeking to balance a realistic appraisal of human nature with the pres-
ervation of an ethically and religiously infused friendship ideal. 'L'amitié,
quoique la plus pure de toutes les unions, a pour objet comme les autres
un échange de plaisirs et d'offices', he argued; 'mais elle n'est pas pour
cela mercenaire.' The underlying motivation of friendship, he insisted, is
a selfless and religious duty: 'de répandre, sur tout ce qui se rencontre de
bien ou de mal dans la vie des amis, certain charme secret qui émousse le
sentiment du mal, et qui aiguise le sentiment du bien.'[25]

Sacy tailored his advice concerning friendship to a world of flawed
individuals. 'Vouloir des amis sans défauts,' he writes, 'c'est ne vouloir
aimer personne.'[26] While following Montaigne in endorsing the
Aristotelian view of the friend as a 'second self', he nonetheless firmly
places duties to friends (and family) third on a hierarchy of duties,
beneath those to God and to 'Patrie'.[27] He suggests precautions to avoid
ruptures in friendship, such as not listening to hostile gossip concerning
friends, and also practical advice in cases when a friendship is irrevocably
broken. In his carefully balanced treatment of his subject, Sacy
attempted to straddle several oppositions characteristic of early eighteenth-century theorisations of human relations: between idealism and
pragmatism; between a vision of endurance and an acceptance of inevitable change; between a celebration of intimacy and an awareness of the
potential danger of such intimacies to public values of patriotism and
law; and, most fundamentally, between a negative view of human nature
as irredeemably self-interested and a commitment to the redemptive
power of faith.

Perhaps the most popular French friendship manual in the early
eighteenth century was the identically titled *Traité de l'amitié* of Sacy's

---

24. Louis de Sacy, *Traité de l'amitié* (Paris, Barbou, 1774), p.42.
25. Sacy, *Traité de l'amitié*, p.62-63.
26. Sacy, *Traité de l'amitié*, p.76.
27. Sacy, *Traité de l'amitié*, p.145-57.

dedicatee, the marquise de Lambert (1647-1733), who between 1710 and 1733 was a leading *salonnière* in Paris. Her literary gatherings on Tuesday afternoons, when she regularly hosted such prominent figures as Fontenelle, Fénelon, Marivaux and Montesquieu, were noted for their propriety, sophistication and prestige. Lambert carefully managed the circulation of wit, aesthetic debate and acquaintances at her home, and also mediated circulation between her Tuesday salon and her equally noted Wednesday afternoon aristocratic gatherings. Her treatise on friendship was first published in 1732, but circulated privately before that date; she also wrote in a humanist vein on other intimate themes such as ageing and motherhood, always emphasising the importance of decorum and wisdom in human relationships.[28]

Friendship, Mme de Lambert asserted, was a basic human need: 'L'homme est plein de besoins; renvoyé à lui même, il sent un vide que l'amitié seule est capable de remplir: toujours inquiet et toujours agité, il ne se calme et ne se repose que dans l'amitié.'[29] Following the established conventions of this genre, she asserted the superiority of friendship over the 'passion turbulente' of love: friendship, she wrote, was the stable, rational form of love: 'l'amour épuré'.[30] Unlike Montaigne, however (whom she cites approvingly), but like Sacy, Lambert sought to accommodate human weaknesses, offering practical guidance to those in search of the consolations of friendship. The choice of friend, she writes, is crucial: a good friend must be virtuous, and friends should be closely matched in age and tastes. At least in the early stage of a friendship, however, an illusory element of idealisation is natural, and helps to establish friendship. With time, though, this should be replaced by the firmer grounding of friendship in reason and realism. Nonetheless, a friend's faults must be accommodated, best of all by not dwelling on them: 'Il ne faut pas se permettre d'examiner les défauts de nos amis, encore moins d'en parler.'[31] A bad friendship nonetheless requires loyalty – this should be accepted as a punishment for choosing a friend too hastily.[32]

Only three years after Lambert's death her treatise was used as the springboard for a mildly scandalous satire on friendship, the piquancy of which was augmented by the fact that its author had been one of her close male friends. The prominent translator and satirist Thémiseul de

---

28. Roger Marchal, *Madame de Lambert et son milieu*, SVEC 289 (1991); Ellen McNiven Hine, 'Madame de Lambert, her sources and her circle', *SVEC* 102 (1973), p.173-92; Craveri, *Age of conversation*, p.263-76.

29. Mme de Lambert, *Traité de l'amitié* (Paris, Pissot, 1736), p.98.

30. Lambert, *Traité de l'amitié*, p.110.

31. Lambert, *Traité de l'amitié*, p.108-10, 114, 123.

32. Lambert, *Traité de l'amitié*, p.130.

Saint-Hyacinthe, who had been a significant participant in Mme de Lambert's salon, in 1736 published his *Recueil de divers écrits sur l'amour et l'amitié, la politesse, la volupté, les sentiments agréables, l'esprit et le cœur*.[33] Included in this volume is the marquise de Lambert's *Traité de l'amitié*, credited only to 'Madame la marquise de * *', but seemingly reprinted without alteration. The impact of her treatise, however, is playfully subverted by the letter that precedes it, presumably by Saint-Hyacinthe himself, but purporting to be a letter to 'Madame la Duchesse de * * *' from an anonymous courtier, recommending the treatise it introduces. At first summarising Lambert's argument, the courtier defines friendship as 'un amour exempt de cupidité', and thus truly noble, in contrast to the 'effervescence du sang' of erotic attraction.[34] He then slowly undermines this opposition, however, through the gentle introduction of materialist argument. If true love is spiritual, the letter argues, then two individuals who truly love each other will know that this love exists on a higher plane than the physical. They may nonetheless experience 'les mouvements involontaires de la cupidité', which will indeed be heightened by true love. These sentiments are neither the cause, nor the purpose of love: precisely because of this, the courtier suggests, what reason can there be not to succumb to these 'petits sentiments de cupidité', and the pleasures, unrelated to friendship itself, that they can bring?[35]

Saint-Hyacinthe's mischievous blurring of the distinction between friendship and love, and, more pointedly, the boundary between platonic and erotic intimacy, deployed a materialist understanding of the body and its passions to mock the moral earnestness and prim respectability of conventional social ethics. His provocation is characteristic of the ways in which erotic or pornographic texts functioned simultaneously as entertainment and as philosophical argument in eighteenth-century France.[36] In introducing these ideas into the friendship debate, however, Saint-Hyacinthe not only challenged conventional Christian morality but also gently destabilised attempts to codify a respectable public ethic of human relationships. This materialist critique of conventional views of friendship was pursued more outspokenly by the marquis d'Argens – the author of the most celebrated materialist

---

33. Elisabeth Carayol, *Thémiseul de Saint-Hyacinthe*, SVEC 221 (1984), p.64-5, 151-7; Marchal, *Madame de Lambert*, p.174-8.
34. Thémiseul de Saint-Hyacinthe, *Recueil de divers écrits sur l'amour et l'amitié* (Paris, Pissot, 1736), p.3-7.
35. Saint-Hyacinthe, *Recueil*, p.41-43.
36. See *The Invention of pornography*, ed. Lynn Hunt (New York, 1993); Jean-Marie Goulemot, *Ces livres qu'on ne lit que d'une main* (Aix-en-Provence, 1991); Darnton, *Forbidden best-sellers*, p.3-22, 85-114.

pornographic novel of the period, *Thérèse philosophe* (1748)[37] – who opened his collected *Nouveaux mémoires* (1745) with an essay titled 'Réflexions diverses et critiques sur l'amitié'.

D'Argens here scornfully rejects the idealised view of friendship advanced in the 'traités pompeux' of Plato, Cicero and the other Ancients, who, he argues, failed to take account of true experience.[38] Most friendships, he writes, are far from reciprocal: more often we are envious of the happiness of our friends. Far from being a selfless impulse, friendship is exclusively based on self-interest, and this is according to d'Argens no bad thing: 'Les amis ne nous paroissent précieux qu'autant qu'ils nous sont utiles. Notre amour-propre exige qu'ils le soient, et c'est le principal et le plus fort lien de l'amitié.'[39] On this theme he takes issue directly with Sacy, refuting his claim that true friendship can transcend self-interest.[40] D'Argens attempts to approach and define friendship through pragmatism and logic, without any recourse to abstract theorising, and in a spirit of pugnacious opposition to received wisdom on this topic. Rejecting the consensus among both Ancient and humanist writers that it is only possible to have one true friend, he argues for having several, because friendships can rupture, but not too many, as this would dilute all affections; and in a similarly combative mode against Montaigne and Charron in particular, he argues that friendship is not indispensable for happiness, notwithstanding the many benefits that it brings.[41] Citing the example of Christina of Sweden, he rejects Montaigne's claim that friendship is not possible with or between women, and suggests that female friendship may even be superior: 'Je crois que les femmes, dans leur amitié, ont quelque chose de plus doux et de plus prévenant que les hommes. Le caractère se fait sentir dans toutes nos actions, et celui des femmes a plus de douceur et d'aménité que le nôtre.'[42]

Despite his attempt to develop a theory of friendship that was free of the naive ungrounded moralism (as he saw it) of more traditional thinkers, d'Argens's essay nonetheless at times draws on a similarly normative moral language, and is in significant respects not dissimilar from the earlier friendship manuals that he repeatedly criticises. In unresolved tension with his view of human nature as inherently self-

37. This text is reprinted in Darnton, *Forbidden best-sellers*, p.249-99.
38. Marquis d'Argens, *Nouveaux mémoires, pour servir à l'histoire de l'esprit et du cœur*, vol.1 (The Hague, Scheurleer, 1745), p.1-13 (13).
39. D'Argens, *Nouveaux mémoires*, p.15.
40. D'Argens, *Nouveaux mémoires*, p.21-23.
41. D'Argens, *Nouveaux mémoires*, p.44-50, 53-59.
42. D'Argens, *Nouveaux mémoires*, p.65-70 (69-70).

interested, he states that seemingly selfless qualities such as good nature, probity and generosity are necessary to sustain friendship, and emphasises the value of friendship in promoting virtuous behaviour: 'Veut-on long-tems conserver un ami, il faut se rendre aimable, en prévoiant tout ce qui peut le satisfaire.'[43] D'Argens based his analysis of friendship in common sense and contemporary observation, and pointedly contrasted this to the airy theorising and ungrounded assumptions of earlier writers on the topic. Despite his methodological distinctiveness, however, in practical terms his overall vision of the nature and value of friendship was much more conventional than was suggested by the self-consciously freethinking tone of his text. His arguments were rhetorically radical, but not in any significant sense socially disruptive. While this may have contributed to the accessibility and popularity of his text, it also highlights something of a deflationary limit to the critical edge of materialist thought when deployed in this manner. The practical aspect of the topic of friendship exposed the outer reach of d'Argens's boldness, and his ultimate dependence on a moralised, improving vision of interpersonal relations that was heavily indebted to the earlier traditions he sought to challenge.

Other more defiantly radical thinkers derived markedly different and more pessimistic accounts of friendship from the materialist view of human nature as inherently self-interested. The marquis de Vauvenargues (1715-1747), whose philosophy was strongly influenced by Spinoza, was particularly vexed by the implications of radical thought for the personal and moral life of the individual.[44] We are drawn to friendship, he wrote, because of our individual weaknesses; but friendship inevitably disappoints, due to the incompatible demands that friends make on each other:

> Est-on seul, on sent sa misère, on sent qu'on a besoin d'appui; on cherche un fauteur de ses goûts, un compagnon de ses plaisirs et de ses peines; on veut un homme dont on puisse posséder le cœur et la pensée. Alors l'amitié paraît être ce qu'il y a de plus doux au monde. A-t-on ce qu'on a souhaité, on change bientôt de pensée.[45]

The attention, even possession, that an individual wants from his friend must, according to Vauvenargues, clash with the attention and possession that that friend wants from him. Reciprocity is chimerical, and friendship, therefore, is doomed.

---

43. D'Argens, *Nouveaux mémoires*, p.64.
44. See J. Israel, *Radical Enlightenment* (Oxford, 2001), p.69-71.
45. Marquis de Vauvenargues, *Introduction à la connaissance de l'esprit humain* (1746), in *Œuvres complètes*, ed. Jean-Pierre Jackson (Paris, 1999), p.1-134 (41).

Claude-Adrien Helvétius devoted a chapter to friendship in his *De l'esprit* (1758), the overall argument of which was to demonstrate that all human passions are reducible to the avoidance of physical pain and the seeking of physical pleasure, and that through appropriate education this principle can be harnessed to promote social virtue. Friendship, he argues, is based on want; and the stronger the want, the stronger the friendship: he thus accounted for this phenomenon in terms of his overall theory of cause and effect. Helvétius presents a man and a woman stranded together on a desert island as a situation that would generate the closest possible friendship, even if they 'se seroient peut-être détestés, s'ils fussent restés à Paris'.[46] Concomitantly, in eighteenth-century society, in which individuals are not united by any common interest, but rather each pursue their own fortunes independently, there is no sufficient motive for us to 'supporter les défauts réels ou respectifs de nos amis. Il n'est donc plus d'amitié.'[47]

Helvétius is unsentimental about this, as would seem to be necessary to sustain conformity with his philosophical system, in which the quest for pleasure and the avoidance of pain has no moral weight, but is simply a fact of human nature. He does not entirely decouple moral values from friendship, however: the best and most faithful friends, he writes, are 'des hommes exempts de toute ambition, de toutes passions fortes, et qui font leurs délices de la conversation des gens instruits'.[48] This ideal strongly echoes Spinoza, and also much earlier ancient and humanist characterisations of the perfect friend. Helvétius's account of such intellectual friendship, however, does not seem to be based on intense want, and thus does not clearly qualify as friendship on his own terms; and his idealisation of such detachment also sits awkwardly alongside his objectivist analysis of the place of the passions in human nature. His treatment of this topic offers a particular but reinforcing perspective of John O'Neal's interpretation of his philosophy as unstable and intermittently fatalistic.[49] In the final analysis, Helvétius seems to baulk from the potentially amoral implications of his theory with respect to close human relationships, and falls back on conventional ideals of virtue for which he does not provide a firm philosophical grounding. As with d'Argens and several other thinkers in the materialist tradition, friendship was a particularly difficult phenomenon for him to account for.

The potentially amoral implications of materialism erupted to the fore in the late 1740s, in the outcry over the extreme Epicurian materi-

---

46. Claude-Adrien Helvétius, *De l'esprit*, ed. Jacques Moutaux (Paris, 1988), p.317.
47. Helvétius, *De l'esprit*, p.319.
48. Helvétius, *De l'esprit*, p.320.
49. O'Neal, *Authority of experience*, p.83-101, 245-50.

alism of the Breton doctor, Julien Offroy de La Mettrie. In his *L'Homme machine* (1748), and equally provocatively in his *Discours sur le bonheur* (1750), La Mettrie seemed to undercut all possible grounds for a notion of virtue beyond the individualistic pursuit of pleasure. This led most other French thinkers associated with materialism, including Diderot and his allies, to hastily repudiate La Mettrie and to seek to affirm their commitment to a secularised public morality.[50] La Mettrie did not give the topic of friendship systematic attention, but he clearly saw it as an important facet of human pleasure, no less glorious for being understood by him, like all pleasure, as derived from biomechanical sensory stimulation. He mentions friendship several times in his *Discours sur le bonheur*, and in his *Système d'Epicure* (1750) lushly celebrates the conversational and social pleasures of 'douce amitié'.[51]

The publication of the first volume of the *Encyclopédie* in 1751 took place against the backdrop of the 'affaire La Mettrie'. While many articles in this volume advanced materialist ideas in semi-veiled form, Diderot and D'Alembert were also concerned, for both pragmatic and political reasons, to disassociate themselves, and the *Encyclopédie* as a whole, from apparently amoral strands of philosophical radicalism such as that of La Mettrie, which they regarded as unproductive or paralysing.[52] The article 'Amitié' in this volume, penned by Claude Yvon, reflects this more cautious aspect of their project. This brief contribution bears no hint of materialism, and dwells not on the pleasures of friendship but on its potential disappointments and mutual responsibilities. Defining friendship straightforwardly as 'l'habitude d'entretenir avec quelqu'un un commerce honnête et agréable', the entry bears more in common with the advice literature of Sacy and Lambert than with the more mischievous texts of d'Argens and Saint-Hyacinthe. While recognising that successful friendships are based on the exchange of satisfaction, Yvon encourages modest expectations from friends, and a vigilant attentiveness to their needs and limits: 'En général, pour ménager avec soin ce qui doit contribuer à la satisfaction mutuelle des amis, et à la douceur de leur commerce, il faut que l'un dans son besoin attende ou exige toûjours moins que plus de son ami, et que l'autre selon ses facultés donne toûjours à son ami plus que moins.'[53]

---

50. Israel, *Enlightenment contested*, p.794-813; Charles T. Wolfe, 'A happiness fit for organic bodies: La Mettrie's medical Epicureanism', *SVEC* 2009:12, p.69-83.

51. Julien Offroy de La Mettrie, *Discours sur le bonheur*, in *Œuvres philosophiques*, ed. Francine Markovits, 2 vols (Paris, 1987), vol.2, p.235-96 (264, 281, 289); *Système d'Epicure*, in *Œuvres philosophiques*, vol.1, p. 351-86 (381) (section 80).

52. Israel, *Enlightenment contested*, p.840-62.

53. *Encyclopédie*, ed. D. Diderot and J. D'Alembert, vol.1 (1751), p.361-62.

The individual who most interestingly brings together the competing strands of French Enlightenment approaches to friendship is Denis Diderot. Drawn to materialist philosophy, and alive to the intellectually challenging potential in rethinking interpersonal bonds, Diderot was nonetheless opposed to what he seems to have regarded as the excesses of materialism. He rejected La Mettrie's Epicureanism, and also considered Helvétius's *De l'esprit* too reductive in its insistence that all human difference could be explained by sensory experience: Helvétius's posthumously published *De l'homme* (1773) prompted him to write a detailed chapter-by-chapter refutation.[54] The precise nature of Diderot's materialism remains difficult to pin down – in his hands this was a dynamic philosophy, and one that he was at pains to differentiate from what he regarded as the voluptuous excesses of Lucretian sensualism.[55] He also keenly perceived, however, a countervailing danger in Rousseau's attitude to society. While opposed to what he regarded as La Mettrie's amorality and Helvétius's overconfident assertion of the power of education to refashion human relations in society, Diderot was equally alarmed by Rousseau's reclusive temperament.

Rousseau's withdrawal from Paris to his rustic retreat at the Hermitage, in April 1756, gave rise a year later to a convoluted quarrel between the two philosophers, ultimately unravelling what had over the previous decade been an intimate and mutually cherished friendship. In the correspondence between them over the course of their rupture we witness an exchange that can be read both as a sequence of petty squabbles and as a serious debate about the nature of friendship and the responsibilities that it entailed. Diderot never explicitly addressed the topic of friendship in his philosophical writings, but, like Rousseau, he was deeply interested in the nature and ethics of close human relations.[56] In their charged exchange they pit contrasting views of friendship against each other, throwing their thinking on the subject into particularly sharp intellectual and personal focus, and offering a notably practical and experiential perspective on Diderot's view of the nature of passionate human bonds.

Simmering tensions between the two men first erupted in March 1757, when Rousseau objected to a line in Diderot's recently published play, *Le*

---

54. D. Diderot, *Réfutation d'Helvétius*, in *Œuvres*, ed. Laurent Versini, vol.1 (Paris, 1994), p.777-923.

55. Wilda Anderson, *Diderot's dream* (Baltimore, MD, 1990); Aram Vartanian, 'Diderot, or the dualist in spite of himself', in *Diderot: digression and dispersion*, ed. Jack Undank and Herbert Josephs (Lexington, KY, 1984), p.250-68; Natania Meeker, *Voluptuous philosophy: literary materialism in the French Enlightenment* (New York, 2006), p.155-88.

56. See Blandine L. McLaughlin, *Diderot et l'amitié*, *SVEC* 100 (1973); William Acher, *Jean-Jacques Rousseau: écrivain de l'amitié* (Paris, 1971).

Fils naturel, which he saw as a gratuitously public attack on him: 'L'homme de bien est dans la société, et qu'il n'y a que le méchant qui soit seul.'[57] This dispute soon became entangled in a grumpy exchange over the state of their friendship, which initially focused on who was to blame for the fact that they no longer saw each other very often. Diderot resented Rousseau's refusal to come to Paris, requiring him, like Rousseau's other friends, to repeatedly make the awkward ten-mile journey to the Hermitage. Probably in order to patch up the quarrel over his play, Diderot later that month rather ill-temperedly agreed to visit Rousseau: 'Vous ne voulez pas venir a Paris. Eh bien, samedi matin, quelque temps qu'il fasse, je partirai pour l'Hermitage. Je partirai a pied [...] Ma fortune ne me permet pas d'y aller autrement.'[58] In response, Rousseau complained that Diderot always broke his appointments, repeatedly keeping him waiting all day in vain – and claimed that this time, if he did in fact keep his promise to come, he would probably be very happy if the journey gave him some minor ailment, 'pour avoir le plaisir de me la reprocher'.[59]

This mundane squabble stirred deep passions in both participants, reflecting not only the intensity of their underlying relationship but also their awareness of more serious issues that lay beneath the surface. Their recriminations soon shifted to this more intellectually substantive register, with Diderot accusing Rousseau of abusing his friendship and mistreating him: 'Oh, Rousseau, vous devenez méchant, injuste, cruel, feroce, et j'en pleurs de douleur.' He sought to remind Rousseau that, within himself, he recognised Diderot's generosity of friendship towards him:

> Une bonne fois pour toutes, demandez vous a vous même, qui est ce qui a pris part a ma santé quand j'ai été malade? Qui est ce qui m'a soutenu quand j'ai été attaqué? Qui est ce qui s'est interessé vivement a ma gloire? Qui est ce qui s'est rejoui de mes succès? Repondez vous avec sincerité, et Connaissez ceux qui vous aiment.[60]

In response to this, Rousseau claimed to be astounded by Diderot's accusations, protesting that he could never do even to his worst enemy everything that Diderot had accused him of having done to him over the past six weeks. He then rejected as irrelevant the basis on which Diderot

57. See Nicholas Cronk, 'Dorval et le dialogue à trois voix: la présence de Rousseau dans *Le Fils naturel* et les *Entretiens*', in *Etudes sur Le Fils naturel et les Entretiens sur le Fils naturel de Diderot*, ed. Nicholas Cronk (Oxford, 2000), p.123-37.
58. Diderot to Rousseau, 14 March 1757, in *Correspondance complète de Rousseau*, ed. R. A. Leigh, vol.4 (Geneva, 1967), p.173 (letter 482).
59. Rousseau to Diderot, 16 March 1757, in *Correspondance*, p.178 (letter 484).
60. Diderot to Rousseau, 21/22 March 1757, in *Correspondance*, p.191 (letter 491).

had asserted his status as his true friend. Authentic friendship, Rousseau insisted, was purely concerned with sentiment, and stood outside and above any accounting of favours and exchanges:

> Vous me parlez de vos Services; je ne les avois point oubliez; mais ne vous y trompez pas. Beaucoup de gens m'en ont rendu qui n'étoient point de mes amis. [...] Tout votre empressement, tout votre zèle pour me procurer des choses dont je n'ai que faire me touchent peu. Je ne veux que de l'amitié, et c'est la seule chose qu'on me refuse. Ingrat, je ne t'ai point rendu de Service, mais je t'ai aimé, et tu me payeras de ta vie ce que j'ai senti pour toi durant trois mois.[61]

Somewhat contradicting this argument, however, later in this letter Rousseau asserted that it was he who had been the more loyal friend, never once having given a thought to the length of the walk, or to the weather, when walking out to Vincennes in 1749 'pour consoler mon ami'.

The relationship between Diderot and Rousseau never recovered from this charged dispute, though in a brief exchange of letters later in 1757 they emphatically addressed each other as friends.[62] Biographers of both men have tended either to attempt to adjudicate in their dispute, generally apportioning some blame on either side, or to interpret their clash as a reflection of the profound temperamental differences between the two *philosophes*.[63] It is more illuminating, however, to consider what this squabble reveals about how both men conceptualised friendship. Rousseau's unstable, whimsical idealism and defensive self-involvement is characteristically evident in this exchange. For Diderot also, however, friendship is revealed here to be a somewhat slippery category. He does not attempt to define the concept in any systematic way, but it is notable that, unlike Rousseau, he places his emphasis on the concrete social obligations that friendship entails. The reciprocal exchanges of friendship, embedded in a wider social matrix, were for Diderot of key importance and value. His analysis, however, is hesitant: he is emotionally engaged with Rousseau, and is by turns resentful, wounded, exasperated and forgiving towards him. Rather than attempting to follow the dispassionate analysis of earlier materialist writers on this topic, Diderot's correspondence reveals a much more flexible approach to human friendships, and is as close in spirit to Montaigne as it is to d'Argens or La Mettrie.

---

61. Rousseau to Diderot, 23/24 March 1757, in *Correspondance*, p.195 (letter 493).
62. *Correspondance*, p.292-93, 296-97 (letters 542 and 544).
63. See Lester G. Crocker, *J.-J. Rousseau: the quest (1712-1758)* (New York, 1968), p.302-306; Arthur M. Wilson, *Diderot* (New York, 1972), p.247-59; Jean Fabre, 'Deux frères ennemis: Diderot et Jean-Jacques Rousseau', *Diderot studies* 3 (1961), p.155-213.

Jacques Derrida's *Politics of friendship* (1994) offers a very suggestive exploration of the problematics of friendship, woven around a sustained interrogation of the puzzling dictum attributed to Aristotle, and revisited by (among others) Montaigne: 'O my friends, there is no friend.' From this starting point Derrida teases out the multiple paradoxes and exclusions that beset the ideal of friendship in the Western political and philosophical tradition. The abstract virtue of unselfish loving – the 'what' of friendship – stands in awkward disjuncture alongside the singularity of the 'who': the individual friend.[64] Perfect friendship is unthinkable: while we aspire to emulate perfection, attaining such a God-like ideal would dissolve the interpersonal mortal needs to which friendship responds. Most potently, perhaps, the private intimacy and trust that most profoundly characterises dyadic friendship awkwardly jars against political ideals of collective friendship, enshrined by the French Revolution as the principle of fraternity. All these visions of brotherhood-based friendship, meanwhile, teeter uncertainly on the rim of homoeroticism, while excluding all other relationalities: friendships between women; friendships between men and women; friendships across generations.[65] Several thinkers of the French Enlightenment attempted to use materialist ideas to overcome these uncertainties that clustered around attempts to make sense of friendship. Ultimately, however, their attempts to establish an unsentimental and rationalist understanding of close human relations proved highly resistant to resolution. Either their uncompromising analysis of friendship led to an extremely bleak or an alarmingly amoral view of human sociability, or, as if to stave off these perils, idealised notions of the nobility of friendship, even if only attainable by very few, tended to creep back into play. Despite the philosophical aspiration to bring interpersonal intimacies within the purview of public and objective scrutiny, this aspect of Enlightenment private life stubbornly remained intellectually and morally awkward.

64. Jacques Derrida, *Politics of friendship*, trans. George Collins (London, 1997), p.1-25.
65. Derrida, *Politics of friendship*, p.221-70.

Captivating Enlightenment: eighteenth-century children's books and the private life of the child

M. O. GRENBY

Children have, for some very obvious reasons, been right at the centre of writing about the history of private life. Volume 3 of the *Histoire de la vie privée* (1986) devotes one of its chapters to 'The child: from anonymity to individuality', and the series deals with aspects of the child's experience pretty much throughout – hardly surprising, one might think, given that the general editor was Philippe Ariès who did so much to reconfigure the history of childhood with *L'Enfant et la vie familiale sous l'ancien régime* (1960; translated in 1962 as *Centuries of childhood*). Historians of private life have looked very interestingly at the material culture of childhood – swaddling, walking frames, clothes, toys and so on – but they have apparently not been much inclined to approach the subject through children's books. This looks somewhat odd, since the development of children's literature as a distinct form in the eighteenth century fits very neatly with Ariès's much-buffeted but never capsized argument about the origins of modern childhood. Children's literature was a classic Enlightenment project, too: most of the mid- to late-eighteenth-century texts, the first recognisably modern children's books, worked hard to instil rationality and a sense of personal and social perfectibility, even religious tolerance and egalitarianism. It seems an obvious question, then, to ask what insight children's literature can give us into Enlightenment-era private lives, and this is what this chapter will be considering. It should be stated at the outset that the focus here is almost exclusively on Britain, where children's literature became established as a separate, flourishing section of print culture more quickly and successfully than elsewhere, and that this investigation will be concerned chiefly with books produced from around the 1770s to the 1820s.

Probably the dominant version of childhood that emerges from the children's literature of the late-eighteenth and early-nineteenth centuries is of middle-class boys and girls immersed in cosy domestic households, surrounded by relatives and neighbourhood friends, and well supplied with the necessities of life as well as with a variety of books, toys and other products designed especially for them. Here, to take one fairly typical example, is the opening of Dorothy Kilner's *The Holyday*

present, published in around 1781. Its moral didacticism and familiar tone
are typical of what is generally referred to as the 'moral tale', the
dominant form of children's fiction in Britain from the mid-eighteenth
century to the 1830s or 1840s. So too is its thoroughly familial setting and
the egregious parental solicitude on display:

> Mr. and Mrs. *Jennet* had six children, three boys, and three girls; the eldest
> boy's name was *George*, the second *Charles*, and the third *Thomas*, and the girls
> names were *Maria*, *Charlotte*, and *Harriet*. In this little book I intend to give
> you some account of each of them; as, I dare say, you will like to read about
> so many little boys and girls, and know which of them were good, and which
> naughty.
>
> Mr. and Mrs. *Jennet* were both extremely fond of their children, and took
> great pains to educate them properly, and make them behave as all little boys
> and girls should do; but notwithstanding all their care, Master *Charles* would
> very frequently give them a great deal of uneasiness, on account of his bad
> behaviour.[1]

Such ostentatious domesticity, it might be thought, is an almost manda-
tory component of children's literature. After all, even with all its blatant
didacticism, this kind of family story can seem fairly similar to many
modern classics of the form – Louisa May Alcott's *Little women* (1868), say,
or Laura Ingalls Wilder's *Little house on the prairie* (1935).[2] But when
contrasted with the sorts of texts that children would have consumed in
the early- and mid-eighteenth century and before, the emphatic domesticity of the later-eighteenth-century moral tale seems a more radical
departure. Other than purely religious texts and books of instruction,
the majority of texts to which children had access before the 1740s and,
for many, long afterwards, were romances, chapbooks and fairy tales, and
in these the domestic is noticeably absent. *Jack the giant-killer*, *Guy of
Warwick*, *Valentine and Orson* and *Dick Whittington* are wanderers, existing
almost wholly in the public sphere. Indeed, their stories are premised on
their readiness to seek their fortunes in the wide world.

What have traditionally been regarded as the first books published
especially for children from the 1740s were equally embedded in the
public sphere. Thomas Boreman's *Gigantick histories* books (from 1740)
were tours of London's public landmarks. John Newbery's books also
took the child outside the home. His famous *Adventures of Little Goody Two-
Shoes* (1765) followed its protagonist's journey into the world after the
death of her parents and her eviction from their house. Family stories
would continue to be published, yet many nineteenth-century children's

---

1. [Dorothy Kilner] *The Holyday present, containing anecdotes of Mr & Mrs Jennett, and their little
   family* (London, J. Marshall & Co., *c*.1790), p.9.
2. For a concise history of the family story see M. O. Grenby, *Children's literature* (Edinburgh,
   2008), ch.5.

books would return the child to the outside world, either in adventure stories such as Frederick Marryat's *Masterman Ready* (1841-1842) or fantasy fiction such as *Alice's adventures in Wonderland* (1865). Although family stories continued to be popular, the domestic setting and ethos of the moral tale stands in contrast with both earlier and later children's books equally. Indeed, one can trace this trajectory from adventures set in the public sphere to those firmly embedded in the private, and back to the public again, just by glancing at the titles of the major books in a single genre, the Robinsonnade. Whereas in Daniel Defoe's *Robinson Crusoe* (1719) the hero finds himself alone in the world, in J. H. Campe's *Robinson der jüngere* (1779-1780) and J. D. Wyss' *The Swiss family Robinson* (1812-1813) the protagonists are cast away as a family unit. Within half a century, though, the heroes are alone again, without their parents, as in the unbounded adventures of R. M. Ballantyne's *The Coral island* (1858) or Jules Verne's *L'Île mystérieuse* (1874-1875).

The fact that most children's books depicted lives confined to the home does not mean, of course, that real children in late-eighteenth- and early-nineteenth-century Britain were so circumscribed. The image of the household that books such as *The Holyday present* offer is rhetorical, not necessarily real. Precisely what kind of idealised domesticity was being presented in children's books is a question that bears further investigation. Most obviously, the child's proper place is shown to be within a close nuclear family: brothers, sisters, father and, most categorically, mother. Even the extended family is usually excluded from this close communion of parents and their children. Servants are certainly debarred – a substantiation of John Locke's influential dictum of a century before that contact with servants, and especially their 'Notions of *Sprites* and *Goblins*', corrupted the minds of children.[3] The French author of moral tales, Arnaud Berquin, was emphatic. The preface to the English translation of his *L'Ami des enfans* (1782) promises that 'Instead of those wild fictions of the Wonderful, in which their understanding is too commonly bewilder'd, they will here see only what occurs or may occur within the limits of their families.' Children reading his book, Berquin continues, will be 'accompanied by none, except their parents, the companions of their pastimes'. Indeed, Berquin mixes short dramas with his stories, designing them for domestic performance, thereby bringing the family together: 'the parents, having constantly some character to play therein,' he says, 'will have the satisfaction of partaking in the pastimes of their little family; while both experience an additional connection in the pleasure felt on one hand, and the gratitude evinced

---

3.   John Locke, *Some thoughts concerning education*, ed. John W. and Jean S. Yolton (1693; Oxford, 1989), p.196.

upon the other.'[4] We are used to thinking of Enlightenment-era reading as having been 'privatised' into a solitary undertaking, designed to foster interiority even as it also brought the reader into contact with a range of externally derived ideas.[5] Children's books could certainly be read alone, and this was sometimes represented as good practice. By and large, however, it seems to have been expected that children would use their books in the company of family members, almost always parents.

Certainly Berquin's moral stories, while attempting to teach various kinds of good behaviour, are fundamentally a protracted exposition of the naturalness, indissolubility and educational efficacy of the family. Motherhood is particularly celebrated, especially tender, interventionist and breastfeeding mothers. 'The little brother', for instance, centres around the first encounter between a little girl called (in the English edition) Fanny Warrington and her newborn brother. She is disappointed because he cannot play or talk and seems so weak, and she doubts that she was ever so incapable. Her father carefully explains how lovingly Fanny's mother had cared for her:

> If you did but know, my dearest Fanny, how much trouble you occasion'd her, you'd be astonish'd; for at first, you were so weak, you could not swallow any thing, and every day, we apprehended you would die. [...] and after she had once found means to make you suck, you soon became quite fat, and were the merriest little creature in the world. For two whole years, 'twas necessary every day and every minute of the day, she should attend you with the same degree of care and caution. Often, after she had dropt asleep thro' absolute fatigue, your crying would awake her. She would then get out of bed and hasten to your cradle. Fanny! my sweet Fanny! would she say, no doubt my pretty babe is dry; and put you to the breast.

The purpose of the story shifts slightly in this passage. Berquin's primary intention was to teach children about the incapacity of infancy, their own and that of others. Here, though, it is the interdependence of the family's members, and the mutual duties each member owes the others, that is being stressed. Fanny's mother sacrificed a great deal for her daughter; the least Fanny can do is to behave well. 'I will never grieve or disobey you for the time to come', she duly promises.[6] We note that this injunction to behave well within the family is not couched as a religious or even moral imperative, but rather premised on a rational calculation about reciprocality. One might almost say that Fanny's obedience is a

4.   Arnaud Berquin, *The Children's friend; consisting of apt tales, short dialogues, and moral dramas; all intended to engage attention, cherish feeling, and inculcate virtue, in the rising generation*, trans. Rev. Anthony Meilan, 8 vols (London, John Stockdale, 1786), vol.1, p.16-17 and 20-21.

5.   See R. Chartier, 'The practical impact of writing', in *Passions of the Renaissance*, ed. R. Chartier, p.111-59 (124-25).

6.   Berquin, *Children's friend*, vol.1, p.38-40, 42 and 45.

duty, not an act of love, and a civic rather than moral duty at that. Fundamentally, such stories offer as forceful an endorsement of family life as Jo March's much more famous exultation in the second part of *Little women*: 'I do think that families are the most beautiful thing in all the world!'[7]

This kind of interdependent, mutually supportive family was new in children's literature, and it was meant to be recognised as such. It was based more on rationality than on traditional religious or moral duty, and it was less patriarchal that we might assume. Michelle Levy even argues that the new 'cross-gendered, intergenerational model of a family' lay behind much of the most pioneering writing of the Romantic period, particularly its writing for children, providing authors with the 'authority for shaping public discourse' and 'progressing reform'.[8] More pessimistically, though, this promotion of the domestic could be rather claustrophobic. In moral tales the outside world is presented as a dangerous place. The furthest a child can go without risk of serious mishap is the immediate vicinity of the house. Indeed, the garden features very prominently in these moral tales, providing what Elise L. Smith identifies as a 'transitional zone' 'at the boundary between home and not-home', 'set apart from the wildness of nature but more flexible, both spatially and socially, than the confined rooms of the home'.[9] Here, often in arbours, bowers or summer houses, children were encouraged to experiment, practising social roles and perhaps playing at being adults, but always remaining under discreet adult observation from the house and safely contained within the clearly demarcated boundaries of the garden.

William Godwin argued that children should not be confined by books, 'shut up forever in imaginary scenes', but that books should enable them to 'live in the world'.[10] Moral tales were designed to allow this, introducing children not to a fantasy world but to people, things and attitudes that they were likely to encounter. But their purview was always very limited. Thus Ellen in *The New doll* (1826) explores the world around her, but never ventures far either physically or psychologically. Using her book, apparently a revision of Oliver Goldsmith's *A History of the earth, and animated nature* (1774), she is able to 'extract knowledge from the most unlettered': the bailiff teaches her about cattle; the plough-boy about snakes; the gardener 'explained the many wonders connected with

7. Louisa May Alcott, *Good wives* (1869; London, 1994), p.339.
8. Michelle Levy, *Family, authority and romantic print culture* (Basingstoke, 2008), p.17.
9. Elise L. Smith, 'Centering the home-garden: the arbor, wall, and gate in moral tales for children', *Children's literature* 36 (2008), p.24-48 (45, 32 and 24).
10. William Godwin, *The Enquirer: reflections on education, manners, and literature* (London, G. G. and J. Robinson, 1797), p.143-44.

insects and vegetable life'. 'Whenever she was puzzled by their provincial diction', she was able to turn to the book, 'which she always examined after such conversations', or, failing that, 'she referred herself to her papa, as the source of perfect information on the subject.' What is noticeable is that Ellen never ventures beyond her father's property, and asks questions only of her father's employees. The book might have connected the child to the world outside her house, but it was not a passport beyond its bounds.[11]

To go beyond the fence was to invite disaster, something that the many moral tales demonstrated with inset cautionary stories that ranged from mildly admonitory to downright grisly. Dorothy Kilner's *The Village school* (*c.*1795), though more shocking than most, is not wholly untypical in its alarmist presentation of what could happen. Home is safe; the school is safe; but the transitional and ungoverned space between them is as dangerous as Red Riding Hood's forest. When Jemmy Flint sits down on a low wall around a well to remove stones from his shoes it is almost inevitable that Roger Riot, 'with a design of frightening him', will push harder than he intends, precipitating Jemmy into the well. He is drowned. His mother and sister rush to the scene, Kilner using every trick she knows to accentuate their grief and force the lesson home.[12] Maria Edgeworth's famous 'The purple jar' (1796) is less gruesome but makes the hazards of the outside world equally obvious. Rosamond is shopping in London and amazed by everything she sees. 'She wished to stop to look at them, but there was a great number of people in the streets, and a great many carts, carriages, and wheelbarrows, and she was afraid to let go her mother's hand.' In this respect she is a wise child, but the story's denouement – Rosamond discovering that the 'purple jar' she had insisted on buying is actually only clear glass filled with foul purple liquid – demonstrates another danger of the outside world – its deceitful trickery – and under-lines the necessity of continual close parental supervision.[13]

If it was certainly the case, however, that 'Children should not wander beyond the bounds allowed them', as Priscilla Wakefield put it in her cautionary tale about the dangers befalling a 'Little wanderer', the importance of contented confinement within the domestic sphere is advanced as a lesson for parents too.[14] Their lives, and especially the

---

11. *The New doll, or Grandmamma's gift* (London, R. Ackermann, 1826), p.22-23.
12. D. Kilner, *The Village school, or a Collection of entertaining histories for the instruction and amusement of all good children*, in *From instruction to delight: an anthology of children's literature to 1850*, ed. Patricia Demers (Toronto, 2004), p.172-75.
13. Maria Edgeworth, 'The purple jar', from *The Parent's assistant* (1796), in *From instruction to delight*, ed. P. Demers, p.177.
14. Priscilla Wakefield, *Juvenile anecdotes, founded on facts* (1795-1798; London, Harvey & Darton, 1825), p.99.

mother's, must revolve around their children and the home. Here, for instance, is Mary Wollstonecraft providing a lecture on weaning directed ostensibly at her infant protagonist; it also speaks to child readers and, over their heads, to their parents:

> When you were hungry, you began to cry, because you could not speak. You were seven months without teeth, always sucking. But after you got one, you began to gnaw a crust of bread. It was not long before another came pop. At ten months you had four pretty teeth, and you used to bite me. Poor mamma! Still I did not cry, because I am not a child, but you hurt me very much. [...] Yes, says papa, and he tapped you on the cheek, you are old enough to eat? Come to me, and I will teach you, my little dear, for you must not hurt poor mamma, who has given you her milk, when you could not take any thing else.

This domestic idyll, a fragment of a children's book left unfinished at Wollstonecraft's death and posthumously published by her husband William Godwin, is especially poignant because it portrays a life they might have lived together had Wollstonecraft survived the birth of their daughter. The determined effort not to condescend to the child yet to remain easily comprehensible is notable. But for all the forced cheerfulness, the text seems constricting, a sort of literary swaddling. The household is enveloped in stillness and silence – the sacred hush of the family – and the characters are so full of mutual love and respect for each other's needs that they move always on tiptoe:

> When I caught cold some time ago, I had such a pain in my head, I could scarcely hold it up. Papa opened the door very softly, because he loves me. You love me, yet you made a noise. You had not the sense to know that it made my head worse, till papa told you. [...]
> You say that you do not know how to think. Yes; you do a little. The other day papa was tired; he had been walking about all the morning. After dinner he fell asleep on the sopha. I did not bid you be quiet; but you thought of what papa said to you, when my head ached. This made you think that you ought not to make a noise, when papa was resting himself. So you came to me, and said to me, very softly, Pray reach me my ball, and I will go to play in the garden, till papa wakes.
> You were going out; but thinking again, you came back to me on your tiptoes. Whisper – whisper. Pray mama, call me, when papa wakes; for I shall be afraid to open the door to see, lest I should disturb him.
> Away you went. – Creep – Creep – and shut the door as softly as I could have done myself.
> That was thinking.[15]

For Wollstonecraft, as for other moral-tale authors, the family is bonded

---

15. 'Lessons' (1798) in *The Works of Mary Wollstonecraft*, ed. Janet Todd and Marilyn Butler, 7 vols (London, 1989), vol.4, p.470 and 473-74.

by an economy of solicitude, premised on an empathy based on rational thought.

In some moral tales, the household was not limited only to the members of the nuclear family, nor quite so sequestered from all impingement of the outside world. For example, in one of the most successful books of the period, John Aikin and Anna Lætitia Barbauld's *Evenings at home* (1792-1796), the household is larger. The book opens with a description of the happy Fairbourne family, a father and mother and their 'numerous progeny of children of both sexes'. 'The house was seldom unprovided with visitors', though – 'the intimate friends or relations of the owners, who were entertained with cheerfulness and hospitality, free from ceremony and parade'. It is the Fairbourne parents and their adult friends alike who write the short texts that are placed in a box, from which they are drawn out one by one to be read by the assembled children. This is all described in the preface; the stories and lessons fill the ensuing six volumes. The action still takes place at home, as the book's title stresses. Indeed, even though some of the children were 'educated at home under their parents' care, and part were sent out to school', we should note that the box is opened only when 'all the children were assembled in the holidays', when the family is whole again. School, in the moral tale, breaks the family unit. It is a necessary separation perhaps, but one that is regarded as an interruption of the child's life, not a normal part of it.[16]

The relative merits and perils of a private and a public education were a matter for sustained debate in the eighteenth century in conduct books, pedagogical treatises, novels and many other forums.[17] The authors of moral tales, though, were more decided than most, continually presenting a hostile, or at the least ambivalent, attitude to public schooling, especially for girls. The 'attendant evils [...] which await a boarding-school education, are such', wrote Dorothy Kilner, that they 'counter-balance the advantages that arise from it.' Schooling outside the home could sometimes be necessary, Kilner conceded, but would always be inferior to an education provided within the private sphere. 'Were your mamma's time at her own disposal, I doubt not but she would gladly dedicate every moment to your improvement; and, by her assiduity, amply supply the place of all other instructions', she explained to the young, female dedicatee of one of her *Anecdotes of a boarding-school* (*c.*1790),

---

16. John Aikin and Anna Lætitia Barbauld, *Evenings at home, or the Juvenile budget opened: consisting of a variety of miscellaneous pieces for the instruction and amusement of young persons*, 6 vols (1792-1796; London, J. Johnson, 1809), vol.1, p.1-2.

17. See Michèle Cohen, 'Gender and the private/public debate on education in the long eighteenth century', in *Public or private education? Lessons from history*, ed. Richard Aldrich (London, 2004), p.15-35.

but other cares, including the education of her younger children, could make this impossible. This suspicious and grudging attitude to education outside the home, reflected in the book's somewhat oxymoronic subtitle, 'an *antidote* to the vices of those *useful* seminaries', points to an intriguing paradox at the root of the school story, a genre of children's literature that Kilner was helping to establish and which has remained popular to this day.[18] The school story, it seems, was founded not on the sort of enthusiasm for school life that one finds later in *Tom Brown's school-days* (1857), Enid Blyton's *Malory Towers* stories (1946-1951) or the *Harry Potter* books (1997-2007), but on the conviction that school life was bad for the child and required an antidote. For the authors of early school stories the solution was often to make the school as much like home as possible. Certainly, girls' schools, as represented in later-eighteenth-century children's books, tended carefully to replicate the family household. Sarah Fielding's *The Governess, or the little female academy* (1749), often called the first school story, provides a surrogate family both for some of its pupils, who are orphans, and for the eponymous Mrs Teachum, a widow whose own children have died. Indeed, the nine pupils are referred to as 'Mrs. Teachum's well-regulated family'.[19]

In some ways, then, the representations of education in moral tales endorse Jacques Gélis's statement that 'There was no contradiction between private child-rearing in the nuclear family and public education.'[20] In the world of the moral tales, though, the supremacy of home education over public schooling was seldom in doubt, even for boys. The hero of *Montague Park, or family incidents* (1825) is the well-mannered Charles. His father explains to the mother of two other schoolboys that 'it would, indeed, be unpardonable in Charles, if his manners had not been refined and polite, as he had been greatly indulged, in never being separated from his mother, and in whose constant society it was natural for him to have acquired that softness of address which is seldom observable in the school-boy.' He goes on,

> Not that I wish it to be understood [...] that I have an antipathy to public schools: far from it; for many are certainly both a pride and national blessing; yet I feel repugnant to the idea of sending boys, at too tender an age, from the parental roof, where they might be well instructed by more tender management, as I am conscious that a contrary plan too often effaces

18. D. Kilner, *Anecdotes of a boarding-school, or an Antidote to the vices of those useful seminaries*, 2 vols (London, John Marshall and Co., *c.*1790), vol.1, p.v-vi (emphasis added). For a brief history of the school story see Grenby, *Children's literature*, ch.4.

19. Sarah Fielding, *The Governess, or the Little female academy*, ed. Candace Ward (1749; Peterborough, Ontario, 1995), p.163.

20. Jacques Gélis, 'The child: from anonymity to individuality', in *Passions of the Renaissance*, ed. R. Chartier, p.309-325 (321).

those generous and amiable feelings, which, by a little more culture, might have been matured into excellence.[21]

Authors were also determined to show that children could receive a much more dynamic education at home than at school, and across a wide curriculum too. In order to teach his children geography, Mr Davenport in Barbara Hofland's *Panorama of Europe* (1813) devises a game in which each child has to masquerade as a different European country, learning and reciting its unique features. Mr Davenport sits on a throne to judge the performances. Beside him sits Mrs Davenport, who, naturally, represents England. She is 'a just representative of a country', says her husband, 'which, like her, not only spreads her matronly arms over her own children, to rear them to virtue, and refine them to elegance, but extends the blessings to strangers also, and bids the children of many a distant land rejoice in her protection.'[22]

Equally, moral tales could openly display a preference for home schooling by some caustic portrayals of public education. Maria Edgeworth's story 'The barring out, or party spirit' (1796) dwells on the eighteenth-century English custom of schoolboys locking themselves into a classroom with enough food and drink to survive a siege by their teacher.[23] Although, as its subtitle indicates, the story's ostensible object is to censure the schoolboy factionalism that has led to the barring-out, it also functions as a reproach to public education. Identification with a group outside the family – with mere school friends for instance – is to be frowned on. A strong identity with the family, on the other hand, is always commendable, as the great majority of Edgeworth's children's stories are designed to demonstrate. The many Rosamond stories, including 'The purple jar', emphasise the bond between the daughter and her parents. The entire didactic scheme in Edgeworth's long-lived *Harry and Lucy* series is premised on the collaboration of two siblings. Lucy, Edgeworth insisted, though scarcely older than Harry, would be the most effective teacher for him, far better than any tutor. Edgeworth's biography was probably at the root of this conviction. Her father, after all, had twenty children, all of whom, from Maria's return from school in 1782 onwards, were educated at home, often by their siblings and most especially by Maria. It has often been asserted that she road-tested her tales on her brothers and sisters, gaining their approval before transfer-

21. A. Selwyn, *Montague Park, or Family incidents* (London, William Cole, 1825), p.36.

22. Barbara Hofland, *The Panorama of Europe, or a New game of geography* (London, Minerva Press, 1813), p.20-21.

23. M. Edgeworth, *The Parent's assistant, or Stories for children: part 1* (London, J. Johnson, 1796), p.149-226. See Rex Cathcart, 'Festive capers? Barring-out the schoolmaster', *History today* 38 (1988), p.49-53.

ring them to paper, and that what she wrote depended on the age of the children being brought up at Edgeworthstown at any given time.[24]

It will be clear by now that, in the moral tales of the late-eighteenth and early-nineteenth centuries, a private, domestic upbringing was almost always promoted as the ideal. The books endorsed children's lives which were led largely at home, presenting the rest of the world to be much like the fairy-tale forest, full of lethal hazards and treacherous predators, threats to both moral and physical well-being. Schools, if well run by parental substitutes, could be tolerated, even welcomed, as an extension of the private sphere. But the best, most effective and innovative education was available at home, in the school holidays if not throughout the year. This was, to rephrase Edgeworth's story title, a sort of 'barring-in'. The child reader was constantly being told, in his or her books, that they were at home only at home. Historians of the private life may claim that the Enlightenment's burgeoning Republic of Letters increasingly provided a sort of rival public sphere to the state – a place for 'the public use of reason by private individuals' – but this was seldom the case for children.[25] Their 'republic of letters', during the early phase of children's literature, was more constrictive. It was not a place where they could forge social links with other children outside their physical ambit, but where the propriety of the home was stridently recommended. Their books were inward-looking, launching children into the world only in incremental stages. Children's books, in effect, were designed to be interposed between the child and the public sphere. This was true for parents too. In the moral tale, parents, and particularly mothers, were urged to look inward not outward, and to regard the nurture and education of their children as their highest, even only, priority. What now needs to be considered is why this was the case.

The answer Philippe Ariès might have given is that this insistence on the domestic accords with a widespread socio-cultural shift towards a society in which the nuclear family formed the basic unit of identity. 'After 1800 individualism declined and the family took on new importance', he wrote: 'The family became the focus of the concerns of even its more recalcitrant members.'[26] This is a convincing argument, but other factors might also be adduced to explain the emphasis given to family and the domestic sphere in early children's books. For one thing, we cannot really understand the children's literature of this period unless

24. Marilyn Butler, *Maria Edgeworth* (Oxford, 1972), p.161.

25. Roger Chartier, paraphrasing Jürgen Habermas, introduction to ch.1 in *Passions of the Renaissance*, p.17. See also Anne Goldgar, *Impolite learning: conduct and community in the Republic of Letters* (New Haven, CT, and London, 1995).

26. Ariès, 'Introduction', p.7-8.

we remember that it was a new and rather vulnerable literary product in the later eighteenth century, only just establishing itself as a commercially viable commodity. Its publishers and authors were anxious to create and cultivate their market, not so much endorsing their own products against those of their rivals within the same sector of print culture (although they often did this too), but attempting to promote the worth of the product as a whole. They needed to please their potential consumers, both those who they imagined bought the books – parents, teachers and other adults – and those intended to use them – children. Pleasing the projected reader was easier. Authors and publishers attempted to make their texts and images, and their pedagogical strategies, appeal to children – to mix 'instruction with delight', as John Newbery famously put it at the very start of what is often claimed to be the first modern children's book, *A Little pretty pocket book* (1744). The promise of education with entertainment was also designed to appeal to parents, but what becomes clear from reading the children's books of the period is that a different propitiatory strategy was also thought to be essential. This was to assure parents that the books being produced for their children were in no way intended as a substitute for the parent, and that the sanctity of the family was certainly not being compromised by this new commodity. Rather, children's books were carefully presented as an augmentation of the family.

The opening of Anna Lætitia Barbauld's *Lessons for children* (1778-1779), a pioneering and influential work but typical in its ostentatious embedding of the text within the family circle, demonstrates this well: 'Where is the pin to point with? Here is a pin. Do not tear the book. Only naughty boys tear books. Charles shall have a pretty new lesson. Spell that word. Good boy. Now go and play.' The start of the second part shows how things have progressed: 'I hope you have been a good boy, and read all the pretty words I wrote for you before. You have, you say; You have read them till you are tired, and you want some more new lessons. Come then, sit down. Now you and I will tell stories.'[27] Barbauld has produced a text which dramatises its own use, and identifies itself as a tool, not a replacement, for mothers. The idea was clearly to create overlap between the fictional parent and the real-life parent reading the book to their children. This is even clearer in Edgeworth's *Harry and Lucy*. It begins with the two children leaping out of bed and preparing for breakfast. Harry is unwilling to make his bed, so his father chides him by telling him that in some countries, and certainly onboard ships, it is men who always perform this task. A footnote demonstrates Edgeworth understood the

27. Barbauld, *Lessons for children* (1778-1779; London, J. Johnson,1801), part 1, p.6 and part 2, p.4.

roles of this fictional father and the adult reading the book as almost entirely merged: 'Here', she advises, 'the child if at a distance from the coast, should be told what is meant by different countries; what a ship is, and what is meant by a sailor, &c.'[28]

By and large, though, it was in the paratextual material – titles, prefaces, dedications, advertisements and so on – that the producers of children's books located their attempts to convince parents that books provided support for existing family structures rather than seeking to replace them. Gérard Genette described 'paratext' as providing 'a "vestibule" that offers the world at large the possibility of either stepping inside or turning back'. It is 'a zone not only of transition but also of *transaction*'.[29] This can be seen very clearly in these children's books. The 'transaction' is with the adult purchaser, not the eventual child reader. The paratext is designed for their benefit, assuring them that they are not being displaced and enjoining them to involve themselves in the deployment of the text. The very title of Maria Edgeworth's earliest collection of children's stories, *The Parent's assistant* (1796), instantly makes this clear. So too do a great many frontispieces to children's books, from *A Little pretty pocket book* on, which insist on the centrality of the mother within the child's 'republic of letters' by subtly amending familiar images of Venus teaching Cupid, St Anne teaching the Virgin or the Madonna teaching Christ to show a mother teaching her child with the very book in which the image itself was appearing. The *mise en abyme* element of these images was not intended merely to amuse, but was designed to draw children unfamiliar with the use of books into the text and to reassure parents that they were not being usurped. They also provided a discreet but insistent directive about the proper contexts and modes of book use. Both children and adults were being told that children's books should be used at home and under parental supervision.

The deference that the producers of children's literature seem to show to parents is remarkable. Authors and publishers make bold claims about the efficacy and value of their books of course, but they are careful to stress that the opinions of the parent should never be subordinate to the authority of the text. In a moral tale called *Virtue and vice* (*c*.1780), for instance, the commendable hero Charles is praised for reading many books, 'but he never did so', the text insists, 'till he had first consulted his parents what were fit for him to read'. This contrasts with Harry Heedless, for whenever he 'thought fit to read, he took the first book that came to hand'. It is no real surprise that Charles ends up rich and

28. M. Edgeworth, *Harry and Lucy* (London, Longman, Brown and Co., 1856), p.4 and n.
29. Gérard Genette, *Paratexts: thresholds of interpretation*, trans. Jane E. Lewin (Cambridge, 1997), p.1-2.

happy while Harry descends into pauperism.[30] The lesson here is aimed at children but, just as often, moral tales seem calculated to shame parents into a better sense of their duty. 'I wish my mamma had leisure to mark for me what she approved as suited to my years'; the precocious Master Brotherton says in Ellenor Fenn's *Juvenile correspondence* (1783), 'but she has so many children, that, although she devotes almost all her time to us, she can not find any for that purpose'. His correspondent, Master Boiscot, is more fortunate, praising his mother for curtailing his choice of books and making extracts of the best authors.[31]

Anxiety about the deleterious effects of removing the child from the home and school stories, such as Kilner's *Anecdotes of a boarding-school* and Fenn's *School occurrences* (1782), lead to concrete strategies which will enable a parent to regulate a child's reading, even at a distance. The first of these books comprises letters from a mother to her schoolgirl daughter that comfort, chide, advise, praise and commiserate. They establish an outpost of the home in the dangerous territory of the public school, both for the heroine of the story and, vicariously, for any actual owners of the book who may have taken it to school with them. *School occurrences*, meanwhile, traces the career of Miss Worthy while she is away from home at school. Fortunately, her books have been marked for her by her mother, the annotations showing those sections which she is permitted to read, and those she is not. She is harshly mocked for sticking to these limits by Miss Pert – 'I vow, I wonder that you have not strings to your eye-lids, and the ends kept in your Mamma's hands' – but Miss Worthy commands the reader's admiration for her steadfastness and obedience. 'I read nothing but what my Mamma supplies me with herself', she steadily declares.[32] This is a lesson in obedience for children but, with an eye to adult co-readers, Fenn was also deliberately comparing parental, school and textual education, and pronouncing that the first of these should take primacy. Above all, texts such as this assure their users, both children and parents, that children remain citizens of the home, as it were, even when they travel in the foreign country of the school.

Some moral-tale authors described a world in which the influence of the home never waned, not even when the child grew up and, in the case of Harriet Ventum's *Charles Leeson, or the Soldier* (1810), joined the army. Even campaigning on the Continent, apparently against Napoleon in the

---

30. *Virtue and vice, or the History of Charles Careful, and Harry Heedless* (1780?; London, J. Harris, 1815), p.10.

31. [Ellenor Fenn], *Juvenile correspondence, or Letters suited to children from four to above ten years of age* (London, John Marshall and Co., [1783]), p.125 and 132.

32. [Fenn], *School occurrences: supposed to have arisen among a set of young ladies, under the tuition of Mrs. Teachwell; and to be recorded by one of them* (London, John Marshall and Co., [1783]), p.88-94.

Peninsular War, Charles is governed by his mother's dicta. 'Your mother again, Leeson!' chides a fellow soldier, echoing Miss Pert in *School occurrences*:

> for pity's sake, do not shew your leading-strings, even if you chuse to wear them – Why man, you will be scoffed at and ridiculed by the whole army, if you are continually quoting the old-fashioned sayings of an old woman. We know very well, all mothers tell us not to do this bad thing, nor the other bad thing; but who minds what they say; they cannot see us; and it is very hard if we, who are exposed to a thousand dangers, and are fighting their battles, may not enjoy a drunken frolic now and then.[33]

It is only letters from Charles' mother that keep him virtuous. For the child reader who might lack such a paragon of motherhood though, it was moral tales such as *Charles Leeson* that were supposed to perform this function, colonising the public sphere with the values, rules and allegiances of the private.

It has been argued that books provide readers with a means of beholding, and even communicating with, the outside world, while they stay, physically, in the home; that reading is 'an event somewhere between the private and the social'.[34] It could be maintained that this is the case with at least some eighteenth- and early-nineteenth-century moral tales for children. Readers of *Charles Leeson* were transported to a military camp on the Iberian Peninsular, for example, and many others were shown what it was like to be at a boarding school. Yet the majority of moral tales confined children to the house or the garden, and even in those which took the child further from the home, its influence remained paramount. The books may have been designed to enlighten children in various areas – morality, horticulture, natural sciences, religion, commerce, politeness and so on – and many of them were undoubtedly captivating, their text and images delighting readers then as they delight collectors now. But they were also captivating in another sense, working to keep readers socially and psychologically confined. For children, books were not a gateway to more extended communities beyond the household, but a cordon around it.

One way of explaining why children's literature was so emphatic about the virtues of home, attempting to expand its influence, domesticating school and even the army, is to place it in a larger context. 'Rather than seeing the public sphere "invading" and "colonizing" the private sphere', Anne K. Mellor writes in *Mothers of a nation* (a book which rather surprisingly fails to consider children's literature in detail), 'I see the

33. Harriet Ventum, *Charles Leeson, or the Soldier* (London, J. Harris, 1810), p.65-66.
34. Markman Ellis, *The Politics of sensibility: race, gender and commerce in the sentimental novel* (Cambridge, 1996), p.16.

values of the private sphere associated primarily with women – moral virtue and an ethic of care – infiltrating and finally dominating the discursive public sphere during the Romantic era.'[35] Certainly, it would not be difficult to understand children's writers' attempts to domesticate the outside world for their readers as part of this larger process. A more prosaic explanation for the wish to circumscribe the world that a child might encounter through reading is the need of authors and publishers to promote their new product by reassuring parents that it supported their role rather than challenging it. Whatever the reason, however, the important point is that reading functioned differently for adults and for children. For adults – or at least for adult men – reading was supposed to expand horizons. For children it was not. This is not to say that real children were always so contained by their reading: memoirs, marginalia and the reprimands of infuriated educationalists clearly show that many children were very capable of subverting the intentions of the moral tales. Publishing for children was generally intended to keep children as children – to prevent them 'being introduced so early into the world', as one moral tale of 1805 put it, that they would 'lose the simplicity and engaging diffidence of youth'.[36] For children, books were intended to be not a key to the wider world but a leash, and the 'republic of letters' was seldom expected to extend further than the garden fence.

35. Anne K. Mellor, *Mothers of the Nation: women's political writing in England, 1780-1830* (Bloomington, IN, 2002), p.11.
36. Elizabeth Sandham, *The Twin sisters, or the Advantages of religion* (1805; London, J. Harris, 1816), p.64-65.

Schiller, gonorrhoea and original sin in the emotional life of a Russian nobleman

ANDREI ZORIN

If we draw a clear dichotomy between 'public' and 'private' lives, individual emotions would definitely belong to the 'private' sphere. In a way, they can even be regarded as the epitome of the private sphere: feelings and emotions are normally perceived as an inalienable property of the person who experiences them even if they choose to share them with others.

Typical descriptions of Romantic love emphasise the role of personal choice rather than social conditioning in the shaping of inner feelings.[1] Yet a more productive analysis departs from the premise that custom and socialisation define the ways in which love, hate, and even grief and laughter are expressed, and also dictate the situations that provoke such emotions and the nature of their experience. The latter approach has become commonplace since the early 1970s, when Clifford Geertz described emotions as 'cultural artefacts', arguing that

> in man neither regnant fields nor mental sets can be formed with sufficient precision in the absence of guidance from symbolic models of emotion. In order to make up our minds we must know how to feel about things; and to know how we feel about things we need the public images of sentiment that only ritual, myth and art can provide.[2]

The role of these 'public images of sentiment' in the formation of individual emotional responses can be understood with the help of the concept of 'event coding' introduced by Dutch psychologists Nico Frijda and Batja Mesquita into their scheme of emotional process. As pointed out by these authors, emotional processes

> are elicited by the particular meaning associated with the event rather than by the nature of an event per se. [...] As cultures possess explicit verbal categories to identify classes of events with particular associated meanings and affective evaluations, a given event [...] may be coded differently in

---

1. See Jacqueline Sarsby, *Romantic love and society* (London, 1983), p.1.
2. Clifford Geertz, *The Interpretation of cultures* (New York, 1973), p.81-82. On the recent historiography of the debate see William M. Reddy, *The Navigation of feeling: a framework for the history of emotions* (Cambridge, 2001).

various cultures. Different encodings may relate similar events to different concerns and thus, give rise to different emotions.

In the process of coding an event the subject of emotion identifies it (not necessarily giving such identification a verbal shape) as danger, insult, seduction, shock and so on. The 'coding' associated with the event suggests a corresponding 'appraisal manifest in fear, anger, wonder etc.'[3] Both the 'event coding' and the 'appraisal', however, are largely determined by the limited pool of patterns available to a given person that must be adjusted to specific experience.

This chapter will try to trace the process of transformation of such 'public images of sentiment', into an individually felt emotion. Our analysis will be based on a case where the event that had to be emotionally encoded and appraised was a manifestly private one. A young Russian noble in his late teens visited a prostitute and contracted gonorrhoea. In order 'to know how to feel about it' he had to attribute to his disease a particular meaning. Both 'the symbolic models of emotion' that he acquired during his adolescence and his own psychological problems needed to be reinterpreted to form a coherent emotional narrative. The process of this reinterpretation as expressed in his private diary reflects a generational (and fundamental) shift in the value systems of the educated Russian public at the turn of the centuries. In a way, it allows us a quick glimpse at the emergence of early Romantic sensibility in Russia.

In mid-January 1800 Andrei Ivanovich Turgenev, an eighteen-year-old graduate of the Moscow Noble Boarding School (Moskovskii blagorodnyi Pansion), an aspiring writer, a leader of a small circle of young Moscow intellectuals and a son of Ivan Turgenev, one of the most prominent Russian Freemasons and the head of Moscow University, was busy trying in his diary to deal with his sexuality and the increasing desire to lose his virginity.[4]

Andrei Turgenev had begun his diary two months earlier, on 9 November 1799. This was for him a major turning point: 'Finally everything of which I have dreamt for so long is going to be fulfilled.

---

3. Nico H. Frijda and Batja Mesquita, 'The social roles and the function of emotions', in *Emotion and culture: empirical studies of mutual influence*, ed. Shinoby Kitayama and Hazel Rose Markus (Washington, DC, 1994), p.57-59.
4. On Andrei Turgenev in English, see Marc Raeff, 'Russian youth on the eve of Romanticism: Andrei Turgenev and his circle', in *Revolution and politics in Russia: essays in memory of B. I. Nikolaevsky*, ed. Alexander and Janet Rabinowitch, with Ladis K. D. Kristof (Bloomington, IN, 1972), p.39-54. His diary, although discovered a hundred years ago, remains unpublished apart from the small part covering early 1802. See 'Iz dnevnika Andreia Ivanovicha Turgeneva', in *Vostok-Zapad. Issledovaniia. Perevody. Publikatsii*, ed. M. Virolainen (Moscow, 1984), p.100-39.

Here I am going to write down all my thoughts, feelings, joyous and sorrowful, am going to deliberate about the subjects that are of interest to me without being afraid of anyone's censure.'[5] Writing the diary was an endeavour not only encouraged, but directly prescribed by the traditional Freemasonic upbringing. The diarist was meant to scrutinise his thoughts and behaviour in order to correct them and achieve moral perfection.[6] In fact, Ivan Turgenev, Andrei's father, translated the most popular manual of this sort: *Self knowledge* by John Mason. The third edition of this book appeared in Moscow in 1800 with a special 'Epistle to my children' attached by the translator to the treatise. Here Turgenev urged his sons to follow the instructions given in the book and 'to acquire the means to pass difficult and unpleasant ways leading to self-knowledge'.[7]

Andrei Ivanovich, Turgenev's elder son, began his diary the same year. There is quite a lot of self-scrutiny and self-depreciation there. It seems unlikely, however, that this diary would have been approved by his father. The young diarist was quite explicit about a chance to express himself 'without being afraid of anyone's censure'. In this notebook he recorded conversations with his friends, books he had read and theatre performances he had seen. The subject that was by far the most 'interesting' to him, however, was his love for the actress and singer Elizaveta Sandunova, a renowned beauty with an improbable past and dubious reputation.[8]

Andrei Turgenev was tortured by what he described as 'Sandunova's enigma'. By this phrase he defined the contradiction between her beauty and angelic voice and less than flattering rumours that surrounded her family life. According to Turgenev, this paradox was also reflected in Sandunova's theatrical repertoire – the actress played both the virtuous maidens and the cynical courtesans. The young admirer regarded her success in different parts not as proof of her theatrical talents, but as a manifestation of the deep ambiguity of her personality. He dreamt of translating for her Schiller's *Cabale und Liebe*, believing that once she

5. 'Итак, теперь может исполниться то, чего я желал так долго. Здесь буду я вписывать все свои мысли, чувства, радостные и неприятные, буду рассуждать о интересных для меня предметах, не боясь ничьей критики.' RORLI (Manuscript Depostary of the Institute of the Russian Literature of Russian Academy of Science, SPb.), fund 309 (Turgenev family), file 271, 2. All further quotations from Turgenev's diaries are from this fund with file and sheet number specified in brackets after the quote. An edition of the diaries is currently under preparation by M. Virolainen, A. Koiten and myself. I am grateful to my co-authors for their permission to use the results of our work.

6. See Lidia Ginzburg, *On psychological prose* (Princeton, NJ, 1991), p.30-33.

7. I. Mason, *Poznanie samogo sebia* (Moscow, 1800), p.iv.

8. The biography and reputation of Elizaveta Sandunova is discussed in Andrei Zorin, 'Catherine II versus Beaumarchais: the scandal at the St. Petersburg court at the time of the French Revolution', in *Russia and the West: missed opportunities, unfulfilled dialogues*, ed. E. Waegemans (Brussels, 2006), p.47-54.

appeared on the stage as Louise she would never be able either to play a
scheming temptress on the stage or to behave like one in real life.

'Sandunova's enigma' not only provoked anxiety in Andrei Turgenev,
but also intensified his erotic desires. His fanatical adoration of Schiller's
plays gave licence to this as well. On 15 November 1799 his deliberations
concerned yet one further quotation from *Cabale und Liebe* (271, 8*v.*):

> 'Oh! it must be more rapturous even to be her licentious paramour than to
> burn with the purest flame for any other! Would she surrender her charms to
> unlicensed pleasure she might dissolve the soul itself to sin, and make
> voluptuousness pass for virtue.'[9] Only now do I understand the full power
> of these words. Probably earlier I was glossing them over without paying
> attention, but suddenly they occurred to me when I was thinking about ...[10]

Needless to say, *diese Mädchen* was totally unavailable to him and he
could only dream 'of fornicating' with her from the distance of the
theatre stalls. The erotic component of his dreams was to be realised *mit
andern*. Schiller provided him with a powerful pattern to see his own
youthful sexuality in a less derogatory light than afforded by the prescriptions of the Masonic quest for virtue.

It is not entirely clear why Turgenev regarded the beginning of his
diary as the fulfilment of 'everything he was dreaming of for so long' and
what had earlier prevented him from keeping it. It seems highly unlikely
that the reasons were of a practical kind. The notebook itself would have
been easily available and affordable. Nevertheless, Andrei Ivanovich used
its pages in an extremely sparing way. When a year later he completed it,
before starting a new one, he carried on writing in the margins and filling
the gaps between earlier entries. Still, there are two completely blank
pages in the notebook. The reverse side of sheet 41 and sheet 42 are left
empty, artificially drawing a dividing line not only between the entry
written on 17 January in the late evening and the next one, recorded
early in the morning of 20 January, but also between two major periods
of his life, that precede and follow 'Fall'. From the dating of entries we
can infer that this earth-shattering event must have taken place on 19
January (271, 42*v.*):

9.   Friedrich Schiller, *Werke*, ed. Julius Petersen, 42 vols (Weimar, 1943-), 5 Neue Ausgabe, 124
     (*Cabale und Liebe*, IV.3).
10. 'O! es muß reizender seyn, mit diesem Mädchen zu buhlen, als mit andern noch so
     himmlisch zu schwärmen! – Wollte sie ausschweifen, wollte sie, sie könnte den Werth der
     Seele herunter bringen, und die Tugend mit der Wollust verfälschen!!' ('Oh! it must be
     more rapturous even to be her licentious paramour than to burn with the purest flame
     for any other! Would she surrender her charms to unlicensed pleasure she might dissolve
     the soul itself to sin, and make voluptuousness pass for virtue') 'Теперь я понимаю всю
     силу этих слов. Может быть, прежде я пропускал их без внимания, но они вдруг
     пришли мне в голову, когда я думал о ...'. Quotations from Turgenev's diary preserve his
     original German spelling.

This night was very remarkable. I woke up quite often and nearly each time was close to despair. Being alone I had time and rest to feel and fully ponder the deplorable consequences and could only pray. I was praying zealously and it seemed to me that at this very moment I was feeling some joy, and finally in the morning – now – in joyous gratitude I am ready to shed tears before my CONSOLER.

The Father of Thy children! The Spirit of goodness and love! Accept these grateful tears from your poor son! I understand that Thou! Thou sent me the sweetness of those tears. Thou showed me that you are the consoler of Thy children. Accept the sacrifice of my tears.

The misfortunes soften the heart; they can transform a caustic cold wit into a sensible, kind, tender brother of his brothers. They help us to feel the sweetness of happiness with a double strength and make us kinder.

I take a firm intention never to stray from the path of chastity; I believe that this example will stay in my memory for long.[11]

It is not too difficult to reconstruct the fears and hopes expressed in this mournful and sweet prayer. For the realisation of his erotic aspirations, Andrei Ivanovich must have turned to paid sex and was desperately afraid of the 'deplorable consequences' of his behaviour – namely of a venereal disease.

To minimise such risks, many Russian and not only Russian noble parents actually encouraged their adolescent sons to start their sexual lives with housemaids and serf girls. During the summer of 1799, several months before he started his diary, Turgenev met young Count Saltykov and was so impressed by their conversation that he chose to record it in his diary in German (276, 35):

He told me without any questions on my part that since he was 14 he kept a girl, but she was taken away from him so now he has F. And so forth. He also asked me several questions on the same topic. Than he took me to his room and showed to me his petite *bibl[ioteque] choisie*.[12]

11. 'Сегодняшняя ночь была очень примечательна. Просыпался очень часто и почти всякий раз был близок к отчаянию. Один, я имел время и покой, чтобы чувствовать и размышлять во всей полноте о плачевных для меня следствиях, и мне оставалось только молиться. – Я молился усердно, и казалось мне, будто в самую ту минуту я ощущал какое-то услаждение: наконец, поутру – теперь – я в радостной благодарности готов проливать слезы перед моим УТЕШИТЕЛЕМ.

Отец чад Твоих! Дух благости и любви! Приими от бедного сына Твоего сии благодарные слезы. Я познаю, что Ты! Ты послал мне сладость этих слез. Ты явил мне, что ты утешитель чад твоих. Приими жертву слез моих.

Несчастья умягчают сердце, они могут сделать колкаго, холоднаго насмешника чувствительным, добрым, нежным братом братьев своих. Они заставляют нас вдвое чувствовать сладость счастия и делают нас добрее.

Я принимаю твердое намерение не удаляться никогда от пути целомудрия; этот пример, думаю, долго останется в памяти моей.'

12. Er entdeckte mir ohne irgend eine Nachforschung von meiner Seite, daß er von seinem 14.ten Jahre ein Mädchen unterhalten habe, daß sie ihm aber weggenommen worden, daß

Turgenev's family, however, belonged to Masonic circles where moral requirements were dramatically more rigorous and young males were supposed to maintain chastity until marriage. This demand was usually accompanied by the threat of sanction as it was an established practice to admonish adolescents about an inevitable outcome of debauchery. For example, at the age of thirteen, Andrei Turgenev was assigned by his parents to translate a 'Biblical moral book for adult children taken from the Books of Solomon', a standard didactic guide for teenagers written by the Danish priest Jacob Friederich Feddersen. As an encouragement for his efforts Turgenev's translation was later published in Moscow. The book is full of characteristic reminders like: 'Chastity gives life and salvation. Debauchery shortens life. Illness tortures those who love its poisonous charms.'[13]

Contemplating the fateful move five days before his sexual initiation, Turgenev had already begun to imagine the worst (271, 36*v*.-37*v*.):

> I think about how I would like to live if I had a disease that would cause me desperation. Having no relatives, no people taking interest in me [...] I would like to rent one room with one servant and a dog, be completely unknown, not to be in any service, not to be dependent on anyone, not to have any obligations and to receive about 1000 roubles of annual income. I would be *alone*, completely *alone* in the whole world and would give joy to my soul solely by helping the poor, especially burdened by a numerous household and small children. To comfort unfortunate fathers, feed hungry babies and give calm sleep to their parents surrounded by poor little children, but never to disclose myself to them, oh! even now it makes me weep; it could bring peaceful sleep to me as well, however desolate and sorrowful I am. But no one should know about me, no one should care for me, I would be alone in a noisy city and experience whether nature, spring can give delight to a lonely, truly unhappy person, to me in this situation. In the morning I would wander here and there to forget myself and would search for the unhappy to give myself a calm rest in the evening. It seems to me one of the most horrible evils, but God's consolation can be found even here.[14]

---

er jetzt die F... habe und dergleichen; [er] machte mir auch einige Fragen, das nehmliche betreffend. Dann führte er mich auf sein Zimmer und zeigte mir seine petite bibl[ioteque] choisie.

13. Jacob Friedrich Feddersen, *Bibleiskaia nravouchitel'naia knizhka dlia vzroslyh detei, v kotoroi predlagav'utsia nastavleniia iz knig Solomonovyh pocherpnytye* (Moscow, V Universitetskoi tipografii u Ridigera i Klaudia, 1795), p.19.

14. 'Я думаю, что естьли бы я имел *отчаянную для меня* болезнь, как бы я хотел жить. – Не имея никаких сродников, никаких людей, интересующихся обо мне, особливо высших меня, желал бы я нанимать с одним каким-нибудь слугой и собакой в одну горенку, быть неизвестным совершенно, не быть в службе, ни от кого не зависеть и не иметь никакого дела, получая в год доходу руб‹лей› 1000.

Я был бы *один*, совершенно *один* в целом мире, услаждал бы душу свою одними

The logic of this weird dream of consolation within despair is quite evident. The disease that is *desperate* for a young nobleman of Turgenev's background excludes him from his community of peers, and confines him to a solitary existence. An income of 1000 roubles per year, however, quite a modest one by the standards of the period, would enable him not only to survive and to keep a servant without whom life would be totally unimaginable, but also to get out of his confinement by performing acts of philanthropy. To be able to do this and avoid the inevitable shame of his position, he has to keep his existence completely anonymous, to renounce his far-reaching career and literary ambitions and his circle of friends and relatives.

Turgenev understood that this bout of masochistic imagination had nothing to do with the real circumstances of his life. Once he had finally sinned he prayed to God several days later to spare him the just punishment, vowing not to 'stray from the path of chastity' and found in the 'sacrifice of his tears' a hope for forgiveness. Unfortunately, these vows and hopes were to be shattered.

Turgenev does not mention any further enterprises of this kind in his diary, but it seems obvious that he did not manage to keep his oath and at least once again committed the same sin shortly afterwards. Unfortunately, he did not escape unscathed. Some three years later in November 1802 he wrote to his friend Andrei Kaisarov from Vienna that in a year and a half he had just one episode of intercourse with a woman, having had it before that also a year and a half ago (840, 49*v*.).[15] The first sexual experience he mentions must date to early 1800, but it is impossible to assess how many times he had 'strayed from the path of chastity'. For instance, on 19 February he wrote in his diary (271, 47*v*.):

благодеяниями неимущим, особливо отягченным многочисленным семейством, малолетними детьми. Утешить несчастного отца – накормить голодных младенцев и доставить покойный сон родителям, окруженным бедными маленькими детьми, но никогда не открываться им – ах! это и теперь заставляет меня плакать, это бы могло доставить мне и самому, бедному и унылому, покойный сон.

Но только никто бы не должен знать обо мне, никому, никому бы не было для меня дела, я был бы один в шумном городе, испытал бы, может ли природа, весна дать наслаждение человеку одинокому, истинно несчастному, одним словом, мне в моем положении. – По утрам я бы скитался по улицам туда и сюда, чтобы заглушить себя, искал бы несчастных, чтобы ввечеру доставить себе покойный, приятный сон.

Это для меня кажется одним из самых ужаснейших зол, но и тут есть утешение Божие!'

15. 'Я, брат, тебе во всем признаюсь. Долго я воздерживался, живучи и в Москве, и в Вене: в 1 ½ года имел я только один раз сообщение с женщиной, имев его перед тем за 1 ½ же года'. Speaking about a second case, Turgenev says that just once he 'forgot about everything, had a moment of weakness, everything ended happily, but for a week' he 'did not have a moment of calm' ('Один раз пренебрег я все, и имел минуту слабости; прошло щастливо, но я целую неделю не знал минуты покоя', 840, 49 ob).

It is a week already since my illness started and I am bearing it with indifference I never could imagine before [...] Is it possible that this also would not become for me a lesson in chastity? [...] The most sorrowful thing in this disease for me is that I have to pretend and deceive my father. This grieves me very much, grieves more than the disease itself and the medicines. Could I think that even for this very disease I would in some way thank God that he sent it to me? Still, it happened this morning. From what dangers in future did it guard me![16]

The mention of worse dangers, symptoms he described and the medicines that were prescribed to him (herbs and almond milk) suggest that the infection he contracted was relatively mild. Luckily for him, by 1793 British physician Benjamin Bell had finally established that gonorrhoea was not an early symptom of syphilis, but a different disease not susceptible to treatment with mercury. Russian medicine was already advanced enough to be aware of these developments.[17] Still, the infection proved to be resilient, lasted for several months and had a tendency to relapse. The option of living alone with no one to know about him or care for him was clearly not realistic for Andrei Ivanovich, who feared that his father might learn of his condition. Ivan Petrovich Turgenev was a renowned Freemason, moralist and didactic writer, 'a Friend of Humanity', as he was called by his friends and admirers, and an object of nearly religious veneration by his son.[18]

Three months later, on 21 April, Turgenev was writing that he had nearly recovered, but (271, 55*v*.-56):

throughout these days had a lot of most despondent minutes. Doubts about bad consequences and thoughts about Richter [the doctor] *who did or yet will say all to my father* [sic] were torturing me. The morning of April 18 was one of the most cheerless. I went to ask Richter, but could not say anything because of tears and a barber and a student who were present and left shedding the most sorrowful tears [...]. Having come home I immediately wrote him a most reassuring letter in which I promised him in God's name that nothing of this sort would happen to me because of my own guilt (important, really important oath!!) and had a reply from him, that he would not compromise me and will speak with me again about it, which did not comfort me. [...] The

16. 'Уже с неделю есть, как началась моя болезнь, и я сношу ее так равнодушно, как прежде и вообразить не мог. [...] Неужели и это не послужит мне вперед уроком в целомудрии? [...] Теперь всего для меня в этой болезни прискорбнее то, что я должен скрываться и обманыв[ать] бат[юшку]. Очень, очень это меня печалит. Печалит более самой болезни и лечения.

    Думал ли я, что и за самую эту болезнь некоторым образом должен я буду благодарить Бога за то, что он мне послал ее? Однако ж это случилось сегодни поутру. От каких опасностей предохранило это меня теперь и впредь!'

17. J. D. Oriel, *The Scars of Venus: a history of venerology* (London, 1994), p.36. See also N. D. Falk, *Traktat o venericheskikh bolezniah* (Moscow, 1800), p.189-96.

18. *Arkhiv bratiev Turgenevyh*, vol.2 (St Petersburg, 1911), p.24.

day before yesterday I sent one more letter to him and he replied again that he won't compromise me, said slightly more decisively and more comforting for me, but still not the way it should be.[19]

Young Turgenev could not imagine that his father had in his turn experienced his share of struggle with his natural dispositions. Yet Ivan Turgenev himself had written the following in the draft of a speech prepared for the meeting of the Masonic lodge, where such public exposures of one's own sinfulness were an institutionalised practice: 'It is from this disposition to gluttony that my disposition for debauchery springs against which I must struggle every day. I am unable to attend that level of sensation where my imagination would be free from that foul vice. This disposition is a product of my brutish soul.'[20] In his private diary for 1788, Ivan Turgenev, who was already a married man and the father of a growing family, recorded his 'mournful experience of fornication'.[21] Andrei Ivanovich was not aware of this and could not use his father's meditations as a pattern for his feelings, but his Masonic upbringing in any case provided him with a clear strategy to deal with his own sinfulness when yielding to bodily temptations – the pattern he followed in his first pathetic diary entry of the morning of 20 January.

Andrei Turgenev was not only a representative of the younger generation of Freemasons. At the same time, he was an early forerunner of Russian *Sturm und Drang*, a fanatical admirer of young Schiller in whose writings he could find a different strategy of 'event coding' and 'appraisal', paradoxically both supplementing and contradicting the one he acquired in the family. And while in the immediate aftermath of his first

19. 'Все еще продолжаю свои лекарства, но почти совсем уже здоров. – В теперешние минуты я довольно спокоен и доволен. Что-то будет далее! – Все эти дни очень много имел самых унылых минут. И сомнения о худых следствиях, и мысли о Рихтере [*who did or yet will say all to my father*] мучили меня. Утро 18-го апреля было одно из самых безотрадных. Я ходил Рихтера просить, но от слез и от присутствия парикмахера и какого-то ученика не мог ничего почти сказать, от него пошел, проливая слезы самые горестные [...] Пришедши домой, тотчас написал к нему преубедительное письмо, где клялся ему Богом, что ничего такого впредь от собственной моей вины мне не случится (важная, очень важная клятва!!) и получил от него в ответ, что он меня не компрометирует, что еще поговорит об этом со мною и проч., что меня не очень утешило. [...] Третьего дни поутру послал к нему еще письмо, он то же отвечал, что не компрометирует, немного решительнее и для меня утешнее, но все не так, как бы должно.'
20. 'От сей склонности к обжорству происходит и склонность моя к блудодеянию, и так сильна во мне, что я каждый день борюсь с нею. Не могу до такого ощущения дойти, чтобы воображение мое чисто было от сего скверного порока. Сию склонность причисляю я к скотской своей душе.' Evgeny K. Tarasov, 'K istorii Russkogo obschestva XVIII-ogo stoletiia. Mason I. P. Turgenev', *Zhurnal Ministerstva narodnovo prosvescheniia* 6:3 (1914), p. 127-175 (158). Quoted in Smith, *Working the rough stone*, p.40.
21. 'В плачевном опыте блудодеяния'. Tarasov, 'K istorii Russkogo', p.158.

sexual endeavour he was following the didactic pattern of religious moralists, he was contemplating the possibility of turning to an alternative model even before the encounter took place.

On 17 and 18 January Turgenev was copying in his diary two of Schiller's poems: 'Freigeisterey der Leidenschaft' and 'Resignation'. He copied the former in full, but was interrupted after having written down only the two first stanzas of the latter. Both poems make a sort of a thematic cycle. Written in 1784, they describe Schiller's love for Charlotte von Kalb who was married to one of his friends. This forbidden passion is interpreted in the poems as a manifestation of the irreconcilable struggle between virtue (*Tugend*) and heart's flame (*Herzens Flammentrieb*) or between hope (*Hoffnung*) and pleasure (*Genuß*).

> Who of these flowers plucks one,
> let him ne'er yearn
> To touch the other sister's bloom[22]

In both poems Schiller finally renounces his claim to virtue and eternity for the sake of passion:

> Having forgot
> before whom should I tremble
> I dare to press her in silence to my bosom, my first kiss burns
> on her lips[23]

However dissimilar the inner struggles of a passionate German poet and of a young Russian noble desperately willing and at the same time afraid to make his first visit to a prostitute, the model established in the poems enabled Turgenev to confer a much nobler meaning and higher dimension on his sexual desires. Undoubtedly his infatuation with the seductive, albeit corrupt, Elizaveta Sandunova also helped him to elevate his dubious intentions in his own eyes.

Cultural intuition did not completely fail young Turgenev. Schiller himself was brought up in the traditions of Swabian Pietism, whose main proponent Friedrich Christoph Oetinger was also quite influential among Moscow Freemasons. The works of Oetinger and other German mystics and Pietists could be found in the library of Ivan Turgenev.[24] It does not seem likely that Andrei Ivanovich actually read them –

---

22. 'Wer dieser Blumen eine brach, begehre / Die andre Schwester nicht Schiller'. *Werke* vol.1, p.163-65.
23. 'vergeßen, / vor wem ich zittern muß, / Wag ich es stumm, an meinen Busen sie zu preßen, / auf ihren Lippen brennt mein erster Kuß.' Schiller, *Werke*, vol.2 II A, p.141-43.
24. I. V. Danilian, 'Masonskaia biblioteka Turgeneva (opyt rekonstruktsii po opisi 1831 g.)', in *Rukopisi. Redkie izdaniia. Arkhivy. Iz fondov biblioteki Moskovskovo universiteta* (Moscow, 1997), p.81-107.

Freemasons rigorously adjusted the program of didactic and theosophical reading of young people to their age and spiritual education. Andrei Turgenev and Schiller, however, were products of a similar moral and intellectual culture, circumstances that made the rebellion of his favourite writer personally compelling. Arthur McCardle in his close study of Schiller's relations to Swabian Pietism regards the two poems copied by Andrei Ivanovich as a testimony of Schiller's final break with his Pietist mentors whose teachings still played a formative role in his earlier plays and essays.[25]

Having committed his sin, Turgenev initially reverted to the original paradigm of interpretation, by praying for forgiveness and vowing to preserve his modesty. Using Frijda and Mesquita's terminology we can say that he 'encoded' his fault as a bodily sin and thus his 'appraisal' of it could consist only of shame and repentance. But even at that moment, the intensity of his remorse brought him tears of 'joyous gratitude' – a clear, if finally misleading, symptom of God's grace. This sudden burst of rapture betrays an ardent fan and translator of 'An die Freude', Turgenev's favourite poem. In an unfinished manuscript of his translation Turgenev filled all the margins with the Russian word 'Радость' ('Joy'), trying to induce in himself the same type of feeling that gave birth to Schiller's masterpiece.

Later on the 'symbolic model of emotion' set by Schiller played an increasingly important role in Turgenev's understanding of his unfortunate sexual experience. He tends to 'encode' it as a 'loss of innocence' or even 'as a transgression of conventional morality', and thus 'appraise' it with nostalgia, passion and even a sort of perverted pride. While before his fall he compared himself to the Schiller of 'Freigeisterey der Leidenschaft' and 'Resignation', taken over by a criminal passion, subsequently he promoted himself to the sort of incarnation of Karl Moor. Three months later, at the end of April, finding out that his illness lasted longer than anticipated, he equated himself to the main character of *Die Räuber* (271, 56):

> No, in no French tragedy would I be able to find what I find in 'The Robbers'. I poured out tears of grief as I read some scenes from it and was ready to cry to Karl Moor: 'My brother'. I felt myself to be completely in him and cried over him and myself. 'The golden May years of my childhood once more revive in the soul of the unhappy' – what can be simpler, stronger and more touching than that! And I was reading the following pages, pouring abundant tears, ~~and~~ and my torturous sorrow became sweeter. [...] I met Peter the postilion and envied his position and later found in 'The Robbers': 'Oh, that I

25. Arthur W. McCardle, *Friederich Schiller and Swabian Pietism* (New York, 1986), p.205-13.

might be born a beggar! No! I would ask for no more, oh ye heavens – than that I might be one of these who earn their daily bread!'[26]

Minor mistakes show that Turgenev was quoting from memory. This is not the sole example in his diary. He knew by heart substantial excerpts from Schiller's plays, but Karl Moor's evocation of his 'Knabenzeit' was one of his favourite moments. Several days later he was drafting in his diary a letter to his friend and complained about his fate (271, 57-57*v*.):

I have great sorrows that become more unbearable to me, because I have to conceal them. I was ill and had to hide my illness. Sometimes despair started to dwell in my soul. I could not find any means of deliverance. My God! How forcefully would then the blessed years of my boyhood, charming scenes of childhood revive in my heart. Then I fell asleep tired with running and playing and not knowing any care. Short lived sorrows had to give place to joy and merriment. Tears stream from my eyes when all blossoms anew in my soul; and each and every place that I can remember, imagine vividly, is a priceless treasure for me and I say with Karl Moor 'Die goldnen Maienjahre der Kinderzeit [correction: der Knabenzeit] leben wieder auf in der Seele des Elenden! – ... My innocence, my innocence!'
My friend! who will return my innocence, who will bring me back my childish joys. Where did my happiness fly forever? Whatever joys I can have now, they will never compensate me what I have lost forever![27]

The keyword in this monologue is 'forever'. Turgenev's fall and subsequent illness finally and irrevocably cut the link connecting him to the lost world of innocence. This world was ever present both in his heart

---

26. 'Нет, ни в какой французской трагедии не найду я того, что нахожу в «Разбойниках». Проливая слезы горести о себе, я читал некоторые сцены и готов был вскричать К[арлу] Моору: «Брат мой!» Я чувствовал в нем совершенно себя! и плакал о себе и об нем. Die goldnen Maienjahre der Knabenzeit leben wieder auf in der Seele des Elenden! – что этого простее, сильнее и трогательнее! И что после следует, читал я, проливая обильные слезы, и мучительная горесть моя услаждалась. – [...], попался мне Петр, форрейтер, и я завидовал его состоянию и после нашел в «Разб[ойниках]»: Daß ich wiederkehren dürfte in meiner Mutter Leib! Daß ich ein Bettler gebohren werden dürfte! Nein, nein; ich wollte nicht mehr o Himmel – daß ich werden dürfte wie dieser Taglöhner einer!' Schiller, *Werke*, vol.3, p.188, 196 (*Die Räuber*, IV.2; III.2).

27. 'Прибавь к этому, что часто я имею великие печали, которые тем становятся для меня несноснее, что я должен был скрывать ее: я был болен и должен был таить болезнь свою. Иногда отчаяние поселялось в душу мою. Я не находил никаких, никаких средств к избавлению; Боже мой! С какою силою оживлялись тогда в стесненной душе моей блаженные леты моего ребячества, милые сцены детства, когда я, утомленный беганьем и игрою, засыпал сладким сном, не зная никаких забот. Минутные горести должны были уступать место веселью и забавам; слезы текут из глаз моих, когда все это расцветет снова в душе моей; всякое место, которое я могу вспомнить, вообразить живо, есть для меня бесценная находка, и я говорю с Карлом Моором: «Die goldnen Maienjahre der Kinderzeit leben wieder auf in der Seele des Elenden! – ... Meine Unschuld! Meine Unschuld!»

Мой друг! Кто возвратит мне мою невинность, кто отдаст мне мои детские радости? – Куда улетело навеки мое счастие?'

and in physical space, it could be memorised and visited, it aroused nostalgia and tender feelings, but it was a lost paradise – nothing could ever bring back the happiness experienced there. Turgenev saw Karl Moor's visit incognito to his former family estate as the ideal pattern of this emotion that in general seems to be paradigmatic in Schiller's theatre.[28] Once again, the main character of Schiller's tragedy – an outcast and a murderer – biographically had very little to do with the actual Andrei Ivanovich Turgenev whose worst crime consisted in catching gonorrhoea during his early sexual encounters. Nevertheless, the protagonist of Schiller's tragedy plays a decisive role in Turgenev's perception of himself, in his *Persönlichkeitideal*, to use Alfred Adler's terminology.[29] Karl Moor endowed Andrei Turgenev with an aura of exclusivity that made his ordeals both more and less painful. Turgenev needed to make sense of his sufferings. The conventional Masonic morality provided a ready-made model: our sins serve as the reminders of our inherent fallibility, of the carnal nature of our flesh. They guard us from pride and direct to repentance and abstinence. In Schiller's world transgression became a sign of a passionate character and of exceptional, if tragic, destiny. No wonder it had such great appeal for a young Russian enthusiast. It was for this reason that Turgenev thus incessantly analysed and interpreted Karl Moor's character and even invented a special term for the emotional pattern he was struggling to reproduce. On 30 January, ten days after his first sexual experience, but before the appearance of first symptoms of his disease, he was discussing with his friend, the poet Alexei Merzliakov, the essence of what they called 'the robber feeling', that constituted for them the emotional essence of Schiller's tragedy (271, 45-45*v*.):

> We have defined already that it consists of the feeling of repentance mixed with something pleasantly sweet strongly affecting our heart. But why repentance? He said this only respecting Karl Moor, but you can say also *the feeling of misfortune*, though it still seems necessary that the misfortune should be produced by our own guilt. The view of innocent children, kind, amiable, playing together can produce this impression. And it seems to be always stronger, when we in our adult age, having lost our childish innocence, purity etc, enter the house where we were brought up in our childhood. What does it cost me to look for example at Savinsky house [the estate of Ivan Lopukhin where Turgenev spend his childhood] where my brother and I lived in fraternal love and concord? Every place, every corner, brings us some tender feelings. But here it can only be just tenderness, without any other feeling. How strongly this feeling is portrayed in Karl

28. Stephanie Hammer, *Schiller's wound: the theater of trauma from crisis to commodity* (Detroit, MI, 2001), p.13.
29. See *The Individual psychology of Alfred Adler: a systematic presentation in selections from his writings*, ed. H. L. and R. R. Ansbacher (New York, 1964), p.94.

Moor, for example when he remembers the dwellings of his childhood, remembers his early age and when he throws himself into Amalia's embrace.[30]

Turgenev reconstructed Karl Moor's emotional patterns to apply them to his own emotions and check to what extent they matched the chosen model. He discovered that, while visiting or remembering the landscapes of his childhood feelings of nostalgia came easily to him, the ability to cherish tender feelings alone was not enough. These feelings should be accompanied by remorse or, at least, by a sense of the strong misfortune caused by one's own guilt. In other words, the final ban from an earthly paradise was to be conclusive. Turgenev interpreted his own sin as analogous to original sin, and his own fall as the Fall of Mankind.

Freemasons regarded the human body and soul as the scene of eternal struggle between the ideal Man created by God and 'Old Adam'.[31] It was necessary to practise penitence, virtue and learning to shed the skin of Old Adam and to return to the primordial wholeness. As M. H. Abrams has shown in *Natural supernaturalism*, the Romantics retained the mythology of the Fall as the core of their poetic universe, but reinterpreted it as the necessary step in humanity's striving for perfection. According to Abrams, Schiller initially expressed this view in his essay *Something concerning the first human society according to the guidance of the Mosaic records*, in which he briefly described how an inner drive unconsciously 'tore him loose from the leading strings of nature [...] and threw him into the wild game of life, set him upon the dangerous road to moral freedom'.[32] These ideas were given more elaborate expression in Schiller's more famous essay *On naïve and sentimental poetry*, where he stated that as 'children of nature we were both happy and perfect; we have become

---

30. 'Мы уже с М‹е›рзл‹я›к‹о›в‹ым› определяли, что оно состоит из чувства раскаяния, смешанного с чем-нибудь усладительным, сильно действующим на наше сердце. – Однако ж – почему раскаяние? Это он сказал только относительно к Кар[лу] Моору, но можно сказать и чувство несчастия, хотя все кажется нужно, чтобы несчастие происходило от нашей собственной вины. – Взор на невинных младенцев, добрых, любезных, играющих вместе, может произвести это чувство. И всегда, кажется, сильнее действует оно, когда мы в взрослые лета, лишившись детской невинности, чистоты и пр., входим в тот дом, где мы воспитывались в детстве своем. Каково мне смотреть, напр[имер], на Савин. дом, на ту комнату, где мы жили в братской любви и союзе с братом. Всякое местечко, всякий уголок приводит нас в какое-то умиление. Но тут, может быть, и одно умиление без всякого другого чувства.

    Как это чувство сильно изображено в Карле Мооре в те минуты, напр[имер], когда он вспоминает о жилище своего детства, о своем младенчестве и когда – бросается в объятья Амалии.'

31. See Stephen Lessing Baehr, *The Paradise myth in eighteenth-century Russia: utopian patterns in early secular Russian literature and culture* (Stanford, CA, 1991).

32. M. H. Abrams, *Natural supernaturalism: tradition and evolution in Romantic literature* (New York and London, 1973), p.206-207.

free and have lost both.' As Abrams puts it, here Schiller incorporated the 'figures of exile and homesickness' into 'a variant form of the parable of a Prodigal son. [...] As in Christian tradition the figure of traveller sick for home is interchangeable with man's "nostalgia for paradise, a state of innocence, a golden age"'. Schiller exhorts the modern poet to 'lead mankind for whom the way back to Arcadia is closed forever, onward towards Elysium.'[33] Schiller, however, developed this optimistic dialectic only in the 1790s under the influence of Herder and Kant. His earlier works still reflect the struggle with his Pietist upbringing and describe the rupture with primordial innocence as a result of tragic predestination, the destiny of the selected few that marks them with the stamp of greatness and doom.[34]

We have no evidence to say whether Turgenev read Schiller's essays of the 1790s, although we know that he strongly preferred his *Sturm und Drang* masterpieces to the works of his classical period. In November 1799 he wrote that, having read Schiller's poems from Musen – *Almanach für das Jahr 1797*, he again found in some of them 'my Schiller, though not the Bard of Joy, but still a great poet' (271, 11).[35] Reservations reflected in words 'again' and 'some' are very revealing. 'Resignation', the poem he started to copy while planning to renounce his age of innocence, starts with a famous formula – 'Auch ich war in Arkadien geboren' – but the inevitable loss of Arcadia leads Schiller not to the search of the future Elysium, but to the tragic conflict between Hope and Enjoyment.

The only way the exiled wanderer can still regain the lost Arcadia is through love. Love, as described in 'Freygeisterey der Leidenschaft' and 'Resignation', is a dangerous passion that brings the age of happy innocence and ignorance to an end, but at the same time it can offer the promise of a return to the lost paradise. These are the feelings of Karl Moor when he, to continue the above quoted entry in Turgenev's diary (271, 45*v*.):

---

33. Abrams, *Natural supernaturalism*, p.214-15.
34. See McCardle, *Friedrich Schiller*, p.137-204; Benno von Wiese, *Friedrich Schiller* (Stuttgart, 1959), p.159-69, 190-218.
35. 'опять нашел в них (в некоторых) своего Шиллера, хотя и не певца радости, но великого стихотворца'. The same attitude is reflected in Turgenev's remarks about Goethe: 'Having read Göthe's [*sic*] poems in Schiller's *Musenalmanach*, I started to read his *Werther* again. What a feeling as if from an unpleasant, barren, cold, alien land I returned to a beloved motherland. Göthe, Göthe, beyond whom you have to fall on your knees, again great, amiable, solemn, in one word Göthe, as he should be.' ('Почитавши стихов Göthe в Schillers "Musenalmanach", принялся я опять за его "Вертера". Какое чувство, точно как будто бы из неприятной, пустой, холодной, чужой земли приехал я на милую родину. Опять Göthe, Göthe, перед которым надобно пасть на колени; опять тот же великий, любезный, важный – одним словом Göthe, каков он должен быть. Какой жар, сила, чувство натуры; как питательно, сильно, интересно! Göthe, Schiller!!!')

throws himself into Amalia's embrace crying: She still loves me, still, I am
pure as Light. She loves me with all my sins (drowning in Joy) The Children
of Light weep in the emraces of the forgiven devils. Hell is destroyed. I am
happy.)!'[36] [...] If in the minute of sorrow and oppression could I listen to
Sandunova playing on clavichord something *to my taste*, what would I feel
then![37]

After his fall Turgenev envisaged for himself the same kind of consolation that Karl Moor could feel in the hands of Amalia. While translating
this monologue in a different notebook, however, he made a significant
change and translated the German 'begnadigter Teufel' as 'forgiven
sinners'[38] (276, 29*v*). Without question he remembered Schiller's text
well enough to quote it correctly in German, and it is obvious that he
knew the meaning of the word he was translating. Such was his identification with Karl Moor that he could not possibly call himself a 'devil'
and downgraded this verdict to that of 'sinner'.

When the young Turgenev was still dreaming about putting an end to
his chastity, the enigmatic Sandunova with her reputation as a seductress
proved to be the ideal person to disrupt his primordial bliss. After his
fall, being cast out of the paradisiacal state, he needed love to reconnect
himself with it. This task of the salvation of the fallen soul required an
entirely different sort of a woman or, to be more exact, a maiden. The
time was ripe for the appearance of a heavenly creature on his horizon. It
is no wonder that she emerged almost immediately. By the end of 1800
Turgenev was remembering the time, exactly a year before, when he
began writing his diary: 'Then I was preoccupied all the time with
Sand[unova], now I hardly think about her'[39] (271, 75), he noticed. He
could afford not to think about Sandunova any more, because he already
had a much more appealing candidate to fill his dreams.

During the last days of April Turgenev several times quoted in his
diary Karl Moor's longing for his boyhood. On 1 May, the day of a
popular spring holiday, he recorded another type of reading and
another type of emotion (271, 58-58*v*.):

---

36. Schiller, *Werke*, vol.3, p.231-32 (*Die Räuber*, V.7).
37. 'бросается в объятья Амалии с словами: "Noch liebt sie mich! Noch! – Rein bin ich wie
    das Licht! Sie liebt mich mit all meinen Sünden! (in Freude geschmolzen) Die Kinder des
    Lichts weinen am Halse begnadigter Teufel – Meine Furien erdroßeln hier ihre Schlangen
    – die Hölle ist zernichtet – Ich bin glücklich!" a.o. [...] Естьли бы я в минуты мрачности
    и горести и притеснения мог слушать С[андунову], играющую на клавикордах что-
    нибудь по мне, что бы я тогда чувствовал!'
38. Помилованные грешники.
39. 'Итак, этой книге уже другой год! [...], – заметил он. – Тогда я все занимался
    Санд‹уновой›, теперь очень мало об ней думаю.'

I am not out strolling? But I don't feel bored. Today I was sitting in hall under the window reading Wieland's *Sympathies* and found there a portrait of my amiable A.
How joyfully do you wander around these lonely bushes, Neither care, nor passinate desires blacken the pure skies of thy soul)[40] [...]

> Blossom, in innocent pleasure
> As tender myrtle in deserted forest

Now your body suffers from severe illness, but good nature will soon cure you. Soon you will sleep again in sweet peace and awake with a joyous smile of innocence. [...] Tender nature will give new pleasures to her favourite.[41]

Wieland's *Sympathien* was a series of philosophical essays written for a small circle of congenial souls. They describe some sort of cosmic attraction that brings these souls together.[42] Amiable 'A' (Anna Sokovnina) was at that time ill, as was Turgenev himself. But her disease had nothing to do with ruinous passions or vice. While her body suffered, her soul remained as innocent as ever. The seeming analogy in their current situations masked the profound rupture between their experiences and destinies.

The scene for the next act of the drama was arranged – the 'forgiven sinner' was to seek happiness in the embrace of the 'child of light'. As we know from the examples of Karl Moor or Goethe's Werther, one can regain lost paradise only briefly and such efforts tend to end tragically. The young Russian diarist followed his models to the end. He died three years later, in July 1803, at the age of twenty-two under highly mysterious circumstances. This, however, is the topic for a separate discussion.

40. 'Я не на гуляньи, но мне не скучно.
   Сегодни читал я, сидя в зале под окошком, Виланд ‹овы› «Симпатии» и нашел там портрет моей любезной А...: Wie froh wandelst du in diesen einsamen Gebüschen. Keine Sorge, keine lüsterne Begierde bewölkt den reinen Himmel deiner Seele.' Christoph Martin Wieland, *Werke*, 40 vols (Berlin, 1879), vol.39, p.448.
41. 'Цвети в веселии невинном,
   Как нежный мирт в лесу пустынном!
   Теперь тело твое страдает от жестокой болезни, но скоро благая натура исцелит тебя! Скоро будешь ты опять засыпать в сладком мире и просыпаться с радостною улыбкою невинности. [...] Нежная природа всем будет радовать свою любимицу...'
42. See John A. McCarthy, *Crossing boundaries: a theory and history of essay writing in German, 1680-1815* (Philadelphia, PA, 1989), p.212-20. Turgenev quotes the fourth essay.

Summaries

Historians and eighteenth-century private life: an overview
Sarah Maza

This chapter provides an overview and discussion of some major historical writings on private life in eighteenth-century Europe since the 1970s. It sets up a contrast between, on the one hand, an older Anglo-American model of family versus marketplace as represented by Lawrence Stone's magisterial history of the English family and, on the other, a French approach, exemplified by the *History of private life* series, in which private life is defined as a set of practices that escape the control of the state, and the opposite of 'public' is not 'private' but 'particular'. Jürgen Habermas' writings on the public sphere, rediscovered from the late 1980s, offer a complex and comprehensive tripartite model – state, private sphere and intimate sphere – which has inspired much of the most innovative recent work.

Intimate, deprived, uncivilised: Diderot and the publication of the private moment
Caroline Warman

This chapter pursues the three distinct meanings of the term 'privé' in eighteenth-century French – 'private', 'deprived' and 'tamed' – through Diderot's writings, from the very public *Encyclopédie* and published works such as the *Lettre sur les aveugles* and the *Bijoux indiscrets*, to unpublished and even secret texts, including his letters to Sophie Volland, the *Rêve de D'Alembert* and *Jacques le fataliste*. It concludes that, in forcing us to consider whether in fact a private life implies a reversion to nature or is an indicator of having been tamed and socialised, Diderot sheds light on tensions and contradictions that we had not even realised were there.

Inventing private lives: the representation of private lives in French *Vies privées*
Olivier Ferret

The French *Vies privées* – a biographical genre that developed from the late 1720s to the 1830s – attempt to publicise aspects of the private life of well-known figures. Authors who pretended to be historians frequently invented details in order to fill gaps in knowledge, blurring the boundaries between historical discourse and fiction. While these texts have a satirical function in denouncing passions and vices, they aim to compromise the public image of the person and to shape public opinion by insisting on the close relationship of the private and the public. This chapter explores how a corpus of *Vie privées* fashions a particular idea of the private at a time when the rise of gossip sheets and newspapers in the public sphere encourages popular taste for knowledge of the intimate.

The private life of criminals
Lise Andries

This chapter treats the lives of criminals active in Paris and its surroundings in the first half of the eighteenth century. It is based on three kinds of documents: broadsheets distributed by pedlars in the streets, criminal biographies and judicial archives. The chapter examines the fascination with different representations of criminality, including the documentary and the mythic. In criminal biographies especially, fact and fiction are so closely linked that it is difficult to distinguish between judicial documents and literature. Although the lives of criminals were widely publicised in pamphlets, songs and novels, they also attracted attention by drawing the public into a private, secret realm. Their lives are indeed a continual pendulum swing between secrecy and scandal: the scandal of their arrest, the scandal of their public condemnation but also the secrets they will or will not reveal under torture, the secrecy and clandestinity of their deeds, the dissimulation of their identity. This growing focus on their private selves reflects a broader cultural trend of the French Enlightenment towards self-examination and a new importance given to the interior life.

La Nouvelle Héloïse and Wolmar's project: transforming passion into 'familiarité fraternelle'
Alison Oliver

This chapter discusses the use of the language of family relationships in Jean-Jacques Rousseau's *La Nouvelle Héloïse* (1761), a novel in which the domestic world becomes a model of social control, an ideal realm of the private in which all players enjoy total transparency to one another. The chapter traces the attempt within this text of a patriarchal figure, Wolmar, to regulate the feelings of individuals belonging to the family group under his control. His aim is to neutralise and transform the potentially disruptive love between his wife, Julie, and her former lover, Saint-Preux, into a different kind of feeling with its roots in family affection. The novel tests to the limit the emotional possibilities of the family group, and the pliability of the private emotions of individuals as social subjects; ultimately, the true nature of all bonds of love, friendship and family affection is called into question.

Private life, personal liberty and sexual crime in eighteenth-century Venice: the case of Gaetano Franceschini
Larry Wolff

This chapter considers the case of a sixty-year-old man in Venice in the 1780s, accused of attempting to have sex with an eight-year-old girl. The case file in the Venetian Archivio di Stato provides a detailed account, including the indictment and defence which focus on issues of private life and the relation of domestic privacy to sexual criminality in the eighteenth century. The defendant affirms his 'freedom' within his private life, a freedom (*libertà*) which relates to the eighteenth-century concept of libertinism. The chapter analyses both the conceptual contours of libertinism in relation to the law, and the controversy surrounding law, privacy and criminality in the Enlightenment, especially after the publication of Beccaria's *On crimes and punishments*.

Handling sin in eighteenth-century Russia
Viktor Zhivov

The chapter describes the influence of religious disciplining (the enforcement of the annual confession) on personal piety and social habits of the Orthodox population in eighteenth-century Russia. The policy of religious disciplining was appropriated by the state during the reign of Peter I and evolved into an element of imperial coercion. As a result, this policy did not produce a new piety (as occurred in some Catholic countries) but generated a widening rift between the public and private spheres in religious life and led to efforts to evade the religious duties imposed on society by the secular and ecclesiastical authorities. In this context, the chapter discusses the difficulty of describing, for Russia, private notions of conscience detached from a sense of communal responsibility.

Writing, ranks and the eighteenth-century Russian gentry experience
Irina Reyfman

Facing modernity, the European aristocracy turned to writing to shape its public and private existence. The Russian elite followed the same path a century later and in circumstances that made the idea of private life radically different: for most of the eighteenth century, lifelong state service was required of every nobleman. A 1762 law released the nobility from this obligation, but the vast majority still served. The chapter explores how obligatory or expected service affected authorial self-image of writers of noble status, and examines three models of authorship as a key to private identity: writing as service; writing as definer of private life; and writing as a dilettante activity, separate from service.

Private walks and public gazes: Enlightenment and the use of gardens in eighteenth-century Russia
Andreas Schönle

Based on evidence from travel literature, geographic descriptions, memoirs and laws, this chapter explores whether gardens in Russia in the second half of the eighteenth century afforded a private space conducive to unstructured sociability and the emergence of public opinion. The evidence suggests that the pastoral setting only thinly disguises differences in power and prestige among the social groups sharing the use of a garden. Even countryside gardens which seemed to suspend social etiquette remain enmeshed in considerations of public representation that compromise their privacy. Gardens are intrinsic to the personalisation of power rampant in court society at all levels.

Embracing and escaping the material: genre painting, objects and private life in eighteenth-century France
Mark Ledbury

This chapter is an exploration of the relationship between people and objects in genre paintings in eighteenth-century France. Exploring works by Boucher, Chardin and Greuze, the chapter asks what we can fathom, if anything, about the relationship between artists and material objects of private life by examining the use of objects and in particular of luxury objects in paintings, and asks whether genre painting's special qualities and purchase might ultimately be derived from the complex relationship between painting as object and practice and painted objects in the intimate sphere of private life.

Eccentricity and the self: private character in English public portraiture
Shearer West

This chapter argues that, despite its ostensibly 'public' nature, English portraiture from the 1770s evinced an increasing engagement with individuality and private life. By investigating portraiture and selfhood in terms of a discourse on privacy, the idea that the Enlightenment witnessed a 'birth of modern identity' will be examined and questioned. This chapter will tackle two neologisms – celebrity and eccentricity – and two fashions – physiognomy and caricature – that coincidentally came together to threaten portraiture's traditional public role, and will conclude with the case study of Joshua Reynolds' portraits of his 'Club' circle, where privacy, individuality and selfhood converged in an unsettling and ultimately unstable combination.

Friendship and materialism in the French Enlightenment
Adam Sutcliffe

In the Enlightenment period, the question of the possibility of authentic friendship as a solution to the division between public and private realms emerged as a complex intellectual terrain, at the intersection of multiply contested boundaries between science and theology, the individual and the social, and private and public life. The chapter examines how several radical thinkers of the French Enlightenment attempted to apply materialist philosophy to the field of social relations, advancing amoral conceptions of human nature and of friendship. Their positions proved to be difficult to sustain, and even more difficult to integrate with any sort of reformist politics or with a viable ethic of friendship as lived experience. Both in theory and in practice, French Enlightenment radicals revealed in their approach to friendship a recurrent slippage from bold materialist analysis to more moderate humanist formulations in the vein of Montaigne.

Captivating Enlightenment: eighteenth-century children's books and the private life of the child
M. O. Grenby

This chapter focuses on British children's literature from 1750 to 1820, examining its emphatic assertion of the superiority of private, domestic experience for the young, over any engagement with public life. This claim for the primacy of private life was new in children's books. It was a contention that was carefully supported, on both moral and rational grounds. The stories exhibit suspicion even of schooling if conducted outside the home; all worthwhile knowledge and experience, they asserted, could be gained within the home and its grounds. When it came to children, it seems, books were supposed to contain the reader at home, not to provide a passport beyond its bounds into a 'republic of letters'.

Schiller, gonorrhoea and original sin in the emotional life of a Russian nobleman
Andrei Zorin

The chapter produces a case study of a Russian nobleman of the early nineteenth century whose diary offers unique material for the history of the emotions in Russia at the end of the long eighteenth century. The discussion treats the diary entries concerning Turgenev's youthful sexual indiscretions and the tension in Turgenev's self-analysis between the moral language of sin and the ideals and language of Schiller in which he casts his plight as a doomed, fallen person. The interplay of these conflicting interpretations organises the semiotic field within which Turgenev patterned and expressed his emotional history.

Bibliography

Primary sources

Aikin, John, and Anna Lætitia Barbauld, *Evenings at home, or the Juvenile budget opened: consisting of a variety of miscellaneous pieces for the instruction and amusement of young persons*, 6 vols (1792-1796; London, 1809).

Alcott, Louisa May, *Good wives* (1869; London, 1994).

Les Amours de Cartouche, ou Aventures singulières et galantes de cet homme trop célèbre, qui n'ont jamais été publiées, dont le manuscrit a été trouvé après la prise de la Bastille (London, n.d. [1798]).

Amours et aventures du vicomte de Barras, ex-membre du Directoire exécutif, avec Mesdames Joséphine de B***, Tallien, la douairière Du Baillet, Mlle Sophie Arnoult, etc., etc., par M. le baron de B***, 3 vols (Paris, n.d. [1815-1817?]).

Amours et intrigues du maréchal de Richelieu, ed. Olga Wormser (Paris, 1955).

Amours secrètes de Napoléon Bonaparte par M. le baron de B***, 2 vols (Paris, 1815).

Angerville, Barthélémy-François Mouffle d', *Vie privée de Louis XV, ou Principaux événements, particularités et anecdotes de son règne*, 4 vols (London, J. P. Lyton, 1781).

Argens, marquis d', *Nouveaux mémoires, pour servir à l'histoire de l'esprit et du cœur*, vol.1 (The Hague, Scheurleer, 1745).

Ash, John, *The New and complete dictionary of the English language*, 2nd edn (London, Vernor and Hood, 1795).

An Authentic detail of particulars relative to the late duchess of Kingston, new edn (London, G. Kearsley, 1788).

Barbauld, Anna Laetitia, *Lessons for children* (1778-1779; London, 1801).

barber, Francis, *More last words of Dr Johnson*, 2nd edn (London, the author, 1787).

Barlow, Frederick, *The Complete English dictionary* (London, published by the author, 1772-1773).

Beauchamp, M. Alphonse de, *Vie politique, militaire et privée du général Moreau, depuis sa naissance jusqu'à sa mort; avec des pièces justificatives et ses discours au tribunal; suivie de son éloge funèbre prononcé à Saint-Pétersbourg et d'une notice historique sur Pichegru, ornée du portrait du général Moreau* (Paris, 1814).

Beaumarchais, Pierre-Augustin Caron de, *Le Barbier de Séville* (Paris, 1965).

Beccaria, Cesare, *On crimes and punishments and other writings*, ed. Richard Bellamy, trans. Richard Davies (Cambridge, 1995).

Berquin, Arnaud, *The Children's friend; consisting of apt tales, short dialogues, and moral dramas; all intended to engage attention, cherish feeling, and inculcate virtue, in the rising generation*, trans. Rev. Anthony Meilan, 24 vols (London, John Stockdale, 1786).

Bogdanovich, I. F., *Stikhotvoreniia i poemy* (Leningrad, 1957).

Bolotov, A. T., 'A. T. Bolotov v Kenigsberge (Iz zapisok A. T. Bolotova, napisannyx samim im dlia svoikh potomkov)', letter 63, accessed from http://bo-ok.ru/lib/memor/bolotov_at.rar on 30 July 2008.

–, *Zhizn' i prikliucheniia Andreia Bolotova, opisannye samim dlia svoikh potomkov*, 3 vols (Moscow, 1993).

Boswell, James, *The Journal of a tour to the Hebrides*, 2nd edn (London, Henry Baldwin, 1785).

–, *Life of Johnson* (Oxford, 1980).

Bromley, Henry, *Catalogue of engraved British portraits from Egbert the Great to the present time* (London, T. Payne, 1793).

Buzhinskii, Gavriil, *Posledovanie o ispovedanii* (Moscow, Moskovskaia tipografiia, 1723).

Casanova de Seingalt, Giacomo Girolamo, *Histoire de ma vie*, 12 vols (Wiesbaden, 1960-1962).

Chagrins domestiques de Napoléon Bonaparte à l'île de Sainte-Hélène; précédé de faits historiques de la plus haute importance; le tout de la main de Napoléon, ou écrit sous sa dictée [...], *suivi de notes précieuses sur les six derniers mois de la vie de Napoléon* (Paris, 1821).

Chevrier, François-Antoine, *La Vie politique et militaire de M. le maréchal duc de Belle-Isle, prince de l'empire, ministre d'Etat de S. M. T. C., etc., etc., publiée par M. D. C**, éditeur du testament et du codicille* (The Hague, Veuve Van Duren, 1762).

Combe, William, *A Poetical epistle to Sir Joshua Reynolds, Knt.* (London, Fielding and Walker, 1777).

A Dictionary of the English language [...] *carefully selected from Sheridan, Walker, Johnson, etc.* (London, W. Stewart, 1794).

Dictionnaire universel des synonymes de la langue française contenant les synonymes de Girard [...] *et ceux de Beauzée, Roubeaud, D'Alembert, Diderot, et autres écrivains célèbres*, 2 vols (Paris, Félix Locquin, 1837).

Diderot, Denis, *Les Bijoux indiscrets*, ed. Jean Macary and Aram Vartanian, in *Œuvres complètes*, ed.

Herbert Dieckmann, Jacques Proust, Jean Varloot *et al.* (Paris, 1975-), vol.3 (1978).

–, *Contes et romans*, ed. Michel Delon *et al.* (Paris, 2004).

–, *Correspondance*, ed. Georges Roth and Jean Varloot, 16 vols (Paris, 1955-1970).

–, *Le Fils naturel*, in *Théâtre du dix-huitième siècle*, ed. Jacques Truchet, 2 vols (Paris, 1974), vol.1.

–, *Jacques le fataliste*, ed. Jacques Proust, in *Œuvres complètes*, ed. Herbert Dieckmann, Jacques Proust, Jean Varloot *et al.* (Paris, 1975-), vol.23 (1981).

–, *Jacques le fataliste*, ed. M. Delon (Paris, 2004).

–, *Lettres à Sophie Volland*, ed. Jean Varloot (Paris, 1984).

–, *Lettre sur les aveugles: à l'usage de ceux qui voient; Lettre sur les sourds et muets, à l'usage de ceux qui entendent et qui parlent*, ed. Marian Hobson and Simon Harvey (Paris, 2000).

–, *Rameau's nephew and first satire*, ed. Nicholas Cronk (Oxford, 2006).

–, *Réfutation d'Helvétius*, in *Œuvres*, ed. Laurent Versini, vol.1 (Paris, 1994), p.777-923.

–, *Le Rêve de D'Alembert*, ed. Jean Varloot and Georges Dulac, in *Œuvres complètes*, ed. Herbert Dieckmann, Jacques Proust, Jean Varloot *et al.* (Paris, 1975-), vol.17 (1987).

–, *Salon de 1761*, ed. Jacques Chouillet (Paris, 1984).

–, *Salon de 1765*, ed. Else Bukdahl and Annette Laurenceau (Paris, 1984).

– and Jean D'Alembert (ed.), *Encyclopédie, ou Dictionnaire raisonné des sciences, des arts et des métiers, par une société de gens de lettres*, 17 vols (Paris and Neufchâtel, Briasson, 1751-1765).

[Doris, Charles], *Amours de Napoléon et des princes et princesses de sa famille: ouvrage rédigé d'après les mémoires modernes et les matériaux authentiques communiqués à l'auteur*, 2 vols (Paris, 1835).

–, *Amours secrètes de Napoléon et des princes et princesses de sa famille, d'après des documents historiques de M. de B***, ornées de gravures historiques*, 2 vols (Paris, 1842).

–, *Amours secrètes des quatre frères de Napoléon, par M. le baron de B***, auteur du Précis historique* [sur Napoléon Bonaparte], *des Mémoires secrets* [sur Napoléon Bonaparte], *de la Défense du peuple français et des Amours secrètes de Buonaparte* (Paris, 1816).

Du Marsais, César Chesneau, *Traité des tropes, ou des différents sens dans lesquels on peut prendre un même mot dans une même langue*, 1st edn (Paris, Vve J.-B. Brocas, 1730).

Edgeworth, Maria, *Harry and Lucy* (London, 1856).

–, *The Parent's assistant, or Stories for children: part 1* (London, J. Johnson, 1796).

–, 'The purple jar', from *The Parent's assistant* (1796), in *From instruction to delight: an anthology of children's literature to 1850*, ed. Patricia Demers (Toronto, 2004), p.177.

Falk, N. D., *Traktat o venericheskih bolezniah* (Moscow, 1800).

Feddersen, Jacob Friedrich, *Bibleiskaia nravouchitel'naia knizhka dlia vzroslyh detei, v kotoroi predlagaiutsia nastavleniia iz knig Solomonovyh pocherpnytye* (Moscow, V Universitetskoi tipografii u Ridigera i Klaudia, 1795).

[Fenn, Ellenor], *Juvenile correspondence, or Letters suited to children from four to above ten years of age* (London, [1783]).

–, *School occurrences: supposed to have arisen among a set of young ladies, under the tuition of Mrs. Teachwell; and to be recorded by one of them* (London, [1783]).

Fielding, Sarah, *The Governess, or the Little female academy*, ed. Candace Ward (1749; Peterborough, 1995).

Forest, Michel, *Chroniques d'un bourgeois de Valence au temps de Mandrin*, ed. Roger Canac (Grenoble, 1980).

Fouché (de Nantes), sa vie privée, politique et morale, depuis son entrée à la Convention jusqu'à ce jour, avec son portrait (Paris, 1816).

Gazette de Cythère, ou Histoire secrète de Mme la comtesse Du Barry (London, chez P.G. Wauckner, 1775).

Girard, Gabriel, *La Justesse de la langue françoise, ou les Différentes significations des mots qui passent pour synonimes*, 1st edn (Paris, L. d'Houry, 1718).

–, *Synonymes françois et leurs différentes significations*, 3rd edn (Paris, Vve d'Houry, 1741).

Godwin, William, *The Enquirer: reflections on education, manners, and literature* (London, G. G. and J. Robinson, 1797).

Graham, James, *Eccentric lecture on the art of propagating the human species* (London, A. Roger *et al.*, 1783).

Granger, Rev. James, *A Biographical history of England from Egbert the Great to the Revolution*, 4 vols (London, T. Davies, 1775).

Granger, William, *The New wonderful museum and extraordinary magazine* [1804], Hope Collection, Ashmolean Museum, Oxford.

Helvétius, Claude-Adrien, *De l'esprit*, ed. Jacques Moutaux (Paris, 1988).

Histoire amoureuse de Napoléon Bonaparte, extraite des mémoires particuliers composés par lui-même pendant son séjour à l'île d'Elbe, et continuée jusqu'au 14 juillet 1815, par un ancien officier de sa maison qui ne l'a quitté qu'au moment de monter sur le Northumberland, 2 vols (Paris, 1815).

Histoire de la vie et du procès du fameux Louis-Dominique Cartouche, et plusieurs de ses complices (Rouen, Pierre Machuel, 1722).

Histoire de la vie et du procès du fameux Louis-Dominique Cartouche, et plusieurs de ses complices (Troyes, n.d.).

Histoire de la vie, grandes voleries & subtilitez de Guilleri et de ses compagnons, et de leur fin lamentable et malheureuse (Troyes, Vve Pierre Garnier, [1728]).

Histoire de la vie privée des Français, depuis l'origine de la nation jusqu'à nos jours, par M. Le Grand [Legrand] *d'Aussy*, 3 vols (Paris, Ph.-D. Pierres, 1782).

Histoire de Louis Mandrin, depuis sa naissance jusqu'à sa mort (Troyes, Vve Garnier, 1755), reprinted in *Histoires curieuses et véritables de Cartouche et de Mandrin*, ed. H. J. Lüsebrink (Paris, 1984), p.157-221.

Histoire du chevalier d'Eon: la vie militaire, politique et privée de demoiselle Charles-Geneviève-Louise-Auguste-Andrée-Thimotée Eon, ou d'Eon de Beaumont, écuyer, chevalier de l'ordre royal et militaire de Saint Louis, ancien capitaine de dragons et des volontaires de l'armée, aide de camp du maréchal et comte de Broglie; ci-devant docteur en droit civil et en droit canon, avocat au parlement de Paris, censeur royal pour l'histoire et les belles-lettres, envoyé en Russie d'abord secrètement, puis publiquement avec le chevalier Douglas [...] secrétaire d'ambassade, [...] ambassadeur extraordinaire [...] et connue jusqu'en 1777 sous le nom de chevalier d'Eon (Paris, Lambert, Onfroi, Valade, Esprit et chez l'auteur, 1779).

Histoire secrète des amours de la famille Bonaparte (Paris, 1815).

Hofland, Barbara, *The Panorama of Europe, or a New game of geography* (London, 1813).

Johnson, Samuel, *A Dictionary of the English language*, 2nd edn (London, J. Knapton, 1760).

–, *The Lives of the English poets*, 3 vols (Dublin, William Wilson, 1780-1781).

–, *The Rambler*, 6 vols (London, J. Payne, 1752).

Kamer-fur'erskii zhurnal (St Petersburg, 1755).

Kilner, Dorothy, *Anecdotes of a boarding-school, or an Antidote to the vices of those useful seminaries*, 2 vols (London, c.1790).

–, *The Holyday present, containing anecdotes of Mr & Mrs Jennett, and their little family* (London, c.1790).

–, *The Village school, or a Collection of entertaining histories for the instruction and amusement of all good children*, in *From instruction to delight: an anthology of children's literature to 1850*, ed. Patricia Demers (Toronto, 2004), p.172-75.

Lambert, Mme de, *Traité de l'amitié* (Brussels, Pissot, 1736).

La Mettrie, Julien Offroy de, *Discours sur le bonheur*, in *Œuvres philosophiques*, ed. Francine Markovits, 2 vols (Paris, 1987), vol.2, p.235-96.

–, *Système d'Epicure*, in *Œuvres philosophiques*, ed. Francine Markovits, 2 vols (Paris, 1987), vol.1, p.351-86.

Lavater, Johann Caspar, *Essays on physiognomy*, 3 vols (London, John Murray, 1789-1798).

–, *Secret journal of a self-observer, or Confessions and familiar letters of the Rev. J. C. Lavater*, 2 vols (London, T. Cadell, 1795).

Legrand, Marc-Antoine, *Cartouche, ou les Voleurs: comédie* (1721); John Gay, *L'Opéra du gueux* (1728), trans. A. Hallam (1750), ed. Christian Biet with Martial Poirson and Romain Jobez (Vijon, 2004).

Lettre à Monsieur de Poiresson-Chamarade lieutenant-général au baillage et siège présidial de Chaumont en Bassigny au sujet des tableaux exposés au Salon du Louvre (Paris, Deloynes, 1741, no. 14).

Ligne, Charles-Joseph de, *Coup d'œil at Belœil and a great number of European gardens* (Berkeley, CA, 1991).

Locke, John, *Some thoughts concerning education*, ed. John W. and Jean S. Yolton (1693; Oxford, 1989).

Lomonosov, M. V., *Polnoe sobranie sochinenii*, 10 vols (Moscow and Leningrad, 1957).

Louis XIV, *Manière de montrer les jardins de Versailles*, ed. Simone Hoog (Paris, 1982).

Mason, I., *Poznanie samogo sebia* (Moscow, 1800).

Les Masques arrachés, ou Vie privée de L. E. Vander-Noot et Van Eupen, de S. E. le cardinal de Malines et de leurs adhérents par Jacques Le Sueur espion honoraire de la police de Paris, et ci-devant employé du ministère de France en qualité de clairvoyant dans les Pays-Bas (London, n.p.,1790).

The Memoires of Monsieur Du Val: containing the history of his life and death, whereunto are annexed his last speech and epitaph (London, printed for Henry Brome, at the Gun near the west end of St Paul's, 1670).

Mémoires pour servir à la vie d'un homme célèbre [Napoléon Bonaparte], *par M. M*** (Paris, 1819).

Mémoires secrets sur la vie privée, politique et littéraire de Lucien Buonaparte, prince de Canino, rédigés sur sa correspondance et sur des pièces authentiques et inédites (Paris, 1815; Brussels, 1818).

Mercier, Louis-Sébastien, 'Cabarets borgnes', in *Le Tableau de Paris*, ed. Jean-Claude Bonnet, 2 vols (Paris, 1994), vol.2, p.180-81.

–, *Théâtre complet*, 4 vols (Amsterdam, Chez B. Vlam; A Leide: Chez J. Murray, 1778-1784).

Montaigne, Michel de, 'De l'amitié',
in *Œuvres complètes*, ed. Maurice Rat (Paris, 1962), p.177-93.

*Napoléon Buonaparte, sa vie civile et militaire réduite aux seuls faits, depuis l'instant de sa naissance, jusqu'à celui de sa retraite dans l'île d'Elbe; avec une foule de détails intéressants et officiels sur les expéditions d'Egypte, d'Espagne et de Russie, suivie d'anecdotes pour et contre ce personnage célèbre, puisées dans les meilleures sources, par Charles D***, auteur des vies de Henri IV et de Sully* (Paris, 1814).

The New doll, or Grandmamma's gift (London, 1826).

Opie, John, *Lectures on painting delivered at the Royal Academy of Arts* (London, 1809).

Pasqualigo, Benedetto, *Della giurisprudenza criminale, teorica e pratica*, vol.1 (Venice, Stefano Orlandini, 1731).

Piozzi, Hester, *Anecdotes of the late Samuel Johnson LL.D.*, 4th edn (London, T. Cadell, 1786).

–, *Thraliana: the diary of Mrs. Hester Lynch Thrale 1776-1809*, ed. Katherine Balderston, 2 vols (Oxford, 1951).

Précis historique sur Napoléon Buonaparte: jugement porté sur ce fameux personnage, d'après ce qu'il a dit, ce qu'il a fait, le tout extrait des mémoires d'un homme qui ne l'a pas quitté depuis quinze ans (1814; Paris, 1816).

Priori, Lorenzo, *Pratica criminale secondo le leggi della Serenissima Repubblica di Venezia* (Venice, Gasparo Girardi, 1738).

Reynolds, Joshua, *Sir Joshua Reynolds: discourses on art*, ed. Robert Wark (New Haven, CT, and London, 1959).

Richardson, Jonathan, *An Argument in behalf of the science of a connoisseur*, in *Two discourses: an essay on the whole art of criticism as it relates to painting* (London, W. Churchill, 1719), p.1-45.

Rousseau, Jean-Jacques, *Les Confessions*, in *Œuvres complètes*, ed. Bernard Gagnebin and Marcel Raymond, vol.1 (Paris, 1959), p.1-656.

–, *Correspondance complète de Rousseau*, ed. R. A. Leigh, vol.4 (Geneva, 1967).

–, *Julie, ou La Nouvelle Héloïse*, ed. Henri Coulet and Bernard Guyon, in *Œuvres complètes*, ed. Bernard Gagnebin and Marcel Raymond, vol.2 (Paris, 1964), p.1-793.

–, *Politics and the arts: letter to M. D'Alembert on the theatre*, trans. Allan Bloom (Ithaca, NY, 1960).

Sacy, Louis de, *Traité de l'amitié* (Paris, Barbou, 1774).

Sade, Donatien-Alphonse-François, marquis de, Marquis de Sade, *L'Histoire de Juliette*, in *Œuvres*, ed. Michel Delon, 3 vols (Paris, 1998), vol.3, p.179-1262.

Saint-Hyacinthe, Thémiseul de, *Recueil de divers écrits sur l'amour et l'amitié* (Paris, Pissot, 1736).

Sandham, Elizabeth, *The Twin sisters, or the Advantages of religion* (1805; London, 1816).

Schiller, Friedrich, *Werke*, ed. Julius Petersen (Weimar, 1943).

Selwyn, A., *Montague Park, or Family incidents* (London, 1825).

Spinoza, Baruch, *Complete works*, ed. Michael L. Morgan (Indianapolis, IN, 2002).

Tableau de la vie politique et privée des députés à la législature actuelle; vie de Laurent Lecointre, député de Seine et Oise (Paris, n.d. [1792]).

Thompson, G., *Newgate calendar containing the lives of the most notorious characters* (London, 1842).

Todd, Janet, and Marilyn Butler (ed.), *The Works of Mary Wollstonecraft*, 7 vols (London, 1989).

Vauvenargues, marquis de, *Introduction à la connaissance de l'esprit humain* (1746), in *Œuvres complètes*, ed. Jean-Pierre Jackson (Paris, 1999), p.1-134.

Ventum, Harriet, *Charles Leeson, or the Soldier* (London, 1810).

Vie criminelle de H.-A. Trumeau, ancien apprenti de l'empoisonneur Desrues (Paris, An XI [1803]).

Vie criminelle et politique de J.-P. Marat, se disant l'Ami du peuple, adoré, porté en triomphe comme tel, projeté saint par la jacobinaille, ou l'homme aux 200 000 têtes, le vampire le plus remarquable de la République française, suivie d'un recueil exact de ce qui s'est passé à son sujet sur plusieurs places publiques (Metz and Paris, n.d. [1795]).

Vie de L.-P.-J. Capet, ci-devant duc d'Orléans, ou Mémoires pour servir à l'histoire de la Révolution française (Paris, Franklin, An II [1794]).

Vie de M. Jean-Sylvain Bailly, premier maire de Paris, dédiée et présentée à l'Assemblée nationale (Paris, Imprimerie de la Liberté, de la Vérité, et surtout de l'Impartialité, 1790).

Vie et aventures de Joachim Murat depuis sa naissance jusqu'à sa mort par M. L. (Paris, 1816).

Vie politique de Jérôme Pétion, ci-devant maire de Paris, ex-député de la Convention nationale, et traître à la République française ([Paris], n.d. [1793]).

Vie politique et privée de Louis-Joseph de Condé, prince du sang (Paris, chez les marchands de nouveautés, 1791).

Vie privée, amoureuse, secrète et authentique de Napoléon Bonaparte et des princes et princesses de sa famille, faisant connaître leurs liaisons particulières et leurs intrigues galantes avec divers personnages de tous rangs et de toute renommée [...], *contenant un grand nombre d'anecdotes curieuses sur des familles et des personnes qui jouent encore un grand rôle dans le monde; ainsi que des lettres de Napoléon et de Joséphine; seul ouvrage impartial et complet publié d'après des renseignements exacts et les divers mémoires du temps et notamment ceux publiés par Constant, ex-valet de chambre de l'empereur*, 2 vols (Paris, 1836).

Vie privée de l'ex-capucin Chabot et de Gaspard Chaumette, pour servir de suite aux vies des fameux scélérats de ce siècle (Paris, Franklin, An II [1794]).

Vie privée de Louis-François-Joseph de Conti, prince du sang, et sa correspondance avec ses complices fugitifs (Turin [Paris], Garin, 1790).

Vie privée des cinq membres du Directoire, ou les Puissants tels qu'ils sont (n.p. [Paris], n.d. [1795]).

Vie privée du comte de Buffon, suivie d'un recueil de poésies, dont quelques pièces sont relatives à ce grand homme (Lausanne, n.p., 1788).

Vie privée du maréchal de Richelieu contenant ses amours et intrigues et tout ce qui a rapport aux divers rôles qu'a joués cet homme célèbre pendant plus de quatre-vingts ans, 3 vols (Hamburg, P.-F. Fauche 1791).

Vie privée et criminelle de Henri-Augustin Trumeau ([Paris], n.d.).

Vie privée et littéraire de Charles Bonnet en réponse à quelques pamphlets (Bern, n.d. [post 1793]).

Vie privée et ministérielle de Calonne, par M. Carra, l'un des rédacteurs du journal Annales patriotiques (Paris, Guillemard, 1791).

Vie privée et ministérielle [Supplément à la] *de M. Necker, directeur général des finances, par un citoyen* (Geneva, Pellet, 1790).

Vie privée et politique de J.-R. Hébert, auteur du Père Duchêne, pour faire suite aux vies de Manuel, Pétion, Brissot et d'Orléans (Paris, Franklin, An II [1794]).

Vie privée et politique du citoyen Lenoir, à ses concitoyens ([Paris], n.d.).

La Vie privée et politique du général Dumouriez pour servir de suite à ses mémoires (Hamburg, B.G. Hoffmann, 1794).

Vie privée et politique du roi Isaac Chapelier, premier du nom, et chez des rois de France de la quatrième race en 1789, Louis XVI étant roi des Français; précédée d'une introduction, et ornée du portrait de Sa Majesté (Rennes, n.d.).

Vie privée et publique de Louis XVI, ou Principaux événements, particularités et anecdotes de son règne, 4 vols (Paris, chez tous les magasins de nouveautés, 1800).

Vie privée et publique du ci-derrière marquis de Villette (n.p., n.d.).

Vie privée, impartiale, politique, militaire et domestique du marquis de La Fayette [...] *pour servir de supplément à la nécrologie des hommes célèbres du dix-huitième siècle et de clef aux révolutions françaises et américaines* (Paris, Bastide, 1790).

Vie privée, ou Apologie de très sérénissime prince monseigneur le duc de Chartres contre un libelle diffamatoire écrit en mil sept cent quatre-vingt un, mais qui n'a point paru à cause des menaces que nous avons faites à l'auteur de le déceler, par une société d'amis du prince ([London], 1784).

Vie privée, politique et littéraire de Beaumarchais, suivie d'anecdotes, de bons mots [...] *propre à faire connaître le caractère et l'esprit de cet homme célèbre et singulier* (Paris, An X [1802]).

Vie publique et privée de Charles Gravier de Vergennes, ministre d'Etat (Paris, Maradan, 1789).

Vie publique et privée de Honoré-Gabriel Riquetti, comte de Mirabeau, député du tiers état de la sénéchaussée d'Aix (Paris, Hôtel d'Aiguillon, 1791).

Vie publique et privée de Joachim Murat, composée d'après des matériaux authentiques, la plupart inconnus, et contenant des particularités inédites sur ses premières années, par M. *** (Paris, 1816).

Vie publique et privée de M. le marquis de La Fayette, avec des détails sur l'affaire du 6 octobre, etc. (n.p., 1791).

Vie secrète de Louise-Marie-Adélaïde Bourbon-Penthièvre, duchesse d'Orléans, avec ses correspondances politiques (London, Werland, 1790).

Vie secrète de Pierre Manuel, ci-devant procureur-syndic de la commune de Paris, et député à la Convention nationale (Paris, n.d. [1793]).

Vie secrète et politique de Brissot (Paris, An II [1794]).

Vie secrète et politique de Louis-Stanislas-Xavier, Monsieur, frère de Louis XVI (Paris, Au manège des Tuileries, 1790).

Vie secrète, politique et curieuse de M. J. Maximilien Robespierre [...] jusqu'au 9 thermidor l'an deuxième de la République [...], suivie de plusieurs anecdotes sur cette conspiration (Paris, Prévost An II [1794]).

Virtue and vice, or the History of Charles Careful, and Harry Heedless (1780?; London, 1815).

Visions, réflexions et aveux de Derues, trouvés dans sa prison, écrits de sa propre main (Amsterdam and Paris, Dessenne, 1777).

Wakefield, Priscilla, Juvenile anecdotes, founded on facts (1795-1798; London, 1825).

The Weekly journal, or British gazeteer (7 November 1724).

Wieland, Christoph Martin, Werke, 40 vols (Berlin, 1879).

Williams, D. E., The Life and correspondence of Thomas Lawrence, 2 vols (London, 1831).

Williams, John [Anthony Pasquin], The Eccentricities of John Edwin, comedian (London, 1791).

Woodward, G. W., Eccentric excursions, or Literary & pictorial sketches of countenance, character and country (London, Allen and West, 1796).

Secondary literature

Abrams, M. H., Natural supernaturalism: tradition and evolution in Romantic literature (New York and London, 1973).

Acher, William, Jean-Jacques Rousseau: écrivain de l'amitié (Paris, 1971).

Adler, Alfred, The Individual psychology of Alfred Adler: a systematic presentation in selections from his writings, ed. H. L. and R. R. Ansbacher (New York, 1964).

Alpers, Svetlana, The Art of describing: Dutch art of the seventeenth century (Chicago, 1984).

Altman, Janet, Epistolarity: approaches to a form (Columbus, OH, 1982).

Anderson, Wilda, Diderot's dream (Baltimore, MD, 1990).

Ariès, Philippe, Centuries of childhood: a social history of family life, trans. Robert Baldick (New York, 1962).

–, and Georges Duby (ed.), Histoire de la vie privée. 5 vols (Paris, 1985-1987).

–, 'Introduction', in A History of private life, vol.3: Passions of the Renaissance, ed. Roger Chartier, trans. Arthur Goldhammer (Cambridge, MA, 1989), p.1-11.

Arkhiv bratiev Turgenevykh, vol.2 (St Petersburg, 1911).

Arkhiv kniazia F. A. Kurakina 7 (1898).

Arnol'd, M. K., Vospominaniia, Golos minuvshego 2 (1917), p.196.

Arquié-Bruley, Françoise,

'Documents notoriés sur Greuze', *Bulletin de la Société de l'histoire de l'art français* 1981 (1983), p.125-54.

Auslander, Leora, *Taste and power: furnishing modern France* (Berkeley, CA, 1996).

Aymard, Maurice, 'Amitié et convivialité', in *Histoire de la vie privée*, vol.3: *De la Renaissance aux Lumières*, ed. Roger Chartier (Paris, 1986), p.455-99.

Backscheider, Paula R., 'Introduction', in *The Intersections of the public and private spheres in early modern England*, ed. Paula R. Backscheider and Timothy Dystal (London, 1996), p.1-18.

Baehr, Stephen Lessing, *The Paradise myth in eighteenth-century Russia: utopian patterns in early secular Russian literature and culture* (Stanford, CA, 1991).

Bailey, Colin B., 'Anglo-Saxon attitudes: recent writings on Chardin', in *Chardin*, ed. P. Rosenberg (London, 2000), p.91-92.

–, 'Details that surreptitiously explain: Boucher as a genre painter', in *Rethinking Boucher*, ed. Melissa Hyde and Mark Ledbury (Los Angeles, 2006), p.39-60.

–, *Greuze: the laundress* (Los Angeles, 2000).

–, 'Surveying genre in eighteenth-century French painting', in *The Age of Watteau, Chardin and Fragonard: masterpieces of French genre painting*, ed. Philip Conisbee, Colin Bailey and Thomas Gaehtgens (Ottawa, Washington, Berlin, 2003-2004), p.2-40.

Banerji, Christiane, and Diana Donald, *Gillray observed: the earliest account of his caricatures in London and Paris* (Cambridge, 1999).

Barker, Emma, *Greuze and the painting of sentiment* (Cambridge, 2004).

Barker-Benfield, G. J., *The Culture of sensibility: sex and society in eighteenth-century Britain* (Chicago, 1992).

Barran, Thomas, 'Ippolit Fedorovich Bogdanovich', *Dictionary of literary biography*, vol.150: *Early modern Russian writers, late seventeenth and eighteenth centuries*, ed. Marcus Levitt (Detroit, MI, 1995), p.29-35.

Barrell, John, *The Spirit of despotism: invasions of privacy in the 1790s* (Oxford, 2006).

Bastien, Pascal, *L'Exécution publique à Paris au XVIIIe siècle* (Seyssel, 2006).

Baxandall, Michael, *Shadows and Enlightenment* (New Haven, CT, and London, 1995).

Baxter, Denise Amy, 'Fashions of sociability in Jean-François de Troy's tableaux de mode, 1725-1738', in *Performing the 'everyday': the culture of genre in the eighteenth century*, ed. Alden Cavanaugh (Newark, DE, 2007), p.27-46.

Beaumarchais, *Le Barbier de Séville* in *Œuvres*, ed. Pierre Larthomas (Paris, 1988), p.265-349.

Bellhouse, Mary, 'Erotic "remedy" prints and the fall of aristocracy in eighteenth-century France', *Political theory* 25:5 (1997), p.680-715.

Bender, John, *Imagining the penitentiary: fiction and architecture of mind in eighteenth-century England* (Chicago, 1987).

Benua [Benois], Aleskandr, *Tsarskoe selo v tsarstvovanie Imperatritsy Elizavety Petrovny* (St Petersburg, 1910).

Berg, Maxine, *Luxury and pleasure in eighteenth-century Britain* (Oxford, 2005).

–, and Elizabeth Eger, *Luxury in the eighteenth century: debates, desires, and delectable goods* (Houndmills, 2003).

–, and Helen Clifford (ed.), *Consumers and luxury: consumer culture in Europe, 1650-1850* (Manchester, 1999).

Berger, Robert W., *In the garden of the Sun King: studies on the park of Versailles under Louis XIV* (Washington, DC, 1985).

Bogdanov, A. I., *Opisanie Sanktpeterburga 1749-1751* (St Petersburg, 1997).

Braudy, Leo, *The Frenzy of renown: fame and its history* (New York, 1997).

Breen, T. H., *The Marketplace of revolution: how consumer politics shaped American independence* (Oxford, 2005).

Brewer, John, *The Pleasures of the imagination: English culture in the eighteenth century* (London, 1997).

Brissenden, R. F., *Virtue in distress: studies in the novel of sentiment from Richardson to Sade* (London, 1974).

Brown, Peter, *Society and the holy in late antiquity* (Berkeley, CA, 1982).

Brownell, Morris, *Samuel Johnson's attitude to the arts* (Oxford, 1989).

Bryson, Norman, *Looking at the overlooked: four essays on still life painting* (London, 2004).

–, *Word and image: French painting of the ancien regime* (Cambridge, 1984).

Bryson, Scott, *The Chastised stage: bourgeois drama and the exercise of power* (Stanford, CA, 1991).

Butler, Marilyn, *Maria Edgeworth* (Oxford, 1972).

Calhoun, Craig (ed.), *Habermas and the public sphere* (Cambridge, MA, 1992).

Campbell, Kimberley Krisman, 'The face of fashion: milliners in eighteenth-century visual culture', *British journal for eighteenth-century studies* 25:2 (2002), p.157-71.

Carayol, Elisabeth, *Thémiseul de Saint-Hyacinthe*, SVEC 221 (1984).

Castan, Nicole, 'Le public et le particulier', in *Histoire de la vie privée*, vol.3: *De la Renaissance aux Lumières*, ed. R. Chartier (Paris, 1986), p.413-54.

Castiglione, Dario, and Lesley Sharpe (ed.), *Shifting the boundaries: transformations of the languages of public and private in the eighteenth century* (Exeter, 1995).

Cathcart, Rex, 'Festive capers? Barring-out the schoolmaster', *History today* 38 (1988), p.49-53.

Cavanaugh, Alden, *Performing the 'everyday': the culture of genre in the eighteenth century* (Newark, DE, 2007).

Chartier, Roger (ed.), *Histoire de la vie privée*, vol.3: *De la Renaissance aux Lumières* (Paris, 1986).

–, *A History of private life*, vol.3: *Passions of the Renaissance*, ed. Roger Chartier, trans. Arthur Goldhammer (Cambridge, MA, 1989).

–, 'The practical impact of writing', in *A History of private life*, vol.3: *Passions of the Renaissance*, ed. Roger Chartier, trans. Arthur Goldhammer (Cambridge, MA, 1989), p.111-59.

Choudhury, Mita, *Convents and nuns in eighteenth-century French politics and culture* (Ithaca, NY, 2004).

Chouillet, Anne-Marie, 'Dossier du *Fils naturel* et du *Père de famille*', SVEC 208 (1982), p.75-166.

Chua, Kevin, 'Painting paralysis: "filial piety" in 1763', *Studies in the history of art* 72 (2007), p.152-77.

Cladis, Mark S., *Public vision, private lives: Rousseau, religion, and a 21st-century democracy* (Oxford, 2003).

Clark, Peter, *British clubs and societies 1580-1800* (Oxford, 2000).

Clément, Pierre-Paul, *De l'éros coupable à l'éros glorieux* (Neuchâtel, 1976).

Clements, Candace, 'The Academy and the other', *Eighteenth-century studies* 25:4 (1992), p.469-94.

Clubbe, John, *Byron, Sully, and the power of portraiture* (Aldershot, 2005).

Cohen, Michèle, 'Gender and the private/public debate on

education in the long eighteenth century', in *Public or private education? Lessons from history*, ed. Richard Aldrich (London, 2004), p.15-35.

Conisbee, Philip (ed.), *French genre painting in the eighteenth century* (New Haven, CT, and London, 2007).

–, Colin Bailey and Thomas Gaehtgens (ed.), *The Age of Watteau, Chardin and Fragonard: masterpieces of French genre painting* (Ottawa, Washington, Berlin, 2003-2004).

Conley, John J., *The Suspicion of virtue: women philosophers in neoclassical France* (Ithaca, NY, 2002).

Connon, Derek, *Innovation and renewal: a study of the theatrical works of Diderot*, SVEC 258 (1989).

Conway, Alison, *Private interests: women, portraiture and visual culture in the English novel, 1709-91* (Toronto, 2001).

Courajod, Louis (ed.), *Livre-journal de Lazare Duvaux, marchand-bijoutier ordinaire du roy, 1748-1758* (Paris, 1873).

Coxe, William, *Travels in Poland, Russia, Sweden and Denmark*, 5th edn, vol.2 (London, 1802).

Cozzi, Gaetano, 'Note su tribunali e procedure penali a Venezia nel '700', *Rivista Storica Italiana* 77:4 (1965), p.931-52.

–, 'Religione, moralità, e giustizia a Venezia: Vicende della Magistratura degli Esecutori contro la Bestemmia (secoli XVI-XVII)', *Ateneo Veneto* 178/179:29 (1991), p.7-95.

Craveri, Benedetta, *The Age of conversation* (New York, 2005).

Crocker, Lester G., *J.-J. Rousseau: the quest (1712-1758)* (New York, 1968).

Crone, Anna Lisa, *The Daring of Deržavin: the moral and aesthetic independence of the poet in Russia* (Bloomington, IN, 2001).

Cronk, Nicholas, 'Dorval et le dialogue à trois voix: la présence de Rousseau dans *Le Fils naturel* et les *Entretiens*', in *Etudes sur Le Fils naturel et les Entretiens sur le Fils naturel de Diderot*, ed. Nicholas Cronk (Oxford, 2000), p.123-37.

Cross, Anthony (ed.), *An English lady at the court of Catherine the Great* (Cambridge, 1989).

Crow, Thomas, 'Chardin at the edge of belief: overlooked issues of religion and dissent in eighteenth-century French painting', *Studies in the history of art* 72 (2007), p.91-103.

–, *Painters and public life in eighteenth-century Paris* (New Haven, CT, and London, 1985).

Danilian, I. V., 'Masonskaia biblioteka Turgeneva (opyt rekonstruktsii po opisi 1831 g.)', in *Rukopisi. Redkie izdaniia. Arkhivy. Iz fondov biblioteki Moskovskovo universiteta* (Moscow, 1997), p.81-107.

Darnton, Robert, *The Forbidden best-sellers of pre-Revolutionary France* (New York, 1995).

–, 'Mlle Bonafon et "La Vie privée de Louis XV"', *Dix-huitième siècle* 35 (2003), p.369-91.

–, 'Readers respond to Rousseau: the fabrication of Romantic sensitivity', in *The Great cat massacre and other episodes* (New York, 1985), p.215-51.

Robert Darnton, *The Devil in the holy water, or the art of slander from Louis XIV to Napoleon* (Pennsylvania, 2009).

Davidoff, Leonore, and Catherine Hall, *Family fortunes: men and women of the English middle class, 1780-1850* (London, 1987).

Démoris, René, 'Chardin and the far side of illusion', in *Chardin*, ed. Pierre Rosenberg (London, 2000), p.99-109.

–, *Chardin, la chair et l'objet* (1991; Paris, 1999).

–, 'De Marivaux à *La Nouvelle Héloïse*: intertexte et contre-texte, entre fantasme et théorie', in *L'Amour dans La Nouvelle Héloïse: texte et intertexte*, ed. Jacques Berchtold and François Rosset, *Annales de la société Jean-Jacques Rousseau* 44 (Geneva, 2002), p.317-39.

Demos, John, *A Little commonwealth: family life in Plymouth colony* (Oxford, 1999).

Denby, David, *Sentimental narrative and the social order in France* (Cambridge, 1994).

Denis, Vincent, *Une Histoire de l'identité* (Seyssel, 2008).

Derrida, Jacques, *Politics of friendship*, trans. George Collins (London, 1997).

Deutsch, Helen, and Felicity Nussbaum (ed.), *'Defects': engendering the modern body* (Ann Arbor, MI, 2000).

Dewald, Jonathan, *Aristocratic experience and the origins of modern culture: France, 1570-1715* (Berkeley, CA, 1993).

Diderot et l'art de Boucher à David (Paris, 1984).

Donald, Diana, *The Age of caricature: satirical prints in the reign of George III* (New Haven, CT, and London, 1997).

Dubiago, T. V., *Russkie reguliarnye sady i parki* (Leningrad, 1963).

Dulau, Anne, Christoph Vogtherr and Ann Eatwell, *Boucher and Chardin, masters of modern manners* (London, 2008).

Eagleton, Terry, *Ideology: an introduction* (1991; London, 2007).

Ehrard, Antoinette (ed.), *Diderot et Greuze: actes du colloque de Clermont-Ferrand, 16 novembre 1984* (Arles, 1986).

Ellis, Markman, *The Politics of sensibility: race, gender and commerce in the sentimental novel* (Cambridge, 1996).

Elshtain, Jean Bethke, *Public man,*

private woman (Princeton, NJ, 1981).

Eriksen, Svend, 'La Live de Jully's furniture *à la grecque*', *The Burlington magazine* 103:701 (1961), p.340-38.

Fabre, Jean, 'Deux frères ennemis: Diderot et Jean-Jacques Rousseau', *Diderot studies* 3 (1961), p.155-213.

Fairchilds, C., 'The production and marketing of populuxe goods in eighteenth-century Paris', in *Consumption and the world of goods*, ed. John Brewer and Roy Porter (London and New York, 1993), p.228-48.

Farge, Arlette, 'Familles: l'honneur et le secret', in *Histoire de la vie privée*, vol.3: *De la Renaissance aux Lumières*, ed. R. Chartier (Paris, 1986), p.580-617.

Fenves, Peter, 'Politics of friendship – once again', *Eighteenth-century studies* 32 (1998-1999), p.133-55.

Ferrand, Nathalie, *Livre et lecture dans les romans français du XVIIIᵉ siècle* (Paris, 2002).

F. G. Volkov i russkii teatr ego vremeni: sbornik materialov (Moscow, 1953).

Flandrin, Jean-Louis, *Familles: parenté, maison, sexualité dans l'ancienne société* (Paris, 1976).

Foisil, Madeleine, 'L'écriture du for privé', in *Histoire de la vie privée*, vol.3: *De la Renaissance aux Lumières* (Paris, 1986), ed. R. Chartier, p.320-23.

Folkenflik, Robert, *Samuel Johnson biographer* (Ithaca, NY, and London, 1978).

Foucault, Michel, *Histoire de la sexualité*, vol.1: *La Volonté de savoir* (Paris, 1976).

–,*The History of sexuality: an introduction* (New York, 1980).

–, 'Technologies of the self', in *Technologies of the self: a seminar with Michel Foucault*, ed. L. H. Martin, H. Gutman and P. M. Hutton (Amherst, 1988), p.16-49.

Franits, Wayne (ed.), *Looking at seventeenth-century Dutch art: realism reconsidered* (Cambridge, 1997).

Frantz, Pierre, *L'Esthétique du tableau dans le théâtre du dix-huitième siècle* (Paris, 1998).

Freeman, Lisa, *Character's theatre: genre and identity on the eighteenth-century English stage* (Philadelphia, PA, 2002).

Friedmann, Herbert, *The Symbolic goldfinch: its history and significance in European devotional art* (New York, 1946).

Frijda, Nico H., and Batja Mesquita, 'The social roles and the function of emotions', in *Emotion and culture: empirical studies of mutual influence*, ed. Shinoby Kitayama and Hazel Rose Markus (Washington, DC, 1994), p.57-59.

Fuller, Lincoln B., *Turned to account: the forms and functions of criminal biography in late seventeenth- and early eighteenth-century England* (Cambridge, 1987).

Gatrell, Vic, *City of laughter: sex and satire in eighteenth-century London* (London, 2006).

Geertz, Clifford, *The Interpretation of cultures* (New York, 1973).

Gélis, Jacques, 'The child: from anonymity to individuality', in *A History of private life*, vol.3: *Passions of the Renaissance*, ed. Roger Chartier, trans. Arthur Goldhammer (Cambridge, MA, 1989), p. 309-25.

Genette, Gérard, *Paratexts: thresholds of interpretation*, trans. Jane E. Lewin (Cambridge, 1997).

Genovese, Eugene, and Elizabeth Fox-Genovese, 'The political crisis of social history: a Marxian perspective', *Journal of social history* 10 (winter 1976), p.205-20.

Georgi, I. G., *Opisanie rossiisko-imperatorskogo stolichnogo goroda Sankt-Peterburga i dostopamiatnostei v*

okrestnostiakh onogo, 1974-1796g. (St Petersburg, 1996).

Gerson, Frédérick, *L'Amitié au XVIIIe siècle* (Paris, 1974).

Ginzburg, Lidia, *On psychological prose* (Princeton, NJ, 1991).

Gladfelder, Hal, *Criminality and narrative in eighteenth-century England: beyond the law* (Baltimore, MD, 2001).

Glebov, A., 'Poezdka v Petergof 22 Iiulia', *Novosti literatury* 26 (May 1826), p.76.

Goehrke, Carsten, *Russischer Alltag: eine Geschichte in neun Zeitbildern vom Frühmittelalter bis zur Gegenwart*, vol.2: *Auf dem Weg in die Moderne* (Zurich, 2003).

Goffman, Erving, *Behavior in public places: notes on the social organization of gatherings* (New York, 1963).

Goldgar, Anne, *Impolite learning: conduct and community in the Republic of Letters* (New Haven, CT, and London, 1995).

Gollerbakh, E. F., *Gorod muz: Tsarskoe Selo v poezii* (St Petersburg, 1993).

Goulemot, Jean-Marie, *Ces livres qu'on ne lit que d'une main* (Aix-en-Provence, 1991).

–, 'Literary practices: publicizing the private', in *A History of private life*, vol.3: *Passions of the Renaissance*, ed. Roger Chartier, trans. Arthur Goldhammer (Cambridge, MA, 1989), p.363-95.

–, 'Les pratiques littéraires ou la publicité du privé', in *Histoire de la vie privée*, vol.3: *De la Renaissance aux Lumières*, ed. R. Chartier (Paris, 1986), p.363-96.

Grafton, Antony, *The Footnote: a curious history* (Cambridge, MA, 1997).

Grantham, G. W., 'Divisions of labour: agricultural productivity and occupational specialization in pre-industrial France', *Economic history review* 46:3 (1993), p.478-502.

Grenby, M. O., *Children's literature* (Edinburgh, 2008).

Grimm, G. G., 'Proekt parka
Bezborodko v Moskve (Materialy
k izucheniiu tvorchestva N.A.
L'vova)', *Soobshcheniia instituta istorii
iskusstv* 4-5 (1954), p.107-35.

Habermas, Jürgen, *The Structural
transformation of the public sphere: an
inquiry into a category of bourgeois
society*, trans. Thomas Burger and
Frederick Lawrence (Cambridge,
MA, 1989).
Hackel, Sergei, 'The religious
dimension: vision or evasion?
Zosima's discourse in *The Brothers
Karamazov*', in *New essays on
Dostoevsky*, ed. M. V. Jones and G.
M. Terry (Cambridge, 1983),
p.139-68.
Hallett, Mark, 'Reading the walls:
pictorial dialogue at the
eighteenth-century Royal
Academy', *Eighteenth-century studies*
37:4 (2004), p.581-604.
–, *The Spectacle of difference: graphic
satire in the age of Hogarth* (New
Haven, CT, 1999).
Hammer, Stephanie, *Schiller's wound:
the theater of trauma from crisis to
commodity* (Detroit, MI, 2001).
Hazlitt, William, 'Character of Sir
Joshua Reynolds', *The Champion*
(30 October and 6 November
1814), in *The Complete works of
William Hazlitt*, vol.18: *Art and
dramatic criticism*, ed. P. P. Howe
(London and Toronto, 1932),
p.54-55.
–, 'On the imitation of nature', *The
Champion* (25 December 1814), in
*The Complete works of William
Hazlitt*, vol.18: *Art and dramatic
criticism*, ed. P. P. Howe (London
and Toronto, 1932), p.74-75.
Hedley, Jo, *François Boucher: seductive
visions* (London, 2006).
Helly, Dorothy O., and Susan M.
Reverby (ed.), *Gendered domains:
rethinking public and private in
women's history* (Ithaca, NY, 1992).
Hesse, Carla, *The Other Enlightenment:

how French women became modern*
(Princeton, NJ, 2003).
Hilles, Frederick W. (ed.), *Portraits by
Sir Joshua Reynolds* (London, 1952).
Hine, Ellen McNiven, 'Madame de
Lambert, her sources and her
circle', *SVEC* 102 (1973), p.173-92.
Hunt, Lynn (ed.), *The Invention of
pornography* (New York, 1993).
Hyde, Melissa, *Making up the rococo:
François Boucher and his critics* (Los
Angeles, 2006).
–, and Mark Ledbury (ed.),
Rethinking Boucher (Los Angeles,
2006).

Iakovkin, Il'ia, *Istoriia sela tsarskogo*,
vol.2 (St Petersburg, 1829).
Iggers, Georg G., *Historiography in the
twentieth century: from scientific
objectivity to postmodern challenge*
(Hanover, NH, and London,
1997).
Israel, Jonathan, *Enlightenment
contested* (Oxford, 2006).
–, *Radical Enlightenment* (Oxford,
2001).
Ivanov, S. A., *Holy fools in Byzantium
and beyond*, trans. Simon Franklin
(Oxford and New York, 2006).
'Iz dnevnika Andreia Ivanovicha
Turgeneva', in *Vostok-Zapad.
Issledovania. Perevody. Publikatsii*, ed.
M. Virolainen (Moscow, 1984),
p.100-39.

James, Susan, *Passion and action: the
emotions in seventeenth-century
philosophy* (Oxford, 1997).
Jardine, Lisa, *Worldly goods: a new
history of the Renaissance* (London,
1996).
Jones, Colin, *The Great nation: France
from Louis XV to Napoleon*
(Harmondsworth, 2002).
–, 'The return of the banished
bourgeoisie', *Times literary
supplement* (29 March 1991), p.8.
Jones, M., *Sexing la mode: gender,
fashion and commercial culture in old
regime France* (Oxford, 2004).

Jones, W. Gareth, 'The Russian language as a definer of nobility', in *A Window on Russia: papers from the V International Conference of the Study Group on Eighteenth-Century Russia, Gargnano, 1994*, ed. Maria Di Salvo and Lindsey Hughes (Rome, 1996), p.293-98.

Josipovici, Gabriel, *Touch* (New Haven, CT, and London, 1996).

Judt, Tony, 'A clown in regal purple: social history and the historians', *History workshop journal* 7 (1979), p.66-94.

Karamzin, N. M., 'Mysli v sadu Pavlovskom', in *Neizdannye sochineniia i perepiska Nikolaia Mikhailovicha Karamzina*, part 1 (St Petersburg, 1862), p.185-86.

–, 'O Bogdanoviche i ego sochineniiakh', in *Izbrannye stat'i i pis'ma* (Moscow, 1982), p.113-36.

Keenan, Paul, 'Creating a "public" in St Petersburg, 1703-1761', doctoral dissertation, SSEES/UCL, 2006.

–, 'The question of access to the Summer Gardens in St Petersburg in the first half of the eighteenth century', *Newsletter of the study group on eighteenth-century Russia* 34 (2006), p.17-22.

Klein, Joachim, 'Bogdanovich i ego "Dushen'ka", in *Puti kul'turnogo importa: Trudy po russkoi literature XVIII veka* (Moscow, 2005), p.459-77.

–, 'Poet-samokhval: "Pamiatnik" Derzhavina i status poeta v russkoi kul'ture XVIII veka', in *Puti kul'turnogo importa: Trudy po russkoi literature XVIII veka* (Moscow, 2005), p.498-520.

Kochetkova, N. D., 'Ippolit Fedorovich Bogdanovich', in *Slovar' russkikh pisatelei XVIII veka*, vol.1: *A–I*, ed. N.D. Kochetkova, et al (Leningrad, 1988), p.104-109.

Kwass, Michael, 'Big hair: a wig history of consumption in eighteenth-century France', *American historical review* 3:3 (2006), accessed from www.historycooperative.org/journals/ahr/111.3/kwass.html on 17 March 2010.

–, 'Consumption and the world of ideas: consumer revolution and the moral economy of the marquis de Mirabeau', *Eighteenth-century studies* 37:2 (2004), p.187-213.

–, 'Ordering the world of goods: consumer revolution and the classification of objects in eighteenth-century France', *Representations* 82 (2003), p.87-116.

Laing, Alastair (ed.), *François Boucher* (Paris, 1986-1987).

Landes, Joan, *Women and the public sphere in the age of the French Revolution* (Ithaca, NY, 1988).

Laqueur, Thomas, *Making sex: body and gender from the Greeks to Freud* (Cambridge, MA, and London, 1990).

Lasch, Christopher, *Haven in a heartless world: the family besieged* (New York, 1977).

Laslett, Peter, *The World we have lost: England before the industrial age* (New York, 1971).

Lavrov, A., *Koldovstvo i religiia v Rossii, 1700-1740gg.* (Moscow, 2000).

Layard, George Somes (ed.), *Sir Thomas Lawrence's letter-bag* (London, 1906).

Lecompte, Denis, *Marx et le baron d'Holbach* (Paris, 1983).

Ledbury, Mark, *Sedaine, Greuze and the boundaries of genre*, SVEC 380 (2000).

Levitt, Marcus, 'Aleksandr Petrovich Sumarokov', in *Dictionary of literary biography*, vol.150: *Early modern Russian writers, late seventeenth and eighteenth centuries*, ed. Marcus Levitt (Detroit, MI, 1995), p.370-81.

–, 'The illegal staging of Sumarokov's *Sinav i Truvor* in 1770 and the problem of authorial status in eighteenth-century Russia', *Slavic and East European journal* 43 (1999), p.299-323.

Levy, Michelle, *Family, authority and romantic print culture* (Basingstoke, 2008).

Lincoln, W. Bruce, *Sunlight at midnight: St. Petersburg and the rise of modern Russia* (New York, 2000).

Linebaugh, Peter, 'The Ordinary of Newgate and his account', in *Crime in England 1550-1800*, ed. J. S. Cockburn (London, 1977), p.246-69.

Linton, Marisa, *The Politics of virtue in Enlightenment France* (Basingstoke, 2001).

Lipsedge, K., '"Enter into thy closet": women, closet culture, and the eighteenth-century English novel', in *Gender, taste, and material culture in Britain and North America 1700-1830*, ed. J. Styles and A. Vickery (New Haven, CT, and London, 2006).

Lloyd, Stephen, 'Intimate viewing: the private face and public display of portraits in miniature and on paper', in *The Intimate portrait: drawings, miniatures and pastels from Ramsay to Lawrence* (Edinburgh, 2009), p.13-23.

Longworth, Philip, *Alexis, tsar of all the Russias* (London, 1984).

Lough, John, *The Encyclopédie* (London, 1971).

Luckhurst, Mary, and Jane Moody (ed.), *Theatre and celebrity in Britain, 1660-2000* (New York and Basingstoke, 2005).

Maccannell, J. F., 'The postfictional self/authorial consciousness in three texts by Rousseau', *Modern language notes* 89 (1974), p.580-99.

McCardle, Arthur W., *Friederich Schiller and Swabian Pietism* (New York, 1986).

McCarthy, John A., *Crossing boundaries: a theory and history of essay writing in German, 1680-1815* (Philadelphia, PA, 1989).

McKeon, Michael, 'Prose fiction: Great Britain', in *The Cambridge history of literary criticism*, vol.4: *The Eighteenth century*, ed. H. B. Nisbet and Claude Rawson (Cambridge, 1997), p.238-263.

–, *The Secret history of domesticity: public, private, and the division of knowledge* (Baltimore, MD, 2005).

McLaughlin, Blandine L., *Diderot et l'amitié*, SVEC 100 (1973).

McLellan, Andrew, 'Watteau's dealer: Gersaint and the marketing of art in eighteenth-century Paris', *The Art bulletin* 78:3 (1996), p.439-53.

Makarov, N., *Moi semidesiatiletniia vospominaniia i s tem vmeste moia polnaia predsmertnaia ispoved'*, vol.1 (St Petersburg, 1881).

Maner, Martin, *The Philosophical biographer: doubt and dialectic in Johnson's 'Lives of the poets'* (Athens, GA, 1988).

Mannings, David, *Sir Joshua Reynolds: a complete catalogue of his paintings*, 2 vols (New Haven, CT, and London, 2000).

Marchal, Roger, *Madame de Lambert et son milieu*, SVEC 289 (1991).

Mariette, P.-J., *Abecédario de P. J. Mariette et autres notes inédites de cet amateur sur les arts et les artistes*, ed. Anatole de Montaiglon and Philippe de Chennevières, 6 vols (Paris, 1851-1860).

Marker, Gary, 'Literacy and literacy texts in Muscovy: a reconsideration', *Slavic review* 49 (1990), p.74-89.

Martin, John, *Myths of Renaissance individualism* (Basingstoke, 2004).

Mascuch, Michael, *Origins of the individualist self* (Cambridge, 1997).

Maza, Sarah, *The Myth of the French bourgeoisie: an essay on the social imaginary, 1750-1850* (Cambridge, MA, 2003).

–, *Private lives and public affairs: the causes célèbres of prerevolutionary France* (Berkeley, CA, 1993).

Meehan-Waters, Brenda, *Autocracy and aristocracy: the Russian service elite of 1730* (New Brunswick, NJ, 1982).

Meeker, Natania, *Voluptuous philosophy: literary materialism in the French Enlightenment* (New York, 2006).

Ménil, Alain, *Diderot et le drame* (Paris, 1995).

Mercier-Faivre, Anne-Marie, 'Les vies privées du chevalier d'Eon', in *The Chevalier d'Eon and his worlds: gender, politics and espionage in the eighteenth century*, ed. S. Burrows (London, 2010).

Merrick, Jeffrey, 'Male friendship in prerevolutionary France', *GLQ: a journal of lesbian and gay studies* 10 (2004), p.407-32.

Michaud-Quantin, P., *Sommes de casuistique et manuels de confession au Moyen Age (XII-XVI siècles)* (Louvain, 1962).

Michel, Régis, 'Diderot et la modernité', in *Diderot et l'art de Boucher à David* (Paris, 1984), p.110-21.

Michels, G. B., *At war with the Church: religious dissent in seventeenth-century Russia* (Stanford, CA, 1999).

Miegroet, Hans J. Van, 'Recycling Netherlandish paintings in eighteenth-century France', in *Collectioner dans les Flandres et la France du Nord au XVIIIᵉ siècle*, ed. Sophie Raux (March, 2005), p.251-88.

–, and Neil de Marchi, *Mapping markets for paintings in early modern Europe 1450-1750* (Turnhout, 2006).

Mills Todd III, William, *Fiction and society in the age of Pushkin: ideology, institutions, and narrative* (Cambridge, MA, 1986).

Moore, Barrington, *Privacy: studies in social and cultural history* (Armonk, NY, 1984).

Mraz, Gerda, and Uwe Schögl (ed.), *Das Kunstkabinett des Johann Caspar Lavater* (Vienna, 1999).

Munhall, Edgar (ed.), *Jean-Baptiste Greuze* (Hartford, 1978), English ed.

Myers, W. D., *'Poor, sinning folk': confession and conscience in Counter-Reformation Germany* (Ithaca, NY, 1996).

Nahirny, Vladimir, *The Russian intelligentsia: from torment to silence* (New Brunswick, NJ, 1983).

Nédélec, Claudine, 'L'argot des gueux aux XVIIᵉ et XVIIIᵉ siècles', *XVIIᵉ siècle* 186 (1995), p.147-54.

Newlin, Thomas, 'Andrei Timofeevich Bolotov', in *Dictionary of literary biography*, vol.150: *Early modern Russian writers, late seventeenth and eighteenth centuries*, ed. Marcus Levitt (Detroit, MI, 1995), p.36-42.

–, *The Voice in the garden: Andrei Bolotov and the anxieties of Russian pastoral, 1738-1833* (Evanston, IL, 2001).

Nikoleva, M. N., 'Cherty starinnogo dvorianskogo byta. Vospominaniia Mar'i Sergeevny Nikolevoi', *Russkii arkhiv* 9 (1893), p.111-12.

Novikov, V. I., 'Masonskie usad'by Podmoskov'ia', *Russkaia usad'ba* 5:21 (1999), p.225-39.

Nussbaum, Felicity, *The Limits of the human: fictions of anomaly, race and gender in the long eighteenth century* (Cambridge, 2003).

Ogée, Frédéric, 'Chardin's time: reflections on the tercentenary exhibition and twenty years of scholarship', *Eighteenth-century studies* 33:3 (2000), p.431-50.

O'Neal, John C., *The Authority of experience: sensationist theory in the French Enlightenment* (University Park, PA, 1996).

*Opisanie dokumentov i del,
khraniashchikhsia v arkhive
Sviateishego Pravitel'stvuiushchego
Sinoda*, 49 vols (St Petersburg,
1869-1914).

'O propuske dlia gulian'ia v
Pridvornye sady po Chetvergam i
Voskresen'iam', in *Polnoe sobranie
zakonov rossiiskoi imperii s 1649
goda, Pervoe sobranie*, vol.14 (St
Petersburg, 1830), no.10.560.

Oriel, J. D., *The Scars of Venus: a
history of venerology* (London, 1994).

Pardailhé-Galabrun, Annik, *La
Naissance de l'intime: 3 000 foyers
parisiens XVIIe-XVIIIe siècles* (Paris,
1988).

Pateman, Carole, *The Sexual contract*
(Stanford, CA, 1988).

Patten, Robert L., 'Conventions of
Georgian caricature', *Art journal*
41:4 (1983), p.331-38.

Pearsall, Sarah M. S., *Atlantic families:
lives and letters in the later eighteenth
century* (Oxford, 2008).

Pekarskii, P. P., *Nauka i literature pri
Petre Velikom*, 2 vols (St Petersburg,
1862).

Pellegrin, Nicole, 'Corps du
commun, usages communs du
corps', in *Histoire du corps*, ed. A.
Corbin, J. J. Courtine and G.
Vigarello, 3 vols (Paris, 2005),
vol.1, p.131-32.

Péveri, Patrice, '"Cette ville était alors
comme un bois": criminalité et
opinion publique à Paris dans les
années qui précèdent l'affaire
Cartouche 1715-1721', *Crime,
histoire et sociétés* 1:2 (1997), p.51-73.

Pigin, A. V., 'K izucheniiu Povesti
Nikodima Tipikarisa Solovetskogo
o nekoem inoke', in *Knizhnye
tsentry Drevnei Rusi. Solovetskii
monastyr'*, ed. S.A. Semiachko (St
Petersburg, 2001), p.303-10.

Piper, David, *The English face*
(London, 1992).

–, *Personality and the portrait* (London,
1973).

Pis'ma russkikh pisatelei, ed. G. P.
Makogonenko (Leningrad, 1980).

Plaisant, Michèle (ed.), *L'Excentricité
en Grand-Bretagne au 18e siècle*
(Lille, 1976).

Plekhanov, George, *Essays in the
history of materialism* (London,
1934).

Pointon, Marcia, *Hanging the head:
portraiture and social formation in
eighteenth-century England* (New
Haven, CT, and London, 1993).

*Polnoe sobranie postanovlenii i
rasporiazhenii po vedomstvu
pravoslavnogo ispovedaniia Rossiiskoi
Imperii* (Sankt Peterburg, 1869-
1915).

*Polnoe sobranie zakonov Rossiiskoi
imperii* [Sobranie 1-e], 45 vols (St
Petersburg, 1830).

Postle, Martin (ed.), *Joshua Reynolds:
the creation of celebrity* (London,
2005).

Preobrazhenskii, A. A., and T. I.
Novitskaia (ed.), *Zakonodatel'stvo
Petra I* (Moscow, 1997).

Price, A. W., *Love and friendship in
Plato and Aristotle* (Oxford, 1989).

Pulcini, Elena, *Amour-passion et amour
conjugal: Rousseau et l'origine d'un
conflit moderne* (Paris, 1998).

Putevoditel' po S.-Peterburgu (St
Petersburg, 1903).

Pyliaev, M. I., *Staryi Peterburg*
(Moscow, 1997).

Raeff, Marc, *Origins of the Russian
intelligentsia: the eighteenth-century
nobility* (New York, 1966).

–, 'Russian youth on the eve of
Romanticism: Andrei Turgenev
and his circle', in *Revolution and
politics in Russia; essays in memory of
B. I. Nikolaevsky*, ed. Alexander and
Janet Rabinowitch, with Ladis K.
D. Kristof (Bloomington, IN,
1972), p.39-54.

Rand, Richard (ed.), *Intimate
encounters: love and domesticity in
eighteenth-century France* (Hanover,
NH, 1997).

Rauser, Amelia, 'Embodied liberty: why Hogarth's caricature of John Wilkes backfired', in *The Other Hogarth: aesthetics of difference*, ed. Bernadette Fort and Angela Rosenthal (Princeton, NJ, 2001), p.240-57.

Reddy, William M., *The Navigation of feeling: a framework for the history of emotions* (Cambridge, 2001).

Requemora, Sylvie, 'L'amitié dans les "Maximes" de La Rochefoucauld', *Dix-septième siècle* 51 (1999), p.687-728.

Retford, Kate, *The Art of domestic life: family portraiture in eighteenth-century England* (New Haven, CT, and London, 2006).

Ribeiro, Aileen, *The Art of dress: fashion in England and France, 1750-1820* (New Haven, CT, 1997).

Rider, Frederick, *The Dialectic of selfhood in Montaigne* (Stanford, CA, 1973).

Roach, Joseph, *It* (Ann Arbor, MI, 2007).

Roche, Daniel, *The Culture of clothing: dress and fashion in the ancien régime*, trans. Jean Birrell (Cambridge, 1994).

–, *Histoire des choses banales: naissance de la société de consommation, XVIIIe-XIXe siècle* (Paris, 1997).

–, *Le Peuple de Paris* (1981; Paris, 1998).

Rochebrune, Marie-Laure de, 'Ceramics and glass in Chardin's paintings', in *Chardin*, ed. Pierre Rosenberg (London, 2000), p.37-53.

Rojek, Chris, *Celebrity* (London, 2001).

Ronsin, Francis, *Le Contrat sentimental: débats sur le mariage, l'amour, le divorce de l'ancien régime à la Restauration* (Paris, 1991).

Rosenberg, Pierre (ed.), *Chardin* (London, 2000).

–, *Chardin, 1699-1779* (Paris, 1979).

Rothschild, Loren, *Blinking Sam: the true history of Sir Joshua Reynolds's 1775 portrait of Samuel Johnson* (Los Angeles, 2002), reprinted in *Age of Johnson* 15 (2004), p.141-50.

Rozanov, N., *Istoriia Moskovskogo eparkhal'nogo upravleniia so vremeni uchrezhdeniia Sviateishego Sinoda, 1721-1821*, 3 vols (Moscow, 1869-1871).

Ruggiero, Guido, *The Boundaries of eros: sex crime and sexuality in Renaissance Venice* (Oxford, 1989).

Sargentson, Carolyn, *Merchants and luxury markets: the marchands merciers of eighteenth-century Paris* (London and Los Angeles, 1996).

Sarsby, Jacqueline, *Romantic love and society* (London, 1983).

Sbornik imperatorskogo rossiiskogo istoricheskogo obshchestva, vol.23 (St Petersburg, 1878).

Scarabello, Giovanni, *Esecutori contro la Bestemmia: un processo per rapimento, stupro, e lenocinio nella Venezia popolare del secondo Settecento* (Venice, 1991).

Schönle, Andreas, *Authenticity and fiction in the Russian literary journey, 1790-1840* (Cambridge, MA, 2000).

–, 'The scare of the self: sentimentalism, privacy, and private life in Russian culture, 1780-1820', *Slavic review* 57:4 (1998), p.723-46.

Schwab, Richard N., W. E. Rex and J. Lough, *Inventory of Diderot's Encyclopédie*, SVEC 80 (1971), 83 (1971), 85 (1972), 91 (1972), 92 (1972), 93 (1972), 223 (1984).

Sennett, Richard, *The Fall of public man* (London, 2002).

Sherman, Nancy, 'Aristotle on the shared life', in *Friendship: a philosophical reader*, ed. Neera Kapur Badhwar (Ithaca, NY, 1993) p.91-107.

Shookman, Erik, 'Pseudo-science, social fad, literary wonder: Johann Caspar Lavater and the art of physiognomy', in *The Faces of physiognomy: interdisciplinary approaches to Johann Caspar Lavater*, ed. E. Shookman (Columbia, SC, 1993), p.1-24.

Shorter, Edward, *The Making of the modern family* (New York, 1975).

Shubinskii, S. N., *Ocherki iz zhizni i byta proshlogo vremeni* (St Petersburg, 1888).

Siegrist, Christoph, '"Letters of the divine alphabet": Lavater's concept of physiognomy', in *The Faces of physiognomy: interdisciplinary approaches to Johann Caspar Lavater*, ed. E. Shookman (Columbia, SC, 1993), p.25-39.

Simon, Robin, *Hogarth, France and British art* (London, 2007).

Sipovskaia, N. V., 'Prazdnik v russkoi kul'ture XVIII veka', in *Razvlekatel'naia kul'tura Rossii XVIII-XIX vv.* (St Petersburg, 2000), p.28-42.

Smirnov, S. I., *Drevne-russkii dukhovnik. Issledovanie po istorii tserkovnogo byta, Chteniia v Imp. Obshchestve istorii i drevnostei rossiiskikh* 2:3 (1914), p.50-63.

Smith, Douglas, *The Pearl: a true tale of forbidden love in Catherine the Great's Russia* (New Haven, CT, 2008).

–, *Working the rough stone: freemasonry and society in eighteenth century Russia* (De Kalb, IL, 1999).

Smith, Elise L.,'Centering the home-garden: the arbor, wall, and gate in moral tales for children', *Children's literature* 36 (2008), p.24-48.

Smolich, I. K., *Istoriia russkoi tserkvi*, 2 vols (Moscow, 1996-1997).

Snoop-Reitsma, Ella, 'Chardin and the bourgeois ideals of his time', *Nederlands Kunsthistorisch Jaarboek* 24 (1973), p.147-243.

Solkin, David, *Painting for money: the visual arts and the public sphere in eighteenth-century England* (New Haven, CT, and London, 1993).

Starobinski, Jean, *Jean-Jacques Rousseau: la transparence et l'obstacle*, 2nd edn (Paris, 1971).

Stemmler, Joan K., 'The physiognomical portraits of Johann Caspar Lavater', *Art bulletin* 75:1 (1993), p.151-68.

Still, Judith, 'Rousseau's *La Nouvelle Héloïse*: passion, reserve, and the gift', *Modern language review* 91 (1996), p.40-52.

Stone, Lawrence, *The Family, sex and marriage in England, 1500-1800* (New York, 1977).

Storch, Henry, *Picture of Petersburg* (London, 1801).

Subbotin, N. I. (ed.), *Materialy dlia istorii raskola za pervoe vremia ego sushchestvovaniia*, 9 vols (Moscow, 1875-1890).

Sutcliffe, Adam, 'Spinoza and friends: religion, philosophy and friendship in the Berlin Enlightenment', in *Love, friendship and faith: intimacy, idioms and institutions in early modern Europe*, ed. Michael Hunter, Miri Rubin and Laura Gowing (Basingstoke, 2005), p.197-220.

Tadmor, Naomi, *Family and friends in eighteenth-century England* (Cambridge, 2001).

Tanner, Tony, *Adultery and the novel: contract and transgression* (Baltimore, MD, and London, 1979).

Tarasovykh, Evgenii K., 'K istorii Russkogo obshchestva XVIII-ogo stoletiia. Mason I. P.Turgenev', *Zhurnal Ministerstva narodnogo prosveshcheniia* 6:3 (1914), p.127-75.

Taylor, Charles, *Sources of the self: the making of modern identity* (Cambridge, 1989).

Tentler, T. N., 'Epilogue: a view from the West', in *Orthodox Russia: belief and practice under the tsars*, ed. V. A. Kivelson and R. H. Greene (University Park, PA, 2003), p.274-75.

Thompson, E. P., 'Happy families', *New society* 41 (8 September 1977), p.499-501.

Thomson, Ann, *Bodies of thought: science, religion and the soul in the early Enlightenment* (Oxford, 2008).

Tolchenov, I. A., *Zhurnal ili zapiska zhizni i prikliuchenii Ivana Alekseevich Tolchenov*, ed. A. I. Kopanev and V. Kh. Bodisko (Moscow, 1974).

Tolstoi, A. K., 'Artemii Semenovich Bervenkovskii', in *Sobranie sochinenii*, vol.3 (Moscow, 1964), p.130-39.

Toutain, J.-C., 'Food rations in France in the eighteenth and early nineteenth centuries: a comment', *Economic history review* 48:4 (2005), p.769-73.

Troyansky, David, *Old age in the Old Regime: image and experience in eighteenth-century France* (Ithaca, NY, 1989).

Trumbach, Randolph, *The Rise of the egalitarian family: aristocratic kinship and domestic relations in eighteenth-century England* (London, 1978).

Tscherny, Nadia, 'Likeness in early Romantic portraiture', *Art journal* 46:3 (1987), p.193-99.

–, 'Reynolds's Streatham portraits and the art of intimate biography', *Burlington magazine* 128:944 (1986), p.7.

Tunstall, Kate E., 'L'aveugle qui suit l'aveugle qui suit l'aveugle qui suit l'aveugle: la philosophie intertextuelle de la *Lettre sur les aveugles*', in *L'Aveugle et le philosophe*, ed. Marion Chottin (Paris, 2009), p.220-28.

–, 'Ethics and the work of fiction: Diderot's answer to Molyneux's problem', in *Fiction at the frontiers of knowledge: law, literature, and philosophy in early modern Europe*, ed. Alexis Tadié and Richard Scholar (Burlington, VT, 2010), p.186-203.

–, 'Pré-histoire d'un emblème des Lumières: l'aveugle-né de Montaigne à Diderot', in *Les Lumières en mouvement: la circulation des idées au XVIIIe siècle*, ed. Isabelle Moreau (Lyon, 2009), p.173-98.

Undank, Jack, *Diderot inside, outside, & in-between* (Madison, WI, 1979).

Uspenskii, A. I., *Imperatorskie dvortsy*, 2 vols (Moscow, 1913).

Van Damme, Stéphane, *Le Temple de la sagesse: savoirs, écriture et sociabilité urbaine (Lyon, France, XVIIe-XVIIIe siècle)* (Paris, 2005).

Vartanian, Aram, 'Diderot, or the dualist in spite of himself', in *Diderot: digression and dispersion*, ed. Jack Undank and Herbert Josephs (Lexington, KY, 1984), p.250-68.

'Vecher i utro, provedennye v Pavlovske', *Syn otechestva* 24:34 (1815), p.41-55.

Verkhovskvoi, P. V., *Uchrezhdenie Dukhovnoi Kollegii i Dukhovnyi Reglament*, 2 vols (Rostov-on-Don, 1916).

Vickery, Amanda, *Behind closed doors: at home in Georgian England* (New Haven, CT, and London, 2009).

Vigarello, Georges, 'Le corps du roi', in *Histoire du corps*, ed. A. Corbin, J. J.Courtine and G. Vigarello, 3 vols (Paris, 2005), vol.1, p.405-406.

Vincent-Buffault, Anne, *L'Exercice de l'amitié: pour une histoire des pratiques amicales aux XVIIIe et XIXe siècles* (Paris, 1995).

Viskovatov, Aleksandr, *Kratkaia istoriia pervogo kadetskogo korpusa* (St Petersburg, 1832).

Vladimirova, I. [Irina Reyfman], M. Grigor'ev [Mark Altshuller] and K. Kumpan, 'A. A. Blok i russkaia kul'tura XVIII-ogo veka', *Blokovskii sbornik*, ed. D.E. Maksimov, vol.4 (Tartu, 1980), p.27-115.

Voeikov, A. A., 'Opisanie russkikh sadov', *Vestnik Evropy* 68 (1813), p.193.

–, 'Progulka v sele Kuskove', *Novosti literatury* 27 (1826), p.103.

Wahrman, Dror, *The Making of modern self: identity and culture in eighteenth-century England* (New Haven, CT, and London, 2004).

Wanko, Cheryl, *Roles of authority:*

thespian biography and celebrity in eighteenth-century Britain (Lubbock, TX, 2003).

Warman, Caroline, *Sade: from materialism to pornography*, SVEC 2002:01.

Weeks, David Joseph, and Kate Ward, *Eccentrics: the scientific investigation* (Stirling, 1985).

Weintraub, Jeff, 'The public/private distinction', in *Public and private thought and practice: perspectives on a grand dichotomy*, ed. Jeff Weintraub and Krishan Kumar (Chicago, 1997), p.1-42.

Wendorf, Richard, *The Elements of life: biography and portrait painting in Stuart and Georgian England* (Oxford, 1990).

West, Shearer, 'The public nature of private life: the conversation piece and the fragmented family', *British journal for eighteenth-century studies* 18:2 (1995), p.153-72.

–, 'Wilkes's squint: synecdochic physiognomy and political identity in eighteenth-century print culture', *Eighteenth-century studies* 33:1 (1999), p.65-84.

Wheeler, David, *Domestick privacies: Samuel Johnson and the art of biography* (Lexington, KY, 1987).

Wiese, Bruno von, *Friedrich Schiller* (Stuttgart, 1959).

Wilson, Arthur M., *Diderot* (New York, 1972).

Wolfe, Charles T., 'A happiness fit for organic bodies: La Mettrie's medical Epicureanism', *SVEC* 2009:12, p.69-83.

Wolff, Larry, 'Depraved inclinations: libertines and children in Casanova's Venice', *Eighteenth-century studies* 38:3 (2005), p.417-40.

–, 'The fantasy of Catherine in the fiction of the Enlightenment: from baron Munchausen to the marquis de Sade', in *Eros and pornography in Russian culture*, ed. Marcus Levitt and Andrei

Toporkov (Moscow, 1999), p.249-61.

–, *Inventing Eastern Europe: the map of civilization on the mind of the Enlightenment* (Stanford, CA, 1994).

Yolton, John, *Locke and French materialism* (Oxford, 1991).

Zakonodatel'stvo Petra I (Moscow, 1997).

'Zapiski grafini V. N. Golovinoi', *Istoricheskii vestnik* 75 (1899), p.801.

Zelle, Carsten, 'Soul semiology: on Lavater's physiognomic principles', in *The Faces of physiognomy: interdisciplinary approaches to Johann Caspar Lavater*, ed. E. Shookman (Columbia, SC, 1993), p.40-59.

Zhivov, Viktor, 'Imperator Traian, devitsa Fal'konilla i provoniavshii monakh: ih prikliucheniia v Rossii XVIII veka', in *Fakty i znaki: Issledovaniia po semiotike istorii*, ed. B. A. and F. B. Uspenskii, (Moscow, 2008), p.245-68.

–, *Iz tserkovnoi istorii vremen Petra Velikogo: Issledovaniia i materialy* (Moscow, 2004).

–, 'Pervye russkie literaturnye biografii kak sotsial'noe iavlenie: Trediakovskii, Lomonosov, Sumarokov', *Novoe literaturnoe obozrenie* 25 (1997), p.24-83.

Zhmakin, V., 'Mitropolit Daniil i ego sochineniia', *Chteniia v Imp. Obshchestve istorii i drevnostei rossiiskikh* 2 (1881), p.257-762.

Zorin, Andrei, 'Catherine II versus Beaumarchais: the scandal at the St. Petersburg court at the time of the French Revolution', in *Russia and the West: missed opportunities, unfulfilled dialogues*, ed. E. Waegemans (Brussels, 2006), p.47-54.

Zysberg, André, *Les Galériens: vies et destins de 60 000 forçats sur les galères de France, 1680-1748* (Paris, 1987).

Index